Silas Mead (1834–1909) and his Baptist family:

'Learning, living, giving Christ'

Edited by

Rosalind M Gooden, Ken R Manley, Stefanie C Pearce

Morling Press, Sydney

2023

Published by Morling Press,
Macquarie Park, Sydney Australia 2113

mp

MORLING
PRESS

ISBN 978-0-6454927-2-9 (paperback)
     978-0-6454927-3-6 (ebook)

Cover and internal design by Impressum
www.impressum.com.au
Cover images: Silas Mead with his adult children, c.1889; Silas and young Cecil, c.1867;
young Silas Mead, c.1861; Silas with grandsons Colin and Bernard Wilson, c.1907.
Photographs supplied by Mead family descendants, Rosalind Gooden, Baptist Mission Australia,
State Library of South Australia
Index by Christopher Brennan
Family tree by Eric Kopittke

Foreword

David Bebbington

'We rejoice', declared Silas Mead towards the end of his life in 1905, 'that all the Churches of the Saviour are co-operating in the effort to make known Jesus Christ as the one Saviour for all mankind.'[1] The occasion was the Baptist World Assembly held in London that gave rise to the Baptist World Alliance, the confessional body that was to bind global Baptists together over subsequent years. Mead was a dedicated Baptist, being chosen not only as one of the speakers at the Assembly but also as the Australian representative on the first committee of the Alliance. His single published book had been entitled *Scripture Immersion* (1867), a resolute defence of the denomination's position on believer's baptism. Yet Mead was conscious of being part of a wider religious community, all those who were members of the movement committed to spreading the gospel. Unlike many of his fellow Baptists, he even believed in opening membership in Baptist churches to all who were able to profess conversion to Christ. Mead was an Evangelical of broad sympathies. His remark about 'all the Churches of the Saviour' was an endorsement of the Evangelical movement that bound together Christians of diverse denominations who shared the conviction that Jesus Christ was 'the one Saviour for all mankind'.

During Mead's lifetime in the second half of the nineteenth century and into the opening decade of the twentieth century Evangelical religion was marked by some fresh developments. In three of them Mead played a prominent part. One was the emergence of the holiness movement. Evangelicals had always believed in cultivating holiness, but from the 1860s there emerged the novel teaching of holiness by faith. After conversion, the new school of opinion held, it was possible to reach a further

---

[1] Silas Mead, 'Missionary Methods–Australian', in *The Baptist World Congress* (London: Baptist Union Publication Department, 1905), 86.

stage of spiritual maturity not through sustained effort but through simple trust. The experience of deeper faith gave a sense of release from the power of sin which supplied a powerful spur to Christian activism. Mead absorbed this teaching during 1868 after reading articles on the subject by the American Robert Pearsall Smith. Although Mead said nothing explicit about his new views, his wife Ann noticed that he 'seemed to realize more of the love of Jesus, and the things that used to vex him now seemed to have no power to do so'.[2] As a result Mead identified with the Keswick movement, named after the town in England, that propagated these convictions. He did not embrace the premillennial teachings usually associated with Keswick, but he did sympathise with the principle upheld by most of its supporters that missions should operate by faith. He sat on the board of the China Inland Mission, a pioneer faith mission, and became principal of Harley College in London, a training institution for faith missionaries. Silas Mead was therefore among the global Evangelicals of the later nineteenth century who was willing to learn fresh ways.

At the same time, in the second place, Mead came to emphasise the place of women in Christian mission. His convictions in this area seem to have crystallised in the year that he accepted the novel holiness views. 'The will of the Saviour', he declared in April 1868, 'was, that those sisters who were brought to God should honour him in an earnest life of Christian service.'[3] Later in the same year he contributed an article to the South Australian denominational magazine commending the idea of appointing deaconesses and his Flinders Street Church in Adelaide took the step of appointing six women to this office.[4] The same principle applied to foreign mission, once the preserve of male agents and their wives. Mead was delighted when two female missionaries were sent out from Flinders Street to Bengal in 1882. One of the two, Ellen Arnold, after returning home, recruited four other women to follow them three years later. That group, celebrated by Mead as 'five barley loaves' who would feed the spiritually hungry of India, became legendary figures in Australian Baptist memory. In a similar way Mead encouraged two of his daughters to attend university. The enlarging of woman's legitimate sphere applied to the secular as well the sacred world. Mead believed wholeheartedly in the advancement of women.

The third development of the later nineteenth century was the growth of missionary work. It was far from being an entire novelty, for Baptists could look back to William Carey's foundation of the Baptist Missionary Society in 1792 and many

---

[2] *Truth and Progress* (hereafter *TP*), May 1875, 55.
[3] *TP*, May 1868, 112.
[4] *TP*, August 1868, 156-60, 171.

other denominational missionary agencies had been created by 1850 in the United States as well as in Britain. But in later decades there was an upsurge of overseas activity. Australia was seen by the Baptist Missionary Society as a field deserving its help just before 1860 and so Mead's departure from England to Adelaide in 1861 was itself part of the mushrooming of global mission. During the first thirty years of his pastorate at Flinders Street, Mead was largely responsible for the foundation of as many as forty-nine Baptist churches in South Australia.[5] In his final years, from 1901 to 1909, he performed a comparable pioneering role in Western Australia. Throughout his ministry, however, Mead was conscious of the needs of lands where British settlers were few or absent altogether. It was at Flinders Street that the South Australian Baptist Missionary Society, the first Baptist foreign mission in the continent, was formed in 1864, soon concentrating its support on work at Faridpur in East Bengal. Mead visited India on four occasions in order to see the mission in progress. Over the pulpit of Flinders Street at the farewell services for the 'five barley loaves' was the scriptural command, 'Go ye into all the world and preach the gospel to every creature'. It was an obligation that Mead consistently honoured.

As an individual Mead attracted personal loyalty by his 'great magnetic force of character'.[6] He possessed notable administrative abilities, but he was also good at teamwork. The minister who was to become his closest friend, John Price, remembered that on his own arrival in South Australia in 1865, Mead welcomed him 'distinctly to a fellowship of work as well as to friendship'.[7] Price joined Mead, for instance, in the editing of *Truth and Progress*, a denominational magazine for the Baptists of South Australia. Mead was the pillar of Baptist activity in his colony. Towards the end of Mead's ministry at Flinders Street, in fact, some of his younger colleagues in the ministry resented his degree of influence. But Mead was particularly keen to encourage the young. He supported the pan-Evangelical Young Men's Christian Association and especially the Christian Endeavour movement that mobilised those in their teens and twenties for playing a full part in their churches. He believed passionately in education. In South Australia he acted as a professor in the Union College that formed a nucleus for the University of Adelaide and in Western Australia he acted as unofficial professor to his denomination, teaching theology, Christian evidences and church history. Mead was appreciated as a man of intellectual weight even in his final years.

[5] JG Raws in 'The Late Rev. Silas Mead, M.A., LL.B.', *Southern Baptist (SB)*, 28 September 1909, 230.
[6] JG Raws, 'The Late Rev. Silas Mead, M.A., LL.B.', *SB*, 28 September 1909, 230.
[7] J Price, 'A Quarter Century's Experience as a Baptist Minister in South Australia', *TP*, June 1890, 93.

Mead was also a family man, and a remarkable feature of this book is its ample coverage of his influence over his children. Lilian, his first daughter, acted as his personal assistant for fifteen years while also serving on the executive committee of Christian Endeavour in South Australia. She married a tutor at Harley College and so remained in England, but published a novel recounting a love story in a missionary setting. Cecil, the only son, told his father when he was eight years old that he would grow up to be a missionary and, having qualified as a doctor, made good his word by becoming a medical missionary in India who deliberately chose to work among people of a low caste. Gertrude, also a doctor, practised in Western Australia, fighting prejudice against female participation in the profession and specialising in the care of women and children while caring for her father in his last years. Blanche spoke for Christian Endeavour, attended a Keswick conference and married a Baptist minister who served in Perth, Western Australia, before other ministries in New Zealand. A final daughter, Flora, died of typhoid at thirteen, but was already a committed Christian. And the same threads ran through the family story in the next generation. Colin, a son of Blanche, also died young, of influenza at the age of nineteen, but he was already a church organist and active in the YMCA. His brother Bernard entered the Baptist ministry and his cousin Roger, the son of Lilian, became a doctor. Cecil's two daughters, Dorothy and Marjory, were baptised in India, followed professional careers in education and promoted the South Australian Senior Girls' Missionary Union. Bernard's son Torrey served as a Baptist minister, concluding his ministry at Flinders Street Church for five years from 2013. The traits of Silas Mead endured to the third and fourth generation.

Silas Mead was therefore a man of profound lasting influence. He was a distinguished Australian Evangelical, certainly the most prominent member of the Baptist denomination in South Australia. Mead displayed adaptability, being drawn into the holiness movement of his day. He championed the role of women inside and outside the churches. He dedicated his life to global mission. And he drew others into the causes he espoused himself, transmitting his concerns to the young. Perhaps his most striking memorial was the persistent moulding power of his priorities over his descendants. Mead's ministry was almost as influential after his death as it had been in his lifetime.

David Bebbington

University of Stirling

Contents

Part 2: The Next Generations   193

Part 3: Conclusion   305

List of Illustrations

Preface

Rosalind Gooden, Ken Manley, and Stefanie Pearce

The name of Silas Mead (1834–1909) has long been honoured among Australian Baptists, especially in South Australia and across the Nullarbor in Western Australia. More widely, his influence in the formation of Australian Baptist societies for 'foreign' missions has been celebrated. Yet no definitive biography of this remarkable man nor of his influential family has been published despite widespread recognition of such a need.

This book is an attempt to tell Silas Mead's story as well as that of his descendants. Whilst Baptists will find special interest in this project, we believe that all those interested in the religious and social history of Australia will value what we believe is a comprehensive and pioneering study. Silas Mead and his family made significant contributions not only in South Australia but throughout the nation. These achievements ranged beyond religious issues to developments in public schools, theological education, medicine, Christian feminism, social political policy and many others. The Mead family motto was apparently 'learn–live–give Christ' and we can see this being born out in the lives and actions of the family members to four generations. All in all, this is a remarkable story of the widespread impact by one family group on Australian life.

The original and long-held vision for this study belongs to Dr Rosalind Gooden. Her missionary service in Bangladesh and elsewhere, her studies in missiology, as well as her long participation in the life of the Flinders Street Baptist Church in Adelaide, founded by Silas Mead in 1861, have fired her vision for this book. Rosalind has known much of the inspiration of this story in a deeply personal way and has been collecting letters, documents and photos for longer than she can immediately recall.

Rosalind has been able to recruit a competent and enthusiastic group of contributors to this project. Two of us agreed to share in editorial responsibilities. Dr Ken Manley has an international reputation as Australia's foremost Baptist historian, and is the author of the definitive two-volume history of Australian Baptists, which demonstrated Mead's importance.[1] He has also long shared Ros's hope for a 'proper' book on Mead and his family. Ms Stefanie Pearce (a great-great-great-granddaughter of George Fife Angas) in Melbourne has guided us in the detailed preparations and disciplines that have been necessary in such a cooperative venture.

Family support has been generous. Rev Torrey Wilson, great-grandson of Silas Mead, and his sisters Raewyn Corey and Colleen Page, have provided valuable family letters and photos whilst a similar passion for maintaining family memories by the late Dorothy and Marjory Mead and the late Mrs Win Wilson has preserved invaluable resources for our book.

But we three contributing editors quickly realised that to achieve the best possible book would require a small army of researchers and writers. We gratefully record the immediate and enthusiastic responses which were received.

Rev Dr John Walker, the leading historian of Baptists in South Australia, although prevented by his pastoral commitments from taking a larger role in this project, has contributed an authoritative introduction and been a helpful consultant on many points. Dr Ken Manley spent many hours researching Silas Mead's origins and his travels. Dr Rosalind Gooden has drawn on her mission studies and her personal friendship with Mead descendants in the Flinders Street Church (FSBC) for her chapters whilst Mr Frank Tucker has contributed important chapters on Mead's wider influence in South Australia, what has been termed 'the Paradise of Dissent'.

Beyond South Australia, as the list of contributors demonstrates, the appeal of Mead to Baptist researchers is immediate. Rev Dr John Olley, whose ministry in mission work and in theological education in Perth parallels the interests of Mead, has written about Mead's influence and ministry in Western Australia.

Mead was a strong advocate of the place of women in church and society and this is reflected significantly in the contributions of his daughters—Lilian, Gertrude, Blanche and Flora—discussed in the chapters contributed by Ms Rebecca Hilton and Ms Stefanie Pearce, and of his granddaughters prepared by Dr Rosalind Gooden. Dr

---

[1] Ken R Manley, *From Woolloomooloo to 'Eternity': A History of Australian Baptists* (2 vols, Milton Keynes: Paternoster, 2006)

Pauline Tudball has written a fresh assessment of Cecil Mead, the 'missionary son' of Silas and Ann Mead. Chapters on the Mead grandsons—Colin and Bernard Wilson, and Roger Brown—together with a personal reflection by a modern descendant, Rev Torrey Wilson, bring further examples of how the impact on Baptist life of one man and his family has now extended over 150 years.

So, here is our story. The influence of Silas from Somerset has reached across the world to Australasia, India and back to England. Professor David Bebbington, a leading historian of Evangelicalism around the world, has been a strong supporter of the project over many years and we are most grateful to him for his foreword.

We also offer special thanks to Morling College Principal, Rev Dr Ross Clifford and all at the Morling Press for their help in producing our book. Mr Eric Kopittke compiled the Mead family trees; the Mead and Wilson family members sourced most of the photos that add so much to our book; Flinders Street Baptist Church and Baptist Mission Australia provided access to valuable archival material and images. Each contributor has also incurred special debts and these are acknowledged elsewhere. To all who have encouraged us to see the 'vision of Ros' come to this conclusion we also record our special gratitude. The generous practical support provided by the Baptist Churches of South Australia, Baptist Mission Australia and donors from around Australia, particularly Mr John Church, enabled us to complete the work with confidence.

We like to think—and hope and pray— that our book will not only stimulate a greater appreciation of how God can use one man and his family in the service of Christ, but also inspire a new generation to make similar commitments. This we pray, just as Silas so frequently prayed in Christian Endeavour meetings, 'for Christ and the Church'.

Rosalind Gooden, Ken Manley and Stefanie Pearce

Acknowledgments

Each of the authors has received particular support and assistance in the researching and drafting of their chapters. They would like to express their thanks and acknowledge that the final text embodies the contributions and help of archivists, librarians, fellow historians and others.

Ken Manley expresses appreciation for the assistance of Emily Burgoyne, Librarian, Angus Library, Regent's Park College, Oxford; Mike Brealey, Librarian, Bristol Baptist College and Lauren McKay, Centre for World Christianity, University of Edinburgh.

John Olley would like to acknowledge the support of Grace Merrells, Baptist Churches of WA Archives Officer and, at Perth Baptist Church, Dr Linda Harris (Senior Pastor) and Dr Carolyn Tan.

Rebecca Hilton would like to thank her parents, Gary and Helen Hilton, and the History and Gender group at the Australian National University for comments on her chapters.

In Melbourne, the assistance of the director of Global Interaction (now Baptist Mission Australia), staff and particularly archivist Pat Barnden in accessing records even during prolonged periods of lockdown was invaluable to Stefanie Pearce and Pauline Tudball. Pauline also sincerely appreciates Dr Rosalind M Gooden's encouragement, experience, and expertise.

Stefanie Pearce owes a debt of gratitude to Ron and Beryl Brown in Sydney who provided months of accommodation and research support when interstate lockdowns kept her from home. She has also been greatly assisted by her fellow authors, particularly John Olley for WA details, and Rebecca Hilton who drove around Canberra looking for Mead Street. John Sampson, the Baptist Union of Victoria Archivist, and Marita Munro, President of the Victorian Baptist Historical Society, seized brief interludes between citywide lockdowns to search for details on behalf of Stefanie and Ros in the Victorian Baptist Union archives.

Ros Gooden would also like to acknowledge David Bebbington's suggestion that a Mead biography was a gap in Baptist history worth filling. She thanks Stuart Devenish for his timely challenge that she needed to collaborate with others if some of her writing topics were to see the light of day. She also wants to acknowledge the delight it has been to work with Ken Manley and Stefanie Pearce. Ken's move from supervision to collaboration made this project feasible. Stef's professional skills have been God's gift. The rest of the team, the two Johns, Rebecca, Pauline and Frank, have filled many Covid weary days with stimulating conversations and thought-provoking challenges.

From years of research Ros's favourite archive is still the Angus at Regent's Park College, Silas Mead's alma mater, and her special thanks goes to Susan Mills, Emma Walsh and Emily Burgoyne.

The South Australian Collection in State Library of South Australia in Adelaide is a fantastic collection of early colonial history and includes significant deposits of Mead, Flinders Street Baptist Church, and early Baptist records. Their photographic library is acknowledged with enthusiastic thanks.

Ros would like to acknowledge the important role that FSBC church has been in her own life (and still is) as well as providing the sphere of influence of the Meads. Finally, the Mead contribution to intercultural (foreign) mission through the specific ABMS/ Global Interaction/ Baptist Mission Australia is part of its specific story. Ros's mission colleagues over the years have shaped her and her appreciation of the Mead story. JD Williams, Trevor Farmilo and Pat Barnden have seen that crucial records are still accessible. Your help Pat has been so timely despite lockdowns.

Finally, she counts it a privilege to have handled so many photos and family treasures. Thank you Torrey and Raewyn.

Introduction

John Walker

One vital concern of nearly all branches of the Christian church which had made their way to the southern shores of Australia was the provision of suitably qualified and energetic ministers who could adapt to the exigencies of colonial life. The Anglican Bishop of Adelaide, Augustus Short, for example, complained in the 1860s to the Society for the Propagation of the Gospel (SPG) in London that, in contrast to the Anglicans, 'Dissenters' were sending ministers to South Australia who were 'clever fellows' of 'high character and considerable ability'. He bemoaned the consequent comparative lack of Anglican progress.[1]

It is highly likely that Silas Mead was one of the ministers Bishop Short had in mind. As Rosalind Gooden's chapter in this volume on Mead's ministry at Flinders Street Baptist Church demonstrates, Mead had an abundantly fruitful ministry there, the most influential Baptist church in Adelaide. Furthermore, as the other authors in this volume make clear, Mead's impact went far beyond his city church, extending to the Baptist and evangelical movements Australia-wide and to the world-wide missionary movement. In South Australia, Mead was sometimes referred to as the 'Baptist bishop', but perhaps a better description of his ministry would be 'apostolic' given his ethos-forming influence among South Australian Baptists and his other wide-ranging contributions.[2] Almost from the beginning of his time in Australia, his ministry displayed apostolic characteristics through his gospel teaching; through his evangelistic, church planting and foreign mission endeavours; and through his church strengthen-

---

[1] Bishop Augustus Short, letters to the Society for the Propagation of the Gospel, 23 March 1863; 30 November 1866. Held in the United Society for the Propagation of the Gospel Papers, Oxford, Bodleian Libraries. I am indebted to Dr David Hilliard for these references.
[2] *Truth and Progress (TP)*, July 1890, 109; *TP*, November 1891, 187.

ing efforts. All these efforts at 'extending God's kingdom'—a popular phrase in Mead's time—were energised by a lively spirituality which drew on new emphases which came to the fore in the second half of the nineteenth century. While the shape of his ministry was moulded by his British background, such was the level and length of his commitment to Australia and such was his embrace of the Australian people and society, he truly can be termed, not just an apostle in Australia, but an 'Australian apostle'.

The South Australian Background

When Mead arrived in South Australia in 1861, twenty-five years after the new British colony had been founded, he encountered a colony which had already reached an estimated population of almost 131,000 and was poised to grow rapidly over the next two decades, increasing to an estimated 359,330 people by the end of 1901.[3] The South Australian Census of 1860 showed that there were 3,424 adult South Australians who described themselves as Baptists. This represented 2.9 per cent of the population. This grew to six per cent in 1901, by far the highest proportion of Baptists in the Australian states.

South Australia was proclaimed a British colony on 28 December 1836, and it was established on the basis that, unlike the other Australian colonies which received convicts from Britain, South Australia was to receive free settlers only. Initially colonists came to South Australia under a scheme of 'systematic colonisation' whereby the sale of land was used to fund immigration.

The land, of course, was not waste and unoccupied land as the South Australia Act, passed in the British Parliament in 1834, claimed it to be.[4] Despite sometimes strong resistance from the First Nations peoples of the new colony, the white invasion dispossessed them of their land, and the catastrophic impacts on the First Nations peoples mirrored those which occurred in the other Australian colonies.[5] Mead, like all colonists, benefitted from this dispossession. Although, as Ros Gooden and Frank Tucker point out in their chapters in this volume, Mead demonstrated considerable spiritual and material concern for Indigenous South Australians, his concern did not

---

[3] W Vamplew, E Richards, D Jaensch, J Hancock (eds), *South Australian Historical Statistics*, (Kensington, New South Wales: History Project Incorporated, University of New South Wales, 1988), 14-15.
[4] This was also the year of Mead's birth.
[5] For the most comprehensive account to this point of the impact of colonialism on South Australian aborigines and their responses, see P Brock and Tom Gara (eds), *Colonialism and its Aftermath: A History of Aboriginal South Australia* (Adelaide: Wakefield Press, 2017).

lead him to question British colonialism. Something of Mead's identification with the goals of British imperialism is evident in an address Mead gave, soon after he arrived in South Australia, on Major General Havelock, a Baptist and an eminent soldier who distinguished himself during the Afghan wars and the 'Indian Mutiny'. Mead, in his hour-long address, agreed with a description of Havelock that portrayed him as 'every inch a soldier and every inch a Christian'.[6]

Baptists were prominent in the founding of South Australia, none more so than George Fife Angas who was one of a small group which was instrumental in bringing Mead to South Australia. Angas was a successful English businessman, banker, investor, promoter of Christian causes and a philanthropist. He was the driving force in founding the South Australian Company which was the largest private investor in the new colony. Angas's biographer, Edwin Hodder, claimed that Angas was the father and founder of South Australia.[7] While this description of Angas's achievements goes too far, Angas's contribution was immense. He played a crucial role in establishing the social and religious ethos of South Australia, one in which colonists could flourish without religious impediment in a place where there was no state-established church and in which there was no state financial aid for religion.[8] He successfully promoted his vision for South Australia as a place of refuge where 'pious Dissenters…could … discharge their consciences before God in civil and religious duties without any disabilities'.[9] Angas also used his influence among English Baptists and other Dissenters to encourage immigration to the new colony, sometimes also employing them to work for the South Australian Company. Among these people was David McLaren, a Scottish Baptist, whom Angas employed as the second manager of the South Australian Company in South Australia. McLaren served as the pastor of the first Baptist church in South Australia in a voluntary capacity.[10] No less significant than Angas's strong encouragement of English Dissenters to make South Australia their new home was

---

[6] *South Australian Register* (hereafter *Register*), 20 September 1861, 2. In the early 1850s, Havelock was involved at an organisational level at Stepney College, the college where Mead trained later in the decade. Havelock died of dysentery in 1857 during the Indian mutiny. Mead was a student at Stepney College at the time.
[7] E Hodder, *George Fife Angas, Father and Founder of South Australia* (London: Hodder and Stoughton, 1891).
[8] For an appreciative summary of Angas's achievements, see RM Gibbs, *Under the Burning Sun: A History of Colonial South Australia, 1836-1900* (Adelaide: Southern Heritage, 2013), 43.
[9] Quoted in D Pike, *Paradise of Dissent, South Australia 1829-1857* (Melbourne: Melbourne University Press, 1957), 130.
[10] On McLaren, see KR Manley, *From Woolloomooloo to Eternity: A History of Australian Baptists, Studies in Baptist History and Thought, Vol. 16:1: Growing an Australian Church (1831-1914)* (Milton Keynes, Paternoster, 2006), 47-49.

his successful attempt to sponsor the immigration of Prussian Lutherans, who were facing religious discrimination, to South Australia. They made their own distinctive contribution to South Australian Christianity and society.[11]

Baptists and like-minded South Australians had to fight hard in the 1840s and early 1850s for the preservation of the religious settlement that was so congenial to them.[12] However, with the victory of those forces who opposed state aid to religious groups in the first election in the new colony in 1851, voluntaryism became the governing principle for church–state relations in South Australia and South Australia became the first British colony in the British empire to end government aid to churches and other religious groups except for the purposes of education. Baptists could revel in a colony which in their view was one in which 'there was freedom, so far as the government is concerned' and in which there was 'fair field and no favour'.[13]

Such was the attraction of South Australia to many religious dissenters such as the Baptists, Methodists and Congregationalists, Douglas Pike called it a 'Paradise of Dissent' in his ground-breaking study of early South Australia.[14] For many Baptists, South Australia seemed like a type of Promised Land. JP Buttfield, one of the first Baptist ministers to come to South Australia, used the prophecy found in Micah 4:4 to refer to South Australia as a 'delightful country, where through the blessing of God they might "sit down under their own vines and under their own fig-trees, none making them afraid"'.[15]

Given the victory of the voluntaryist forces, Silas Mead, when he arrived, entered a society where Baptist principles on church–state relations had become established in a way that British Baptists were still longing for and were never to achieve. He would soon make his way in a community where Baptists were both unhindered and unaided by the government, one in which Baptist voluntaryist principles would be put to the test. Mead was also faced with a situation in which, unlike some other denominations such as the Anglicans and Congregationalists who were able to draw on funds from denominational bodies in Britain, no similar funds were forthcoming for Baptists.

---

[11] Gibbs, *Under the Burning Sun*, 96-100. Angas personally financed both the fares and the purchase of land for the German Lutherans. In the end he made good profits from the loans he advanced them for purchase of land.

[12] See, for example, the petitions from several Baptist churches in 1847 against state aid to churches in *Register*, 4 August 1847, 3.

[13] *TP*, November 1871, 147.

[14] D Pike, *'Paradise of Dissent'*.

[15] *Adelaide Observer (AO)*, 1 December 1849, 2.

As Tucker has alluded to in chapter six of this volume, prior to Mead's arrival in South Australia Baptist work had been fragmentary and divided. Not only was this occasion for lament among South Australian Baptists who had envisioned that the Baptist cause would flourish in South Australia given the congenial environment, but members of other denominations provided negative commentary.[16] In response, one Baptist, while conceding that Baptists were not as united as other denominations, claimed this was because Baptists exercised the right of private judgement 'whilst many others allow their pastors to think for them'.[17]

Not only did doctrinal and practical divisions over issues such as open and closed membership and communion prove a hindrance, but impediments such as a lack of continuity in supply of able ministers, shortfalls in finances and the high mobility of the population had telling effects. A general 'pan-evangelical' spirit which led to a willingness on the part of evangelicals to cooperate with other evangelicals across denominational lines also resulted in some 'Baptists' making their spiritual homes in 'union churches' (non-denominational churches which included people from different evangelical churches) or in evangelical churches which did not identify as Baptist.[18]

A particular disappointment for some influential Baptists who supported open-membership principles was that there was no flourishing Baptist church of any variety to the south of the River Torrens in what is now known as the central business district of Adelaide but what was then called South Adelaide. This was in contrast to North Adelaide where two stable open-membership Baptist churches (Kermode Street and LeFevre Terrace) existed prior to Mead's arrival and which showed promise of future growth. A failed attempt to establish a Baptist open-membership church south of the River Torrens in 1857–58 possibly underlined to those who initiated the call to Mead the need for a fresh, well-resourced effort to plant a new church with a hand-picked minister. The failed effort was led by the former Congregational minister of Ebenezer Chapel in central Adelaide, Edward Dewhirst, a learned, energetic and able man who had come to embrace Baptist beliefs and was baptised by George Stonehouse, pastor of Lefevre Terrace Baptist Church in North Adelaide. Despite the backing of Stonehouse and Angas (who later were on the committee that brought

16 *Register*, 4 November 1850, 4.
17 *Adelaide Times*, 19 November 1850, 3.
18 See JS Walker, 'The Baptists in South Australia, 1863-1914', Bachelor of Theology honours thesis, 1990, 6-7. On pan-evangelicalism in England see RH Martin, *Evangelicals United: Ecumenical stirrings in pre-Victorian Britain 1795-1830* (Scarecrow Press, New Jersey, 1983).

Mead to South Australia) this venture came to naught in little over a year.[19] Discouraging, too, was the failure of the South Australian Baptist Home Missionary Society, formed by Kermode Street Baptist Church in 1860, to generate any momentum.[20] There had been talk of forming some type of Baptist association for at least a decade and the efforts of this church represented little advance.[21]

Mead the evangelical

Mead, typical of many young evangelicals of the Baptist variety, was converted and baptised as a youth. And as Manley claims in the next chapter of this volume, Mead's evangelical faith was deep and lasting. Many attempts have been made to define the essence of evangelicalism including by David Bebbington in his widely influential definition which delineates four central features of British evangelicalism.[22] These include commitment to the authority of the Bible, an emphasis on the salvific significance of Jesus' death on the cross, the necessity of individual conversion, and both evangelistic and social activism whereby the gospel is proclaimed and applied for human betterment. Bebbington summarises these as biblicism, cruci-centrism, conversion and activism.

As is evident throughout this volume, Mead was manifestly an evangelical in all these senses, even archetypical. Evangelicalism has never been monolithic and, as is apparent in this volume, while Mead was more conservative theologically than some of his fellow South Australian Baptists on issues such as the doctrine of scripture, he was often innovative in methodology. He was open to any initiative that could both aid the cause of Christ and could be justified on the basis of scripture or, at least, not be contradicted by it.

Mead too was a man of his times. As Bebbington has demonstrated, part of the reason for the success of evangelicalism, particularly in the nineteenth century, was its ability to register shifts in the wider culture but remain true to its core beliefs and val-

---

[19] *Register*, 18 April 1857, 3; 4 June 1857, 1; 29 October 1858, 3; *Adelaide Times*, 1 August 1857, 3. Dewhirst, a classics specialist, went on to have a long and distinguished career as an educationalist for the South Australian government, becoming Second Inspector of Schools in 1860. *Register*, 10 August 1860, 2; 5 February 1904, 6.

[20] *Register*, 1 May 1861, 2

[21] For an early call to form a Baptist denomination in South Australia, see *Register*, 16 April 1851, 2. This society seems to have existed only briefly and it became redundant with the formation of the South Australian Baptist Association in 1863.

[22] D Bebbington, *Evangelicalism in Modern Britain: A History from the 1730s to the 1980s* (London: Unwin Hyman, 1989).

ucs.[23] While Mead rejected ideas about the perfectibility of human beings or society, his optimistic perspective on the advancement of the kingdom of God throughout the world reflected the optimistic spirit of the age which itself was largely shaped by a confluence of Enlightenment, Romanticist and biblical ideas.[24] Mead, too, as Manley explains in chapter four, was an early participant in the holiness movement. This emphasis on the necessity of the experiential side of Christian life sat well with the Romanticist embrace of emotion and the mystical in rebellion against what was seen as the soulless rationality of the Enlightenment.[25] Mead, to use a twentieth century term, successfully contextualised the gospel in his ministry.

Mead on baptism and church membership

Mead arrived at a time when South Australia was experiencing significant growth and this expansion continued until the middle of the 1880s when a long-lasting economic downturn began to affect many aspects of South Australian society. Key to the expansion from the late 1860s to the middle of the 1880s was the opening of land for settled agriculture that had hitherto been used for pastoral purposes by colonists. Within the context of this expansion, Mead was a dominant figure in establishing an open-membership policy among South Australian Baptists whereby Christians from paedo-baptist churches could become members of Baptist churches if all other requirements of membership were met. This policy aided the establishment of Baptist churches in areas, particularly agricultural ones, where Baptists were not numerous and paedo-baptist churches did not exist. JD Bollen characterises this approach as an expression of 'liberal denominationalism'.[26] He argues that South Australian Baptists, comfortable in a society they helped to create, were the prime example among Austra-

---

[23] Bebbington, *Evangelicalism in Modern Britain*, chapters 2 and 5.
[24] The Enlightenment mood was an optimistic one which placed great reliance on the belief that the application of reason to every field of human endeavour would bring enlightenment and progress. While this mood was frequently not inimical to religious belief, some 'enlighteners' contrasted reason with what they regarded as the superstitions of revealed religion. The Romanticist temper, while also generally being optimistic, rejected what was seen as the cold rationality of Enlightenment belief and emphasised the importance of the spiritual, the mysterious, and human feeling and intuition. For short explanations of the Enlightenment and Romanticism, see Bebbington, *Evangelicalism in Modern Britain*, 50-54, 80-81.
[25] For the influence of Romanticism on the holiness movement, see Bebbington, *Evangelicalism in Modern Britain*, 80, 167-69.
[26] JD Bollen, *Australian Baptists: A Religious Minority* (London: Baptist Historical Society, 1975), 27-32.

lian Baptists of a denominational approach which rejected sect-type religion in favour of a more accommodating denominational style.

In the late 1860s and early 1870s, legislation in the South Australian Parliament opened vast swathes of land to settled agriculture. By 1870, Mead was greatly troubled by the competitive rush of evangelical churches to establish their own congregations in new areas. He believed that this often resulted in several struggling evangelical congregations when one strong united evangelical church could have a much greater impact for the kingdom of God. Accordingly, Mead proposed to the South Australian Baptist Association that a conference be held with representatives of the Congregational and Presbyterian denominations in order to discuss amalgamation. Mead believed that suitable arrangements on the administration of baptism could be made on the basis of forbearing love.[27] Mead's proposal, though, received virtually no support from the South Australian Baptist Association. In the second half of the 1870s and in the 1880s, Mead retreated from his earlier position. Indeed, in 1888 he went as far as to claim that infant baptism was 'seriously detrimental to the interests of Christ's Kingdom' because the 'vital truths' of the gospel are all 'especially involved, enfolded and exhibited in the proper administration of the ordinance of the believer's immersion'.[28]

Overall, Bollen's claim that Mead emphasised baptism as the justifying principle of the denomination while minimising its religious importance goes too far.[29] Certainly, Mead's flirtation with denominational amalgamation in the 1870s, his strong advocacy of open membership, and his willingness to work cooperatively in evangelical non-denominational organisations such as Christian Endeavour display not only a biblically inspired desire for the spread of the gospel but more than a touch of the type of Enlightenment-influenced pragmatism that Bebbington has identified.[30] At the same time, his thorough arguments in his small book, *Scripture Immersion* and his enthusiasm for the establishment of a Bible translation society in South Australia that would use the word 'immersion' instead of 'baptism' reveal strong views on baptism from which he never deviated.[31] In addition, his stress on the symbolic function of baptism, and the fact that he baptised over 1900 people during his ministry at

[27] *TP*, November 1870, 129.
[28] *TP*, 1 May 1888, 67.
[29] Bollen, *Australian Baptists*, 28.
[30] Bebbington, *Evangelicalism in Modern Britain*, 65-66.
[31] Silas Mead, *Scripture Immersion: Or Arguments Showing Infant Baptism to be Unscriptural and Believers' Baptism to be Exclusively Scriptural and Obligatory* (Adelaide: Andrew, Thomas and Clarke, 1867).

Flinders Street Baptist Church point to a different interpretation to that of Bollen. For Mead, baptism was the justifying principle of the denomination because of its religious significance.

Throughout his long career Mead did not waver from a liberal-denominational stance. As Olley shows in his chapter on Mead in Western Australia, Mead was also a strong advocate of open membership in Western Australia. GH Cargeeg, a successful businessman who was prominent in Western Australian Baptist circles (he had also been a member of Flinders Street Baptist Church in Adelaide when Mead was pastor), feared that the advocacy of Mead (whom he called the 'old prophet') for open membership—like that of his son-in-law, AS Wilson—would put a 'clog in the wheel of progress' in reconciling the Baptists of Western Australia who were still struggling to fully overcome differences over membership issues.[32] This did not prove to be the case, and Mead was no 'doctrine bigot' as Cargeeg seemed to imply, but Mead did not shift from his position that 'no Baptist church has the right founded on Christ's teaching to withhold the fellowship of living brotherhood from those on whom the Lord himself bestows it'.[33]

The final South Australian years and after

In the final dozen years of Mead's ministry in South Australia, an economic downturn meant that the South Australian Baptist Association struggled for funds and was often unable to offer much financial help to struggling churches, many of which had found it difficult to sustain a fulltime pastor from the beginning. Furthermore, as the suburbs of Adelaide continued to grow, even with the economic recession, Flinders Street Baptist Church did not quite have the preeminence it once did. The Baptist church at Norwood which Mead had played a leading part in establishing, for example, began attracting crowds in the 1890s which thronged to listen to the socially oriented sermons of its minister, Charles Bright. While both Mead and his church had been the brightest stars in the South Australian Baptist firmament, other luminaries now shone brightly as well.

Gooden in chapter five and Tucker in chapter six reveal the sad end to Mead's ministry in South Australia. Although greatly respected, his influence within the

---

[32] CH Cargeeg to JR Fowler, 10 September 1907, Fowler Papers, PRG 34/29/6/16, State Library of South Australia (SLSA).
[33] S Mead in Preface in AS Wilson, *What is a Baptist Church?* (Perth, 1906). Mead followed the arguments of an English Baptist theologian and leader from an earlier generation, Robert Hall.

Flinders Street congregation and the South Australian Baptist Association was in decline. Mead was honoured on his departure from South Australia, but his last year there was decidedly not one of 'finishing well'. By insisting on his continued occupancy of the church manse despite his successor John Raws becoming the new pastor, he lost the support of many congregational members and even that of many of his closest friends and advisers.[34] But even so, too many South Australian Baptists lacked the type of generosity of spirit that had characterised Mead in his ministry in South Australia. Mead and his family were deeply wounded by the events that unfolded during this time.

Mead's wider ministry was not finished though. As Manley in chapter six makes clear, Harley College in London provided Mead with ample opportunity to exercise his gifts and pursue his missionary passion by educating young students training for missionary work. Similarly, as Olley demonstrates, Mead made a substantial contribution in Western Australia along similar lines to those that had been prominent throughout his life. Advancing age and declining health limited him in both London and Western Australia, but his passion for the extension of God's kingdom burned bright until the end.

The Mead generations: Making heaven and earth richer

In his will, Mead left an 'undivided share of a father's love'.[35] Although, as Ros Gooden reveals in chapters three and five, Mead's commitment to his duties and his ties in England often meant he was away from his children, his love for them and his dedication to their spiritual, educational, and all-round welfare meant that they had a start in life upon which each one of them was able to build in their own way. Cecil Mead's passionate spirituality and missionary enthusiasm, which Tudball enlarges on in her chapter, echoed Silas's own relationship with God, his evangelistic vision for the spread of the gospel throughout the world, and his humanitarian concerns. Mead's fatherly concern was not just for his son Cecil, but for his daughters too. He ensured that his daughters had a good education, an education that they used well. As Rebecca Hilton discusses in her chapter on Lilian Mead, Lilian, the only female ever to

---

[34] Letters: G Hogben to JR Fowler, 17 September 1897, PRG 34/29/21, SLSA; JR Fowler to S Mead, 6 August 1896, PRG 34/31/1/3, SLSA; JR Fowler to L Fowler, 12 August 1896, PRG 34/31/1/3, SLSA. AO, 16 January 1897, 43.
[35] *Southern Baptist (SB)*, 12 October 1909, 249.

enrol at Prince Alfred College, a Methodist boys' school, argued publicly in support of female education and a wider role for women beyond the domestic sphere. 'God and not man is the end of existence', she declared.[36] Lilian was outspoken in support of women's suffrage and had a further impact through the fiction books she authored. Lilian and her sister Blanche both married and raised families and Blanche's ministry as a daughter, sister, wife of a pastor and as a mother and grandmother of pastors followed more traditional lines than those of her adult sisters. As Hilton points out though, her contribution too should be celebrated and not underestimated. Not only was she a homemaker for her pastor husband, Alfred, but for her medical doctor sister Gertrude. Gertrude is the only one of her siblings to have an entry in the *Australian Dictionary of Biography*. Stefanie Pearce's chapter on Gertrude Mead demonstrates her immense pioneering contributions to public health in Western Australia and her untiring efforts to elevate the status and circumstances of women both in the medical profession and in the general community. Her death at a relatively early age was a momentous loss.

Pauline Tudball in her chapter on Cecil Mead refers to Silas's prayer for his son Cecil and Cecil's wife Alice at their wedding in India in 1896. Silas prayed for them that they would 'work out a destiny that shall make heaven and earth richer'.[37] The chapters in this volume on Silas's children reveal his continuing influence in them as they sought, in their own ways, to 'make heaven and earth richer'. As Gooden makes plain in chapters sixteen and seventeen and as Torrey Wilson, Mead's great-grandson, shares in chapter eighteen, members of subsequent generations have worked out their own destinies and have given substance to God's promise found in Psalm 103:17–18 that the Lord's love and righteousness is with the children's children who keep his covenant and obey his precepts. Silas's apostolic influence reached not only Australia, Bengal and Britain but through many decades among his own descendants.

---

[36] Lilian S Mead, *The Awakened Woman: Paper Read at the Seventh Annual Convention of the Woman's Christian Temperance Union of South Australia* (Adelaide: Woman's Christian Temperance Union, 1895), 24-25.
[37] Silas Mead and WT Whitley, *Our Indian Trip: Notes and Impressions of a Visit to Several Mission Stations from November 1895 to March 1896* (Melbourne: Bible and Tract Repository, 1896). Copy held in Baptist Mission Australia collection of Mead files, Moore Potter House, Melbourne.

PART 1

Silas Mead

Silas Mead

2

The Formation of Silas Mead

Ken R Manley

Silas Mead (1834–1909) was born on 16 August 1834 at Curry Mallett, a small village nestling in the beautiful Somerset countryside.[1] His parents were Thomas Mead (1791–1851) and Honor Uttermare (1796–1860). The Mead family had a local farming history stretching back several generations.[2]

The West Country had long been a powerful centre of Dissenting influence. The Baptist church in Hatch Beauchamp, five miles south-east of Taunton and less than two miles from Curry Mallett, is thought to be the oldest Baptist cause of its kind in West Somerset, dating from 1630. During the Commonwealth period Baptists were active in this region although they were severely persecuted in the succeeding reigns of Charles II and James II when Baptists were forced to meet illegally.[3] Not surprisingly, the Monmouth rebellion of 1685 had many supporters among Baptists and other Dissenters. Sampson Clarke, pastor of Lyme Regis Particular Baptist church in the town where the rebellion had begun, was executed as a result of his involvement in the uprising. Taunton, the nearest large town to the Mead farm, some seven miles away, had been the site of the notorious 'Bloody Assize' conducted by Lord Chief Justice Jeffreys (known as 'the hanging judge') when hundreds were either hanged or trans-

---

[1] Several local places were named 'Curry' which comes from the Celtic word *crwy* meaning boundary.
[2] See the family tree in the appendix to this book.
[3] W Fisher, 'The Baptists of Hatch Beauchamp', *Baptist Quarterly* 12:1-2 (1946), 34-40; WM Wigfield, 'A Short History of the Baptist Churches at Isle Abbots (1808-1968) and Fivehead (1868-1968)', typescript, 1968. (Copy available on the Fivehead church's website.)

ported to the West Indies.[4] How much young Silas learned about this is unknown but certainly the Dissenting tradition was clearly important for him in later years.

Only scattered details of Silas's early life are extant, mainly from occasional public personal references and treasured family memories. Family tradition, for example, claims that he once won a prize for ploughing the straightest plough.[5] Much later in life, on 4 December 1905 when giving a lecture to a number of Indian Babus (local Indian leaders) at a missionary convention at the Australasian Baptist field conference at Brahmanbaria, Silas spoke about 'The Story of a Happy Life'. He testified that 'early in life he had followed the plough, and that it was only then that he became a Christian and devoted himself to the ministry'. As a reporting missionary observed, this was 'just the right thing to tell these men who are taught to despise labour, and to regard all Englishmen as "Christians"'.[6]

Silas was baptised at the age of fifteen. Years later, two of his children, Blanche and Cecil, made a pilgrimage to the site of his baptism, near Welinge Bridge. A relative gave them details: 'It was not in a church but in the open air, a spot surrounded by trees, and the ice had to be broken over the water before the candidates could be immersed. They drove to the place in an open vehicle (2 or 3 miles) and had to return in their wet clothes'.[7] This remained a memorable experience for Silas who later devoted considerable energy to the promotion of immersion as the real English meaning for the Greek word usually translated as 'baptism'.

Silas never forgot those Somerset beginnings of faith. In January 1875 he visited Curry Mallett, spoke at a Sunday School meeting and baptised two young Sunday School teachers in the following August.[8] On his return to England in 1897 Silas again visited the site of his baptism and also preached at the Hatch Beauchamp church.[9]

Young Silas had clearly developed an alternative ambition to following the plough. His evangelical faith was deep and lasting. He helped in the building of the

[4] BR White, *The English Baptists of the Seventeenth Century* (Didcot: Baptist Historical Society, 1996), 133; AR Cross, 'Baptists, Peace, and War: The Seventeenth Century British Foundations', in *Baptists and War. Essays on Baptists and Military Conflict, 1640s–1990s*, ed GL Heath and MAG Haykin (Eugene, Oregon: Wipf and Stock, 2015), 24-25; M Watts, *The Dissenters* (Oxford: Clarendon Press, 1978), 256-58.
[5] Marjory Mead, 'Rev Silas Mead', *AB*, 22 April 1959, 11.
[6] *OB*, December 1905, 7.
[7] Letter, M Baker to R Gooden, 3 October 1993.
[8] Letter, Rev HE Watkins, Minister, Hatch Beauchamp Church, citing Minute Book of the Curry Mallet Sunday School, to M Mead, 5 October 1964 (in possession of R Gooden).
[9] Letter, M Baker to R Gooden, 3 October 1993.

chapel at Curry Mallett and regularly walked all the way to Taunton for evening classes so that he could prepare for admission to a Baptist College.

The name 'Silas' recalled the biblical figure, a devoted believer who had been a significant assistant to the apostle Paul, as recorded in Acts, and later acted as an amanuensis for Peter (1 Peter 5:12). Whatever the reasons for giving him this name, it proved to be prophetic: Somerset Silas developed a deep love for Christ and an apostolic missionary zeal.

Late in his ministry at the Flinders Street Baptist Church in Adelaide, when Silas was sixty, an irreverent review of a Sunday service was published in the Adelaide weekly paper *Quiz and Lantern* which proclaimed itself as 'a satirical, social and sporting journal'. Complaining of a funereal atmosphere in the church, the observer suggested that Silas Mead had been severely handicapped throughout life:

> When his parents resolved to christen him Silas [something a Baptist parent would never do, it should be observed] his career was fixed. It was impossible for the boy to grow up anything but a parson. It was not in the nature of things. The very name has an apostolic sound. Mr Mead's aspirations, if he had any, were crushed shortly after his birth. But for the action of his parents he might have been an honest and a hard-working mechanic...But 'Silas' prevented all but one consummation. The boy launched into the world with such a handle to his patronymic had either to be a parson or die. Mr. Mead chose the lesser of two evils.[10]

Perhaps there was also reference to Silas's West Country accent in the observer's further complaints about some of Silas's pronunciations: 'Victoria becomes Vic-toe-reear. God is sometimes given as Go-ard, again as Gard, and then again as Gawd. Because becomes bc-kars, Lord is Lo-ard, and so on'.[11]

With his biblical name and a developing apostolic vision, young Silas embarked on a determined course of spiritual and academic preparation that would take him to an unexpected life in a far distant country.

---

[10] *Quiz and Lantern*, October 1894, 8.
[11] Mead was said to have a 'speech disqualification' when applying to Stepney College.

Silas Mead at Stepney/Regent's Park College (1854-59)

Silas undertook ministerial studies at a significant period in the development of Baptist training institutions in England. There was a widespread tendency for an 'academy', which offered only training in basic skills, to transform into a more ambitious role as a 'college' which fostered a broader scholarship. Several such institutions developed into larger bodies. Basic facilities were transformed into grand facilities, especially at Stepney in London which during Silas's time moved into the salubrious area of Regent's Park. The instruction in these colleges became more scholarly and quite advanced, as Silas's own experience demonstrates.[12] The only English universities at Oxford and Cambridge were not open to Dissenters and to obtain a degree many men studied in Scotland or Germany.

William Mead (1823–1877), Silas's older brother by some eleven years, had earlier entered the Baptist ministry.[13] The example of this older brother must have had some impact on the younger sibling. William's initial ministerial study was supervised by a local minister, Rev Alfred Day, and then he spent 'two or three years' in the 'Academy for the Training of Young Men for the Dissenting Ministry' with a small band of students under the guidance of Rev John Jackson of Taunton Baptist.[14] In 1845 William was accepted as a student at Bristol Baptist College which since 1720 had become the training institution for many Baptists, especially those from the West Country. In 1812 the College had developed a purpose-built property in Stokes Croft, Bristol. When William entered Bristol, the Principal was Thomas Crisp (1788–1868) who was remembered as a rather uninspiring lecturer, content if students simply reproduced his material in their examinations. Fortunately for the College, Dr FW Gotch (1808–1890), a distinguished Biblical scholar, commenced as tutor in 1845, the year that William began his course.[15]

---

[12] D Bebbington, 'The Baptist Colleges in the mid-Nineteenth Century', *Baptist Quarterly* 46.2 (2015), 49-68.

[13] *TP*, July 1877, 80. Details presumably supplied by Silas.

[14] Jackson was minister of the Taunton Baptist Church from 1840 until 1845 and had established his Academy in nearby Mount Street: I Kember, *Taunton Silver Street: A Baptist Chapel and its Town. The Early Years 1814-51* (Taunton: privately published, 1988), 30. The Academy did not continue after Jackson left.

[15] NS Moon, *Education for Ministry. Bristol Baptist College 1679-1979* (Bristol: Bristol Baptist College, 1979), 42-47.

After his second year, William proposed leaving Bristol to study in Germany. Significantly, the College Committee in January 1848 tried to dissuade him, desiring it to be distinctly understood 'that in their opinion Mr Mead's going to study at a German University is not adapted to improve his fitness for preaching the Gospel in this Country'.[16] This recalls the deep suspicion of German biblical scholarship which many British evangelicals felt during this period even though several later Baptist leaders studied in Germany.[17] William then changed his ideas and followed many other English Dissenters by attempting to study in Scotland, moving to Glasgow. However, after a few months he was 'seized with cholera' and nearly died. He recovered but never really enjoyed good health. William became pastor at Truro but was forced to resign because of his health. He later supplied Somerton Congregational Church and another church at Oakhill but resigned in 1875. He died two years later, leaving behind a widow, two sons and a daughter.

William's unsettled experience is perhaps the reason why Silas resolved to seek admission to Stepney College in London, rather than the closer College at Bristol. Like William, Silas clearly was determined to study at the most advanced level that was available to him.

Baptists in London established in 1810 'The Baptist Academical Institution in Stepney'.[18] The property was located near Whitechapel Road and consisted of two large houses with what was known as King John's Tower in between. The premises were never ideal as the heating and ventilation were recurring problems. Stepney, however, gradually gained the confidence of the churches and offered a broad-based course in general education as well as theology.

One major development in the history of the college was the foundation of the University of London (in which a number of Baptists had been involved).[19] The University was established by royal charter in 1836, as a degree-awarding examination

[16] Bristol Education Society, committee meeting Minutes, 2 October 1845 (courtesy of M Brealey of Bristol College).
[17] JHY Briggs, *The English Baptists of the Nineteenth Century* (Didcot: Baptist Historical Society, 1994), 190-92.
[18] For the history of the College, see RE Cooper, *From Stepney to St. Giles'. The Story of Regent's Park College 1810-1960* (London: Carey Kingsgate Press, 1960); AJ Clarke and PS Fiddes, *Dissenting Spirit. A History of Regent's Park College 1752-2017* (Oxford: Regent's Park College, 2017).
[19] See JHY Briggs, 'Baptists and Higher Education in England' in WH Brackney and RJ Burke (eds), *Faith, Life and Witness: The Papers of the Study and Research Division of the Baptist World Alliance 1986-1990* (Birmingham, AL: Samford University Press, 1990, 92-114); HH Bellot, *The University of London: A History* (London: London University, 1969).

board for students holding certificates from University College and King's College London and 'such other Institutions, corporate or unincorporated, as shall be established for the purpose of Education, whether within the Metropolis or elsewhere within our United Kingdom'.[20] Stepney began discussions about joining the University from 1840 and this gave Stepney students opportunity to obtain a degree without going to Scotland or Ireland or Germany. Bristol Baptist College also affiliated with London in 1841. Baptist students could now matriculate and graduate with a recognised degree. Stepney was careful to insist that such academic study would not interfere with 'the great object of the Institution' of preparing ministers.

Despite these encouragements, the 1840s had been difficult for Stepney whilst Dr Benjamin Davies was President from 1844–47.

The advent of Joseph Angus (1816–1902) as President in 1849, when he was still only 33, initiated a new era for the College. Angus had studied at Stepney and Edinburgh where he had won the gold medal in moral philosophy and the University English prize. He was pastor at the New Park Street Church in Southwark from 1838–40, following the long years of John Rippon as pastor.[21] This was the church that Silas attended whilst in London and where a young Charles Haddon Spurgeon came in 1854, the same year Silas began at Stepney.[22] Whilst at New Park Street Angus was secretary of the Stepney committee where he was a leading figure in negotiations with the University of London. Then in 1840 he became full-time secretary of the Baptist Missionary Society. Angus brought this missionary knowledge and passion to Stepney and was to be a key figure in Silas Mead's life.

The report of Stepney for 1854 records that thirteen ministerial applications had been received and seven had been accepted, including 'Mr Mead from North Curry, near Taunton'.[23] Evidently special attention was given to Silas because of his speech 'disqualification'.[24] The only full-time teacher in that year was Angus who was assisted by tutors in classics, mathematics and philosophy.[25] Students also had access to classes and lectures at University College and New College. Benjamin Davies, the former President, returned in 1857 to teach Classics, Old Testament and Hebrew. The

---

[20] Clarke and Fiddes, *Dissenting Spirit*, 51.
[21] Clarke and Fiddes, *Dissenting Spirit*, 40. For Rippon and this church, see KR Manley, *'Redeeming Love Proclaim': John Rippon and the Baptists* (Carlisle: Paternoster, 2004).
[22] *TP*, 3 March 1892, 67.
[23] The Report of the Committee of the Baptist College of Stepney for MDCCLIV (London, 1854), 8.
[24] Gooden, 'Silas Mead', 70 (citing a minute from Regent's Park College records).
[25] *Report*, 7; Clarke and Fiddes, *Dissenting Spirit*, 64.

academic status of both Angus and Davies is reflected in that in the 1880s both were involved in the preparation of the Revised Version, Angus with the New Testament and Davies with the Old. EA Payne has argued that under Angus at Regent's Park, 'without any overt breach or crisis men came to appreciate the newer ways of thought and interpretation'.[26]

A later student at the College describes Angus as a courteous, scholarly, saintly figure with a domed head and long ragged beard. He was essentially a kind man, if a little remote, but could deflate any self-confidence in a student with a penetrating remark. Davies was a man of a more boisterous, approachable temperament and was described as 'a great, rolling, lovable, elephantine figure of a man, like Samuel Johnson'.[27]

Silas's first year course was listed in detail. That year two men had matriculated at the University (presumably one was Silas). Students had 'gone through a great part of Latham on the English language, and Milner's English History'.[28] In logic they had read 'Whately, books i, ii, and iii' and in Theology they had studied Angus's own *Bible Handbook* (published only as recently as 1853), including portions on the history of the sacred text, the canon and Christian Evidences.[29] 'Sketches of sermons have been prepared by each member of the class during parts of the session'. Details of what had been read in Greek and Latin Classics, in Mathematics and in German were also listed.

This was a broad and challenging course with more classical content than modern students are given. Silas evidently thrived on it all. In the report for 1855 there were 27 students and four (not named but may well have included Silas) were contemplating 'a life of missionary labour among the Heathen'. Silas's close and lifelong friend George H Rouse (1823–1909), later a leading BMS linguist and missionary in India, was certainly one of these four.[30] The second-year course (1855) included studies of

[26] EA Payne, 'The development of nonconformist theological education in the nineteenth century with special reference to Regent's Park College' in Payne, *Studies in History and Religion* (London: Lutterworth Press, 1942), 246.
[27] JF Makepeace, as cited by Cooper, *From Stepney*, 62.
[28] RG Latham, *The English Language* (London, 1841); T Milner, *The History of England* (London, 1853).
[29] R Whately, *The Elements of Logic* (1825); J Angus, *Bible Handbook* (1853).
[30] For Rouse, see B Stanley, *The History of the Baptist Missionary Society* (Edinburgh: T & T Clark, 1992), 160, 180, 369-70.

the influential Butler's *Analogy*,[31] Genesis 1–7 in Hebrew, John 1–5 in Greek, and further studies in Classics and German.

Undoubtedly the most exciting event during Silas's time was the move from Stepney to Regent's Park in 1856. The old site had become increasingly unhealthy and a location closer to the new University was desired. Moreover, it has been suggested, the move reflected the social aspirations of Nonconformists alongside the growing respectability of society.[32] A quest for 'a more healthy and convenient neighbourhood' had commenced in 1854. Eventually the College moved to the much more promising site of Holford House, a private house erected in 1832 as part of a grand design to build substantial classical villas in Regent's Park. Angus appealed to wealthy Baptists to support this exciting venture in which the well-known Baptist Member of Parliament and millionaire Sir Morton Peto (1809–1889) played a key role. The extensive property was leased for the next seventy-eight years as it was Crown land and could not be purchased.[33]

Regent's Park College had an impressive entrance, with a wide portico and by comparison with Stepney was 'much more spacious with almost a rural feel'.[34] Some thirty to forty rooms could be used immediately. Gradually, the 'Academy' became known as Regent's Park College and the community became 'more ecumenical, more academically focussed and more diverse'.[35] (This name was retained when the College began relocating to Oxford from 1920.) An increasing number of 'lay' students were admitted, a development which Angus had encouraged prior to the relocation.

Silas, as College students often do, must have known much of how all this was achieved. Did he perhaps learn a valuable lesson about how to organise and lead sympathetic laymen to support a Baptist venture?

All these important developments at Regent's Park were experienced by Silas. In the 1859 Report he was listed as one of six students who had completed their course and his MA was 'in the division of Mental Philosophy'. He also gained a LL.B. degree although precisely why he undertook this course is unclear; possibly with a view to a different career if that proved necessary. Family tradition claims that he studied Eastern languages, including Syriac, to the level of a Doctor of Divinity and that he tied

---

[31] J Butler, *The Analogy of Religion, Natural and Revealed, to the Constitution and Course of Nature* (1736).
[32] D Bebbington, as cited by Clarke and Fiddes, *Dissenting Spirit*, 60.
[33] Clarke and Fiddes, *Dissenting Spirit*, 62–64.
[34] Clarke and Fiddes, *Dissenting Spirit*, 58.
[35] Clarke and Fiddes, *Dissenting Spirit*, 63.

in fifth place. But at that time London could not award theological degrees and 'when this was changed in 1900 the authorities would not make the retrospective award'.[36] Certainly Silas was a successful, capable and highly motivated student.

He developed many strong friendships among fellow students, notably with George Rouse. When he returned to England in 1874 many old College friends, such as Robert Caven, then at Southampton, gave him a warm welcome home.[37]

In 1860 Silas was among the list of ministers trained at the College, although no place of church settlement was recorded. He was in fact acting as pastor at Fivehead, near his hometown.[38]

But Silas's life soon moved in a new and unexpected direction. His Principal was to be a key figure in this exciting development.

Joseph Angus, George Angas, Silas Mead and Adelaide

Joseph Angus proved to be a highly significant figure in the formation of Silas Mead in at least four ways. This influence embraced careful scholarship, missionary enthusiasm, a comprehensive theology of the local church and included personal guidance.

Angus's scholarship constituted a model for Silas whose own academic achievements were of the highest order. Silas's mind was well trained and his pastoral leadership always evidenced an appropriate confidence in his own judgments. He was widely respected as a scholar and theological teacher at Union College in Adelaide which he helped establish.[39] In every report of his activities in Adelaide he was always listed as 'Rev Silas Mead, MA, LLB'. At one time there was an unfounded rumour that he was moving to teach at a proposed Baptist College in Victoria.[40] Later in life, his academic credentials, as well as his long life in ministry and mission advocacy, commended him for his appointment as Principal of Harley College, a missionary training college in London, in 1897.

---

[36] Marjory Mead, 'Rev Silas Mead', *AB*, 22 April 1959, 11.
[37] *Freeman*, 18 September 1874, 460; 2 October 1874, 479.
[38] *Baptist Magazine*, 1861, 296.
[39] For details of Union College, see later chapter.
[40] *TP*, May 1885, 57.

Early in his time in Adelaide his book on baptism is clear evidence of his scholarly ability to analyse and develop a convincing case for his position.[41] Although Silas wrote regularly in denominational and other religious publications, this was his only published book. A later chapter will consider this study in the context of Silas's ministry in Adelaide but, in brief, his book was a convincing and scholarly production in the style of the period. Almost 3,000 copies had been published by November 1868.[42] His book was well reviewed:

> But though simply an answer to another work, we are constrained to say that we never saw a book in which the views of Baptists, especially upon certain particular passages, are so fully and ably displayed…a complete declaration of Baptist sentiments on the most disputed passages of the Holy Scriptures.[43]

As will be later discussed, Silas established a Bible Translation Society in South Australia and this also reveals the passion for exact translation that Angus had inculcated in his students.

That scholarly habits were pursued by Silas is found in his confession when he retired from FSBC in 1897:

> I have always been a student and a conscientious reader. Seldom has my judgment allowed me to spend time in reading other than first-class books…If anyone has doubts on this point I can easily inform them of each book I have read since I first landed on South Australian shores.[44]

The missionary enthusiasm and knowledge of Angus as a former secretary of the BMS also impacted Silas. Stepney/Regent's Park was to develop a rich legacy of graduates who served in 'foreign' mission fields, notably with the BMS.[45] According to a later statement, based on Silas's own input, he had discussed his future with Angus and proposed continuing studies in theology and Oriental languages at London University. He told Angus of his interest in some missionary or colonial sphere but that

---

[41] Silas Mead, *Scripture Immersion: Or Arguments Showing Infant Baptism to be Unscriptural, and Believers' Immersion to be Exclusively Scriptural and Obligatory, Intended as a Reply to the Rev. John Hannah's Book entitled 'Infant Baptism Scriptural and Immersion Unnecessary' and Issued at the Wesleyan Conference, London* (Adelaide, 1867).

[42] *TP*, November 1868, 233.

[43] *Baptist Magazine*, 1868, 111.

[44] *SB*, 4 February 1897, 27.

[45] Cooper, *From Stepney*, 116 notes that between 1810 and 1958 some 750 students were trained by the College and of these 153 served in the mission field, mostly with the BMS, including 67 to India and Pakistan, 26 to China, 25 to the West Indies and 6 in Ceylon.

there was 'one difficulty which then stood in the way…a difficulty which only the hand of death could remove'.[46] 'This was a family matter and when his mother died in February 1860 Silas felt free to pursue a course of 'foreign' ministry. Clearly he had also used his time to develop a friendship, and possibly an 'understanding', with a Miss Ann Staple (1839–1874) of Stoke-sub-Hamdon, Somerset. Silas had been instrumental in Ann receiving her 'first deep religious conviction' when she was only fourteen and before he went to College. She was baptised by Rev James Price of Montacute, Somerset on 4 December 1857 and later travelled to Adelaide to marry Silas in 1864.[47]

Angus also had written extensively on the nature of the church. As a youthful minister he had defended the voluntary system of the church in 1839 and in *The Christian Churches* (1862) insisted that the crucial question to be asked of church membership was whether its members were a converted people and insisted that the church was 'a theocracy administered through the conscience and heart of Christians'.[48] He also argued that women could be deacons and that women could pray and speak in public. These became important principles in Silas's ecclesiology.

Silas's time with Spurgeon at New Park Street also gave him an outstanding model of how a local ministry could have an evangelistic ministry, such that one member recalled that in the earliest days of FSBC the church had 'a passion for saving souls' and that it was a 'real Salvation Army'.[49]

All these emphases were evidenced in Silas's leadership both in Flinders Street and more widely among South Australian Baptists.

The 1858 Report of Stepney recorded the development which was to have a direct bearing on Silas's future:

> From the Hon. G.F. Angas, of Australia, a sum of £120 has been received for the support of two students who purpose giving themselves to the work of God, in Australia or other dependencies. Failing such students, the amount is to be appropriated to the general support of the Institution. This

---

[46] *The Handbook of Flinders Street Baptist Church, Adelaide 1865*, 3 (clearly either written or authorised by Mead).
[47] Details from her obituary in *TP*, June 1874, 76-79.
[48] Briggs, *The English Baptists of the Nineteenth Century*, 20-21, 285-86.
[49] *TP*, September 1886, 137.

sum he intends securing to the College annually, to found, in perpetuity, two scholarships for the purposes named.[50]

George Fife Angas (1789–1879) was a Baptist deacon, businessman and philanthropist who had a long interest in the colony although he only arrived personally in 1851. His vision and influence were pervasive in the development of South Australia.[51] After his arrival in Adelaide Angas recognised the need for a new and open Baptist church with a strong and visionary pastor. He wrote to Angus, who was naturally keen to help his College's benefactor and recommended Silas.

Accordingly, Angus approached Silas who was then warmly commended to Angas and his friends as 'a very favourable character, of high collegiate attainments, a moderate Calvinist, earnest and zealous, of conciliatory manners, possessing firmness and prudence; and not tainted with Germanism in theology'.[52] This reveals a shrewd assessment by Angus and these were precisely the attributes that the committee led by Angas were seeking. A 'moderate Calvinist' suggested the theological soundness of Silas but also implied that he was free of the narrow and divisive tendency that had marred many extreme Particular Baptists. 'Germanism' implied a belief in the higher critical analysis of Biblical texts and a general tendency towards modernism. Angus discerned the exact qualities that would lead Silas to become the undoubted leader and a major formative influence in the development of the Baptist movement in South Australia, as the subsequent chapters will demonstrate. Whilst reflecting on this invitation Silas went to London to meet with Charles Goode (1827–1922), a highly successful Baptist merchant and philanthropist in Adelaide and London, who assured him that Adelaide would be a wonderful opportunity.[53]

Angas and his committee members were quickly persuaded of the wisdom of Angus's choice. Silas accepted the challenge and left aboard the *Parisian*, arriving at Port Adelaide on 13 July 1861.[54]

---

[50] *Report for 1858*, 14. 'The money was given annually, rather than coming from investment income, and although the intention was to ensure scholarships in perpetuity this did not happen': Clarke and Fiddes, *Dissenting Spirit*, 67.

[51] See 'Angas, George Fife (1789-1879)', *Australian Dictionary of Biography*, National Centre of Biography, Australian National University, https://adb.anu.edu.au/biography/angas-george-fife-1707/text1855, published first in hardcopy 1966; KR Manley, *From Woolloomooloo to 'Eternity': A History of Australian Baptists* (2 vols, Milton Keynes: Paternoster, 2006), 46-49.

[52] Extract from letter, 14 November 1860, in FSBC archives.

[53] *TP*, September 1881, 99; *SB*, 4 February 1897, 26.

[54] *Register*, 15 July 1861, 2.

On his first Sunday in Adelaide, Silas preached at the Ebenezer Independent Chapel in Rundle Street on the prayer of Jesus in Matthew 26:39: 'O my father, if it be possible, let this cup pass from me'.[55] Does this reflect how deeply Silas felt at this time with so much of his future uncertain and so far from home? However, he soon clearly embraced the example and commitment of his Saviour, affirming 'nevertheless not as I will, but as thou wilt'.

Silas stayed at first with GF Angas and soon became the founding pastor of what became the Flinders Street Baptist Church. Just a few years later Silas praised the advantages of serving in the colony: 'More freedom, life, liberality, and enterprise'.[56] He had found the time and the place for his life's ministry.

---

[55] *Register*, 15 July 1861, 2.
[56] Letter from Mead, dated 27 April 1865 in *Freeman*, 19 July 1865.

The Foundations in South Adelaide, 1861-75

Rosalind Gooden

Silas Mead, c.1865

Preparation for the new minister

Silas Mead arrived in Adelaide on Saturday 13 July 1861, and went to stay with George Fife Angas at Prospect Hill for the next three months.[1] Angas had paid his travel costs and offered initial hospitality. Before Silas arrived a committee had been very active, attempting to answer Silas's suggestions and conditions.[2] They had reassured him that the number of ministers labouring in Adelaide was far from adequate and he was needed. He told them:

---

[1] *Register*, Monday 19 May 1879, 6.
[2] See Ken Manley, *From Woolloomooloo to 'Eternity'*, 98-99.

I can scarcely pretend to say whether I come up to your standard in ministerial qualifications—of course it would border on presumption were I to attempt it. I may say however that I enjoy good health—am a 'thorough Baptist',—believe very conscientiously in 'open communion', as to reading sermons, I attempted it once and failed! As to the rest you must look to Dr Angus and others.[3]

They pledged Silas to raise £500 towards a building, and so match the gift offered by George Fife Angas and they promised a stipend of £250 for the first year. They added other well-known Baptists to their committee: Charles Todd (of overland telegraph fame) and Christopher Giles, a pastoralist. David Fowler, a wholesale grocer, was appointed treasurer to collect promised donations.

George Shaw (draper) and William Kyffin Thomas (newspaper proprietor) agreed to look for a half-acre block of land in a central location.[4] They were offered the Methodist New Connection's chapel at Hilton, but Angas did not approve that purchase. A block in Victoria Square was too small and the adjoining owner wanted too much for extra land. They considered blocks in Wakefield Street and Franklin Street, but their final choice was 'town acre block number 273, 67 x 270 feet' on Flinders Street and Divett Place for £410 owned by the SA Company. They negotiated to buy the land for £400 with three months to complete the payment, and the manager agreed to see water from the roof of the adjourning building was redirected.[5] Trustees of the property were initially Charles Todd, David Fowler, John Beeby, James Holden, George Shaw and William Kyffin Thomas.[6]

A group of women, organised by Mrs George Shaw, agreed to raise incidental money for the building and met alternate Wednesdays for that purpose.[7] A prayer meeting was commenced on Wednesday evenings in Zion Chapel.[8] The committee made arrangements to use Zion Chapel's premises for week-night activities until their

---

[3] FSBC Meeting Minutes, Preliminary Meeting Minutes, 16 January 1861.
[4] FSBC Meeting Minutes, 5 February 1861.
[5] FSBC Meeting Minutes, 14 May 1861.
[6] FSBC Meeting Minutes, 21 March 1861.
[7] FSBC Meeting Minutes, 14 May 1861.
[8] An independent evangelical congregation located in Pulteney Street between Wakefield and Flinders Street. RC Petersen, 'Zion Chapel', SA History Hub, History Trust of South Australia, https://sahistoryhub.history.sa.gov.au/organisations/zion-chapel,.

own building was available. For the two services expected on Sundays they hired White's Assembly Hall.[9]

They asked architect Robert Thomas,[10] brother of William Kyffin Thomas, to prepare 'plans, elevations and specifications of a Chapel, cost not to exceed £3,000, including platform, baptistery, pewing etc.'[11] Five days later Thomas showed them plans of chapels and churches he had built in England. This was to be the earliest of his significant buildings in the colony. At the same time Fowler reported that by the following Friday he would have paid in £500 to the Bank. They agreed to inform Angas of the financial situation and of their building plans.[12]

On 9 July at the final committee meeting before Silas's arrival, Fowler reported a payment of £544/9/10, with £160 promises yet to be collected; Mr White had agreed to the Assembly Hall for two services on Sundays for 500 or more for £1/6/- per week for six months, and two hours of gas lighting would be 10/- per week. Also, they approved plans for the building except for the upper part of a tower and spire, and Thomas was instructed to draw up the specifications. They agreed to purchase a contribution box for use at the services, and in order to report on its suitability at the next meeting each of the committee was to buy a copy of *Psalms and Hymns* (1858), the hymnal Silas suggested as suitable for congregational use.

[9] White's rooms were opened in June 1856 and for many years were the only place of public entertainment in Adelaide.
[10] Christine Sullivan, 'Thomas, Robert George', Architecture Museum, University of South Australia, 2008, Architects of South Australia, http://www.architectsdatabase.unisa.edu.au/arch_full.asp?Arch_ID=62.
[11] FSBC Meeting Minutes, 14 May 1861.
[12] FSBC Meeting Minutes, 19 June 1861.

Silas as a young man

Silas Mead arrives

Silas arrived on Saturday 13 July 1861, and on Sunday morning he preached at Ebenezer Independent Chapel, Rundle Street for Rev FW Cox and in the evening at the Baptist Church pastored by Rev Stonehouse in LeFevre Terrace, North Adelaide.[13]

On Tuesday 16 July Silas attended the next meeting of the committee, and it was down to work after he had prayed. They adopted Silas's suggested hymn book, subject to the confirmation of the Church once it was formed. They went through the list of those invited to be members. They suggested that it might be possible to form the Church on Monday 5 August, less than three weeks from Silas's arrival.

On Wednesday the notice of Sunday 21 July's services was in the Thomas-owned *Register* and repeated in other Adelaide papers. Stonehouse preached in the morning. Before his sermon he stated:

> [This] was the commencement of a Baptist cause in South Adelaide on Congregational principles in which the doctrine as held by the Baptist Union in England would be upheld.[14]

---

[13] Ebenezer Chapel was a Congregational Church pastored by FW Cox, who had arrived in the colony in 1857.

[14] 'Opening Services–White Assembly Rooms', *Register*, 21 July 1861.

Silas spoke in the evening. Seven hundred were seated, and a further 100 stood. Silas took for his text 1 Corinthians 2:2: 'I am determined not to know anything among you save Jesus Christ and Him crucified'. He directed an earnest appeal to 'men of business, to the followers after pleasure, to young men and women to seek for peace and satisfaction where alone they would be found' in Jesus Christ.[15]

Another two committee meetings were held in the following week, talking through the basic principles of membership. It was agreed that all trustees and office bearers must have been immersed on profession of their faith in Christ. Open communion was defined as to include the principle of open fellowship. They were still looking for trustees. Silas was suggested and he was to approach Angas. Silas was also asked to talk with Stonehouse about the doctrinal requirements for Trust Deeds. Angas declined trusteeship and Stonehouse suggested that Silas and he be omitted, placing the trustee responsibility on the businessmen. The North Adelaide congregation provided two further names.

A delegation from a congregation that met in Stephens Place, under the leadership of Henry Hussey[16] asked to be received and enquired about the constitution, church government and doctrines of the new church. Hussey reported back that there was a difference of opinion over their church uniting with the new cause, and it was to be left to individual action. George Duke was one of the earliest from there to request membership.[17]

The church is founded

Monday 5 August 1861 was the set date; the place LeFevre Terrace Baptist Chapel; the people, twenty-six Baptist believers. Before their meeting these twenty-six had signed the following declaration:

> We, the undersigned, professed Disciples of Christ, feeling it to be our duty to unite in Church fellowship, for the purpose of mutual edification and the observance of the Divine Ordinances, hereby request to be now constituted and recognised as a

[15] 'Opening Services—White Assembly Rooms', *Register*, 21 July 1861.
[16] GL Fischer, 'Hussey, Henry (1825-1903)', *Australian Dictionary of Biography*, National Centre of Biography, Australian National University, Vol 44 (MUP) 1972, https://adb.anu.edu.au/biography/hussey-henry-3829/text6077, published online 1972.
[17] George Duke married Jessie Melvin, one of the foundation members, on 8 November 1866 at the house of her sister Mrs Beeby. They were later dismissed to Parkside Baptist Church as founding members.

Baptist Church. Feeling the importance of this step we commend ourselves to the care and guidance of Him who is able to keep us from falling and to present us faultless before the presence of His Glory with exceeding joy. Dated at Adelaide in province of South Australia this Monday, the fifth day of August One Thousand eight hundred and sixty-one.[18]

They were: Silas Mead, Christopher Giles, George and Mary Shaw, William Kyffin and Mary Thomas, Mary Jane Thomas, Mary Maria Thomas, Helen Rosetta Thomas, Thomas and Elizabeth Monck, Anne E Browne, David and Jessie Fowler, George Swan and Margaret Fowler, Wilhelmina Melvin, Jessie Melvin, James and Isabella Whiting, John and Margaret Beeby,[19] Elizabeth Mildred, Martha Morris, James A and Mary Holden, Sarah Phillips.[20] This was not just a list of individuals, but of families, and friends, of differing ages, ten men and sixteen women.

They met round the 'Table of Remembrance'. Rev Stonehouse addressed them on the constitution of a Christian Church. Revs Tuck and Buttfield prayed and Silas Mead read out the declaration. Stonehouse offered them the right hand of fellowship. Rev John Hannay of Angaston addressed the newly formed church on the duties, responsibilities and privileges of a Christian Church. The ordinance of the Lord's Supper was conducted. Silas Mead closed in prayer.

The church was constituted as a Congregational or Independent Baptist Church, on open fellowship principles; all office-bearers to have been immersed in order to eligibility to office.[21].

Building a congregation

Two nights later those members met, and Silas was elected 'chairman for this and any succeeding meeting at which he may be present'.[22] The meeting accepted a membership recommendation for Charles Hulls from Earl Street Baptist Chapel, London. They appointed visitors for three more who desired to join. They took over responsibility from the building committee. They discussed plans for a Sunday School including a place to meet, forms and fittings, Bibles and hymn books needed. They

---

[18] Handwritten copy held in SA collection for FSBC.
[19] Isabella Whiting and Margaret Beeby were sisters to Jessie and Wilhelmina Melvin.
[20] Sarah Phillips was the mother of Mary Holden.
[21] *The Handbook of Flinders Street Baptist Church, Adelaide, 1864* (Adelaide: Andrews, Thomas and Fisher, 1865), 4.
[22] FSBC Members Meeting Minutes, 7 August 1861.

decided that the Lord's Supper should be held at the conclusion of every Sunday morning service.

A week later they met again, and continued setting parameters for their corporate life. Brother Shaw was to find a leader for singing; they endorsed the use of *Psalms and Hymns* and agreed to take up a collection for the poor after the next Sunday's communion. Brother Fowler reported that the ladies had already collected £38/2/7d and that the Sunday offerings for three Sundays had been £38/11/5d. Deacons were elected on 27 August: Christopher Giles, William Kyffin Thomas, George Shaw and David Fowler,[23] men who were to become involved in pastoral care and leadership of the congregation. They divided the membership among the deacons for pastoral contacts.[24] Silas expected his members to be actively involved in the work of the church, as busy as himself. A united monthly missionary prayer meeting was programmed for the first Monday in every month, and George Duke and Allan Webb (who were later going to be dismissed to new causes) became members.

Their first baptismal service was organised for Friday 6 August when Silas baptised three members of other churches, as well as those from Flinders Street. They planned on holding monthly church meetings, monthly baptisms (if necessary), quarterly members' social tea meetings and a weekly Sunday prayer meeting before the morning service.

Plans were made to lay the foundation stone of the new building on 18 December 1861 with special celebrations featuring Rev Isaac New from Albert Street, Melbourne. Silas conducted his first marriage—Sarah Lambell to David Melvin—by special licence at the residence of the bride's father, on 26 November 1861, the first of many. [25]

A special church meeting was held on 27 November 1861 in conformity with the Trust Deeds, to elect a pastor. A warm letter of invitation was unanimously endorsed.[26] Silas responded:

> Having a great sense of the responsibility of the solemn step and yet having faith in God, who hitherto has upheld me, I now accept as in His sight the office of Pastor over you. May the great

---

[23] FSBC Members Meeting Minutes, 27 August 1861, 55.
[24] FSBC Deacons Meeting Minutes, 7 May 1862, 25.
[25] *Register*, 27 November 1861, 2.
[26] Hand-written copy of minutes of Special Church Meeting, moved by Brother Beeby and seconded by Brother Fowler. Gooden/Mead collection.

head of the Church sanctify this union between Pastor and the flock...[27]

The foundation stone was laid by David Randall[28] (instead of GF Angas who believed that the sanctuary building was too expensive and grand for their needs—£3,500 was his desired estimate—and asked that 'he must be excused from giving my public sanction to proceedings which, in my opinion are at variance with prudence and sound direction'. Yet he still continued to honour his promised financial support.)[29] During those special public meetings before a number of ministers, Baptists and others, Rev New gave a special address to Silas on his ministerial duties and responsibilities, setting him apart for the ministry of FSBC.[30]

Flinders Street Baptist Church before the erection of the manse, c. 1873. [SASL B7853]

Providing the facilities

Buildings loomed large in the life of that early congregation. Plans for the sanctuary and vestries were modified, a tender accepted from the building firm English and

[27] Copy of hand-written letter, Grote Street Adelaide, 27 November, 1861. Gooden/Mead collection.
[28] David Randall, an early settler, friend of GF Angas and resident of Mt Crawford.
[29] Rosalind Gooden, '"In the city but not of the city": Reflections of 150 years of Baptists in Adelaide'. A presentation on the occasion of the 150th Anniversary of FSBC, 22 May 2011, 5. The copy of Angas's letter is found in the South Australian collection Box SRG 465/44/33.
[30] 'New Baptist Church', Register, 21 December 1861, 3. https://trove.nla.gov.au/newspaper/article/50080870.

Brown, a loan of £1,500 negotiated,[31] foundation stone laid and local Glen Osmond stone used. The first use of the vestry was for a prayer meeting on 28 November 1862. At the following Members' social, Silas suggested various prayer groups to meet in the first rooms finished: groups for wives with unconverted husbands, for young men, and the group regularly distributing tracts.[32]

> The chapel was opened for worship by a prayer meeting on April 24th, 1863 and Rev [James] Taylor of Melbourne preached the first two sermons in it the following Sunday. The number of sittings provided…is a little less than 700. The cost is …£7,291/8/10.[33]

The financing of it came from generous gifts from GF Angas (£1,600), subscriptions of £4,288/13/9, salary sacrifice by Silas (£312/10/-) and £1,066/15/1 from the work of the women, and special gifts for the baptistry (£23/10/-). The general funds for the work of the church were received from a system of weekly offerings, and averaged £8/3/4 per week for the first year, £8/16/9 for the second, £11/4/10 in the third, and £12/8/6 in 1865. The total given in the first four years was £2,113/9/1. 'It ha[d] exceeded expectations of many; yet now that the principle is better understood, it is felt that there is room for considerable improvement.'[34]

In 1865 membership was fifty-eight.[35] It grew to 502 by 1882. The statistical records in 1865 provide an insight into the early pastoral pattern established by Silas; for the acceptance of individuals, dismissals, discipline, readmissions over the four years:[36]

> Total net increase, beyond the original 26, during four years, 208. Total number lost 35. Of these 6 have died; 13 have been dismissed to other Churches or have received honourable certificates of membership; 11 have left without moral Church censure, of whom 3 have returned; 5 have been subject to the discipline of the Church, one of whom has been restored to fellowship.[37]

---

[31] Members had 'agreed to amount not exceeding 2,000 pounds sterling at an interest rate not exceeding 10 pounds per centum per annum'; FSBC Members Meeting Minutes, 3 December 1862, 125.

[32] FSBC Members Social Meeting Minutes, 29 November 1862, 122.

[33] *Handbook,* 1865, 5.

[34] *Handbook,* 1865, 6.

[35] It is unfortunate that there are not summaries and reports in the printed lists of members of August 1871 and 1873 to give us the developing picture.

[36] FSBC Deacons Meeting Minutes, 27 November 1867, 27, 30.

[37] *Handbook,* 1865, 10.

At the quarterly social meeting of 13 May 1862, after hearing encouraging news of Sunday School numbers reaching 112 (with attendance ranging between 45 and 85), members were informed that a further £300 had been added to their debt in order to add another storey above the vestries. This was to provide accommodation for an infant school room and five classrooms for older scholars. More land was purchased adjoining the sanctuary and in 1867 another hall with sixteen classrooms upstairs was added to the property.[38]

The acoustics in the sanctuary were poor and they experimented unsuccessfully with red drapes, then in 1873 agreed to add a gallery for acoustic effects. GS Fowler disagreed with that decision, but once decided, he gave his substantial donation.[39] Plans were prepared for the building of a manse in 1869 but it was delayed at Silas's request. A 'keeper's cottage and extensive sheds and stabling' were also added. [40]

Flinders Street Baptist Church interior with organ [SASL B8702]

Building-wise it would seem that an extra western door was added to the sanctuary linking sanctuary to courtyard for the 50th Jubilee of the church after Silas Mead's death. An extra house was obtained next door to the manse and later given to the Bap-

---

[38] *Register*, 1 June 1870, 3.
[39] John Price, *Memoir of George Swan Fowler. Christian Merchant.* (Adelaide: ES Wigg & Sons, 1897), 25-26.
[40] *Register*, 1 June 1870, 3.

tist Association. Much later, as preparation for the Centenary, the hall was upgraded, floor flattened, renamed Mead Memorial Hall and used for worship for months while the sanctuary was beautifully redecorated.

A family man

Soon after the opening of the sanctuary Ann Staple arrived from Somerset in 1864 and went to stay with Rev and Mrs HL Tuck in Kenton Valley. She and Silas were married there on 25 May 1864 (with a young Tuck daughter as bridesmaid). By the end of that year the initial church building was debt free, and the women of the church were keen to build the family a manse.

Ann Staple Mead

The Meads' first daughter, Lilian Staple Mead, was born 30 June 1865. The birth notice for Cecil Silas on 18 October 1866 was still from rented premises at 4 Clara Terrace, Franklin Street. Gertrude Ella was born 31 December 1867, and Annie Blanche on 8 January 1870. They lost John Angel (born and died 12 October 1871) in infancy, but welcomed Flora Beatrice on 20 January 1873. Obviously, Ann spent much of her time pregnant and caring for this growing family, but she also had a significant ministry in the congregation.

Ann Mead with baby Cecil, c. 1866

At a needed election for an additional initial deaconess in 1868, Silas explained:

> with regard to Mrs Mead it was unnecessary for numbers to record any votes for her, as on account of her relationship to the pastor, she already virtually filled such an office: therefore, if any members thought of voting for her, they had better substitute some other name.[41]

In 1873 Silas received a request from the Baptist Association to visit England to 'seek to bring out some ministers from Baptist colleges' for the work in South Australia.[42] He decided that then was not the time to be away but wrote to the FSBC deacons requesting fifteen months leave from December 1874 intimating that he would fulfil an undertaking to Ann to visit her relatives.[43]

---

[41] FSBC Members Meeting Minutes, 1 July 1868, 129.
[42] Letter HJ Lambert, Secretary SABA, to S Mead, 27 October 1873.
[43] Letter Silas Mead to deacons of FSBC, 4 November 1873. Ann's contribution to Silas's ministry is covered more fully in chapter 4.

Dismissing to new churches

One of the noteworthy features of Silas's ministry was his dismissal of members to other churches. Before the sanctuary was even opened in July 1862, Flinders Street Church was offered the use of Queenstown Independent Chapel for nominal rent. The matter was referred to Allan Webb who was under Silas's tutelage and assisting some Baptists in that area. He requested dismissal and was called to be the pastor of Alberton church on its formation on 6 October 1862.[44]

In April 1864 Daniel Melvin requested dismissal so he could join two friends in the formation of a Baptist Church at Moonta.[45] Five more members were released to Kapunda when a church was formed with eighteen members in September 1865.[46] Similarly another four were dismissed to Gawler where Silas Mead gave seven new members the right hand of fellowship on 16 September 1866.[47]

In December 1867 Silas inducted twenty-four members into the Norwood Baptist Church, of whom twenty-three were members released from Flinders Street, and the other was Rev HJ Lambert, who was to be their pastor for nearly twenty-one years.[48] Silas and he were to be close associates and friends. Norwood was a growth area of Adelaide and the formation of Norwood Baptist Church was the culmination of a seven-year period of prayer and activity in the rapidly developing eastern suburb.[49]

The suburb Hilton had been a preaching point with a Sunday school from FSBC since 1862.[50] In May 1871 local members asked for dismissal to form a church. The Flinders Street deacons resolved that, although believing the step inexpedient because there were so few men to unite in the formation of the church, yet if the formal application [were] received, they would undertake to bring it to the church.[51] Ten foundation members all came from FSBC and Wilton Hack, who later became a missionary to Japan, was their first pastor.[52]

---

[44] FSBC Members Meeting Minutes, 1 October 1862, 113. H Estcourt Hughes, *Our First Hundred Years: The Baptist Church of South Australia* (Adelaide: SA Baptist Union, 1937), 74-75.
[45] FSBC Members Meeting Minutes, 27 April 1864, 240. Hughes, *Our First Hundred Years*, 89.
[46] Hughes, *Our First Hundred Years*, 92.
[47] Hughes, *Our First Hundred Years*, 93-94.
[48] Hughes, *Our First Hundred Years*, 101-02.
[49] Copy of Mead's pastoral letter of dismissal in the FSBC Members Meeting Minutes, 11 December 1867, 89.
[50] FSBC Quarterly Members Tea Minutes, 18 February 1862, 92.
[51] FSBC Deacons Meeting Minutes, 15 November 1871, 204.
[52] Wilton Hack, Rev Stonehouse's son-in-law, is part of the mission's story. See Chapter 8.

Former members of FSBC who had moved north made up eight of the fifteen Baptists who formed the Georgetown church, the first in the northern regions of the expanding Colony.

Women's evolving role

In the initial membership of FSBC there were six couples, one, the Thomas family, with three unmarried daughters, who also joined the church. Their fourth daughter, Rosetta Jane, was one of the first Sunday School scholars, and became important in the suffrage movement.[53] There was a family cluster of four sisters, one married to John Beeby and another to James Whiting, a third who later married George Duke. There were four older women, including Mrs Browne, a widow, who ran a Girls' School, and Sarah Phillips, mother of Mary Holden. Mary Shaw had already organised a group of women and offered to raise money towards the funding of the property; an offer that was readily accepted even before Silas first arrived. Women's fund-raising ability was significant and they bargained with the men on what they would do on condition the men took their responsibilities.[54] They advocated that the pastor not forego his salary for the building fund, and they argued for the provision of a manse. They wrote to the deacons proposing that:

> Feeling it desirable that a manse should be erected as soon as possible, we are willing ...to undertake from the date the money being loaned to pay all additional interest above the sum of £60 now paid for rent, and to strive strenuously to pay off the principal by successive instalments.[55]

One of the major tasks of the early membership was the processing of every application for church membership. Initially two deacons were appointed as visitors who reported back to members meetings. In November 1861 Miss Melvin was asked to visit Mrs Newell and Miss Lipsett, the first woman appointed to do so.[56] Women, even the younger ones like Laura Fowler and Ellen Arnold became regular visitors.[57]

---

[53] Rosetta Jane (née Thomas) Birks married her older sister's widower.
[54] A group of FSBC women offered £500 towards the debt, so that the pastor's stipend does not go to the debt. FSBC Deacons Meeting Minutes, 23 September 1863, 125.
[55] FSBC Deacons Meeting Minutes, 3 July 1867, 15. At this time the Meads had two children, Lilian and Cecil.
[56] FSBC Members Meeting Minutes, 13 November 1861, 70.
[57] Laura Fowler was to become the first female medical graduate of the University of Adelaide. Ellen Arnold was later one of the pioneer missionaries sent to India in 1882. Both women were visitors while they were students.

Initially the women were allowed to report by letter to the meetings, but men visitors could speak. In 1868, following a case involving 'untruthfulness' by a young woman, there was a discussion of the wisdom of two women dealing with these issues. Soon after this incident, two sisters were appointed as sole visitors, and reported to the members meeting by letter.[58] On 28 January 1891 (as the debate on suffrage in South Australia involved women's capabilities) the church agreed 'that the lady members of the church instead of writing their reports of intending candidates for membership be allowed to report _viva voce_ at the meeting of the Church'.[59]

Well before then Silas had given a significant address at Morphett Vale Baptist Church in April 1868 advocating the appointment of deaconesses, as recognised and authorised leaders in the Church.[60] That same month William Kyffin Thomas prepared the notice of motion for FSBC:

> That the Church appoint by ballot six sisters for one year, whose duty it shall be to exercise spiritual oversight over the whole Sisterhood of the Church, with the concurrence of the Pastor, such elected sisters to have no charge or authority in connection with the business matters of the Church.[61]

The motion was passed unanimously in June.[62] At the following meeting five women were elected, who were required to signify their acceptance in writing by the next meeting and due to a tie for the sixth a further one needed to be nominated and elected. Following these appointments it was suggested to appoint a group of elders, whose 'special duty [be] to visit the male members and attend exclusively to spiritual work'.[63] At the next election the deaconesses were elected for three years. But it does not seem that the proposed election of elders with these responsibilities occurred for ten years, until 1878 after Silas's trip. Concepts could be introduced early but Silas was prepared to wait for their development.

For counselling enquirers he suggested the desirability of two men and three sisters joining him and staying behind after services.[64] Mrs Beeby, Mrs Leyburn and Mrs Glandfield were appointed for such duties.

---

58 FSBC Members Meeting Minutes, 1 April 1868, 113.
59 FSBC Members Meeting Minutes, 28 January 1891, 487.
60 The address was printed in *TP*, August 1868, 156-60.
61 FSBC Members Meeting Minutes, 29 April 1868, 121.
62 FSBC Members Meeting Minutes, 3 June 1868, 123.
63 FSBC Deacons Meeting Minutes, 29 July 1868, 57.
64 FSBC Members Meeting Minutes, 12 November 1873, 192.

Prayer was another area of church life where Silas was forthright, leading by example. His own life was said to be organised so that he could be up at 5 a.m. for his own commune with God. His vestry at the church was often lit late at night as he and others prayed. Even before they were using the sanctuary Silas indicated:

> he did not think it right that their devotions should be exclusively led by the elder members of the Church, but those also who had recently given their hearts to Christ should be encouraged to engage in prayer publicly, and he asked their sympathy on behalf of the young members.[65]

At the same meeting Silas mentioned that in answer to the complaint that he had not seen some in their own homes that the deacons were to relieve him of some visitation. His priority was evangelism, especially of the young.

City ministry

City ministry was often on the Church's agenda, whether it be in cooperation with others or as a specific ministry of the church. Richard Parkin, one of Silas's early students, did supervised practice in the city, until he became Baptist State evangelist and then moved to Magill as its first pastor in 1865.[66] In 1864 Miss Agnes Gillies was appointed to city ministry. She had come from Edinburgh and was seen as answered prayer.[67] Initially she reported to the minister, then to two deacons, and there were suggestions that she serve the Female Refuge. But she continued to serve the church until ill health in 1866 caused her resignation. She left the colony for England by April 1867 with a letter of dismissal, commendation and recommendation of her usefulness as a missionary.[68]

The church agreed that two workers were necessary for the city. They appointed William Brown for part-time work. Mrs Trick was recommended to them by Collins Street church (Victoria), and she was supported as a Bible woman by a Christian friend, but with decline in health in 1870 she requested an open dismissal and com-

[65] FSBC Quarterly Meeting Minutes, 28 May 1863, 163.
[66] FSBC Quarterly Meeting Minutes, February 1864, 220. See also Hughes, *Our First One Hundred Years*, 73.
[67] FSBC Quarterly Meeting Minutes, 16 May 1864, 247.
[68] FSBC Members Meeting Minutes, 3 April 1867, 42.

mendation in order to return to Melbourne.[69] In May 1870 Mrs Bunn replaced Mrs Trick.[70]

In the interim

The sudden death of Silas's wife, Ann Mead, from typhoid occurred on 15 June 1874, just five months after the enrolment of eight-year-old Cecil at Prince Alfred College. In response to her death, and Silas's decision to seek the recommended medical treatment overseas, the deacons formed a committee, including the deaconesses and another thirteen women, to collect a testimonial. £533/14/7 was raised of which £263/9/7 came from FSBC and £100 from GF Angas.[71]

While the pastor was away, they arranged that William Kyffin Thomas would attend the church 'on Wednesday and Sunday evenings to meet with anxious people and those who desired membership'.[72] He was also to conduct the weekly Bible class. Local ministers would be used for services, and the deaconesses were expected to meet and continue their visiting as usual, and to appoint a President to act during the pastor's absence and make necessary communication with Mr James Smith.

Silas sent back a suggestion that attendance records at communion services be collected and the deaconesses undertook to see to it.[73] Mrs James Kentish provoked a discussion on the spiritual state of the Church and the conduct of the prayer meeting and as a result one of the decisions that was taken was:

> That the sister members be respectfully requested to take part in our prayer meetings. We sincerely trust they may see their way clear to do so, as we doubt not a blessing will follow.[74]

The years 1875 and 1876 saw drops in church membership. The Mead children were living in Norwood while Silas was away. He arrived back in Adelaide mid-November 1875.

---

[69] FSBC Members Meeting Minutes, 13 April 1870.
[70] FSBC Members Meeting Minutes, 25 May 1870.
[71] FSBC Deacons Meeting Minutes, 17 June 1874, 343; 15 July 1874, 354.
[72] FSBC Deacons Meeting Minutes, 17 June 1874, 343.
[73] FSBC Deacons Meeting Minutes, 13January 1875, 391.
[74] Report on the Prayer Meeting of the Church, Members Minute Book, 3 March 1875, 254-56.

4

Loss, Holiness and Travel, 1874-75

Ken R Manley

Silas Mead's prominent place in the FSBC and among South Australian Baptists was happily assured when a sad personal tragedy disrupted his life. Ann, his beloved wife of ten years, contracted typhoid fever and died after just a few days on 15 June 1874.[1] A bereft Silas had five children (Lilian, Cecil, Gertrude, Blanche and Flora) to care for and was naturally overwhelmed by his loss.

Young Mead children:
Lilian, Gertrude, Blanche and Cecil (baby Flora is not included), c. 1874

---

[1] *TP*, July 1874, 77.

An impressive and deeply moving funeral was held at Flinders Street on 17 June. Several of Silas's ministerial friends—JM Day, HJ Lambert and S Fairey—shared in the service, whilst J Langdon Parsons gave the address, affirming, '"The Lord gave and the Lord hath taken away"; nor will we refrain from adding, "Blessed be the name of the Lord"'. On the following Sunday both services featured eulogies for Ann Mead.[2] In the morning Lambert (1836–1924) of Norwood, a graduate of Regent's Park College, reported that Ann had come to faith through the influence of a young Silas, was later baptised and had come to Adelaide to marry him. Her strong faith and her support of her husband in his ministry were emphasised as well as her compassion for the poor. What was also significant in Lambert's address were the details he reported of how, four years previous to her death, Ann had come to 'the conscious enjoyment of that perfect "rest through faith", which is usually characterized as the "higher Christian life" and which results from the entire consecration of self to the Lord'. This holiness emphasis reflected what had become the dominating feature of their shared spirituality.

In the evening J Langdon Parsons (1837–1903), of North Adelaide, another Regent's Park man, also stressed Ann's deep faith, noting that she was 'a true pastor's wife: rarely gifted by God with tenderness, patience, tact, meekness, prudence…She was the light of this Flinders-street Church.' He rehearsed her care for young people, her visiting women in gaol and service on the Committee of the Female Refuge and the Reformatory. Approaching death, Parsons recalled, she had sung in a faint voice,

'My Father's house on high.
Home of my soul HOW NEAR'
(these last words being sung with much emphasis.)[3]

The funeral services must have brought comfort to Silas, but he was unable to resume preaching at Flinders Street. The church, noting his poor health as well as his bereavement, granted him a leave of absence for fifteen months and urged him to 'avail himself of the advantages of a hydropathic establishment'.[4]

In fact, the church had earlier agreed in November 1873 to a request from the Baptist Association to grant Silas fifteen months leave in order for him to visit England with a view to recruiting ministers to come to the colony.[5] He had planned with Ann to leave in December 1874 to visit their families as well as travel to America and Palestine. Sadly, these hopes were dashed by Ann's untimely death.

---

[2] TP, July 1874, 77-79.
[3] TP, July 1874, 79.
[4] TP, August 1874, 85.
[5] FSBC Deacons Meeting Minutes, 12 November 1873.

Because these plans had already been made, Silas was quickly able to commence his leave. Just one month after Ann's death, the church on 15 July gathered to farewell Silas. The gifts, as detailed in the previous chapter, which enabled Silas to undertake an extensive travel itinerary, were a generous recognition of all that he had contributed to the development of Flinders Street. As was then noted, some 874 members had been added to the church since the church's formation in 1861. His leadership of the denomination had been pivotal to its growth and effectiveness. At this farewell, for the first time since Ann's death and with his children present, Silas spoke to the church 'with greater calmness and composure than it was supposed he would command'. He evidenced a 'tone of entire submission to the Lord' and strongly urged 'the cultivation of loving consideration as between husbands and wives, remembering how speedily the tie may be dissolved'.[6]

One reason why Silas was able to leave on this lengthy overseas break was that Ann's sister Sarah had travelled to Adelaide and married Frank Hann in FSBC on 15 November 1866. They were members of the Norwood Church but readily agreed to care for the children. Most probably this had been part of the plan when Silas and Ann were hoping to travel. He does not seem to have considered just how traumatic the loss of mother and the absence of father would affect the children—Flora was only eighteen months old. He debated whether to travel via Cape Horn or to journey 'through the heat' of the Red Sea region, but at the last moment decided to go 'home' by 'the mail', 'thinking that the heat for eight or nine days would be less perilous than the delay and the cold of the passage by the Horn'.[7] The Suez Canal had been opened in 1869 but it remained a long and tiring journey. Silas departed by the mail steamer, leaving Adelaide on Thursday 16 July 1874 and arrived in London on 3 October.[8] He was to be away until December 1875, well over the fifteen months that had been granted.

Experiencing and promoting holiness: 'the missing stone in the arch of God's truth'

Whilst Silas had many hopes for his long tour a prominent concern was to learn more about the holiness or 'higher life' movement that was already sweeping through much of world Evangelicalism. Indeed, Silas was one of the first in the Australian colonies to discover this teaching and to embrace the central experience of the 'rest of

---

[6] *TP*, August 1874, 85-86.
[7] *TP*, August 1874, 85.
[8] *AO*, 10 October 1874, 5.

faith' that was the key message of this theology.[9] All through his life, Silas was keen to learn of the latest movements that were influencing the worldwide church and because of his reading and experiences, he became an ardent apostle of this message—in his home, in his church, in his denomination and indeed throughout the world. Just as he had advanced the missionary cause among Baptists through the example of his single-minded devotion and persuasive powers, so now he promoted this understanding of Christian living.

To appreciate just how important this issue was for his travel plans some review of how Silas had come to understand what was later popularly known as the Keswick tradition needs to be outlined. Keswick is a beautiful tourist centre in the Lake District of England and is where an annual convention for the deepening of the spiritual life was first held in the summer of 1875. But the movement began well before that Keswick gathering.

The quest for holiness is, of course, an ancient and honoured Christian ambition. Two major traditions were followed widely among Australian Protestants: the Calvinist and the Wesleyan, with most Baptists following the former. Calvinists and all mainstream Protestantism taught that spiritual growth came from a steady and disciplined effort in order to grow in grace.[10] Spurgeon was one leading Baptist who advocated this basically Puritan understanding of holiness. By contrast, the Keswick model emphasised an immediate experience of holiness by simple faith. Just as one received salvation by faith, so holiness was also an experience of immediate change by simple faith. This 'rest of faith' was the new way to find holiness.

Wesleyans had a popular model of 'entire sanctification' which was fostered by revivalism and promoted a view that whilst this usually came after a long quest it was obtained by true faith and not human effort.[11] Indeed, perfect love was possible but only came through a crisis, an equivalent to conversion. But this sanctification could be lost and needed faith to sustain the experience. One of the more controversial dimensions of this Wesleyan tradition was that sinless perfection was attainable and this became a major point of dispute by Calvinists against the Wesleyan tradition.

What precisely did the new style of attaining 'the higher life' involve? Where did it come from? The new spirituality, in many ways a product of the age of Romanticism, was a transatlantic import deriving from the revivalist tradition of North

---

[9] See DW Bebbington, *Evangelicalism in Modern Britain A History from the 1730s to the 1980s* (London: Unwin Hyman, 1989), 151-80; D Bebbington, *Holiness in Nineteenth Century England* (Carlisle: Paternoster Press, 2000), 73-90.

[10] Bebbington, *Holiness*, 29-50.

[11] Bebbington, *Holiness*, 51-72.

America. One definitive text was WE Boardman's *The Higher Christian Life* (1858).[12] Boardman (1810–1866) was an American pastor and teacher whose book urged readers to move on by faith to a superior form of spirituality and 'the higher Christian life' became a popular catchphrase of the movement. Boardman was active in England and his book was also extremely influential in Australia.

Indeed, in 1868, the first year of *Truth and Progress*, the monthly magazine for South Australian Baptists that Silas and his friend John Price edited, a full review of Boardman's book by J Langdon Parsons was included. Parsons noted that Boardman advocated 'a second conversion' wherein the believer 'trusted Christ for sanctification and entire holiness'. Whilst Parsons was critical of this idea of a second conversion, and indeed the whole concept of 'the higher Christian life', his review indicates that the book and much similar literature was being read in the colony.[13] Many articles, all sympathetic to the new teaching, appeared throughout the succeeding issues of *Truth and Progress*. For example, in October 1869 a paper by AB Earle (1812–1895), an American pastor and evangelist, titled 'An Imperfect Christian resting in a Perfect Saviour' dated the exact moment of his consecration after which 'Jesus has been my all since then'.[14] There is no doubt that Silas and Price influenced many Baptist readers to accept this model of 'the higher life'.

Silas was frankly evangelistic in his zeal for this new model of spirituality. At a church meeting at FSBC on 1 February 1869, with Price by his side, Silas referred to 'his own religious experience'. He felt obliged to make a personal explanation 'in order that the church might understand more fully the style of remark they heard from him Sabbath to Sabbath' and which he admitted were 'in some respects different from what it was at one time'. What he meant was illustrated by reference to an article in *Truth and Progress* on 'The Way of Holiness', by Robert Pearsall Smith which had been extracted from *The Revival* magazine.[15] There was an air of expectation and perhaps some anxiety in the meeting, as Silas was leaving for Melbourne the next day to support the Collins Street Baptist Church 'during its present time of trial'.[16] Perhaps because of this religious and moral disaster in Melbourne Silas felt an urge to explain his own new-found peace and adoption of 'the higher life' model.

[12] WE Boardman, *The Higher Christian Life* (Boston: Henry Hoyt, 1858). A facsimile edition was published in 1984 by Garland Publishing.
[13] *TP*, September 1868, 173-75.
[14] *TP*, October 1869, 197-98.
[15] *TP*, May 1869, 33-35, 48-53.
[16] *TP*, March 1869, 59. Rev James Taylor (1814-1896), a leading evangelist and church leader in Melbourne, had preached at the opening of Flinders Street Church in 1863 but had suddenly resigned from the Collins Street Church amidst what the local press called 'the clerical scandal'. See Manley, *From Woolloomooloo*, 72-73.

Robert Pearsall Smith (1827–1898) and his wife Hannah (1832–1911) were American Quakers who were profoundly blessed by Methodist sanctification teaching in 1867.[17] They became revivalist evangelists for the holiness/deeper life movement. Pearsall Smith's article, published over two issues of *Truth and Progress*, shows his direct and engaging style. He appealed to readers who had a sense of deficiency in their experience and set out in a clear biblical exposition his understanding of holiness. He offered step-by-step prayerful guidance on how to receive the rest of faith so that when temptation comes the believer would be able 'to hide behind the shield of faith'. He urged his readers to recall how they had trusted Christ for salvation and urged them now to trust him for sanctification. You have failed, Christ has not, he insisted. This paper had special significance for Ann Mead, as we shall see.

Another article by Smith appeared in the May issue, 'The way of holiness' in which he concluded, 'I do not present this secret of the Lord as a doctrine to be discussed, but as a *life* to be enjoyed'.[18]

Silas's sermon on 11 April 1869 on 'Service of Holiness' showed how deeply he had embraced the new teaching.[19] He addressed the question of whether a Christian can be sinless and lamented that few Christians actually sought to live such a sinless life: this was a form of Antinomianism, Silas insisted. We are to be righteous in everything we do, and this only seems impossible because we do not believe what the New Testament teaches, that all who are 'in Christ' can do all things. The idea that Silas held to a notion of sinless perfection is suggested here but he was always cautious about claiming this in debates on the topic. Indeed, in October 1870 he answered the question, 'Does the "old Nature" cease to exist on our becoming united to Christ?'. His answer was 'No!'. Through negligence and unbelief, 'the old enemy gains a hold' but with confession and faith the rest of peace may be regained.[20]

An insight into just how powerful this teaching had become for both Silas and Ann Mead is revealed in a letter which Ann wrote to her brother-in-law ('E') on 30 March 1869.[21] When he was in England Silas was given this letter and he had it published as 'it so very clearly expressed her conception of the bright life of faith in Jesus'. As a pastor's wife she could not give such 'an open testimony to the great change wrought in her spiritual life', but Silas was glad that it could now be publicly shared.

---

[17] For the Smiths, see ME Dieter, 'Smith, Hannah Whithall and Robert Pearsall' in T Larsen (ed), *Biographical Dictionary of Evangelicals* (Leicester: Inter-Varsity Press, 2003), 616-18.

[18] *TP*, May 1869, 98.

[19] *TP*, June 1869, 101-04.

[20] *TP*, October 1870, 110.

[21] 'E' was Ebenezer Drayton who had married Ann's sister, Martha Staple.

Her intimate letter shows the depth of her religious experience and her relationship with Silas.[22]

Ann told 'E' that she felt that she had preserved 'a guilty silence' for three months in 'not testifying to the grace of Christ in me'. She was afraid that some would think of her as appearing holier than others, but she felt obliged to share her story. For years she had felt despair as she heard others speak about 'abiding in Christ' and 'overcoming the world'. She continued:

> Some months ago I noticed a change in my dear husband. He seemed to realize more of the love of Jesus, and the things that used to vex him now seemed to have no power to do so. I marked this change but said nothing, and he said nothing except that it came out in sermons, &c. Well, when we were going to take our trip up the Murray I thought I would ascertain what made him so different to myself. We had much quiet converse, but I did not open my mind, and returned home more miserable than ever.

Sometime later, after Silas had again preached on this theme, Ann confessed the bitterness of spirit that had overcome her. Silas did not argue but quietly gave her a copy of 'The Way of Holiness' by Pearsall Smith. Feeling quite resentful, Ann read it but then happily made the 'glorious discovery' and proclaimed, 'Saviour, I must, I will trust Thee'. When they met for tea she joyfully told Silas, 'I've got it. I live, yet not I but Christ liveth in me…It just seemed to me as if Jesus had only been half a Saviour before'. She asked that the piece by Smith be placed in *Truth and Progress* (as it was in the May issue).

It is clear that during all of 1869–70 the topic of holiness was discussed in almost every meeting of the Baptist Association. Price rejected any idea that a couple of Adelaide ministers wanted to gather them together since they had discovered some new truth, yet he affirmed that an old truth could be hidden by indistinct forms of expression. However, it is clear that many had come into a new appreciation of this doctrine. Several ministers made strong statements of how their lives had been changed. JM Day of Kapunda, for example, spoke at length about how Silas's advice and his gift of a booklet had changed his life and ministry.[23] This kind of testimony was repeated in many lives and was a key factor in the growth of the movement.

In the same month that Ann wrote to her brother-in-law, the Meads wrote directly to Pearsall Smith on 30 March 1869, and began an encouraging correspondence which, after Ann's death and whilst Silas was overseas, appeared in the Adelaide

---

[22] The full text of the letter is in *TP*, May 1874, 55.
[23] *TP*, November 1869, 222-23.

Baptist paper. Smith was pleased that 'the antipodes does not break or change the fellowship of Jesus'. His warm and friendly letters greatly encouraged Ann and Silas. 'I feel myself more and more impelled to present the privilege as an *immediate step*—an abandonment of soul to Jesus never to be recalled or modified'.[24] Silas had always been an avid reader and kept up to date with what was happening overseas through a large range of periodicals and books. His testimony from 'the antipodes' was greatly appreciated by Smith: 'I wish I could convey the loving communion I feel towards you and your dear wife, the sense of oneness in Christ—the holy fellowship'.

In January 1873 Smith declared to the Meads, 'We have, I believe, found the missing stone in the arch of God's truth, and I know not what we may hope for in the future if the universal church will receive the message. God grant it!'[25]

Certainly, Silas Mead embraced this vision and hope. This was an insight that he had not discovered in all his advanced study at Regent's Park. He and his close friend John Price who was in the midst of a revival at the mining town of Moonta did all they could to proclaim this message. Commenting on this phenomenon, so early in the story of the spread of the holiness movement, David Bebbington observed, 'They were practising Keswick spirituality before Keswick began'.[26]

Clearly the trip to England that Silas and Ann had planned together had included meeting Smith and other leaders in the holiness movement. Silas retained this hope for his personal visit. His undoubted highlight was meeting and hearing Smith as well as his wife Hannah and, of course, many other higher life speakers who unambiguously taught that sanctification and the victorious life was not a matter of strenuous effort but of peaceful trust.

Travels and meetings

Meeting leading figures in the holiness movement and gauging its effectiveness was an important objective for Silas Mead's trip but this was not his sole concern as he left his family and friends in Adelaide. He anticipated visiting his and Ann's family as well as renewing friendship with College friends. Sharing in denominational events and meeting leading preachers as well as a deep interest in everything connected with global mission were high on his agenda. He was also charged with trying to find a senior minister for the North Adelaide church and, of course, planned to visit numer-

---

[24] *TP*, August 1874, 90.
[25] *TP*, August 1874, 91.
[26] D Bebbington, *Victorian Religious Revivals. Culture and Piety in Local and Global Contexts* (Oxford: Oxford University Press, 2012), 224.

ous famous sites, not least in the Holy Land. His trip was an exhausting but extremely rewarding adventure for Silas and his health was largely restored.

Silas was careful to write to his family and friends as frequently as he could, and some of his letters together with press reports of his activities help in constructing a reasonably comprehensive account of his itinerary and experiences.

His ship left on 16 July 1874, arriving at Galle in Sri Lanka on 4 August.[27] Silas disembarked at Bombay on 12 August, because he wanted to see mission work in India, especially the South Australian work. He wrote home from Calcutta on 17 August with a comprehensive report.[28] He had endured a tiring rail journey to Calcutta (over fifty-nine hours, Silas reported) where he met his college friend GH Rouse who helped plan his ongoing itinerary. He left the first evening by train for Goalundo where he was met by Samuel Buksh, an elderly 'native Christian teacher', who accompanied him on a rather hair-raising boat journey of twenty-two miles to Faridpur. Silas was pleasantly surprised to find the town 'such a pretty place'. He was delighted to meet Punchanon Biswas, 'our youngest native teacher', who was to play a strategic role in the development of Australian Baptist mission work.[29] His first-hand contact with Faridpur was to be of great help for the South Australian mission.

After meeting local dignitaries, Silas returned to Calcutta where he attended services at the historic Circular Road Baptist Church (on the same site as the Baptist Missionary Press) where Rouse preached. In the evening he visited William Carey's church at Lal Bazaar. He next made the short trip to Serampore and inevitably was deeply moved to see the sites associated with Carey and his colleagues. Silas was also impressed by the schools conducted by Rev and Mrs George Kerry and by the 'Duff Institute' which had 1,200 boys enrolled as part of Alexander Duff's emphasis on the role of English-medium education in winning the Bengali elite for Christ.[30] Silas then visited Benares and Delhi before boarding his ship at Bombay on 28 August. His two weeks in India had been an exhausting but instructive time for the missionary enthusiast.

Finally, he reached Southampton on Saturday 26 September where he was warmly greeted by the local pastor, Rev Robert Caven, a Regent's Park College friend. Sympathy for the bereaved pastor was warm and caring. Silas preached on the follow-

[27] *Freeman*, 1 September 1874, 444.
[28] *TP*, October 1874, 119-20.
[29] For Biswas and the beginnings of Australian Baptist missions in India, see T Cupit, R Gooden and K Manley (eds), *From Five Barley Loaves. Australian Baptists in Global Mission 1864-2010* (Preston, Vic: Mosaic Resources, 2013), 1-18.
[30] Kerry (1826-1906) was a LMS missionary. For Duff (1806-1878) see ID Maxwell, 'Alexander Duff' in *Biographical Dictionary of Evangelicals*, 197-99 and MA Laird, *Missionaries and Education in Bengal 1793-1837* (Oxford: Oxford University Press, 1972).

ing Sunday evening and he found it 'a pleasure to preach but the physical exertion seems to have been too much'.[31] Silas left the next day for London where he saw a Dr Wheeler who advised him to go to a hydropathic establishment at Forres in the north of Scotland, about twenty-five miles from Inverness. Silas had been advised in Australia to seek this form of treatment which was a method of 'water cure' rapidly growing in popularity. The Cluny Hill Hydropathic establishment at Forres in Morayshire was a state-of-the-art centre housed in a splendid facility opened in 1865.[32] Silas did not take this cure immediately but visited family and friends in the Somerset region, proceeded to the Baptist Union autumnal meetings in Newcastle and thence to Forres.[33] His only recorded comment about the water cure is that he enjoyed some talk about the holiness movement with other patients whilst there.[34] Whether this cure greatly helped him or not, Silas did recover a greater measure of strength and undertook a demanding program in England and abroad.

The rest of his busy time was taken up with making family connections, visiting leading Baptist figures, touring in Europe and the Holy Land as well as active involvement in the holiness movement.

Silas was happy to travel down to Somerset and catch up with his family and relatives. The foundation stone for the new chapel at Curry Mallet, 'on a site kindly granted by the Prince of Wales', had been laid by Silas's brother William on 7 August 1873 and the chapel was opened on 27 May 1874. Silas gladly preached at services there on 3 January 1875 and spoke about Australia to several meetings during the week. A special pleasure towards the end of his time in England was to baptise his niece Mary Baker and his two nephews, Baxter Baker and Samuel Mead, at Curry Mallet on 2 August 1875.[35]

Silas was also welcomed at the autumnal Baptist Union Assembly in Newcastle where he made a brief but 'deeply interesting speech'. He brought greetings from South Australia, declaring that 'we are a small people there, but nevertheless we are glad to feel a oneness with your Union here'. He hoped that 'increasing sympathy' for their work could be found. In the missionary conference he shared details of his recent time in India and hoped a large number of men would go to India.[36] Silas later commented that he was surprised at how few ministers were at the meetings and that there

[31] *Freeman*, 18 September 1874, 460; *TP*, December 1874, 145.
[32] See J Bradley, M Dupree and A Durie, 'Taking the Water-Cure: The Hydropathic Movement in Scotland, 1840-1940', *Business and Economic History*, 26.2 1997, 426-37. The Centre is today an education centre.
[33] *TP*, December 1874, 145.
[34] *TP*, February 1875, 21.
[35] Minutes of Hatch Beauchamp Baptist Church (kindly supplied by R Gooden).
[36] *Freeman*, 9 October 1874, 496; 16 October 1874, 498.

was insufficient time for business and too much time taken up with papers. It was a 'conference' with no time for real discussion. He also deplored 'the absence from the agenda of the great, vital, and pressing questions of real Church life, and of Christian service'.[37] He evidently had in mind the holiness question which was all-consuming for him. The contrast with the smaller and more personal meetings in South Australia was apparent.

Whilst in the north of England, Silas went to Sheffield where he met and heard the former Chartist Henry Vincent (1813–1878) give eloquent lectures on Wycliffe and Civil and Religious Liberty. He was also impressed by Sir Wilfrid Lawson (1829–1906), the Liberal temperance campaigner, who spoke on the Permissive Bill intended to give each parish the right to refuse the issue of licences to sell intoxicating liquor. He was impressed with the enthusiasm for temperance and observed that he was not in practice a total abstainer, 'but I wish to be if my health would justify it'.[38]

From Sheffield Silas went to the Baptist College at Rawdon, near Leeds where he met with the Principal Dr Green and the students. On Sunday he was at Manchester where he heard Alexander Maclaren preach a 'most splendid sermon' and was 'converted' to the place of organs in worship, 'I strongly wish we could have one at Flinders-street'.[39] He also heard Mr Birch at the Manchester Free Trade Hall and in the evening he was seated on the platform when some seventy orphans were present and sang some Sankey's hymns. A deeply moved Silas observed, 'I confess I could hardly look upon them at first without a great gulping sensation in the throat. It was positively hard work not to weep'.[40] In the afternoon Silas had gone out in the rain to hear Neal Dow of Maine, another temperance enthusiast who gave a 'Yankeeish' address on the topic.[41]

From Manchester Silas went to Liverpool, being unimpressed with the dirty city that he found. Staying with another Regent's Park friend, PG Scorey, he joined with most of the Liverpool ministers in a meeting with 'Mr Sale the missionary of Barisal'.[42] After visiting several churches Silas returned to London where he joined in

---

[37] *Freeman*, 23 October 1874, 528.
[38] *TP*, February 1875, 19.
[39] *TP*, February 1875, 20.
[40] William Birch founded 'Cornbrook Orphanage' in Manchester. He migrated to New Zealand in 1889 and was a controversial minister at the Auckland Baptist Tabernacle. Birch was for a short time at the Burton Street Baptist Church in Sydney but returned to Auckland. He later migrated to California where he died in 1900: J Ayson Clifford, *A Handful of Grain. The Centenary History of the Baptist Union of NZ, vol 2 1882-1914* (Wellington, NZ Baptist Historical Society, 1982), 28-30.
[41] *TP*, February 1875, 20. Dow (1804-1897) was an ardent Prohibition advocate and politician.
[42] John Sale and his wife Elizabeth were important in establishing the Zenana missions and greatly assisted Australian Baptist missionaries in this work. They worked in Barisal in Bengal.

a conference for about seventy former students at Regent's Park College. He greatly enjoyed greeting 'several old faces that I did not expect to see again'.[43]

On 4 February 1875 Silas left for his 'grand tour' of Europe and Palestine which would take until the end of May.[44] This exciting but strenuous trip was to have deep significance for Silas at many levels. It would increase his knowledge of history and mission work as well as create a store of rich memories for later speaking. Travel in his times, especially in deep winter, could often be quite unpredictable and even dangerous but he undertook his great adventure with faith and a keen fascination for everything that he saw and experienced.

After crossing to Calais, Silas left for Rome via Paris, Macon, Turin, Milan, Venice and Florence. On the Sunday morning he witnessed the Mass at the impressive Lateran Church, in the afternoon an English-speaking Presbyterian Church and in the evening shared in a 'religious conversazione' where Silas and several others spoke. The next morning, he met up with James Wall, an English Baptist who helped establish the Baptist movement in Italy and was supported by the BMS. With evangelist 'Father' Paolo Grassi, whom Silas also met, Wall held a meeting of about eighty people on the Wednesday evening in his own house where Silas was one of the speakers. The Baptist work in Italy greatly impressed Silas.[45]

From Rome his touring group sailed to Cairo where warmer weather was welcomed and although he enjoyed seeing the pyramids and other famous sights his main interest was naturally in Christian work in Egypt. He was especially pleased to meet missionary Mary Louise Whately (1824–1899), daughter of the late Archbishop of Dublin, Richard Whately (1787–1863), whose book *Ragged Life in Egypt* (1863) Silas had (of course) read. He visited the schools conducted by Whately for some 300 children although he was, however, unimpressed with the general squalor of Cairo which reminded him of Ceylon and Bengal.[46]

From Cairo he and his party travelled to Palestine, landing at Jaffa (Joppa, 'the filthiest town I was ever in') where he visited the supposed house of Simon the Tanner (Acts 9:43). Overland travel brought them to Jerusalem where he saw the well-known sights of the holy city and Bethany. Then to Bethlehem, the Dead Sea and Jordan. Silas enjoyed 'two dips in the clear water' of Lake Galilee but after two days in that region they encountered a severe rainstorm as they travelled further. Tents were blown

43 *TP*, February 1875, 20.
44 *Freeman*, 12 February 1875, 79.
45 *TP*, May 1875, 56; for Wall, Grassi and Baptist work in Italy see B Stanley, *The History of the Baptist Missionary Society 1792-1992* (Edinburgh: T & T Clark, 1992), 220-22; AW Wardin (ed), *Baptists Around the World* (Nashville: Broadman & Holman, 1995), 277-78.
46 *TP*, July 1875, 78.

away, thunder and lightning alarmed many in the group as the guides struggled to find the way. Eventually they reached Caesarea Philippi where Silas preached a short sermon. The way to Mount Hermon was blocked with snow (indeed, some of 'the Thomas Cook party' had been snowed in for three days).[47] Eventually, Silas's group reached Damascus and thence to Beirut where to Silas's great disappointment the ruins of Baalbek could not be visited because of 'four hours of fierce storms of hail, sleet, and snow'.[48]

Despite these adventures Silas confessed in Athens on 20 April 1875 that he was 'exceedingly well', better than he had felt for many years.[49] The party had left Beirut by small steamer and Silas was disappointed that it was not possible to visit Tarsus as no one else was willing to travel from the port with him. He did, however, see Smyrna and Ephesus which brought special pleasure. Sailing through the Aegean Sea was a relaxing experience, a fortnight of 'luxuriant idleness', visiting islands like Rhodes although he missed seeing Patmos. Silas enjoyed his time in Athens, being 'delighted beyond my expectation' with a visit to the Acropolis.[50]

From Athens they sailed to Constantinople and then to Venice. They visited Prague, Dresden, Berlin and Hamburg. Silas met up with yet another Regent's Park former student Joseph Lehmann in Berlin. He was, however, grieved at what he saw as 'the general absence of Christian life in Germany'. Many shops were open on Sunday and the great bulk of the people 'give themselves to pleasure-seeking'. Silas returned to London, feeling well and with a mind filled with memories and ideas for preaching.[51]

His holiness advocate friend Robert Pearsall Smith had been holding successful meetings in Berlin, but Silas missed seeing him there. He was able to purchase a book about the Oxford meetings which had been highly successful and where Smith had been a major speaker. Silas promised to see that copies were sent to Adelaide, but he was disappointed that his Berlin friend Lehmann was not in sympathy with this movement.[52]

Indeed, for most of the time that Silas had been in England the holiness movement had been prominent in his mind. During the conference for former students at Regent's Park College Silas had been 'electrically delighted' to hear the question privately raised, 'Could we not have a little meeting of those interested in the subject of holiness?' Silas returned the next week to talk with any of the students who were inter-

---

[47] Baptist local missionary Thomas Cook (1808-1892) had begun his tours in 1841.
[48] *TP*, July 1875, 78.
[49] *TP*, August 1875, 88.
[50] *TP*, August 1875, 88.
[51] *TP*, August 1875, 88.
[52] *TP*, August 1875, 88.

ested and found that several had been at the Oxford Conference. A few testified to the change that had come into their lives and, as Silas commented, 'I don't know anything that could have made my heart so rejoice'.[53] In general, he had been disappointed at the prejudice and opposition he had encountered on this subject. But as he travelled he did not fail to raise the subject and in all kinds of places found willing listeners.

The highlight of all Silas's time in England was undoubtedly the 'Convention for the Promotion of Holiness' held at Brighton over eleven days from 29 May 1875.[54] This was the peak of the American revivalists' influence in Britain. The later Keswick meetings, it has been observed, simply 'substituted the Wordsworthian Lakes for Regency Brighton'.[55] The Brighton convention was attended by over 5,000 people who had been attracted by the invitation to all who sought 'a life of maintained communion and victory in a degree hitherto unlooked for'. The secret was 'an entire surrender to and trust in the Lord'. Phoebe Palmer and the Pearsall Smiths were key speakers.

Personal responsibility for sanctification was the theme of Pearsall Smith's short but powerful speech in which he raised the familiar theme of the movement in true revivalist style:

> If there are any present who are doubtful as to whether or not they have brought their all to Christ, who have any lurking uncertainty, any twilight, under the shade of which they do not know whether some things are God's or their own—if there are any such I beseech you at once to give yourself wholly to God. A complete consecration is an easy life of rest and ease to the soul, and a partial consecration is the very opposite—a hard and difficult life.[56]

Under such emotional pressure, reinforced by suitable hymns and extended prayer gatherings, many traditional Evangelicals adopted this new understanding of sanctification. The climax came on the sixth day when Pearsall Smith placed great pressure on his hearers to embrace 'here and now' the experience that had been talked about so much.

Silas had been fully involved. He chaired some sessions and on another occasion gave his own testimony about his experience in Australia. He concluded:

---

53 *TP,* February 1875, 20.
54 *Record of the Convention for the Promotion of Scripture Holiness at Brighton 29 May to 7 June 1875* (London, 1875).
55 J Kent, *Holding the Fort: Studies in Victorian Revivalism* (London: Epworth Press, 1978), 341.
56 Kent, *Holding the Fort,* 343.

> What I want to press upon you is what Christ asks you to do
> tonight, to enter upon the promised land of glorious, beautiful
> rest. Here it is, take God at his word; He says you are in Christ
> Jesus, believe it, lift up thy heart and say, 'Lord Jesus, I thank
> Thee that I am in Thee, because Thy word says it'...Christ will
> cause to flow into your heart a stream of living water.[57]

The report of his talk in the *Christian World* added that Silas 'had accepted the "perfectionist" theory in its extreme form'. The *Truth and Progress* editor denied that this was really so.[58]

Pearsall Smith was obliged to leave at the end of the Convention and indeed the movement more generally because of a rather vague moral allegation against him. Details are unclear but the leaders were quite emphatic in their dismissal of this key leader.[59] This was naturally most distressing for his supporters and one wonders whether Silas himself ever had quite the same enthusiasm for the movement.

Certainly, back in Australia, especially in Victoria, a holiness convention movement along the lines of Keswick was later begun with many key Baptists involved.[60] This Australian style of convention, like Keswick, was not revivalist in its theology and style of meeting and appealed to the cultured Evangelical. Not all Australian Baptists embraced the higher life movement. WT Whitley, for example, the founding principal of the Victorian Baptist Theological College in 1891, opposed the movement's theology, asking what exactly a 'lower' kind of Christian life might be.[61] In this Whitley was echoing the criticisms of the holiness movement made by many Evangelicals from the Reformed tradition in England.[62]

That Silas Mead maintained his holiness position is undoubted. Indeed, on leaving Adelaide one of his confessed disappointments was how few had adopted this doctrine and how rarely it was preached.

Doubtless his memory of that significant trip abroad, not least his active participation in the Brighton meetings and the way it had refreshed his ministry and life at a time of deep personal loss, remained a powerful force in his ministry. His children

[57] *TP*, September 1875, 104.
[58] *TP*, September 1875, 105 (quoting *Christian World*).
[59] See Kent, *Holding the Fort*, 355 and JC Pollock, *The Keswick Story: The Authorized History of the Keswick Convention* (London: Hodder and Stoughton, 1964).
[60] Stuart Piggin and Robert D Linder, *The Fountain of Public Prosperity: Evangelical Christians in Australian History 1740-1914* (Clayton: Monash University Publishing, 2019), 446-52; Manley, *From Woolloomooloo*, 123; D Paproth, 'The deeper life movement in Victoria 1880-1914', *Our Yesterdays*, 10 (2002), 53-77.
[61] *Victorian Baptist*, May 1894, 101-02.
[62] Bebbington, *Holiness*, 86-90.

and congregation welcomed him home with great enthusiasm and many a tale was told of his experiences during 1874–75.

Silas was disappointed that the two ministers he had approached about coming to North Adelaide had both declined. He certainly had aimed high by speaking with two leading pastors, John Clifford of Paddington and JG Greenhough, then at Cotham Grove in Bristol. Both were liberal in theology and it is interesting that Silas should have selected them, and not one of Spurgeon's graduates. Perhaps this was more a reflection of his judgment on what North Adelaide was seeking. Both men later toured Australia.[63]

Just a few years later, on 22 October 1878, Silas married Mrs Mary Leighton (née Pitty), herself a widow who had been baptised by him. She was partially paralysed by a stroke a year after marriage but remained a great support to Silas. Sadly, Mary died on 21 March 1886.[64] Once again Silas experienced personal loss. By this time, he must have begun to wonder what he might do with the rest of his life.

[63] TP, October 1875, 122; Manley, From Woolloomooloo, 126, 128-29, 225, 178.
[64] TP, 1 April 1886, 50-51.

Work, Prayer and Blessing: FSBC, 1875-97

Rosalind Gooden

Welcome home

Silas Mead was warmly welcomed home by both church and family. He arrived on 19 November 1875 by *SS Northumberland* (a smart trip of just 51 days London to Melbourne) then steamer to Adelaide. He preached twice on 28 November and attended a welcome home on Wednesday evening including a large number of pastors from the city. All welcomed his return to health and anticipated his fruitful ministry for years to come. Silas acknowledged the kind assistance given by ministers of various denominations in filling the pulpit during his absence and noted that the congregations had been well sustained. He felt that here was proof of the unity existing among the several denominations by the readiness with which different ministers had consented to act in his absence.[1]

Whether the family lived in Norwood at the Hanns' or the Hanns moved in with them is unknown but after Silas's return he and his young family lived in Osmond Terrace, Norwood, a much greater distance from the church buildings. Silas needed a horse for transport. Costs of children's education were growing. Even before his return FSBC had determined that a manse needed to be built adjoining the church in FSBC, and a number of women promised to raise necessary finance. Economic times were depressed and added to pressures. A series of fund-raising lectures was arranged and

---

[1] *TP,* 8 January 1876, 8.

Silas gave lectures of his travels. One of the first was 'Athens'.[2] At the deacons' meeting in February 1876 there was the suggestion of need for a co-pastor, and Silas was asked to write to John Price with the knowledge of the deacons.[3] This was another instance of delay before action. A co-pastor came in 1895.

Money matters

Silas had left the care of his family with the Hanns. He had been blessed with considerable monetary gifts as a testimonial from a variety of sources. Silas had reckoned that during his absence the expenses for his children had cost £6/10/0 per week. In June 1876 he raised with the deacons that his income did not meet his expenditure, nor had it for a number of years. In July 1877 he wrote giving reasons why he was £100 a year out of pocket.[4] Subsequently he withdrew the comments (a practice he used at times in negotiating business) but those details give insight into Silas's philosophy of life and ministry. He had spent money on furniture and fittings for the Norwood property that he claimed would be unrealisable when the family relocated.[5] He did admit to obtaining a piano for £50, something he had wanted but delayed for years. He argued that the life insurance paid by the Church should be designated as a payment by the Church for insurance of the pastor's life and not salary. He reckoned that £50–£60 a year was spent on books and petty expenses in service of the Church. He claimed the horse had cost him £50. His reason for raising the matter was 'his existing obligation to his family'.[6]

At the following meeting of the deacons when his earlier statement was withdrawn, he submitted:

> Assuming...that it is the wish of some of the deacons that I should be absent from, or if present, to be silent at Deacon's [sic] meetings when money matters are discussed, I think it right to submit the following statement: I much regret that now for the first time in my 16 years pastorate I should feel it necessary to state what I conceive to be my obligations in regard to Deacons' meetings. I cannot but be aware that financial affairs

[2] *Chronicle*, Saturday 18 October 1876, 9.
[3] FSBC Deacons Meeting Minutes, 28 February 1876, 436.
[4] FSBC Deacons Meeting Minutes, 27 July 1877, 507.
[5] This suggests that while he was away the children lived in the Hanns' house and when Silas returned he had to set up house for them all.
[6] FSBC Deacons Meeting Minutes, 2 July 1877, 507.

play a very important part in the machinery of church life either to its advantage or disadvantage, therefore I think that in what so closely concerns the welfare of the Church the pastor should have a voice in the deliberations of the Diaconate.[7]

Silas included in his reasons the role of the pastor in raising funds and therefore his obligation to donors for their use. He claimed that this was scriptural. He wrote:

I know that under special circumstances ...the Apostles chose to hand over to deacons the charge of the common fund for the daily maintenance of the disciples—virtually a poor fund—but I am not aware of any evidence in scripture that this practice was perpetuated in the first churches. Beside there is the completest evidence that Paul did not act upon this principle. Substantially he made himself the Chief Mover and Director of the funds raised. Nor is it the practice of British Baptist Churches to exclude the pastor from such diaconal discussions of financial matters.[8]

But in the hope of promoting smoother working of FSBC operations Silas offered:

...to waive my right of taking part in Deacons' meetings when financial affairs are discussed for one year from this date, if requested by the deacons to do so. In the event of this being done it will be necessary to rearrange Deacons' meetings defining those at which I should be present and those from which I should be absent...I hope it will in future be regarded as a function of the Diaconate to labour to stimulate the people to liberality...I trust also that prompt and practical measures will be adopted ...with the view to meeting the Church debt in April 1880...As to the future I have no other wish than to honour Christ in my judgements and decisions.[9]

He was an astute negotiator, but the deacons' reaction must have disappointed Silas. They felt it was inadvisable to bring before the church any fresh scheme for raising money for church or manse debts, they did not recommend any increase in salary for the pastor, nor did they adopt any plans to eliminate the debt of £2,800 by 23 April 1880. But they did resolve:

---

[7] FSBC Deacons Meeting Minutes, 11 July 1877, 513.
[8] FSBC Deacons Meeting Minutes, 11 July 1877, 503.
[9] FSBC Deacons Meeting Minutes, 11 July 1877, 513.

That it is not desirable to exclude the pastor from discussing financial matters but that the Deacons consider he should not initiate them nor take a prominent part in them.[10]

At the following meeting Silas voiced his objection to the principle of the assigning to the pastor a position of inferiority inconsistent with his pastoral office, without him conceding his danger of conflict of interest.[11]

At the same time the SABA was talking of finding a paid secretary, a policy that Silas felt would hinder the work of the Association by siphoning too many resources into a salary rather than help needy churches in country areas.

The leadership group with whom he had worked so vigorously initially were no longer at FSBC. George Fife Angas had shown 'a discreet wisdom of abstinence' from the congregational life of FSBC from the beginning.[12] His membership was at Angaston and he died in 1879. David Fowler had returned to England (dying in 1881), and George Swan Fowler and James Alexander Holden were key leaders at Norwood BC. They met Silas at Association meetings, with many of those meetings held on FSBC property, which was virtually the SABA headquarters. William Kyffin Thomas, who had sustained so much of the work in Silas's absence, had moved from nearby Wyatt Street to Glenelg, and died on 4 July 1878.[13] Times had changed and possibly so had Silas.

At the church anniversary in 1878 Silas, reading the annual report, said that in the light of their lack of progress in membership or in tackling debt it was his belief that it was not God-honouring to ignore that large debt. He explained:

It is not often that ministers give in their resignations and yet go on in hearty co-operation with the Church. I have not resigned my pastorate of this Church, nor have I any present intention of doing so...But I am free to acknowledge to-night, that any thought of final separation from the church seems farther off than ever. Yesterday, as you know, I gave in two resignations—the first resignation was of my salary to the Church, the second resignation was of myself into the Lord's hand and care.[14] I feel

[10] FSBC Deacons Meeting Minutes, 11 July 1877, 513.
[11] FSBC Deacons Meeting Minutes, 18 July 1877, 517.
[12] Comment made in: 'The Late George Fife Angas', *TP*, June 1879, 65.
[13] The sermon preached by Mead on the Sunday following WK Thomas's death was published in *TP*, August 1878, 88-89.
[14] During the initial financing of the building of the sanctuary, he had also foregone his salary for a time.

relieved and much more happy this day than on Saturday. The thing is now off my mind and I feel at ease about it...[15]

Later he acknowledged that the elections of deacons and deaconesses had been fulfilled 'without a jar'. He concluded: 'I trust…both Pastor and Church will earnestly and cheerfully work together, pray together, be blessed together.' This was his standard of ministry—working, praying and being blessed together.

New manse and new marriage

In 1877 the family with Lilian (12), Cecil (11), Gertrude (10), Blanche (7) and Flora (3) and a house-keeper moved back into the city into the newly finished manse. Intriguingly nothing is known of the early education of the girls, but Cecil continued at Prince Alfred College.

FSBC church and manse, c. 1905 [SASL PRG 631_2_1800]

At that time Silas described his pattern of life and ministry as:

to read so as to keep abreast of the literature of the day, to spend the best part of two days in preparing sermons for the Sunday, take one day's rest out of seven, devote such time as duty demands to his own household, hold a public position on

15 *TP,* July 1878, 105.

committees in the city, work for the Denomination, prepare for
Literary Club meetings, Bible Class, Greek Testament Class,
Wednesday evening prayer meetings, attend funerals, go to the
homes of the sick and visit 470 members...[16]

His answer to the impossibility of such visitation was that this work of primary
pastoral visitation should be done by the deacons and deaconesses.

Later he commented on his reading habits as:

I have always been a student and a conscientious reader...I have
ever believed that my supreme work was to unfold the truths of
the Bible. So I have read chiefly high class authors who could
throw any light on any part of Scripture. To be always abreast of
the times as they concern God's kingdom on earth I have made
myself familiar with the new crude theories which perpetually
issue from the press.[17]

At the deacons' meeting on 2 September 1878 the secretary, Henry Bowen, read
a letter from Silas indicating that he was engaged to Mary Leighton and that they
would marry towards the end of October. Mary was the widow of sea captain George
Leighton and the eldest daughter of Catherine and George Pitty of Maldon, Victoria.
Mary had come to Adelaide to help her aunt, Mrs Reid. She became convinced of
the need for baptism and was baptised by Silas. They were married in FSBC on 22
October 1878 by John Price.[18] She was commended for membership by the pastor of
the Presbyterian Church at Maldon.

Mary Mead entered upon a very busy life, both in presiding over the household,
and in the various relations which a pastor's wife was expected to sustain. She was well
regarded by the congregation, and the manse maintained its warm, extensive ministry
of hospitality.

---

[16] *TP*, September 1877, 106.
[17] *Register*, Tuesday 12 January 1897, 7.
[18] *TP*, 1 April 1886, 50.

L to R standing: Blanche, Cecil, Lilian, Gertrude;
seated: Mary (Leighton) Mead, Flora, Silas, c. 1878

But her active usefulness soon received a melancholy check. About a year after her marriage, she was stricken by paralysis, which for a little while seemed to threaten her life. The Lord, however, partially raised her up again from that attack, but she was not restored to her former strength and soundness. One side of the body was found to be permanently affected by the stroke and for the remainder of her life she was disabled in the arm, and partially so on the whole side. Notwithstanding this very serious infirmity, Mrs Mead did a good deal of visiting, for which in various ways she was suited in a marked degree.[19]

Silas was called away to minister to a nephew at the beginning of 1886 when Mary's health deteriorated. After the nephew's death Silas returned home to a dangerously ill wife, who lingered for several weeks. She died at 6 am on Sunday 21 March 1886 and was buried the following day. Her funeral was conducted by ministerial friends of Silas.[20] Both Lilian and Gertrude were overseas when their stepmother died and were still away when Flora died of typhoid on 9 September 1886. Cecil and Blanche who were ill at the same time both survived.[21]

---

[19] *TP,* 1 April 1886, 50.
[20] *TP,* 1 April 1886, 51.
[21] 'Obituary for Flora', *TP,* 1 October 1886, 146-47. See also chapter 15.

Hospitality of home, pulpit and advocacy

The Mead household was known for its hospitality of visiting dignitaries. Mary's obituary emphasises this, despite her limitations. On 25 August 1880, Rev HL Tuck came to Adelaide from Stockport with Mrs Tuck to seek medical advice. They were invited by Silas to stay the night to break the fatigue of the journey.[22] Tuck's health deteriorated on the Thursday and he died that evening. His funeral was held in Stockport on the Saturday with Silas and a number of Baptist pastors participating. Silas was signatory to the appeal for help for his widow.[23]

Both GS Fowler and CH Goode were also widely noted for their hospitality in Baptist circles. Goode returned to Adelaide from England in 1879 and, although a member of North Adelaide Baptist Church, he almost immediately accepted responsibility for a weekly Bible Study group for young men at FSBC.[24]

Silas knew and often quoted Charles H Spurgeon whose son, Thomas, came to Australia in 1878

> ...seeking to benefit his health, and with the idea if the climate and conditions were favourable of commencing business, but from the very first his original intention had to be abandoned. Thanks to the publicity given to CH Spurgeon's hint that his son 'could preach a bit'...he has been from his arrival [in Adelaide]... preaching at least once every Sunday, in addition to holding services and attending meetings through the week in different parts of the country.[25]

He had accompanied Silas to visit Jamestown. His last preaching service in SA was held on Sunday evening, 13 January, at the Town Hall, Adelaide, the largest building in the city being packed to its utmost capacity.[26] At a further farewell event chaired by GS Fowler, Silas spoke:

> the object of the meeting not merely being to say farewell to the son, and to show a token of respect for the father, but to mark our sincere and deserved regard for the guest of the evening. ...He was presented with a souvenir—an Emu Egg Inkstand...

[22] 'Rev HL Tuck', *TP*, 1 September 1880, 181.
[23] 'Funeral of Rev HL Tuck', *TP*, 1 September 1880, 104.
[24] Goode was still conducting this class at the Jubilee of FSBC in 1911. See *Souvenir Brochure Flinders Street Baptist Church (Incorporated)* (Adelaide: Hussey & Gillham Ltd, 1911).
[25] *TP*, February 1878, 13.
[26] *TP*, February 1878, 13.

with the following inscription—'A token of Christian regard and a memento of Mr. Thomas Spurgeon's visit to South Australia, presented at Adelaide, 14th January, 1878'. [27]

Thomas went on to significant Christian ministry in Auckland, New Zealand before returning to London after the death of his father.[28] There was a suggestion that he would be interim pastor at FSBC while Silas visited India, but that visit was postponed. [29]

George Müller of Bristol, founder of boys' homes, addressed the SABA Assembly Meetings in 1887 while on his twelfth international tour.[30] The London evangelist Henry Varley, after special religious services in Adelaide, travelled to the South-East, en route to Melbourne, accompanied by Silas in August 1878.[31] In 1885 Harry Grattan Guinness (son of Henry Guinness, founder of Harley College) addressed the FSBC Annual Social and conducted several services for Silas.[32]

As mentioned in reference to 'foreign' missions, Silas was regularly introducing visitors to the Baptist scene in SA: James Chamberlain Page (1865), Punchanon Biswas (1881), Rev George and Mrs Kerry (1886), Joy Nath Choudhury (1892), Ruprecht Bion (1885), and the streams of missionaries either in transit to India to be farewelled in FSBC or on 'deputation' in the churches.

After 1886 Lilian, Gertrude and Blanche handled domestic arrangements and continued that ministry of hospitality. Lilian left university. The pipe organ was installed in 1886, and this added to the Church's debt. Cecil became organist. There is a record that:

> a gathering...took place at the Flinders-street Manse...About forty ladies and gentlemen members of the Furreedpore Mission...were present, and the capacity of Mr. Mead's dining room was tested when the whole party sat down to tea at once. After tea an adjournment was made to the drawing-room... Mr. Mead mentioned a conversation he had had with a native (Indian) missionary now in the colony on a visit. This brother had told him that there was a danger of the English missionaries

---

[27] *TP,* February 1878, 13.
[28] Craig Skinner, *Lamplighter and Son* (Nashville: Broadman Press, 1984).
[29] *TP,* September 1890, 143.
[30] *TP,* 1 November 1887, 166. See also Arthur T Pierson, *George Müller of Bristol and His Witness to a Prayer Hearing God* (London: Pickering & Inglis, 1899).
[31] *TP,* July 1878, 75; September 1878, 104.
[32] *TP,* 1 September 1885, 117, 131, 148.

looking down on the native pastors. The latter were not allowed
to preach in the large churches, nor were they permitted to take
any practical part in business matters. [33]

Silas used this propensity to racism to advocate the need for specific missionary training including language learning, systematic biblical study and missionary literature.

Dr Alexander MacLaren, whose father David McLaren had been so important in the forming of SA, brought his daughters to SA in 1889, staying with GS Fowler, and fitting in nostalgic visits to McLaren Vale, organised by Silas, and to the McLaren Wharf at Port Adelaide.[34] He preached to a packed audience at FSBC on the evening of his one Sunday in Adelaide.[35]

In July 1890 the Meads provided hospitality for Rev Samuel and Mrs Chapman from Melbourne; Chapman at the time was ill from overwork.[36] Chapman had called Silas 'the Andrew Fuller of Australia'[37] and this had been linked in a report of his visit to FSBC fitting the description 'Churches live two lives, one here and another in the Indias'.[38]

Silas entertained ministers to a meal to meet newly arrived Rev and Mrs Shackleford in August 1889, on their arrival to replace Lambert at Norwood.[39] When Charles Bright and his wife arrived to take up the pastoral responsibility at Norwood they stayed initially with the Mead family.

There were special evangelistic meetings in October 1889 but Silas was sick and could not attend. He himself needed help. *Truth & Progress* reported:

we are grieved to report, [Mead] is still unwell, and unable ... to
resume his pastoral duties...Our esteemed friend has preached

---

33 *TP*, August 1888, 110.
34 *TP*, 1 November 1888, 157. Mead was one of the delegates to meetings in Melbourne for BUV Jubilee, where Dr MacLaren was the special speaker. There is dispute as to the spelling of McLaren's name. John Briggs says that he used the form 'McLaren' when signing his name but 'Maclaren' in all his publications. He is Maclaren in the BWA book of 1905. McLaren Vale in SA is named after the father. JHY Briggs, 'McLaren (Maclaren), Alexander' in T Larsen (ed), *Biographical Dictionary of Evangelicals* (Leicester: Inter-Varsity Press, 2003), 397.
35 *TP*, 1 November 1889, 174. See also H Estcourt Hughes, *Our First Hundred Years: The Baptist Church of South Australia* (Adelaide: SA Baptist Union, 1937), 288–89.
36 *TP*, July 1890, 109.
37 *TP*, 1 June 1889, 86.
38 *TP*, 1 June 1889, 85. Andrew Fuller was the advocate for BMS in England while William Carey served in India.
39 *TP*, 1 August 1889, 135.

but once during the month, and then suffered a serious relapse in consequence. As we go to press it has been arranged for Mr. Mead to take a six weeks' trip to New Zealand in company with Mr. C. H. Goode and Mr. C. Proud...Trying as it may be to the church at this juncture to part for so long a time from its pastor, and indeed for all of us to lose his wise and inspiring presence, we are, nevertheless, sincerely glad that this is arranged; and all will be most deeply grateful to our Heavenly Father for our brother's return to us in his usual brightness and strength.[40]

Returning early in 1890, Silas acknowledged the help his companions Goode and Proud had been in defraying his travel expenses and they spoke of shared tourist experiences in New Zealand.[41]

General William Booth of the Salvation Army stayed with Goode when visiting Adelaide in 1891 and held meetings in the Exhibition Building. Silas was suffering from bronchitis at the time and Booth called and interviewed him.[42]

The following report was printed in the November 1890 edition of *Truth and Progress*:

LUNCHEON AT MR. MEAD'S. Luncheon was provided at the close of the morning session by Rev. S. Mead at the Flinders Street manse. The usual vote of thanks was accorded to the reverend host, who generously passed it on to his daughters, who he said had most to do in preparing the repast. ...Our bishop has a widespread reputation for hospitality.[43]

There were two other very significant international visits for Silas, FSBC and the SABA: Hudson Taylor, founder of the China Inland Mission (CIM) in 1890 and Dr Francis E Clark of the Christian Endeavour Movement (CE) in 1892. Hudson Taylor attended and spoke at the Missionary Breakfast at the Baptist Association meetings to farewell Bertha Tuck, Lucie Kealley and Annie Hearn for service in India.[44] FSBC also had Alfred C Rogers, one of its members, applying to the CIM and Taylor was able to meet and commend him at the time.[45] Taylor also addressed the Baptist minis-

---

[40] *TP*, December 1889, 193.
[41] *TP*, March 1890, 43.
[42] *TP*, December 1891, 205.
[43] *TP*, November 1890, 180.
[44] Lucie Kealley was a SA missionary who was to be supported by Tasmanian Baptists. See Chapter 8.
[45] *TP*, November 1890, 183.

ters—'all of Christ, *His* faithfulness, *His* love'. Silas was to serve on the CIM Council in SA until he left the Colony.

Woman evangelist—Emilia Baeyertz

Emilia Aronson was a Welsh Jewess, who was sent to her sister in Victoria, Australia to recover health following the breakdown of her marriage arrangement in 1864. She met and fell in love with Charles Baeyertz, an Anglican bank manager. Without telling her family, she married him in 1865 on the condition that he would never attempt to convert her. The family disowned her. They had two children, Charles and Marion. Her husband died from a shooting accident in 1871. Later she grew to understand and accept the Christian faith and gradually her own giftedness as an evangelist.[46]

Silas was keen for wider Australian Baptist links. In September 1880 Rev WC Bunning was fraternal visitor from Victoria to the SABA meetings. His specific topic was evangelism and Bunning spoke of Mrs Baeyertz, whom he had baptised five years earlier.[47] He knew of her ministry in Melbourne among factory girls and had seen her in action in crusades in Geelong and Ballarat. He 'stated his conviction that Mrs Baeyertz would probably consent to pay a visit to Adelaide if she was invited'.[48]

Next day an *ad hoc* committee, Silas included, during a picnic at the close of those Assembly meetings, sent the invitation.[49] Within days Baeyertz arrived in Adelaide and conducted meetings for three weeks.

> Her first service was held in Flinders-street Baptist Church… where the place was crowded. She created a good impression, and has continued to deepen it through the series of services. Meetings have been held in North Adelaide, Norwood, and Parkside Baptist Churches, which were crowded to excess.[50] She also held meetings in the Town Hall, when about 2,000 persons were wedged into the building, and hundreds had to go away. Beside her Sunday services, she has conducted week night

---

[46] Betty Baruch and Amanda Coverdale, *This is My Beloved: The Story of Emilia Baeyertz, Jewish Christian Lady Evangelist* (Melbourne: Emilia Baeyertz Society, 2017).
[47] Baptised at that same service in Aberdeen Street Geelong were Marie Gilbert and Marion Fuller, early Baptist women missionaries.
[48] *TP*, 1 October 1880, 120.
[49] *TP*, 1 October 1880, 120.
[50] Norwood and Parkside Baptist churches had been formed with initial members from FSBC.

meetings, and held special afternoon gatherings for women and girls.[51]

Emilia held a final tea for converts and those restored to fellowship in FSBC. Afterwards more than 120 converts sat in their allotted portion of the Church. The majority of converts were

> young, only twenty or thirty over twenty years of age. Some ten or twelve were men, two or three of middle age...twenty lads and boys, the remaining fourteen to twenty women, the rest girls. She had ministered to both women and men.[52]

On the wharf as the ministers farewelled her they handed her a letter endorsing her work among them. They wrote:

> We are equally confident...in testifying not only to our esteem for you as a sister in Christ Jesus, but to our conviction that God has eminently endowed you with gifts for the setting forth of His precious truth both to Christians and Non-Christians.[53]

They concluded their letter: 'You know...how ardently we entertain the hope of your returning to labour afresh in and around Adelaide as well as in the country districts'.[54]

Mrs Baeyertz returned to South Australia in August 1881 and ministered in various Baptist and other congregations until the end of 1883. There were detailed reports of her addresses and of the converts' testimonies, particularly of men. Reporters were careful to note her lack of sensationalism and referred to her messages as 'natural' and 'varied' and called them Bible readings rather than sermons.

But no matter how described in a place where women were facing the criticisms made of women in the burgeoning suffrage movement she was accepted as a public evangelist. It is worth noting that South Australian women were granted both the vote, second only to New Zealand, and also the right to sit in parliament in 1894, and FSBC women were involved.

Baeyertz was used by the churches to hold evangelistic events in the tradition of visiting evangelists of that time. John Walker concludes: 'Over the next thirty years no

---

[51] *TP*, 1 January 1881, 8.
[52] *TP*, 1 January 1881, 8.
[53] *TP*, 1 January 1881, 8.
[54] *TP*, 1 January 1881, 8.

other evangelist gained the acceptance and exposure which Mrs Baeyertz had enjoyed among South Australian Baptists.'[55] Following her return to Victoria she moved to evangelistic crusades in other colonies, New Zealand, and later to ministry in both USA and England.

Young Peoples' Society Christian Endeavour

FSBC had not lacked groups, societies, organisations and activities for its younger members. The Sunday School was in operation before the church was even built.[56] Young Men's Literary Society, sporting groups (cricket, football, tennis clubs, athletics), Temperance Leagues and Mothers' Dorcas Society and girls' groups were formed, all reporting regularly to the Members' Socials. But perhaps the group that most excited Silas was Christian Endeavour, an organisation founded in USA by Dr Francis Clark.

> Francis E Clark (12 September 1851 - 26 May 1927) is considered by many to be the founder of modern youth ministry. Concerned with the disconnection of young adults from his congregation he created a segregated youth prayer ministry. ...Armed with an "iron-clad" pledge, a weekly newsletter and the incessant travels of the founder, the society grew to be a worldwide organization.[57]

The FSBC Young Peoples' Society Christian Endeavour was formed on 24 April 1888, with a membership of eight, the oldest CE Society in South Australia, and the third in Australia. Silas's name was the first on the roll and he was naturally President. Silas also had the honour of being the first Australian CE President.[58]

> Of the other pioneer members it is interesting to note that one is a Baptist minister—Rev AS Wilson; three went out as foreign missionaries—Dr CS Mead, Miss Hearn (now Mrs Summers) and Mr AC Rogers; and one is a home missionary—Miss Nellie Koehncke. The remaining two were Miss Paqualin, who passed

[55] John Walker, 'The Baptists in South Australia, 1863-1914' (Thesis for Honours degree in Theology, Flinders University, South Australia, 31 October 1990), 41.
[56] See *Souvenir Brochure Flinders Street Baptist Church (Incorporated)* (Adelaide: Hussey & Gillham Ltd, 1911), 24.
[57] Jason Lanker, 'Francis Edward Clark', in 'Christian Educators of the 20th Century', Talbot School of Theology, Biola University, accessed at www.biola.edu/talbot/ce20/database/francis-edward-clark, 1.
[58] Formed in 1891.

away soon after the formation of the Society, and Miss Bridgland (now Mrs Lenthal).[59]

CE's 'iron-clad pledge' incorporated so much of Silas's principles: prayer, daily reading of Scripture, church loyalty, regular attendance and participation: [60]

> Trusting in the Lord Jesus Christ for strength, I promise Him that I will strive to do whatever He would like to have me do; that I will make it the rule of my life to pray and to read the Bible every day, and to support the work and worship of my own church in every way possible; and that just so far as I know how, throughout my whole life, I will endeavor to lead a Christian life. As an active member I promise to be true to all my duties, to be present at and to take some part, aside from singing, in every Christian Endeavor meeting, unless hindered by some reason which I can conscientiously give to my Lord and Master, Jesus Christ. If obliged to be absent from the monthly consecration meeting of the society, I will, if possible, send at least a verse of Scripture to be read in response to my name at the roll call.[61]

There was the egalitarian expectation that both young women and young men would prepare talks, pray and take part. CE resulted in missionary enthusiasm, financial support and service. All served on committees.

In October 1890 twenty-six FSBC endeavourers had a studio photo taken to make a presentation to Bertha Tuck, Annie Hearn and Alfred Rogers, leaving for overseas. Cecil and Blanche Mead, Alf Wilson and his two sisters are in the photo but neither Lilian nor Gertrude Mead.

At the same time as there was the excitement for the sending of missionaries overseas, the church continued to search for those who could be missionaries to Adelaide city. Miss Nesbit, EM Bridgland, Annie Green, Nellie Koehncke, and later Ada Tapson, all served for a time, and eventually it was from the fruit of the YPSCE that both Halifax Mission in East Adelaide and the West End Mission were established.

---

[59] Miss Paqualin was an early convert of Mead, who served as first secretary of the newly formed Adelaide YWCA, and died 6 October 1886: *TP*, 1 March 1889, 45. Mrs Lenthal joined the church in 1874, *Souvenir Brochure*, 45-46.
[60] This was the expected CE structure.
[61] World's Christian Endeavor Union, 'The Christian Endeavor Pledge', accessed at www.worldsceunion.org/files/the_christian_endeavor_pledge.pdf.

FSBC Young Peoples' Society Christian Endeavour presentation photo, 1890

Clark writing of his time in Adelaide in 1892 said:

> A week's [CE] convention was held in Adelaide...Here I was the
> delighted guest in the home of Rev Silas Mead, who has been the
> beloved pastor of the Flinders Street Baptist Church of Adelaide
> for more than thirty years. The Flinders Street Church, in fact,
> is not only a Church, but a missionary head-quarters, a tract
> repository, a theological seminary, and a Christian Endeavour
> office all in one. [62]

He commented on Silas's busy round of duties, beyond being pastor of the
Church, adding that these roles were

> Surely enough to occupy the heart and hand of any one man but
> he is one of the busy men who can always find time for something
> else if he is convinced that it is the Master's work.[63]

Later that year, Cecil Mead, hurrying to catch his boat [to London] at Colombo,
Ceylon, met Dr and Mrs Clark and son Eugene, also catching theirs. After a few
hearty greetings, and the hope that they would meet at the British CE Conference,
shouted across the water, they lost sight of one another, regretting no doubt that their
visit to Colombo was unknown to each other.[64]

---

[62] *TP,* 16 February 1893, 54.
[63] *TP* 16 February 1893, 53.
[64] *TP,* March 1893, 85.

Associate minister and conclusion of Silas's ministry

In August 1891 at a special meeting of elders and deacons and others, GS Fowler referred to an interview he had had with Silas respecting future ministry at FSBC. He thought that: 'Mr Mead might occupy a kind of Bishopric and another pastor be obtained as coadjutor with him in the ministrations at Flinders St, and which he might state had Mr Mead's approval'.[65] Fowler felt that the first step was to get rid of the floating debt [on property and organ] towards which he was willing to give £150, understanding that about £606 was needed. He would also give £250 per annum towards the new minister's salary.

Further promises were received, £465 including Fowler's for the debt and £450 for the salary of the new minister. By the next deacons' meeting the debt fund had reached £615 and they appointed an English selection committee of Dr MacLaren, Rev James Stuart and Rev FB Meyer.[66] Later they asked Rev Samuel Chapman who was on a world trip to join the group. However, plans were delayed and at the Anniversary Social in 1893 GS Fowler restated his belief that Silas needed an assistant to leave him more free time for denominational work. (Fowler also referred to the luxury of foreign missions until the home base was better established.)[67]

Eventually a committee of Dr MacLaren, Rev Meyer, Dr Clifford, Rev James Stuart together with GS Fowler and John Darling from Adelaide (who were in London) suggested Rev JG Raws then at Harrogate.[68]

The Members' meeting of 7 November 1894 accepted unanimously the nomination of John Garrard Raws. His credentials were widely circulated.[69] He, his wife and five children arrived in Adelaide on 24 March 1895 for a two-year appointment and were warmly welcomed. Raws asked from the church—trust, help and prayer. He was quickly accepted by both church and the Baptist community, he was added to the Clergy Marriage Register and invited to speak at the next Association meetings.[70] He was asked to do more and more of the weekly preaching.

[65] FSBC Special Meeting Minutes, August 1891, 239-40.
[66] FSBC Deacons Meeting, 1 February 1891, 241.
[67] TP, 17 August 1893, 245.
[68] John Price, *Memoir of George Swan Fowler: Christian Merchant* (Adelaide: ES Wigg & Son, 1897), 107.
[69] *Advertiser*, 4 August 1895, 7; *SB*, 18 April 1895, 96; *SB*, 30 May 1895, 130.
[70] *SB*, 18 April 1895, 89.

Seven months later Silas left Adelaide on 6 November 1895 to visit Perth and then to meet up with Dr William Whitley for their delayed visit to India to survey missions. He was away from Adelaide until early 1896. By then daughter Gertrude was caught up in an Adelaide University dispute and had to relocate to Melbourne to complete her medical degree. Blanche was planning her marriage to AS Wilson, who was already in Perth. Cecil was in India.

The discussion of Silas Mead's resignation from the pastorate of the church was a protracted affair. On 26 June 1896 Silas wrote a letter to Henry Bowen, secretary of FSBC to clarify an interview they had had.[71] The suggestion was that Silas be given the title of honorary pastor, a salary of £100 pa for the work of the Mission and denomination and from 15 February he would vacate the manse. He counter-suggested that instead of the salary he be able to occupy the manse. He suggested that from 6 February 1897 he hold the position of honorary pastor and Mr Raws the position of pastor. The issue threatened to divide the congregation, and a number of individuals spoke to Silas to help resolve the issue. He mentioned GS Fowler, Stow Smith, James Cowell, and particularly James Fowler. He eventually agreed to withdraw his demands and sent in an unconditional resignation. On 19 August 1896 it was moved:

> That the church accepts the resignation of Rev S Mead, MA LLB as pastor of the Flinders Street Baptist Church Incorporated as per his letter of Aug 7 1896: the manse to be vacated by him on Feb 15 1897.[72]

The meeting went on to grant Silas £100 pa annuity for life, and the position of honorary pastor without duties or responsibilities and to request the SABU to grant him life membership.[73]

A split was averted. In August 1898 after Silas had left Adelaide it was reported that:

> Rev. John G. Raws has proved to be a pastor well qualified for the position he was called to fill. He had many difficulties to contend with at the beginning, but they have gradually given way before him, and he is now well established in the affections and confidence of the people.[74]

---

[71] Incorporated in the minutes of FSBC Members Meeting, 8 July 1896.
[72] FSBC Special Church Meeting Minutes, 19 August 1896.
[73] The South Australian Baptist Association (SABA) changed to South Australian Baptist Union (SABU) in 1895.
[74] *SB*, August 1898, 181.

Silas Mead had made the transition but with anguish. He went on to further usefulness, despite some feeling that 'Mr Mead made the fatal error of clinging too long to his post. A new generation has arisen with new ambitions and a hankering after novelties which would have palled upon their fathers and mothers'.[75]

At the CE farewell to Silas and Lilian on Christmas evening 1896 in Pirie Street Wesleyan Church Silas said 'Foreign missions and Endeavourism were dear to his heart. He believed he was now called to devote himself to these two objects, and to this larger service he would consecrate the remainder of his life'.[76] New challenges lay ahead.

SA), 4 March 1898, 3. In the same article the writer made a similar
'riend Rev FW Cox.
1.

6

Silas and
South Australian Baptists

Frank Tucker

The breadth of ministries Silas was directly involved in was extensive and impressive. Prior to 1863 there was little Baptist denominational identity in South Australia and local churches did not see the need to surrender their independence and particular doctrinal distinctives. With Silas's arrival this was about to change.

The South Australian Baptist Association

At the time of Silas's arrival in South Australia, there were twenty-one Baptist church buildings and nine ministers in South Australia but there was no cohesive relationship between them.[1] Most British Baptist sects were represented. There were 'Scotch Baptist, Strict and Particular and "Fullerites"....There were differences over Calvinism, church order, open and closed membership, open and closed communion, as well as millenarian views.'[2] Closed membership churches would only admit to membership people who were believers baptised by immersion. Closed communion meant that only immersed believers could participate in the Lord's Table. Although the churches shared much in common, independence and isolation were treasured. The lack of association was denying the unity of the denomination.

---

[1] D Hillard, quote by John Walker, 'The Baptists in South Australia, 1863-1914' (Honours Thesis, Flinders University, 1990), 2.
[2] Manley, *From Woolloomooloo to 'Eternity' A History of Australian Baptists. Vol 1: Growing an Australian Church (1831-1914). Studies in Baptist History and Thought, vol 16:1* (Milton Keynes, UK: Paternoster, 2006), 45.

Independence threatened the survival of the small rural churches. Some people from a Baptist tradition had joined other denominations and seemed content to stay there. John Hannay, the son-in-law of George Fife Angas and a Baptist pastor of the Union Church at Angaston where Angas worshipped, [3] observed that the 'Baptists here have no bond of union...and unless *something is done soon* to give the *denomination a start,* it will be quite lost.'[4]

The mood for cooperation changed with the presence of Silas Mead. Silas's theological views were clearly evangelical and evangelistic, which influenced his ministry.[5] Evangelicals in the nineteenth century were largely influenced by a biblical paradigm. Consequently, evangelicalism was involved in social transformation of local communities, transcending denominations and confessional boundaries.[6] Silas embraced this evangelicalism (as discussed in the Introduction).[7]

The inauguration of Flinders Street Baptist Church in 1861 marked the beginning of a new era in the history of Baptist churches in South Australia.[8] Silas's leadership challenged the factionalism and independence that had been part of Baptist identity in South Australia. While each Baptist church was an autonomous entity, it was deemed valuable for the churches to cooperate and support one another rather than relate on an *ad hoc* basis. George Stonehouse, the pastor of a North Adelaide Baptist Church, had attempted to form an Association earlier but it had not materialised.[9]

> The work of denominational extension throughout the colony may be said to date from the arrival of Mr. Mead. Before 1861 very little success had crowned any efforts that had been made for the establishment of new churches. It could scarcely be said that denominational unity existed. Circumstances had frustrated any attempts that had been made in this direction. But with the

---

[3] The Union Church was evangelical and inclusive of people from various Protestant denominations.
[4] Quoted by Manley, *From Woolloomooloo*, 97-98.
[5] Evangelical refers to the central belief that people are saved by the grace of God through the sacrificial death of Jesus on the cross. Evangelism is the proclamation of this good news to people who do not yet believe, with the intent that they will respond.
[6] Edwin Orr, *The Light of the Nations: Progress and Achievement in the Nineteenth Century*. The Paternoster Church History, vol. 8 (Exeter: Paternoster Press, 1965), 26.
[7] See also David Bebbington, *The Dominance of Evangelicalism: The Age of Spurgeon and Moody* (Leicester: Intervarsity Press, 2005).
[8] H Estcourt Hughes, *Our First Hundred Years: The Baptist Churches of South Australia* (Adelaide: South Australian Baptist Union, 1937), 50.
[9] Walker, 'The Baptists in South Australia, 1863-1914', 11.

establishment of a strong metropolitan Church there was a centre of influence and a bond of unity.[10]

Silas Mead's influence amongst Baptist churches in South Australia, and the perceived need for such an association, generated a critical mass for change.[11] Consequently, the South Australian Baptist Association was formed on 26 May 1863.[12] The Flinders Street Baptist Church became the focal point of the Association and the location of many of the Association meetings. A number of the members of FSBC became leaders in the Association.

The forming of the South Australian Baptist Association (SABA) was not without problems. The Association brought together disparate, isolated Baptist churches in the colony. It enabled cooperation and made mutual support possible. There were other key people besides Silas involved who shared the vision and responsibility, including CH Goode, T Barnes, James Smith, WK Thomas, W Scott and Rev. G Stonehouse who, together with Silas, made up the first committee of the Association.[13] However, Silas's presence and influence provided the impetus. It may be wondered if the formation of the Association and associated ministries would have occurred without him. Silas was 'able to multiply his own efforts by imparting to others the spirit which animate[d] himself.'[14] His dynamism, organisational ability, his imparting of vision, collaboration, commitment to the mission of God and his firm spiritual leadership were the catalysts if not the initiators of numerous ministries.

It was not easy for strongly independent churches to surrender any of their independence. The intentions of the opinion makers like Silas Mead, George Fife Angas, John Price and George Stonehouse[15] was that the Association should be made up of open membership churches although church leaders were to be believers baptised by immersion. This open policy was a problem for the closed membership churches. Silas and other Association members were hopeful that the 'Christian Churches' would join the Association. These churches, started by Thomas Playford,[16] were Baptist in

---

[10] 'The Reverend Silas Mead', *Colonist*, 17 January 1890, 5, http://nla.gov.au/nla.news-article214701923.
[11] 'The Reverend Silas Mead', *Colonist*, 17 January 1890, 5.
[12] Hughes, *Our First Hundred Years*, 82.
[13] 'Farewell Meeting to Rev. Silas Mead, M.A., LL.B.', *SB*, 4 February 1897, 26.
[14] 'The Rev Silas Mead, MA, LL.B.', *Colonist*, 17 January 1890, 5, http://nla.gov.au/nla.news-article214701923.
[15] George Stonehouse withdrew from the Association soon after its formation (Walker, 'The Baptists in South Australia, 1863-1914', 83).
[16] Thomas Playford (also known as Tom Playford) was the great grandfather of a former state Premier.

polity and theology. However, they rejected denominational labels as sectarian. They had not noticed that they were being sectarian by remaining independent.[17] Their isolation led to their decline.

In later years Silas reflected on these times and stated that believers could become members without being baptised by immersion but many of the unbaptised later were baptised by immersion. In an interview in London in 1899 Silas observed that some Baptist churches had practised open and closed communion on alternate weeks.[18]

In 1880, Silas read an article in a UK newspaper in which the author was impressed with the willingness of a Baptist church in Bowden, near Manchester in England, to accept Christians from other church traditions. He was constrained to respond with a letter to the editor of the *Christian Colonist*.[19] He pointed out that this should not have been a surprise to the observer. It was the very policy advocated by Baptists in South Australia. From his perspective, any Nonconformist Christian can join a Baptist church in South Australia irrespective of the nature of their baptism.[20] It was this open policy championed by Silas that troubled Baptist churches in other states.

The formation of the Association enabled organised cooperation in interchurch ministries, which could not easily be addressed by independent local churches alone. It enabled the provision of aid for Baptist churches to build their own sanctuaries and for struggling churches to pay their debts.[21] It also provided the impetus for serving together to enhance shared Baptist services not possible alone. The combined initiative supported local training of ministers to augment the tenuous supply from the UK. A Ministers' Association and a Lay Preachers' Association were also formed but it was not until 1880 that an Aged Ministers' Relief Fund was functioning.[22]

In 1868 an Association library at the Flinders Street Church was established. It was built up largely by donations particularly from Silas's own collection with the hope that further gifts would follow. This library could have been a useful resource but was under-utilised.

[17] Walker, 'The Baptists in South Australia, 1863-1914', 28.
[18] 'Chat With a Baptist Enthusiast', *SB*, 1 June 1899, 114.
[19] 'Freedom of the Baptist Churches', *Colonist*, 9 January 1880, 3, http://nla.gov.au/nla.news-article214680901.
[20] 'Freedom of the Baptist Churches', *Colonist*, 9 January 1880, 3.
[21] 'Grant in Aid of Churches', *TP*, 4 February 1893, 39.
[22] 'South Australian Baptist Aged Minister's Relief Fund', *TP*, 3 March 1880, 33.

A denominational periodical, *Truth and Progress*, was also started in 1868 to enhance communication between the Baptist churches and create a sense of belonging together. It encouraged a corporate identity for Baptists. Silas Mead and his friend, John Price, were the first editors of the paper. The title was instructive. Silas and John chose *Truth* to refer to the truth of Scripture and *Progress* to refer to the application of this truth to the ministry amongst the Baptist churches.[23] Producing such a newspaper required a significant effort in the nineteenth century since it was labour intensive.

With the formation of the Association it became possible to collectively form a Baptist Mission Society in 1864.[24] This was in keeping with Silas's sense of calling and passion for mission. The Association provided regular news for Baptist churches to stimulate specific prayer and financial support for their national workers.

Silas's promotion of open membership, the shared disdain for creedal statements and the emphasis on freedom and responsibility for individuals to interpret the Scriptures was consistent with his evangelicalism. Creeds were restrictive.[25] The Bible was the Baptist statement of faith.

This perspective left the church open to diverse interpretations of the Bible and potential conflict from within. However, the strong leadership of Silas discouraged sectarian opposition within SABA in its early days. He was a strong advocate of believer's baptism by immersion and maintained that that was the New Testament practice. This was clearly expressed in his paper titled, 'Bible Baptisms'.[26] However, his understanding of the unity of the Body of Christ would not limit inclusion only to people of that persuasion in the organised church. The openness on church membership avoided isolationism and sectarianism but could become fertile ground for divergent views to be expressed within the church.

Silas was active in ongoing leadership of the Association. He was appointed President in 1867, 1872 and 1879. 'Four times he was prevailed upon to accept the honorary position of General Secretary of the Union, covering a period of eight years, and he was Financial Secretary more than once.'[27] In the capacity of President, Silas presented papers on various doctrinal issues which are elaborated below. He frequently

---

[23] 'Our Work', *TP*, January 1868, 1.
[24] See chapter 8 for more on missions and the development of the mission societies.
[25] 'The Baptist Association', *EJ* (second edition), 26 October 1871, 3, http://nla.gov.au/nla.news-article197660864.
[26] Silas Mead, 'Bible Baptisms', *SB*, 1 no 3, 31 January 1895, 27. See also a sermon by Silas on baptism, 'Dean Stanley on Baptism', *TP*, vol 13 no 3, 3 March 1880, 30-32.
[27] 'Farewell Meeting to Rev. Silas Mead. M.A., LL.B.' *SB*, 4 February 1897, 26.

visited other Baptist churches, including those in rural areas such as at Laura, Lyndoch Valley, Saddleworth, Kapunda, Minlaton and Jamestown. It was also common for him to participate in the preaching at other churches.

> As the years passed, Mead acquired patriarchal status and was commonly lauded as the father of South Australian Baptists. He was the most influential figure among Baptists of the colony and probably in all Australia during the nineteenth century. It is noticeable that the first period of major growth among Baptists of the colony, from 1863–1885, coincided with the time of Mead's dominance.[28]

His leadership skills, his influence and the respect with which he was held within the Association earned him the appellation 'Baptist Bishop'.[29] However, that would not remain to be so in the 1890s.

Various doctrinal contributions to SABA

It was the custom for the president of the SABA meetings to speak on a relevant topic.[30] At the fourth annual meeting of SABA in 1867, Silas chose to speak on conversion as the basis of church membership.[31] He believed that conversion involved a change of heart and conduct, a turning from self and Satan to God: 'It is the relinquishing of a life of opposition to God for a life of loving obedience to Him.' He asserted that this was a work of the Spirit. Baptism declared that the person baptised has died to sin and is alive to Christ while participation in the Lord's Supper reflected the inner union with Christ resulting from his sacrificial death. Silas stated that this is for the Lord's people alone: 'Christ's Church is solely for Christ's disciples.'[32]

On 18 September 1872 Silas, as chairman elect, chose the subject of 'Doctrine and Church Life' at the evening meeting of the Association's ninth annual gathering.[33] He was concerned about the notion of churches having no doctrinal position as though that was unimportant. He argued that the church teaches from a particular

---

[28] Walker, 'The Baptists in South Australia, 1863-1914', 79.

[29] Walker, 'The Baptists in South Australia, 1863-1914', 12.

[30] It was the practice for men to be appointed to leadership in the Union during this era. There is no reference to the appointment of women.

[31] 'The Baptist Association', *Advertiser*, 11 October 1867, 3, http://trove.nla.gov.au/newspaper/article/28801577.

[32] 'The Baptist Association', *Advertiser*, 11 October 1867, 3.

[33] 'The Baptist Association', *EJ*, 18 September 1872, 3, http://nla.gov.au/nla.news-article196743184.

theological position which shapes Christian practice. The church is to guard the truth and avoid 'strange doctrines'.[34] However, he was aware that a commitment to a doctrinal statement can lead to either good or harm.

It is difficult for anyone, in a particular cultural context, to formulate the truth of the Scriptures without bias, nevertheless, he believed that every truth of scripture should 'be subject to human inquiry'.[35] He considered that some teachings of the church, such as that concerning baptism, the Lord's Supper and the rites of worship were based on church tradition rather than the Bible. This is apparent in the development of different church polity and different rituals.

At a half-yearly meeting of the Baptist Association, held at Kapunda in April 1874, Silas addressed the subject of baptism. His paper drew on the content of his book, *Scripture Immersion,* written in 1868 (see chapter 7).[36] Later he had, on several occasions, opportunity to address this topic.

Ministerial training in South Australia

The training of ministers in the new colony presented some challenges to be solved. It was an important task for the survival and continuation of the denomination. Trained ministers from the UK could be invited to South Australia. There were potential problems with such appointments since it was uncertain whether a minister was suitable for the colonial environment, and the Christian community in Australia had to rely on the decision of agents in the UK. Several ministers had been solicited from the UK to pastor prospective Baptist churches but these mostly proved to be unsatisfactory.[37] Some other colonies had started informal theological training but the number of experienced ministers from other colonies was limited. The third option was the appointment of local untrained lay preachers. With the formation of an Association, collaboration in local training of suitable candidates for ministry became feasible.

The Adelaide Baptist Theological College began to train people for the ministry in 1869.[38] At the inception of the College, George Stonehouse was appointed President and Silas Mead became a Board Member and lecturer. Silas was to teach Greek

---

[34] 'The Baptist Association', *EJ*, 18 September 1872, 3.
[35] 'The Baptist Association', *EJ*, 18 September 1872, 3 and *TP*, October 1872, 109-112.
[36] 'On Baptism', *TP*, May 1874, 49-51.
[37] Hughes, *Our First Hundred Years*, 261.
[38] Hughes, *Our First Hundred Years*, 261.

and Hebrew.[39] The examining body of the College was drawn from qualified and experienced people from outside the denomination.

Lectures were conducted in rented accommodation and sometimes in the lecturer's place of work. The Adelaide Baptist Theological College was a catalyst for better things to come.[40] It combined with the Congregationalists and Presbyterians in 1872 to form the Union College of South Australia.[41] This College was an innovative one since it was not confined to one denomination,[42] although the Wesleyans and Anglicans were not included and it was not connected to a university since there was no university in South Australia at the time.[43] Each denomination represented was expected to provide its own distinctive emphases for their candidates.[44] Union College offered pastoral training and general subjects for lay people. Initially, fifty-three students were enrolled.[45] Silas became a council member of Union College and lectured in Greek Testament until the death of his wife and his overseas travel in mid-1874.[46] He resumed teaching in 1876.

In 1874 Walter W Hughes, a pastoralist and mining magnate, donated £20,000 from his estate to the Union College.[47] The College Board decided that it would be best used for the establishing of a university.[48] From that time the College focused on pastoral training and hoped that there would be lay preacher and Sunday School teacher candidates to make it viable.[49] The Presbyterians withdrew in 1886 to attend to their ministerial training at the recently formed Victorian Presbyterian College.[50] The Congregationalists also withdrew. The remaining Baptist and Bible Christians, who joined in 1877, found the College unsustainable. Subsequently, a Baptist college was reformed in 1891. Silas, with others such as Rev John Price, Rev Bell and Rev Charles Bright, continued training Baptist pastors: 'The chairman, in his opening

[39] Hughes, *Our First Hundred Years*, 263.

[40] Walter Phillips, 'Studies: Union College Adelaide, 1872-1886: A Brief Experiment in United Theological Education', in *The 'Furtherance of Religious Beliefs': Essays on the History of Theological Education in Australia,* ed. Geoffrey R Treloar (Sydney, NSW: Centre for the Study of Australian Christianity, 1997), 60.

[41] 'General Intelligence', *TP* 5:4, April 1872, 45.

[42] Phillips, 'Union College', 59.

[43] Phillips, 'Union College', 60.

[44] Phillips, 'Union College', 61.

[45] 'Baptist College Work in South Australia', *SB* 1:2, 17 January 1895, 15-16.

[46] 'Union College', *TP* 7:10, October 1874, 123.

[47] Phillips, 'Union College', 62-63.

[48] 'Union College', *TP* 8:5, May 1875, 52.

[49] Phillips, 'Union College', 63.

[50] Phillips, 'Union College', 67.

remarks, bore testimony to the earnestness and persistency with which Rev. S. Mead all along had laboured for [the] good of [the] college.'[51]

The planting and support of new Baptist churches

The period of 1860–1885, which coincides with Silas's influence, was one of significant consolidation and growth of the Baptist denomination in South Australia.[52] He was active in church extension in the suburbs of Adelaide and in rural regions. His significant role in planting urban churches was an extension of the ministry of Flinders Street Baptist Church. In addition to that, Silas capitalised on Flinders Street members moving out to rural locations and supported the planting of a number of rural churches.

The planting of rural churches was facilitated by the appointment of Rev D Badger, as the Association church planter of new rural churches.[53] The planter's 'mission was to visit the places unsupplied with ministers, and occasionally remaining at one place a month or two, visiting from house to house during that time.'[54]

Silas and other Association leaders also supported the smaller rural churches through the provision of lay ministers where local preachers were unavailable. This activity consolidated and strengthened these churches. The circuit practice of the Methodist Church, where a minister would be appointed to pastor several local churches, was not adopted by Baptists due to independence and congregational government.

Such was the respect for Silas that many times he had the opportunity to speak at various country and urban churches on occasions. He was able to attend the Northern District Baptist Association meetings and had personal contact with the pastors. In his leadership capacity in the SABA he also had input into key topics of the regional meetings.

Silas's contribution to the Association meant that the denomination grew. However, after 1885 the denomination, particularly the rural churches, was affected by the years of economic depression when the churches battled for survival. Expansion was not in focus then.

---

[51] 'South Australian Baptist College Celebration', *SB* 1:24, 12 December 1895, 284.
[52] Walker, 'The Baptists in South Australia, 1863-1914', 79-83.
[53] 'Denominational Evangelist', *TP* 4:5, May 1871, 46.
[54] 'South Australian Baptist Association', *Register* 29 October 1868, 4, http://nla.gov.au/nla.news-article41389587.

Church unity as a gospel witness

There was an occasion in 1868 when union between the Congregationalists and Baptists was proposed. They had a close association, a shared polity and similar theological heritage. The two denominations had also shared important events, and union negotiations had been considered.[55] However, the barrier to union proved to be the significant difference over baptism.[56]

In 1868 some Baptist members of the Association considered that cooperation would be preferred to union. Silas Mead and John Price were agreeable to union if the Congregationalists could accept believer's baptism.[57] Congregationalists, while practising infant sprinkling, were known to have immersed believers amongst their constituency so it was presumed that a commitment to believer's baptism by immersion was not insurmountable. However, the proposed merger in 1868 failed. Later, in 1870, Silas considered it may be negotiable without compromise if both views on baptism could be accommodated but such a perspective was not supported by the Baptist Association.[58] He withdrew his proposal but much later lamented that denominations were a concession to human worldliness and a stumbling block to the unsaved.[59]

Silas commended

After many years of service, Silas was recognised for his contribution to the Baptist denomination in 1885, and for his years of service and sacrifice. Charles H Goode presented him with an oil painting of Silas on behalf of the South Australian Baptist Union (SABU).[60]

The painting was a good representation depicting Silas at a point of passing a resolution at an AGM but facing opposition to the resolution. It was painted by Andrew MacCormac.[61]

---

[55] 'The Deputation From the Baptist Association to the Congregational Union', *TP*, May 1870, 55.
[56] 'Congregationalists and Baptists', *TP*, May 1868, 91.
[57] Walker, 'The Baptists in South Australia, 1863-1914', 30.
[58] Walker, 'The Baptists in South Australia, 1863-1914', 30-31.
[59] Walker, 'The Baptists in South Australia, 1863-1914', 31 referring to *TP*, February 1873, 13.
[60] The South Australian Baptist Association (SABA) changed to South Australian Baptist Union (SABU) in 1895.
[61] South Australian portrait painter Andrew MacCormac (23 December 1826 – 13 August 1918) was a Baptist.

> [He] intended it to represent Mr. Mead the moment after, in face
> of opposition, he had successfully carried a resolution at the
> Annual Meetings. He (Mr Goode) suggested to the artist he ought
> to have seen Mr. Mead when he failed to carry a resolution ... a
> real representation of Mr. Mead would be somewhere between
> these two expressions.[62]

Goode hoped that Silas would then present the painting to the denomination to remain as a memorial of his ministry, and a smaller copy was to be made for him. In his reply, Silas stated that he regarded that FSBC and the denomination was his memorial enough.[63]

Portrait of Silas Mead by Andrew MacCormac, 1885

[62] 'At the Annual Meetings', *TP* 18:10, 1 October 1885, 121.
[63] 'At the Annual Meeting', *TP* 18:10, 1 October 1885, 129.

SABA leadership change

Having invested much time and effort into the South Australian Baptist Association, Silas was saddened by the liberal theological drift of a considerable number within the Baptist Union away from the conservative evangelicalism that he had embraced. He had advocated in 1892 that the denomination adopt a theological statement and desired that acceptance of such a statement be a condition of membership.[64] He was not advocating that a creed be imposed upon individuals, but considered that if the Union had an agreed statement of faith it would help the denomination stem the tide of more liberal views. However, this proposal was soundly rejected by the majority of Union delegates.[65]

After thirty-five years Silas was respected but no longer had the influence amongst Baptist leaders that he had had in earlier years. Furthermore, he had hoped to serve the SABU in a voluntary capacity when he stepped down as the senior pastor of Flinders Street Baptist Church but this never eventuated. In addition, to the dismay of many who had benefitted from Silas's denominational leadership, a motion for the South Australian Baptist Union to provide a retirement annuity for Silas divided delegates at the Baptist Assembly in the spring of 1896.[66]

Was it time to simply move on? Had Silas overestimated his role? Some of the emerging ministerial leaders, such as John Sexton, James Fowler, John Paynter and George Hogben, were restless for change. They lobbied for a change in Union polity, believing that too much member church independence was stifling the development of the denomination.[67] They sought a more connexional form of church government. Silas, however, expressed the opinion that the Union already had sufficient influence amongst the Baptist churches.[68]

The new leaders wanted to assert their influence and could not do that while Silas was still 'at the helm'. They considered that Silas had wielded too much power for too long so could not agree to his offer to serve the Union in a voluntary capacity.[69]

---

[64] 'The Baptist Association', *EJ*, 18 September 1872, 3, http://nla.gov.au/nla.news-article196743184.

[65] 'SA Baptist Association', *Register*, 29 September 1892, 6, http://nla.gov.au/nla.news-article48535482.

[66] 'SA Baptist Association', *Register*, 29 September 1892, 6, http://nla.gov.au/nla.news-article48535482

[67] John Walker, 'The Baptists in South Australia, circa 1900 to 1939' (PhD thesis, Flinders University, 2006), 337, referring to a letter from J Fowler to JG Raws in footnote 5.

[68] For a discussion of the clash between Silas Mead and a younger group of ministers over theological issues, see John Walker, 'The Baptists in South Australia, 1863-1914', 44-52.

[69] JR Fowler reported by John Walker, 'The Baptists in South Australia, circa 1900 to 1939', 3.

Silas was also aware that there were people who considered that he was too zealous to see people saved, and other members of the Union appeared to lack interest in his future ministry. '[T]here has been a growing feeling amongst the Ministers, which latterly had developed into a strong opposition to Mr. Mead because of the influence he wielded or was supposed to wield on Committee' expressed the depth of opposition concerning Silas's influence within the leadership of the SABU.[70] Rather than cause dissension, Silas withdrew.[71]

In honour of Silas Mead

Silas Mead's contribution to the Baptist denomination was significant. He laid the foundation for its ongoing identity and ministry and saw the need for theological education in South Australia. However, his influence extended beyond the state and Australia to a global dimension.

At the farewell to Silas in 1897, Charles Goode commended Silas for being selfless in the multiplication of churches, for the growth of the Baptist denomination in South Australia was largely due to his energy.

The YMCA expressed appreciation for his valued contribution at a leadership level and his work outside of the denomination. Rev Bell spoke on behalf of the Baptist College, which was sustained by Silas's energy. The College students held Silas in high esteem and an indebtedness to him for the years of service.

George Hogben, who studied for the ministry under Silas, and 'for 18 or 19 years' had worked together with Silas in the Baptist Union 'in the truest sense', stated that Silas's 'organisational ability and his devotion to the Church was only exceeded by his devotion to Christ'.[72] Even his associate at FSBC, Rev JG Raws, acknowledged Silas as a scholar and organiser, despite their 'delicate' relationship.

Among the tokens of appreciation given to Silas at the farewell was an illuminated address presented to him by Rev EH Ellis on behalf of both the Furreedpore Mission and the Baptist Union. The wording of the address was reprinted in the *Southern Baptist* and lists many of Silas's achievements on behalf of South Australian Baptists:

---

[70] JR Fowler in a letter addressed to David Murray, 13 October 1896. Personal communication from John Walker, 22 October 2021.
[71] 'Farewell Meeting to Rev. Silas Mead, M.A., LL.B.', *SB* 3:3, 4 February 1897, 26-27.
[72] 'Farewell Meeting to Rev. Silas Mead, M.A., LL.B.', *SB* 3:3, 4 February 1897, 26.

Dear Mr. Mead—On the occasion of your approaching removal, at least for a time, from South Australia, we desire to express our high appreciation of the services you have so long and so honourably rendered to the Baptist denomination in this colony. We recognise that in all the denominational extension here in the work on the foreign field you have been throughout the leading spirit. It was very largely through your efforts that the Baptist Union as a strong band of brotherhood and an efficient agency of work came into being. You have taken such a position as to the training of young men for the University that one-half of our present pastors owe their tuition very largely to you. It was through your Christian enthusiasm that our Foreign Missionary Society was founded in 1864, and since then no one has more earnestly kept its claims before the Churches. Our denominational magazine originated with you, our Building Fund and Aged Ministers' Fund have always found a friend in you, and with you originated numerous schemes for establishing Churches in different parts of the province. Having worked long by your side, we feel keenly the thought of your separation from us. We shall ever remember with pleasure our association with you. Wherever it may be the Master's will that you spend your future years, our sympathies, our love, our prayers will be with you.[73]

John Price, a close friend of Silas, was not able to attend the farewell but wrote his thoughts to be read at the farewell. Price reflected that they had shared their personal lives and ministry for thirty-two years. He described Silas as 'ever the evangelist'.[74] Silas had implemented many useful plans for the Baptist churches but had not sought any recognition for this. Through him, there was a spirit of expansion, including FSBC producing a number of 'daughter churches' in the suburbs. Price concluded:

My own view of the matter can only be summed up by expressing my conviction that there is no man in the history of Australasia who has, in his own person, accomplished so much in the Southern Hemisphere for the denomination to which we belong.[75]

[73] 'Farewell Meeting to Rev. Silas Mead, M.A., LL.B.', SB 3:3, 4 February 1897, 27.
[74] 'The Rev. Silas Mead, M.A., L.L.B.', Colonist, 17 January 1890, 5, http://nla.gov.au/nla.news-article214701923.
[75] 'Letters Read at Rev. S. Mead's Farewell Meeting', SB 3:5, 4 March 1887, 60.

7

Silas and
South Australian Society

Frank Tucker

Introduction

Silas understood that the mission of the church included evangelism and social reforms. These reforms were an outcome of the social conscience of revived Christians of the eighteenth and nineteenth century.[1]

Evangelicals were able to minister with others of different theological emphases without compromising perceived beliefs and practices. This understanding of religious tolerance meant that each person could adhere to their beliefs and practices whether their beliefs were considered to be valid or not.[2]

Advocacy on social issues

A high proportion of colonists were dissenters and Christians were well represented amongst State parliamentarians. However, the young colony was unable to avoid social ills and inequalities and failed to achieve the 'paradise of dissent' to which

---

[1] Edwin Orr, *The Light of the Nations: Progress and Achievement in the Nineteenth Century*. The Paternoster Church History, vol 8. (Exeter: Paternoster Press, 1965), 26.
[2] Harold A Netland, *Dissonant Voices: Religious Pluralism and the Question of Truth* (Grand Rapids, MI: William B Eerdmans Publishing, 1991), 301–14. The meaning of tolerance has changed in a postmodern world to mean acceptance of contrary beliefs.

its Christian founders aspired.[3] Silas Mead took an active role in promoting an evangelical view of social reform.

Christian education in state schools

The use of the Bible in public schools was a long drawn out, complex and controversial saga in which Silas participated. The year 1875 marked the inauguration of a state system of education. The state parliament insisted that a compulsory education system should be non-sectarian. The Education Act disallowed reading or teaching the Bible in schools during instruction time. And the use of the Bible outside teaching time was permitted but required parental approval.[4]

Many of the colonists were Nonconformists. They were resistant to government endorsed and sponsored churches and government interference in religious issues. However, Silas did not understand religious education in secular schools as government interference in religious issues, he believed that the Bible was foundational to society.

The issue of biblical education in schools was fought on two fronts: in the parliament, and with the churches that were opposed to Bible lessons in state school time. To address this issue a meeting of the interested public was called. At that meeting Silas proposed, 'That a society to be called the Bible in State Schools Society be formed, with the object of securing systematic Bible reading and teaching during school hours in the State schools.'[5] Silas became the chairman of this Society formed in 1881.

Silas argued that the use of the Bible need not lead to the favouring of any church by the state. He argued that morality cannot be properly taught without reliance on the Bible. For that to happen, explanation of the text was needed.[6] Silas believed this was important for the wellbeing of society so it was a state issue. It was the role of the government to educate children to be citizens of the country and not be ignorant of the basis of national morality. The alternative would be to advocate secularism. Silas

---

[3] D Pike, *Paradise of Dissent: South Australia 1829-1857* (Melbourne: Melbourne University Press, 1957).

[4] 'The Education Commission and the Bible in State Schools', *AO*, 12 May 1883, 39, http://nla. gov.au/nla.news-article159561956.

[5] 'Bible in State Schools', *ET* (second edition), 4 October 1881, 4, http://nla.gov.au/nla.news-article208195213.

[6] Silas Mead, AT Magarey and Joseph Nicholson, 'Letter to the Editor—Scripture League and Ministerial Manifesto', *ET* (second edition), 23 March 1893, 4, http://nla.gov.au/nla.news-article208383794.

thought that the criticism of religious bias, raised by some Nonconformists, was not supported by the experience in NSW. In any case, any student who objected to the Bible lessons should not be required to participate.[7]

In the National Scripture League and Ministerial Manifesto, Silas referred to Joseph Cook saying, 'What ever puts the Bible out of the schools takes its place.'[8] In that case, secularism could become a state sponsored religion and the curriculum would provide secular explanations for reality which would discourage exploring a biblical viewpoint.[9]

To gauge community concerns about Bible reading in state school, the Society conducted a colony-wide survey of parents in 1882.[10] The response was overwhelming—90% of responses supported Bible reading and explanation of the text.[11]

On 26 June 1883, the Hon. John Colton[12] presented a petition in the House of Representatives on behalf of Silas as Chairman of the Bible in State Schools Society. He stated, 'praying the Board to so amend the Education Act as that the Bible may be read and explained in the state schools of this colony during school hours and as part of the ordinary course of instruction.'[13]

Despite such petitions from citizens, the government saw no need to change the Act. However, a state referendum on the issue was held in 1896. The government thought that the results supported the choice of no change to the existing practice.[14] The lobbyists had lost their cause. At this time South Australian politics was becoming increasingly secular[15] and parliament recognised that there was no agreement amongst the churches. The battle had been lost on this occasion.[16]

---

[7] Mead, Magarey and Nicholson, 'Scripture League', *ET*, 23 March 1893, 4.
[8] Mead, Magarey and Nicholson, 'Scripture League', *ET*, 23 March 1893, 4.
[9] Secularism should be understood not as areligious but rather as a non-transcendent religion. In that case there is no neutrality.
[10] 'Bible in State Schools Society's Meeting', *ET* (second edition), 26 September 1882, 2, http://nla.gov.au/nla.news-article208267332.
[11] Ronald George Slee, 'The Politics of Religious Education in South Australia' (MA Dissertation, University of Adelaide, 1979), 22-23.
[12] John Colton was the South Australian Parliamentary representative for the Noarlunga electorate.
[13] 'House of Assembly', *Register* 27 June 1883, http://nla.gov.au/nla.news-article42001166.
[14] Slee, 'The Politics', 28.
[15] Condon, Brian. 'Dissent in Paradise: Religious Education, 1840-1940: An Historical Outline', in *Dissent in Paradise: Religious Education Controversies in South Australia*, 2nd ed., ed. PC Almond and PG Woolcock, 3-18 (Magill: Murray Park College of Advanced Education, 1978), 7.
[16] Condon, 'Dissent in Paradise', 7.

Government grants to Christian schools

In 1889 Silas wrote in the *South Australian Register* expressing his concern over a proposal to make government grants to denominational schools.[17] He considered that this would result in discrimination. Such a concern, he observed, was supported by contemporary experience in Boston, USA.

Silas's contribution to higher education

Silas was a Board member of the Union College (see chapter 6) at a time when a significant donation for the College was received from Walter W Hughes in 1874. The Board of the College determined to apply the donation to general education (rather than theological education) which led to the establishment of The University of Adelaide. Through this connection Silas became a member of the University Senate.[18] In that capacity he advocated for a school of medicine and the inclusion of women students. Three children of Silas and Ann Mead became students at the University. It was an innovative university in that it accepted women as students and offered degrees in science.[19] However, Silas's intimate association with its formation enabled him to realise that the university was hampered by being structured in a similar way to those in England.[20]

A response to gambling

The subject of gambling in local sports was drawn to the attention of the monthly meeting of the Adelaide Ministerial Association in December 1894.[21] Silas was one of the committee members who prepared and published a sweeping 'manifesto' on the subject. It stated that, in the first instance, the church should not be tainted by gambling and should set an example by not using raffles. Preachers and teachers should advise students of the harm caused by dishonest gains. Playing for money in homes, irrespective of the amounts, was to be discouraged due to its effect on children. The

---

[17] 'Grant to Denominational Schools', *Register*, 23 July 1889, 7, http://nla.gov.au/nla.news-article54591664.
[18] Alison Mackinnon, *The New Women: Adelaide's Early Women Graduates* (Adelaide, SA: Wakefield Press, 1986), 201.
[19] Alison Mackinnon, *The New Women*, 21.
[20] See further in Chapter 10.
[21] The Adelaide Ministerial Association on Gambling', *SC*, 8 December 1894, 7, http://nla.gov.au/nla.news-article93856704.

manifesto also stated that gambling should be banned in employment venues. Legislators and leaders of society needed to conduct themselves with due honour and not act with duplicity by promoting and participating in the practice. The manifesto finally requested that the State Governor should withdraw patronage from events that promoted gambling since such practices had a moral consequence and were not a good example to the young. It is not known if the agenda was implemented.

A response to alcoholism

Alcoholism was a social problem in the colony and contributed to the need for female refuges. In the early colony, there were few controls on production and consumption. In 1872 the leadership of the South Australian Evangelical Alliance included Silas Mead (President) and WK Thomas, FW Cox and James Jefferis LLB amongst others. The Evangelical Alliance was concerned with social reforms. It addressed the lack of supervision and proliferation of inferior 'public houses' that sold alcoholic beverages and were associated with other vices that were tempting young men. The Evangelical Alliance proposed a bill to present to the state parliament to restrict the number of these public houses.[22] It was also proposed that there be a limited tenure to such houses, which had to be renewed, and that they close on Sundays. The Evangelical Alliance advocated that churches should conduct annual prayer sessions regarding the problem of alcoholism.[23]

The organisation also sought cooperation with the Temperance League and the Temperance Alliance, which provided education on the problems of alcoholism. Silas influenced the Alliance as a member of the state executive of the Alliance from 1883 until at least 1893 apart from the time of his absence from the state.[24]

Branches of the Temperance Alliance (composed of women and men) were established in a number of churches. One of these was at FSBC. It was also noted that increasingly churches were using unfermented wine for communion.[25]

[22] 'Evangelical Alliance', Advertiser, 22 May 1872, 5, http://nla.gov.au/nla.news-article28685674.
[23] 'Evangelical Alliance', Advertiser, 22 May 1872, 5, http://nla.gov.au/nla.news-article28685674.
[24] 'Temperance News', SC, 28 March 1891, 9; and 'South Australian Alliance', Chronicle, 4 March 1893, 8. http://nla.gov.au/nla.news-article92304073.
[25] 'The Temperance Movement', Chronicle, 24 March 1894, 7, http://nla.gov.au/nla.news-article92862398.

Support for the needy

Silas was concerned about destitute people in society, consistent with his evangelicalism. A report on government food rations for destitute people was carried in the *South Australian Register* on 15 March 1867. Silas endorsed the criticisms in the report by affirming that these rations had to be broken up with a hammer (literally) in order to be eaten. He cited the case of a woman who declared the rations inedible and was reliant on other help to survive. From Silas's experience this was a common problem.[26] He said that if recipients complained about the food there were repercussions. There were times when cash had to be given because the food provided was inedible. His concern was that the government did not deliver on its own undertaking. He argued that while non-government charities were available for assistance they should be reserved for cases not covered by the government rations.

Christian unity

In the colony of South Australia there were many independent churches. Evangelicalism generally sought to unite believers in devotion to God and service but not necessarily organically connected. Silas, being an active evangelical, shared this notion of unity. In South Australia the Evangelical Alliance was an agency that promoted evangelical action through seminars and lectures, and advocated evangelical unity; Silas joined in 1869 and was an active member.[27]

Silas believed that the divisions between denominations gave the 'unregenerate an excuse to continue in unbelief'.[28] For him, the church was much broader than individual denominations. He could disagree with other believers over theological issues and still show grace towards them. This demonstrated a unity in shared ministry without sacrificing personal convictions.

Local evangelical ecumenical missions

Soon after his arrival, Silas became involved in local mission, the Aborigines' Friends' Association, and the mission to colonists through the South Australian Bush

---

[26] Silas Mead, 'Government Rations', *Register*, 15 March 1867, 3, http://nla.gov.au/nla.news-article39178006.
[27] 'The Evening Meetings', *TP*, November 1869, 222; 'Evangelical Alliance', *Advertiser*, 22 May 1877, 6, http://nla.gov.au/nla.news-article33748864.
[28] 'The Spirit of Denominationalism', *TP*, February 1873, 14.

Mission. This was consistent with Silas's sense of calling to participate in God's mission and concurred with his association with George Fife Angas and FW Cox.

Aborigines' Friends' Association (AFA)

When Silas arrived in Adelaide in 1861, there were few local Kaurna people remaining on the Adelaide plains and those who did were a tragically decimated, demoralised people.

There remained, however, a significant number of Ngarrindjeri living around the lower lakes near the mouth of the Murray River.[29] Concerned colonists[30] had formed the Aborigines' Friends' Association (AFA) in 1858 to address the spiritual, social and physical needs of these people.[31] It was holistic in its intent and 'civilising' (westernising) was part of the agenda. In 1862, Silas identified with these advocates for the indigenous people.

At a meeting of the AFA held in 1863 the Rev FW Cox, a Congregationalist and close associate of Silas, reported on the 'Narrinyeri' ministry.[32] He acknowledged that mission amongst these people was difficult and discouraging. The real discouragement was mainly due to the apathy of colonists. Silas attended the meeting and urged that more funding be made available for the 'spiritual and social improvement of the Aborigines.'[33] He acknowledged that he had not had the opportunity to visit Point Macleay but had met believers and Mr Taplin from the mission and was impressed with them.[34]

Silas had not allowed his opinion to be influenced by the dominant colonial impressions of the dispossessed and victimised remnants of the Kaurna people encountered in Adelaide.[35] Silas shared views held by a minority of colonists and missionaries who worked with the Ngarrindjeri people. He told the meeting:

---

[29] Graham Jenkin, *The Conquest of the Ngarrindjeri: The Story of the Lower Murray Lakes Tribes* (Adelaide: Rigby, 1979), 37.
[30] The use of the terms, 'settler' and 'colonist' are not intended as a statement about the ethics of European presence.
[31] South Australian Museum Archive, 'Aborigines' Friends' Association', https://www.samuseum.sa.gov.au/collection/archives/provenances/aa1.
[32] 'Aborigines' Friends Association', *Advertiser*, 27 November 1863, 5-6, http://nla.gov.au/nla.news-article31830403.
[33] 'Aborigines' Friends Association', *Advertiser*, 27 November 1863, 6.
[34] 'Aborigines' Friends Association', *Advertiser*, 27 November 1863, 6.
[35] 'Aborigines' Friends Association', *Advertiser*, 27 November 1863, 5.

the natives were our brothers and sisters, and their place in the next world may be as high or higher than ours. We were quite ignorant of the history of the aborigines of the world, and only knew that they possessed the same faculties as ourselves.[36]

Silas viewed Aboriginal people as fellow humans worthy to hear, and needing to hear, the gospel. The AFA mission was about converting the Ngarrindjeri to Christianity and included socio-cultural transformation from a western cultural perspective. It was a Christian mission and a 'civilising' mission.[37] John Harris writing about advocates for Aboriginal people could equally apply to Silas:

[These people] were not perfect. They were ethnocentric. They saw the world through what have been called 'cultural spectacles'. They were people of their time, influenced by the spirit of their age, but they were also the best of their age.[38]

Well-meaning Christians, including Silas, were also participants in the collective colonial social action that deprived Aboriginal people of land.

A number of years later, in 1887, a group of between 150 to 200 Ngarrindjeri people from Point Macleay visited Adelaide and attended the AFA meeting. On Sunday they participated in Christian worship at the Kent Town Methodist Church in the morning and then at FSBC in the evening.[39] At the latter service Silas Mead's text was 'And they shall come from the east, and from the west, and from the north, and from the south, and shall sit down in the kingdom of God'.[40] In his sermon, Silas stated that the past century of missionary efforts had brought this verse to fruition and noted that indigenous people from Australia, India and Africa had been amongst the first to receive Jesus as saviour. He had moved beyond his earlier understanding that Aboriginal people needed to become culturally western to be Christian. Silas demonstrated continued development and was a man before his times.

[36] 'Aborigines' Friends Association', *Advertiser,* 27 November 1863, 6.
[37] 'Narrinyeri', *TP,* vol 7 no 7, July 1874, 75-76.
[38] John Harris, *One Blood: Years of Aboriginal Encounter With Christianity: A Story of Hope.* 2nd ed. (Sutherland: Albatross Books, 1994), 184.
[39] 'Aborigines Friends Association', *ET,* 21 November 1887, 3, http://nla.gov.au/nla.news-article207710568.
[40] Luke 13:29 (RSV).

The YMCA in Adelaide

The Young Men's Christian Association (YMCA), an interdenominational Christian youth organisation, was started in London in 1844 by George Williams.[41] It was 'born in evangelism, prayer meetings, and Bible Study.'[42] Also, it recognised the need for the 'development of the whole man—Body, Mind, and Spirit', and had as its central objective the 'winning of young men and boys to Christ'.[43] The Adelaide branch of the London YMCA was formed in 1850 for the improvement of the 'spiritual condition of young men'.[44] It was the first YMCA to be formed outside of the UK. The initial meeting was held at Rev Stow's Congregational church. Charles H Goode, a close associate of Silas, became secretary at its inception.

The missional and evangelistic emphasis of the YMCA during its early days appealed to Silas. It aligned with his commitment to global mission and provided a means for young people to engage in an inclusive mission of the church. This would complement Christian Endeavour at FSBC. He helped draft the YMCA constitution in 1878 and participated in state leadership, being the Vice-President for several years. During 1894–95 he was the South Australian YMCA President.[45]

A new Bible translation

The South Australian Auxiliary of the Bible Translation Society[46] (later Bible Translation and Revision Society) was re-formed in 1864 to support the promotion and provision of English language Bible translations and provide Bengali Scriptures for the people of Faridpur in East Bengal. The committee included prominent Baptists, such as Silas, A Webb, G Fowler, John Price, G Prince and Charles H Goode.[47] The committee made a point of stating that the Bible Translation Society was not intended to compete with the British and Foreign Bible Society,[48] but the British

[41] Jack Massey, ed., *At Milestone 50: A Brief History of the Y.M.C.A. in Adelaide from 1850 to 1930, including the Fiftieth Annual Report* (Adelaide, YMCA, 1930).
[42] Massey, *At Milestone 50*, 4.
[43] Massey, *At Milestone 50*, 4.
[44] Massey, *At Milestone 50*, 4.
[45] 'The Rev Silas Mead', *Register*, 12 January 1897, 7, http://nla.gov.au/nla.news-article54471447.
[46] 'South Australian Auxiliary of the Bible Translation Society', *Chronicle*, 16 July 1864, 2, http://nla.gov.au/nla.news-article92259103.
[47] 'The Bible Translation and Revision Society', *TP*, April 1868, 78-80.
[48] 'Instruction for bible translation', *TP* 3:1, January 1891, 28-44. In Australia the British and Foreign Bible Society has been renamed the Bible Society in Australia.

and Foreign Bible Society had withdrawn assistance from the Bengal project due to Baptist insistence on using the word 'immersion' in place of 'baptism'.[49] The British and Foreign Bible Society had insisted on transliterating the Greek word *baptizo* to *baptism.* Silas asserted that such Greek words would be unintelligible to the people of India.[50] However, Silas believed that this should not affect the relationship between the Translation Society and the British and Foreign Bible Society.[51]

At the meetings, he reported on the progress made in 're-translating the Word of God by the American Bible Union'.[52] A revision of the King James Version of the New Testament became available in America from 1850, so in 1868 the committee ordered 1,000 copies from the American Bible Union.[53] The Society also undertook to distribute Bengali Bible portions for the people of Faridpur.

In a report to the Baptist Association in 1882, Silas updated the news of the new translation and was particularly concerned that the majority of the twenty-five revisers were not Baptists. Dr Joseph Angus, Silas's Principal at Regents Park College in London, was the only Baptist New Testament scholar on the committee.[54] Silas thought that the new version was a great improvement but still left some issues unresolved. Despite the shortcomings, he supported the Revised Version of the New Testament. The translation of the Old Testament had not yet been completed at the time.

Silas did not consider that religious language needed to use antiquarian English as though that was sacred language. His driving concern was that the Bible needed to be understood in the common language people use. He regarded that effective communication of the gospel was important for evangelism and discipling.[55]

Using the print media

Newspapers were the usual public media of the day. Silas was not reluctant in making his views known and addressed a number of subjects. It was an era when Christian topics were featured in printed newspapers, some of which were owned by

[49] 'South Australian Auxiliary of the Bible Translation Society', *Chronicle*, 16 July 1864, 2.
[50] 'Furreedpore Bible Society', *TP*, 1 March 1881, 30–31.
[51] 'South Australian Auxiliary of the Bible Society', *Chronicle*, 16 July 1864, 2.
[52] 'Bible Translation and Revision Society', *TP*, February 1868, 44.
[53] 'Bible Translation and Revision Society', *Advertiser*, 10 January 1868, 2, http://nla.gov.au/nla.news-article31974068.
[54] 'The Revised Version and the Baptist Position', *Register* (supplement), 29 September 1882, 2, http://nla.gov.au/nla.news-article43328303.
[55] 'The Bible Translation and Revision Society', *TP* 23:1, January 1891, 28–30.

Christian publishers such as William Kyffin Thomas and later his son, Robert, who were close associates of Silas.

It was said of Silas Mead, 'He used his pen very extensively.'[56] It was used for such diverse topics as university endowments, state interference in the church, the marriage bill before parliament, martyrdom in China, and state responsibility for secondary education. His pen was busy.

Scripture Immersion–a response to John Hannah's writings

The only book written by Silas was *Scripture Immersion,* in 1867. It provides insight into his incisive thinking, his logic, the documentation of evidence and a willingness to agree with an opponent where agreement was appropriate.[57] His argument was comprehensive, based on his study of the Scriptures and biblical languages. He cogently put the case for a biblical understanding of believer's baptism by immersion.

The occasion for writing the book was a paper titled *Infant Baptism Scriptural and Immersion Unnecessary* by John Hannah, an English advocate for infant baptism, presented at the Wesleyan Conference in London, and published in 1866.[58] This document was distributed to the Wesleyan Church in South Australia. A review of Silas's book was published in the London *Baptist Magazine* in February 1868.[59]

In his book Silas quotes John Hannah liberally. He wrote to reassure readers that believer's baptism by immersion was legitimate and biblical. From Hannah's understanding, the Greek word *baptizo* should not be translated as 'dip' since baptism is used in situations where 'dip' is clearly not meant. Silas responded with a defence of scriptural teaching and sought to show that infant baptism was invalid:[60]

> Mr. Mead gives plain and satisfactory...convincing answers to all his adversary's 'arguments', and besides bringing forward overwhelming Scripture evidence, to the utter confounding of his antagonist's 'logic', his observations are enforced by

[56] 'Rev. Silas Mead, MA, LLB', *PA* (Adelaide), 1 June 1892, 90, http://nla.gov.au/nla.news-article230506956.
[57] Silas Mead, *Scripture Immersion: Or Arguments Showing Infant Baptism to be Unscriptural, and Believers' Immersion to be Exclusively Scriptural and Obligatory, Intended as a Reply to the Rev. John Hannah's Book entitled 'Infant Baptism Scriptural and Immersion Unnecessary' and Issued at the Wesleyan Conference, London.* (Adelaide, SA: Andrews, Thomas and Clarke, 1867).
[58] 'Review of "Scripture Immersion"', *TP,* August 1868, 165.
[59] 'Review of "Scripture Immersion"', *TP,* August 1868, 165.
[60] Mead, *Scripture Immersion,* 2.

well selected quotations from Christian authors of every denomination.[61]

Silas countered Hannah's claim that infant baptism was valid.[62] Silas argued that the immersion of believers was scriptural and obligatory.[63] Certainly, as Silas concedes, the word for baptism was used in contexts other than immersion in water; however, he states that these are figurative uses of the word.[64]

Hannah argued his case from an analogy with the Lord's Supper where the quantity of bread and wine was not important. Hannah claimed that the two sacraments can be compared; Silas rejected this claim.[65] He also argued that the classics favour immersion for the meaning of *baptizein*. In Silas's opinion Hannah's evidences were 'sharp swords that fatally wound his own theory.'[66]

Silas appealed to some Episcopalians who claimed that in the New Testament baptism was administered by immersion representing 'death to the life of sin, and then raised from this momentary burial to represent resurrection to the life of righteousness.'[67] He argued that it was unfortunate that in the Authorised Version the translators capitulated to King James' opinion that 'baptism' be used rather than the English equivalent.[68]

It was stated by Hannah that while there is no evidence in the New Testament that the disciples of Jesus baptised children yet he considered that they would have done so. This is argued from the assumed attitude of Jewish parents not to exclude children, and a supposition from early church practice.[69] Silas countered this argument stating that the rite of baptism was restricted to believers, irrespective of age.[70] He supported this by writing: 'We believe there are "no differences" in the eternal safety of the baptised and unbaptised infant.'[71] The notion of baptismal regeneration or any special blessing implied in the practice of infant immersion was dismissed by Silas since there was no evidence in the Scriptures for such a claim.

---

[61] 'Review of "Scripture Immersion"', *TP,* August 1868, 165.
[62] Mead, *Scripture Immersion,* 5–6, 12.
[63] Mead, *Scripture Immersion,* 6, 9.
[64] Mead, *Scripture Immersion,* 16–17.
[65] Mead, *Scripture Immersion,* 6.
[66] Mead, *Scripture Immersion,* 10.
[67] Mead, *Scripture Immersion,* 12.
[68] Mead, *Scripture Immersion,* 23.
[69] Mead, *Scripture Immersion,* 40.
[70] Mead, *Scripture Immersion,* 41.
[71] Mead, *Scripture Immersion,* 42.

The debate also raised the question of Immersion of households in the case of Cornelius's household (Acts 10).[72] There is no mention of infants in the text and their participation cannot be inferred from silence. Those who believed were baptised. The same applies to Lydia's household (Acts 16:13–15). Silas cited several early writers stating that the practice of infant baptism was not known until at least 150 CE.

Scripture Immersion also dealt with the question of people who falsely profess faith and are baptised.[73] Hannah considered that this practice is an inconsistency on the part of Baptists. However, Silas contended that occurrence of incidences do not negate the practice of believers' baptism by immersion. He regarded such a claim as offensive because of its generalisation.[74] Silas was disturbed by the accusation that Baptist motives were questionable and that their understanding of baptism was being used to 'entrap' people.[75]

John Hannah also raised the question of rebaptism. He accused other churches (meaning Baptists) of rebaptising people who had been infants at the time of being 'baptised'. Hannah regarded such rebaptism as being without the authority of Jesus. In response to such a claim, Silas agreed that the 'subsequent baptism of believers... is to be condemned'.[76] However, '[w]hen a Paedobaptist minister sprinkles, or pours water on, or immerses an infant, the Lord's ordinance is not administered.'[77] Therefore, subsequent immersion on profession of faith was not rebaptism. Silas stated that the burden of proof of any claim must lie with the claimant.[78] That was absent from John Hannah's writings or any other supporter of infant baptism.[79]

In summary, Silas countered the claim that infant baptism was valid and argued that the immersion of believers was scriptural and obligatory.[80] This subject was often dealt with by Silas in speeches, sermons, presentations and in writing.

In 1868 Silas's *Scripture Immersion* was printed for distribution. It was reprinted at least twice more (at least 3,000 copies) due to popular demand.[81] A German edition was also made available. This later edition was possibly intended for the German im-

---

[72] Mead, *Scripture Immersion*, 47.
[73] Mead, *Scripture Immersion*, 43.
[74] Mead, *Scripture Immersion*, 43.
[75] Mead, *Scripture Immersion*, 65.
[76] Mead, *Scripture Immersion*, 61.
[77] Mead, *Scripture Immersion*, 62.
[78] Mead, *Scripture Immersion*, 66.
[79] Mead, *Scripture Immersion*, 66.
[80] Mead, *Scripture Immersion*, 5-6, 12.
[81] 'Baptist Association', *AO*, 31 October 1868, 5, http://nla.gov.au/nla.newsarticle158933957.

migrants to South Australia. He was competent in the German language, evidenced by remarks about his preaching in German at the Pirie Street Lutheran Church during his first year in South Australia.[82]

Other writings

Other contributions on a range of issues were included in public newspapers. He wrote about religious education in schools, the need for Bible translation and issues related to social discrimination and abuses. He also contributed articles on theological issues that were deemed of interest to a wider readership than that of the Baptist Association. In some cases his writing took the form of disputation. They revealed his concerns and his careful documentation. Other writings related to the Baptist Association were confined to denominational periodicals.

Concerning ritualism

As President of the Baptist Association in September 1879, Silas delivered an address on the subject of ritualism. He recognised that ritual was important in Christian practice but he was concerned about ritualism since it shifts an inner heart response to God to an external one. Ritualism 'may be defined as the attachment of excessive importance to external religious rites in regarding them as the necessary and procurative means of imparting the gifts of salvation.'[83] Silas was concerned about the emphasis on ritualism since it externalised faith, it would result in salvation through ritual. Silas stated that salvation achieved through the ritual observances of the church was an unscriptural concept. To him, it was a 'spiritual mischief'[84] and diametrically opposed to the teaching of Scripture. His address on the subject, given at the Baptist Association meeting, was published in the public domain.[85]

****

Silas's influence as a leader was widely acknowledged. It was a spiritual leadership in that it was directed by his inclusive understanding of the gospel.

---

[82] 'Lutheran Church', *Advertiser*, 26 March 1862, http://nla.gov.au/nla.news-article31808980.

[83] 'Ritualism' *AO*, 4 October 1879, 10, http://nla.gov.au/nla.news-article160125046.

[84] 'Ritualism' *AO*, 4 October 1879, 10.

[85] 'Ritualism', *AO*, 4 October 1879, 10.

In his ministry to the wider South Australian society and nationally, Silas demonstrated continuity with the evangelical movement. His participation in local missions expressed his concern for the unevangelised and his commitment to Christian mission.

He had a heart for marginalised people. His support for welfare and missional programs and the extent of his advocacy for social reform demonstrated his desire to contribute to the development of South Australia and to see people enter the Kingdom of God.

'Missions on Heart and Brain'

Rosalind Gooden

Silas Mead arrived in Adelaide in 1861 well informed of the William Carey tradition of Baptist Mission history (BMS), committed to missionary service, and keen for local action. At the time most Australian denominations were finding missionary enthusiasm focused on Pacific islands through auxiliaries of British societies. Silas Mead refocused Baptist commitment to Bengal in India.

Silas Mead's roles in South Australia

Prayer

Silas's first action to encourage missionary fervour (a decision taken in the first month of the FSBC's existence) was to establish a missionary prayer meeting.[1] The first Monday in the month was a rich British Baptist tradition from the call to prayer in 1784 in Northamptonshire even before the formation of the BMS:

> The grand object in prayer is to be that the Holy Spirit may be poured down on our ministers and churches, that sinners be converted, the saints edified, the interest of religion revived and the name of God glorified. Don't confine your requests to our own societies; or our immediate connection; Let the whole

---

[1] FSBC Members Meeting Minutes, 27 August 1861, 55. Marjory Mead, *God Building Flinders Street Baptist Church 1861–1961* (Adelaide: Flinders Street Baptist Church, 1961), 37.

interest of the Redeemer be affectionately remembered and the spread of the gospel to the most distant parts of the habitable globe be the object of your most fervent request.[2]

John Price, who shared Silas's missionary passions, wrote:

For success in every enterprise [Mead] has unconquerable faith in prayer. When all other means fail he regards prayer a resource that cannot fail; and thus he often undertakes enterprises that seem a very forlorn hope...because he puts unbounded trust in the living God; and his faith is not deceived.[3]

He was known 'to pray around the globe naming each needy country in turn'.[4] Bertha Tuck, one of the FSBC missionaries, said:

I doubt not that Mr Mead's best weapon in making missionary enthusiasts was his habit of prayer...I don't remember many missionary sermons...but his missionary prayers entered deep into my soul...A person not interested in missions was once heard to say, 'Would it not be a treat to hear Mr Mead pray just once without naming India, China, and Africa'...Mr Mead well knew what preaching on missions may not do, the taking of worshippers by prayer into the presence of the Eternal Father would do.[5]

Voluntary society not an auxiliary

The South Australian Baptist Association (SABA) was established on 29 October 1863,[6] and twelve months later on 10 November 1864, while discussing needed decisions, responsibility for missions was raised:

Rev. H. L. Tuck addressed...the importance of forming an Australian Baptist Missionary Society in preference to establishing an Auxiliary of the Baptist Missionary Society of London, and proposed–'That to-night it be submitted to the general meeting that a separate South Australian Baptist Missionary Society be

[2] Anthony R Cross, *Useful Learning: Neglected Means of Grace in the Reception of the Evangelical Revival among English Particular Baptists* (Eugene, Oregon: Wipf and Stock, 2017), 320.
[3] John Price, 'The Rev Silas Mead MA LLB', *The Baptist Magazine* July 1890, 289-92.
[4] Marjory Mead, 'Silas Mead', *AB*, 22 April 1959, 11.
[5] BS Tuck, 'The Late Rev Silas Mead MA LLB', *OB*, November 1909, 2.
[6] *South Australian Advertiser (Advertiser)*, 31 October 1863, 2.

formed.' Rev. S. Mead seconded. Mr. D. Fowler proposed as an amendment, and Mr. Shaw seconded–'That special efforts be made to raise funds for foreign missionary work, and that the Committee of the Association be empowered to expend the funds.' The amendment and motion having been put there was a tie, and the Chairman gave his casting vote in favour of Mr. Tuck's motion.[7]

That evening at the full Association meeting Silas spoke on 'The Work of Missions':

...He held it to be their duty to endeavour to do something for the heathen abroad, and he submitted to them a proposition to the effect that those present should form themselves into a Society to promote this end.[8]

He further explained:

Missionary labour [is] a glorious undertaking...His own feelings pointed to India, and he believed...that a glorious harvest was awaiting that land;...that although the seed might be long in germinating, it would ultimately bud forth and grow up to maturity; and that there would be collected, not a few scattered sheaves, not the gleaning, but the grand and glorious harvest... He would move:–That this meeting, appreciating the duty of assisting foreign mission work, hereby constitutes itself into a Society to promote this object.[9]

That new society needed to determine a specific field. They had two influences. James Smith, a BMS missionary from Delhi, forced by ill-health to recuperate in Victoria, Australia in 1858 and 1861, had stirred missionary concern.[10] The newly formed SABMS contacted Smith and promised help of £60 to finance four or five native preachers in and around Delhi. Second, there was interest in the South Seas. Rev AW Murray, LMS missionary to Samoa, had been baptised in Sydney in 1862 and desired support from Australian Baptists.[11] A letter to him was unanswered when

---

[7] *Register*, Wednesday 24 October 1864, 2.
[8] *Register*, 24 October 1864, 2.
[9] *Register*, 24 October 1864, 2.
[10] Tony Cupit, Ros Gooden and Ken Manley, *From Five Barley Loaves: Australian Baptists in Global Mission 1864-2010* (Preston, Vic: Mosaic Press, 2013), 8.
[11] Ken Manley, *From Woolloomooloo to 'Eternity': A History of Australian Baptists* (2 vols, Milton Keynes: Paternoster, 2006), 242.

the Society met for their first annual meeting in September 1865. At that time Rev. J Chamberlain Page, BMS missionary from Barisal, Bengal was visiting Adelaide.[12]

Silas opened his pulpit to him, announcing an open collection in aid of missions he advocated.[13] The Church meeting amended the decision so that the 'whole of the contents of offering boxes be given in aid of Missions' that Sunday.[14]

Page met with the SABMS Committee and at that first annual meeting they announced their decision to support work in Faridpur, a district of East Bengal unoccupied by any missionaries. They decided to support four native preachers and a schoolmaster, under Page's supervision. Page went on to Victoria and rekindled the enthusiasm stirred by James Smith and the Victorian Baptist Missionary Society was also formed adopting interest in Mymensingh District of East Bengal. He also visited New South Wales and held stirring meetings, but at that time no society resulted.

Directions were set for Australian Baptist missions for eighty-five years. East Bengal became the specific Australian Baptist territory. It was not until after the Second World War that they commenced new work in the Pacific.[15]

Advocate and theorist

Silas's chief role was as advocate, reminding churches of the great population for which they were the sole Christian mission. The SABMS published letters from their agents, they organised prayer and fund-raising. Silas as editor with John Price of the journal *Truth and Progress* (*TP*) published information on missionary activity.[16] GH Rouse, a fellow-student of Silas's at Regent's Park College, contributed extensive articles on Baptist work in India.[17] These shaped the early understanding of SA Baptists. By 1880 the SABMS was featuring a specific missionary page in each *Truth and Progress*. Silas intended all to recognise the validity of Mission beyond their own setting.

[12] 'An Epitomized Report of the South Australian Baptist Missionary Society' (1865), Baptist Mission Australia archive; Cupit, Gooden and Manley, *From Five Barley Loaves*, 10; Rosalind M Gooden, 'Awakened Women: Initial Formative Influences on Australasian Baptist Women in Overseas Mission 1864-1913', (M Theol thesis, Melbourne College of Divinity, 1997), 55.
[13] FSBC Members Minutes Book 1, 13 September 1865, 319.
[14] FSBC Members Minutes Book 1, 13 September 1865, 318.
[15] Cupit, Gooden and Manley, *From Five Barley Loaves*, 195.
[16] 'The Devil-Worshippers', *TP*, March 1869, 44-48; 'Foreign Missions', *TP*, 1869, 149-56; 'A.L.O.E. in India', *TP*, 1876, 102.
[17] GH Rouse, 'The Results of Mission Work in India Compared with the Triumphs of the Early Church Pt 1', *TP*, September 1869, 161-67; Pt 2, *TP*, 1869, 186-92; 'Missions in India—The Field of Labour', *TP*, 1869, 230-34.; etc.

The text 'Go ye into all the word and preach the gospel to every creature' was over the FSBC pulpit at least on special occasions:[18]

> [The Mission] is small, but it is the best we can do; and being our best, we are warranted in expecting that God will bless the work of our hands.[19]

Silas was enthusiastic for evangelism of other nationalities along with his commitment to grow his own church from his 'world'. Evangelism in Adelaide and abroad had his passionate interest but he recognised the need for bite-size pieces and sufficient continuity. As early as November 1868 he mentioned the newly developing work among women in the zenanas of India. In 1868 Silas expressed the hope that soon no one, particularly isolated women, would be debarred from hearing the truth.[20]

Silas at FSBC preparing to farewell the 'barley loaves', showing the text above the pulpit, 1885
[BMA]

Recruiter

Silas believed that there was a need for European missionary supervision of their Indian/Bengali workers. Initially he hoped that SABMS might engage Page's services.[21]

---

[18] For example, the farewell to the five 'Barley Loaves' in 1885.
[19] 'Report of Half Yearly Meeting of Baptist Association', October 1867, 85.
[20] 'South Australian Baptist Missionary Society', *TP*, December 1868, 263.
[21] *TP*, January 1868, 17.

But with his unavailability Silas 'hoped that as there was no prospect of a missionary being sent from Europe, they might send one…'[22] He argued that Australian settlers were very suited to missionary service because of Australia's proximity to the large mission fields—they had personal experience of sea travel—and that the rugged life of colonies fitted 'for a speedy adaption to the new mode of life in other countries'.[23]

He reasoned that nine out of ten Australians were acquainted with the Gospel and that the dispatch of fifty men from the colonies would not in the long run materially diminish the total amount of spiritual agency put forth and any gaps temporarily caused would speedily be filled.[24] This was at a time when the colonies were struggling to find pastors for their own ministries. He resisted the plea that there were sufficient heathen at their doors.[25] He pleaded passionately that South Australian Baptists should be senders, and answered the excuse that there were no suitable men offering:

> No, and never will in adequate numbers, till with yearning sympathies, the churches open their eyes to behold vast harvest fields calling for labourers. The conviction and feeling must be evoked within our churches that we ought to respond to the mute but almost overwhelming appeal of these six hundred millions of our fellow-beings who nationally are our neighbours. When the churches think aright, feel aright and pray aright … young men filled with the Spirit of Christ will not be backward in declaring, here are we; send us to India or to Japan or to China.[26]

Not surprisingly, the first recruits came from FSBC. But that was still years away. Silas's vision was for South Australia's local resources to serve global needs. Bertha Tuck wrote:

> Mead was a missionary enthusiast and made others enthusiasts. How did he do it? Partly because to think missions was as natural to him as being. When Mr Mead talked missions there was that tone about the conversation which prevented one supposing it was unthinkable to be a missionary.[27]

Silas 'had India both on the heart and the brain'.[28]

---

22 'The South Australian Baptist Missionary Society', *TP*, June 1873, 69.
23 'Missions', *TP*, June 1873, 61-62.
24 'Missions', *TP*, June 1873, 61.
25 Mead, despite his support of work among First Nations people, did not integrate them in his thinking. Geography was the defining concept; foreign missions was the criteria.
26 'Missions', *TP*, June 1873, 61.
27 BS Tuck, 'The Late Rev Silas Mead MA LLB', *OB*, November 1909, 1.
28 'Missionary Page South Australian Baptist Missionary Society', *TP*, 1884, 68.

Japan Baptist Mission

Wilton Hack, a former member of FSBC and Baptist minister in SA, applied to the SABMS in 1872, but was unconvinced of a call to India. He eventually decided the climate of Faridpur was unsuitable for his family.[29] He resolved instead to go to Japan and asked the Committee to support him but they did not feel justified in changing focus.[30] Even so, Silas suggested to FSBC that as Hack was going to Japan, some recognition should be made of his party, and a tea meeting was held where Hack explained:

> ...it was his duty to go. From his earliest years it had been his desire to work among the heathen...and it had been his object to seek out fields of labour not tended by others.[31]

Letters gave news of the party's travels, arrival in Nagasaki, the purchase of a printing press. Hack mentioned the need for £400 to pay off the press.[32]. He was emphatic that his method of tract production was appropriate and his lack of language study justified. He believed that his church in Hiroshima was the first church in all Japan outside of a port. He used his printing assistant as pastor and taught through interpretation.

By 1876 he needed help to pay off £1,000 on the press and mission house. Donations were to be sent via Silas.[33] That appeal was unsuccessful and Hack visited England and Australia in 1876 to raise more support. George Fife Angas gave £100.[34] The FSBC congregation gave £12.[35] Some Victorian Baptists showed interest in supporting him.[36] Hack named Silas as one of the trustees for the property. By 1877 there were rumours of the closing of the Japan mission and there was relief in South Australia that they could concentrate on Faridpur.[37] However Hack returned to Japan and contributions were divided and the SABMS found it difficult to maintain ministry even on a limited scale. Silas mentioned an approach to the LMS to take over the work in Faridpur.[38] Nothing came of this.

[29] 'The South Australian Baptist Missionary Society', *TP*, June 1873, 69.
[30] 'The South Australian Baptist Missionary Society', *TP*, 1874, 66.
[31] 'Immersions, Hilton and North Adelaide', *TP*, 1873, 131.
[32] Frederick Searle 'Correspondence–Rev W Hack', *TP*, 1874, 69.
[33] Wilton Hack, 'Correspondence, The Rev Wilton Hack and Japan', *TP*, 1876, 94.
[34] 'Mr Hack and His Work in Japan', *TP*, September 1876, 99.
[35] FSBC Members Meeting, 2 August 1876, 341.
[36] Basil Brown, 'A Century of Australian Baptist Overseas Missions', *Foundations*, 1964, 62.
[37] 'Denominational News–Baptist Missionary Society', *TP*, 1877, 82.
[38] 'Denominational News–Baptist Missionary Society', *TP*, 1877, 81.

The leaders in whom Hack had placed faith proved to be unreliable and without necessary finance the mission was wound up and virtually disappears from the corporate memory of Australian Baptists. Brown alone mentions it.[39] Hack was later to become a theosophist, shunned by Baptist friends.[40]

Refocusing vision

By 1878 revitalising focus was needed. Reports reminded supporters of the appointment of their first agents in 1866. Their first convert, Punchanon Biswas, baptised in 1871, studied in Serampore and returned to Faridpur as one of the supported preachers.[41] Silas, as he travelled to England, wanted first-hand information in order to be an even more effective advocate of missions. His nineteen days spent in India in 1874 gave him a sharpened vision. Silas met the BMS missionaries in Calcutta who were mentors for the Victorian and SABMS Indian workers. He wrote to Calcutta to arrange a visit to Adelaide of Punchanon Biswas.[42]

Australian women offer

On Friday 5 January 1877 Lady Elizabeth Lush chaired the Baptist Zenana Mission (BZM) Committee in London. The minutes record:

> Letters were heard from a Miss Marie Gilbert of Geelong in Australia offering herself for Zenana work in India and Mrs [Hannah] Martin of Melbourne and Rev Bunning of Geelong speaking of her fitness for the work and high Christian character.[43] It was thought advisable to send copies of the letters to Mrs Lewis of Calcutta, in case she...should feel urged by the want of agents to send for Miss Gilbert at once...and it was besides resolved to write Miss Gilbert and Mrs Martin encouraging the idea of Miss Gilbert's becoming an agent but laying upon the friends at Melbourne and Geelong that as much as possible they should bear all the expense of such an Agent...[44]

---

[39] Basil Brown, 'The Australian Japanese Mission', *The Baptist Quarterly* 19:7, 1962, 309.
[40] Gooden, 'Awakened Women', 65-66; Manley, *From Woolloomooloo to Eternity*, 383-84, 593-94.
[41] 'South Australian Baptist Missionary Society', *TP*, 1878, 134.
[42] 'Correspondence–The Furreedpore Bible Society', *TP*, June 1881, 71.
[43] Bunning was the advocate for Emilia Baeyertz to SABA in 1880.
[44] Minute Book of the Zenana Mission No 1, 5 January 1877, BMS archives, Oxford.

Nothing developed. There is no further mention of Gilbert, Martin, Geelong and Australia for six years until 11 February 1883, when we read:

> A letter was read from Rev Silas Mead in Adelaide, S Australia, stating that they had just sent out two young ladies to India for work at Furreedpore,[45] a Miss Gilbert and a Miss Arnold - the former having applied to our Society a few years ago but as the Melbourne Church was not then prepared to do much her application had fallen through. That now in consequence of the greater expenditure attending this effort Mr Mead suggested that the money supplied...to Calcutta by the friends at Melbourne...should be added to that contributed at Adelaide. Mr Martin concurred in the propriety of this suggestion that our Society consented to give up the money. Mrs [Amelia] Angus was requested to write to Mead and say that the request was reasonable...and to express a cordial sympathy and good wishes for the new effort.[46]

Silas Mead and Victorian Baptist mission interests were linked, in the eyes of the BZM. Silas had studied under Joseph Angus, Amelia's husband. He had met some of the enthusiasts of zenana work in 1874–75.

Fund raising

Silas was an effective fund raiser. FSBC gave regularly to missions. As early as 1862 the Sunday school had contributed £9/10/6 to the New Hebrides mission and resolved to maintain a national missionary in India.[47] They also gave to Australian indigenous mission work. Silas expected each member to contribute something, however small, and regularly. He knew that work had to be regulated by the amount of money raised.[48]

---

[45] Indian place names were anglicised in various ways at various times, and today in many places have been renamed. In general, the names of the period have been used in this volume. Faridpur is the preferred option, but Furreedpore is used for the incorporated name of the Society. Calcutta, Pabna, Mymensingh are treated similarly.
[46] Minute Book of the Zenana Mission No 1, 11 February 1883, Regent's Park College, Oxford. Rev James Martin, husband of Hannah Martin, acting on behalf of the Baptist Zenana Mission (BZM) in Victoria.
[47] 'FSBC Report of First Annual Social Meeting August 5 1862', FSBC Members Minutes Book 1, 105.
[48] 'Report of Half-yearly Meeting of the Baptist Association', TP, October 1867, 85.

Giving for missions was often personalised. Different groups knew which agent they were supporting.[49] Silas appealed to various motives for giving: the importance to India as a nation; their joint membership of the British Empire; the duty of the English (having taken over India); the supply of a good education system; that the mission belongs to the denomination, and not any particular church.[50] He used the shame factor—'some churches had not helped this year'; and comparison with others like the Presbyterians and Congregationalists.[51]

FSBC in 1878 decided on four annual designated collections: March for the Baptist Association, June for the Sunday School, September half for City Missions and half for work at Point McLeay with the Ngarrindjeri nation, and in December for the SABMS.[52] So he taught a balance in giving—church support, city needs, local and regional ministries and overseas.

Silas early recognised the effectiveness of women as collectors of funds. FSBC formed an Auxiliary for the SABMS appointing a group of men as committee,[53] with authorised collectors, all single women! Silas believed that no church was the worse, but, on the contrary, both better and better off for the funds they gave away.[54] He was justified in his belief. They gave systematically, they gave for special needs. So did the Baptist Association, despite hard economic times.

Visits to India

Silas made four visits to India. The first in 1874 was only nineteen days, two of which were at Faridpur.[55] He saw a number of other missionary programs but wished he had allowed 6–8 weeks. He was convinced

> Religiously India is far worse than I was able to imagine. I confess my heart is deeply pained to see how very little the gospel of Christ has so much as touched or reached the idolatry and Mahommedanism [sic] of India. It is all nonsense that people write about idolatry waning, and caste ceasing. Unless the

[49] 'Baptist Missionary Society', *TP*, May 1871, 47.
[50] 'Missions–South Australian Baptist Missionary Society' *TP*, 1876, 67.
[51] 'South Australian Baptist Missionary Society' *TP*, 1879, 68.
[52] FSBC Members Meeting Minutes, 19 July 1876, 337.
[53] FSBC Members Meeting Minutes, 31 October 1877, 41.
[54] 'Missionary Page South Australian Baptist Missionary Society', *TP*, June 1884, 69.
[55] 'South Australian Baptist Missionary Society', *TP*, 1874, 133.

church of Christ works far more successfully than heretofore, it will take a hundred centuries to bring India to the feet of Christ.[56]

Silas's time in England in 1874 also added to his mission perspectives. He seconded the paper of Wenger 'The History of Bible Translation in India' and of Trafford 'Education and Missions' at the BU Annual Assembly and pleaded for more workers—fifty men in five years.[57] He met missionaries on leave and attended meetings addressed by practitioners.

Silas visited India again in 1895–96 as an official delegation with William T Whitley, principal of the Victorian Baptist College and secretary of the VBFM.[58]

On leaving FSBC in 1897 he again visited Bengal, spending time particularly with the Australian Baptist work and his son. Finally, he spent a longer time there in 1905 following his attendance at the World Baptist Conference in London.[59]

Silas and WT Whitley in Bengal, 1896.
L to R: Bertha Tuck, Silas, Alice Mead, WT Whitley, Agnes Pearce [BMA]

[56] 'Missions in India', *TP*, 1874, 133.
[57] 'The Autumnal Meetings of the Baptist Union', *TP*, January 1875, 7.
[58] Manley, *From Woolloomooloo to 'Eternity'*, 123-24.
[59] 'Missionary Methods. Australian', *The Baptist World Congress. London, July 11-19, 1905* (London: Baptist Union Publication Department, 1905), 86-92.

Mentoring missionaries

In 1881 Punchanon Biswas, SABMS's first convert, whom Silas met at Faridpur, visited South Australia. Income increased, and laid the foundations for sending out Marie Gilbert and Ellen Arnold.

In June 1882 Silas recommended Marie Gilbert, a member of FSBC but teaching at Moonta, as 'suitable for the work, and…willing to go to India as a Zenana Missionary'.[60] She had not lost her call since the letter from Geelong to BZM in 1877. Silas also took the initiative and spoke to Ellen Arnold, another schoolteacher in his congregation.[61] She too was accepted by the Committee, and he arranged for the two to do medical observation at the Adelaide Hospital. Silas spoke on their behalf at their farewell.[62]

Silas nurtured Arthur Summers, the first male missionary for the SABMS, and his fiancée Annie Hearn, a member of that first YPSCE. Silas suggested service with VBFM to Abia Neville.[63] He suggested to Fanny Denness that she serve with the NSWBMS. The biographers of Amy Parsons and Bertha Tuck write of Silas's influence.[64] Tuck wrote of Silas's advocacy for all missionaries:

> Have any missionaries left Australasian shores without Mr Mead's sympathy, prayers and blessing?…Not only was Mr Mead ever on the look-out for recruits, but also he earnestly sought to help those who went forth to realize what a holy, happy and dignified service they were called to.[65]

Edith King, one of the early women from Western Australia, wrote:

> To us missionaries Mr. Mead was always kind and sympathetic, and it was always a help to talk to him about one's own work, for he entered into it so heartily, and made one feel that he was more than merely interested. I shall never forget some of Mr. Mead's prayers…How he used to pray for a spiritual awakening to come to India, for the dead bones to live![66]

[60] 'The Baptist Missionary Society', TP, June 1882, 68.
[61] ABFM, The Missionary Heritage of Australian Baptists (Sydney: Australian Baptist Publishing House, 1937), 9.
[62] 'Furreedpore Zenana Mission', TP, November 1882, 134-35.
[63] Abia Neville, White unto Harvest: An Account of the Mission in Mymensing, East Bengal (Geelong: Victorian Baptist Foreign Mission, 1898), 81.
[64] Irene Dover, Pathway to India (London: Poona and Indian Village Mission, 1958), 16-17. ABFM Annual Report, What God Hath Wrought, 1933, 6.
[65] BS Tuck, 'The Late Rev Silas Mead MA LLB', OB, November 1909, 1-3.
[66] 'Goalundo Mission', WAB, 15 November 1909, [n.p.].

Silas also influenced Laura Hope née Fowler to spend much of her life in India.[67]

Roles in other colonies

Baptists were more numerous in South Australia and Victoria than in the rest of the Australian colonies until 1900. Both groups formed their missionary societies in the 1860s, financing agents in Faridpur and Mymensingh. Silas hoped that SA and Victoria would cooperate to finance a European or Australian superintendent for both programs.[68]

From 1877 there were regular exchanges of delegates at the annual Association meetings between NSW, Victoria and SA. Silas in Melbourne in 1881 optimistically announced that while the wedding of the colonial associations had not yet taken place, he looked upon them as 'engaged'.[69] This exchange of views of delegates laid the foundation for discussion of possible federal activities.

In 1902 and 1903 inter-colonial Baptist conferences were held, and Silas chaired both.[70] They discussed the formation of a federal body for Baptists, a federal paper, federation of missionary work, and the establishment of a federal College.[71] But before such federation, missionary societies were formed in NSW, Tasmania and Queensland, chiefly through Silas's initiative.

Victoria

Contact between the Victorian and South Australian Baptist missions dates from their inception in 1865 with common influences, but adoption of different spheres. In 1885 Ellen Arnold spent time in Victoria and met Ruth Wilkin from Castlemaine and Marion Fuller at Aberdeen Street Geelong, who became Victorian missionaries. Later, Abia Neville, a member of FSBC, recommended by Silas and deacons, transferred mem-

---

[67] Helen Jones, 'Hope, Charles Henry Standish (1861-1942)', *Australian Dictionary of Biography*, volume 14 (Carlton: Melbourne University Press, 1996), 491.
[68] Silas Mead, 'Our Foreign Missions', *TP*, June 1872, 61.
[69] It was to be a long engagement: Australian Baptist federation did not happen until 1926. Basil Brown, *Members One of Another: The Baptist Union of Victoria 1862-1962* (Melbourne: The Baptist Union of Victoria, 1962), 91.
[70] 'Baptist Federation', *The Baptist. The Organ of the Baptist Denomination in New South Wales*, 1 October 1902, 1.
[71] Gerald B Ball, 'The Australian Baptist Mission and its Impact in Bengal 1864-1954' (MA Thesis, Flinders University, SA, 1979), 26.

bership to Collins Street Baptist Church in Melbourne and became Victoria's first male missionary.[72]

Victoria and South Australia combined in sending a delegation to Bengal in 1895—Silas and William T Whitley. Their joint delegation report, printed in *Southern Baptist*, indicated agreement on missionary methodology. Silas was senior to Whitley by twenty-five years, and in fact Whitley and Silas's son Cecil were more contemporaries. Silas wrote: 'We went not as mere tourists…We went as lovers of Mission work'.[73] They visited mission stations of many denominations.[74] They brought encouragement to both missionaries and national Christians at Australian centres. They believed that to maintain separate missions in adjoining areas was a wasteful use of personnel and means and both advocated federated action to eliminate lack of continuity and to maintain good practice in handling agents.[75]

Arnold Crusade

Ellen Arnold and Marie Gilbert, the first Australian Baptist missionaries, departed for India in October 1882. Within eighteen months Arnold returned to Adelaide broken in health. Her return to India was delayed on medical grounds. Silas recognised her giftedness in stimulating enthusiasm. After time in SA, Silas sent her to the other colonies, preceded by a letter to pastors, deacons, superintendents, Sunday-school teachers and churches of mainland Australia, Tasmania and New Zealand.[76] This circular contained Silas's philosophy of missions by the 1880s. It was a case for work in contiguous areas, using such phrases as 'one compact great mission field', 'the united energies of the… churches, a federated union…for mission purposes'.[77] Silas commended action, in dependence on the power of God, for facing the challenge of the millions in India and in the light of the BMS's inability to staff adequately their own work in India and elsewhere.

Each colony gave Arnold a good hearing. She spoke in most Australasian Baptist churches and challenged several women to offer for India.[78] She developed her missiology and maintained women were a necessary first step for Australian Baptists, and not

[72] FSBC Members meeting, 17 June 1891, 495.
[73] Quoted by Marjory Mead, 'Silas Mead', *AB*, 22 April 1959, 11, 14.
[74] 'Chat With a Baptist Enthusiast', *SB*, 1 June 1899, 114.
[75] Brown, *Members One of Another*, 72
[76] Silas Mead, 'Foreign Mission', *The Victorian Freeman*, February 1885, 42; 'South Australian Baptist Missionary Society', *TP*, January 1885, 16; *The New Zealand Baptist*, January 1885, 10-12.
[77] Ball, 'The Australian Baptist Mission and Impact in Bengal 1864-1954', 25.
[78] 'Preached' may even be an appropriate term.

just a zenana mission.[79] She argued for women on the basis of essential roles, cost effectiveness, ability to supervise pastors, competent decision makers.[80]

Meanwhile, Silas corresponded with BMS's George Kerry, indicating developments in Australia. The BMS staff rejoiced at the growing missionary spirit among the Australian Baptist churches.[81]

The churches were stirred by Arnold, but they were not ready for corporate action. They formed independent societies with individual territories. Four women accompanied Arnold to East Bengal in 1885: Alice Pappin from South Australia, Marion Fuller and Ruth Wilkin from Victoria and Martha Plested for Queensland. They became known as the 'five barley loaves' and took up initial residence in the SABMS property at Faridpur. A grand farewell was held for them in FSBC where Silas referred to the five barley loaves, so few for such a task.[82] New Zealand sent Rosalie Macgeorge the following year.

The five 'barley loaves', L to R: Marion Fuller, Martha Plested, Ruth Wilkin, Alice Pappin (later Mead), Ellen ('Nell') Arnold [BMA]

[79] Rosalind M Gooden, ' "Mothers in the Lord": Australasian women missionaries at the intersection of cultural contexts 1882-1931' (PhD (Theology) thesis, Tabor College of Higher Education, Adelaide, 2016), 129.
[80] Gooden, 'Awakened Women', 154.
[81] TP, January 1885, 17.
[82] Cupit, Gooden and Manley, From Five Barley Loaves, 15.

New South Wales

Baptists in New South Wales were slower to take up the challenge. Page visited them in 1865, generating enthusiasm but no decisive action. Silas had a profound influence on Allan Webb, an early member of FSBC. Webb moved to New South Wales and was significant in the formation of the Baptist Association. In 1871 he gave a paper on foreign missions. Like Silas he favoured work in India and also opposed becoming a mere auxiliary for the BMS. He urged a field abutting Faridpur.[83] Webb was to move on to ministries in New Zealand, North Adelaide, Melbourne and Geelong where he was known for his support.

Another minister from SA, one-time member of FSBC William Clare moved to NSW in 1881.[84] He read a paper to NSW Baptists advocating the formation of a Foreign Missionary Society. The matter was referred to their executive.[85] Rev Frederick Hibberd had represented NSW Baptists in Adelaide for the Association meetings of 1880.[86] He and Silas differed over the question of open or closed membership, but agreed that the colonies should unite together in an Australian Missionary Society. He said 'He would not be satisfied until the colonies united in such enterprises'.[87]

Ellen Arnold was recuperating in Monghyr, West Bengal when she heard of NSW's possible interest. She and BMS's Thomas Evans wrote to Silas suggesting the district of Tirhoot as the field for NSW.[88] These letters arrived while Rev Fenwick, the NSW delegate, was in Adelaide with instructions to discuss inter-colonial missions. Silas passed on the suggestion. The NSW Baptist churches decided to occupy Tirhoot with agents supported by their colony, sending money to Evans at Monghyr.

Kerry and Rouse in Calcutta did not favour Tirhoot, but a field adjacent to Mymensingh. Arnold was in NSW when that advice arrived and it was decided to conduct zenana work.[89] Their committee interviewed six applicants, but none proved

---

[83] Alan C Prior, *Some Fell on Good Ground* (Sydney: Baptist Union of NSW, 1966), 88–189.

[84] FSBC Members Meeting, 23 March 1881, 168.

[85] Prior, *Some Fell on Good Ground*, 189.

[86] 'Report of the Annual Meetings of the South Australian Baptist Association Incorporated–September 1880', *TP*, October 1880, 117.

[87] 'Report of the Annual Meetings of the South Australian Baptist Association Incorporated–September 1880', *TP*, October 1880, 117.

[88] 'India–Tirhoot District', *TP*, February 1884, 17.

[89] 'History of the NSW Mission (as far as I know it)': Arnold's notes based on original notes she gave to EE Watson, just a few months before her death and signed by Watson 13 September 1939. Baptist Mission Australia Archives.

suitable. They asked Arthur Jewson, BMS missionary at Comilla, to superintend work of two national workers for NSW.

Later in January 1887 Arnold was transferred by SABMS to do zenana work alongside the Jewsons. She set about supervising the building of a brick mission house for the zenana workers at Comilla.

Arnold's relationship with NSWBMS was complicated by that building. Silas Harding from Geelong had been a very generous supporter of mission housing in Bengal. In 1888 Silas communicated with NSW that an interest-free loan of £1,000 was available for four years for Comilla. NSW accepted the loan and agreed to meet the guarantee; Queensland undertook half the responsibility. Later, the donor converted the loan to a gift. Silas communicated with NSW and Queensland and said he took it to be £500 to each and advised Queensland to start a separate station. Unfortunately, this caused misunderstanding between the two colonial committees effectively preventing union (according to Arnold) and Martha Plested moved to start work in Noakhali. Arnold also proved unable to work harmoniously with NSW staff (who had come actually from South Australia and FSBC) and returned to work at Pabna with the South Australian Mission.[90]

Following the delegation in 1896 both Silas and Whitley visited NSW and proposed various schemes for united actions.[91] NSW favoured Whitley's rather than Silas's suggestions. This may be due to those earlier experiences over the loan, differences over closed and open membership, or the fact that Silas was now in his sixties and would be absent for the next five years, before returning to Western Australia.

Queensland and Tasmania

Silas's role in Queensland and Tasmania was more limited or less documented. In 1880 William Poole arrived in Queensland after effective ministries in Victoria.[92] He cited the forwardness of SA Baptists as a shining example. He called on Queensland to support two native preachers on an Indian field.[93] Arnold fanned the missions interest on her visit in 1885.

[90] Minutes of the NSW BMS, 7 August 1891.
[91] SB, 13 August 1896, 177. Mead had just resigned from Flinders Street Baptist Church at the time.
[92] Poole was one of the founders of the Baptist Association of Victoria. Brown, Members One of Another, 34.
[93] John E White, A Fellowship of Service: A History of the Baptist Union of Queensland 1877-1977 (Brisbane: Baptist Union of Queensland, 1977), 108.

Martha Plested heard Arnold, offered for service and joined those going to India in 1885. Martha spent her first year at Faridpur, then went with Arnold to Comilla and then in 1888 opened up work in Noakhali for Queensland. Thus, Arnold's visit resulted in three things: the formation of the Missionary Society in Queensland, the offer of service of Plested and their adopting work in Comilla and then Noakhali District.

In 1885 Arnold also visited Tasmania.[94] She influenced Mary and William Gibson, wealthy Baptist pastoralists. They formed the first committee in Launceston with Rev Alfred Bird.[95] Tasmania became an auxiliary of SABMS, adopting Lucie Kealley, a South Australian missionary as their own responsibility. SABMS changed their name to Furreedpore Baptist Mission to acknowledge this partnership.

Australasia

Silas's proposal for contiguous missions in East Bengal included New Zealand.[96] His circular endorsing Arnold's visit was published in full.[97] He, himself, visited Auckland early in 1885 and spoke fervently of possibilities.[98] Arnold followed in February 1885, visiting almost all the Baptist churches in three months and finding great interest.

Many NZ Baptist churches held regular monthly missionary prayer meetings, and BMS boxes were in many homes. Arnold's plea was for an even deeper prayer support and a willingness to take a share in the 'Mead plan'. The fire was kindled.[99]

There was a growing conviction that New Zealand Baptists ought to take their part in the missionary endeavour alongside the Australians. However, there was no agreement about Silas's greater plan for the federation of all that work. The *NZ Baptist* expressed itself in favour of the idea but doubted its practicality. New Zealand showed sturdy independence. Their work began and continued as an independent effort. Their staff were part of the annual conventions, taking their share in hosting and accepting office. In 1913 when the separate Australian societies federated, they did not join. However, the fruit of their work remained linked in the East Bengal Baptist Union, giving the one Union two missions to handle.

---

94 *TP*, December 1884, 135.
95 Laurie Rowston, 'One Hundred Years of Partnership in Foreign Missions Pt 1: Serajgunge for Christ', *Tasmanian Baptist Advance*, May 1991, 9.
96 SL Edgar and MJ Eade, *Towards the Sunrise: The Centenary History of the New Zealand Baptist Missionary Society* (Wellington: New Zealand Baptist Historical Society, 1985), 5.
97 *The New Zealand Baptist*, January 1885, 10.
98 *The New Zealand Baptist*, February 1885, 28.
99 'New Zealand Baptist Missionary Society Celebrates', *AB*, 11 January 1961, 10.

Mission roles in Western Australia

Silas's son-in-law, AS Wilson, was minister of Perth Central Church and while Silas was visiting India in 1896, Silas wrote to Wilson urging that WA Baptists become involved in missions possibly in conjunction with the SABMS. Both Cecil and Silas wrote suggesting WA concentrate efforts in the East Bengal District of Bogra. A committee was formed with Wilson as chairman, and at its first meeting in April 1897 they decided to send £15 to Cecil 'to enable him to go thro' Bogra with tracts & gospels and report the results to us'.[100] The Victorian committee, under Whitley, wanted WA to assist them in Mymensingh, pointing out the money and personnel needed for a new work. But Silas's move to WA in 1902 provided the driving force. Silas encouraged WA Baptists to undertake work in Goalundo and they adopted Rajbari.[101] Two of their first missionaries, Carrie and Grace Brown, were from Wilson's church where Silas was the associate pastor.[102]

Silas and Cecil Mead at the Goalundo Mission Meeting in Perth Baptist Church, November 1901

---

[100] R Moore, ed., *Baptists of Western Australia. The First Ninety Years* (Perth: Baptist Historical Society of WA, 1991), 150.
[101] Ball, 'The Australian Baptist Mission and its Impact in Bengal 1864–1954', 19.
[102] GS Freeman, 'First Permanent Minister of Perth Baptist Church', *WB* 3:3 (1988), 10.

Brown applied to Silas (then their Missions committee President) in May 1903. Her application was accepted immediately with the request that she do some Biblical studies with Silas from June.[103] He organised for Walter F White to complete his preparation at Harley College. George Menzies in his tribute to Silas Mead wrote 'He had the honorary position in Western Australia of Professor to the student missionaries.'[104] Edith King summed it up:

> ...we love to think of [Mead's] great strong hopes for the future of Goalundo. I shall never forget his turning to me and rather abruptly asking me if I had faith enough to believe that someday we should have a college, a hospital, a training school for Bible women, a strong Christian community, etc. at Rajbari. Then with that characteristic smile and nod of his, said, 'I do.'[105]

So, Silas Mead had primary roles in the formation of missionary societies in South Australia in the 1860s, and forty years later in Western Australia.

Claims

Many claims have been made of Silas's significance in Baptist missions. His close colleague John Price wrote '...Mead has humanly speaking been the chief inspiration of missionary movements throughout Australasia'.[106] The South Australian Baptist Missionary Society (SABMS) in its annual report 1908–09 said:

> Under God, to [Mead's] enthusiastic devotion our Society owes its origin...From the first Mr Mead's wise statesmanship, cheery optimism, and tireless energy were ungrudgingly given to the work of this society, and he crowned all by the surrender of his only son, Cecil Mead, to this great work.[107]

Within two years of his death the Western Australians had erected a church in Rajbari, East Bengal and wrote on the memorial tablet:

---

[103] Moore, *Baptists of Western Australia*, 153.
[104] *The Daily News* (Perth), 9 October 1909, 3.
[105] 'Goalundo Mission', *WAB*, 15 November 1909, [n.p.].
[106] John Price, 'History of the Furreedpore Mission Supported by the Colonies of South Australia and Tasmania' in John Price, Silas Mead and Samuel Vincent, *The Centenary Volume 1792-1892: The South Australian and Tasmanian Baptist Missions of Furreedpore and Pabna* (Adelaide, 1892), 5.
[107] Annual Report for 1908-1909, 96.

> This church is dedicated to the glory of God and to the memory of REV S MEAD MA LLB, Father of Australasian Missions In India, who for many years sought to lead Baptists of Australia to give their best of life and service in India, and who was the inspirer, advisor of and intercessor for the Goalundo Mission.[108]

With typical Australian parochialism, this was misquoted, or reinterpreted by Miss Florence Barker, a visitor at that opening, and by FG Benskin, minister at FSBC, in a demonstration 'Sunrise in India' written in 1924.[109] Silas became 'Father of Australian Missions in India', an interesting claim.[110] The CMS may have sent their first woman to India about the same time as SABMS in the early 1880s. It wasn't until the 1890s that the Australian Churches of Christ and the Poona and India Village Mission (PIVM) began their Indian work.

The claim for Silas was resized by the General Secretary of the Australian Baptist Foreign Mission, Frank Marsh, at the 90th Anniversary of the commissioning of the first Australian Baptist missionaries held in FSBC on 26 October 1972. He remarked:

> How fitting it is that this event should be celebrated...in this church whose pastor for many years before and after was the inspiring genius of that event and who has substantial claim to being regarded as the Father of Australian Baptist missions.

Silas was a significant figure in Australian Baptist, Australasian Baptist and even Australian missionary history and its roots are early in Adelaide, twenty years before the first recruits, which is the date far too often claimed as the origin.

Conclusion

Silas's understanding of missions developed. He became very involved in the Christian Endeavour movement, rejoicing in its ability to foster missions and missionary service. He resonated with the work of Hudson Taylor and the China Inland Mission (CIM). As early as 1873 he wrote of the 'whole plan and genius which characterise what is known as "the China Inland Mission"'. He was attracted by the faith principle, where financial support was sought from God not donors and even more by the attempts that their missionaries made to identify with the culture and mode

---

[108] *Souvenir and Programme of the Opening Ceremony of the Silas Mead Memorial Church, Rajbari, 2 December 1911.*
[109] FJ Barker, 'The opening of the Mead Memorial Church', *OB*, January 1912, 9.
[110] FG Benskin, 'Sunrise in India: A Missionary Demonstration', Adelaide, 1924.

of life of the Chinese.[111] He was a member of their Board.[112] In 1890 Alfred Rogers, a member of FSBC and that first CE Society, was one of the first group of Australians to go to China.

Further broadening of Silas's missions vision resulted from his contacts with Dr Grattan Guinness, who preached at FSBC in 1885.[113] As discussed in the next chapter, Guinness invited him to become principal of Harley College in London in 1897. A group of his students formed the Bihar Mission, a new field for Guinness's Regions Beyond Missionary Union. In Silas's India visit of 1905 he spent time with those students.

Earlier on that same trip he was invited to address the Baptist Congress in London, speaking on 'Missionary Methods—Australian'.[114] He spoke of the unity of home and field in the missionary task. He also said:

> We often speak of the mass of people [to be won] as heathen. I do not like this term...I think neither our Lord nor Paul employed [it] in the sense we use it today. The more appropriate term is the Nations, and Nations spelt with a capital N. The Mohammedans (sic), Buddhists, Chinese, Japanese and Hindus are more accurately described as Nations...Their literature commands the best respect of our ablest scholars, however much we dissent from their teachings...Not only are our Scriptures translated into all the languages spoken by the sons of man, but there are to be found among all tribes some true believers in the Lord Jesus Christ ...who constitute, however few in number the Church of God.[115]

Methods may become outdated. New 'Nations' may become the focus of new or redirected effort, but ultimately Silas's certainty was caught up in that confident vision of the whole earth joining in adoring praise. May that continue to be true of Australian Baptists, through Baptist Mission Australia as they seek to empower communities to develop their own distinctive ways of following Jesus.[116]

[111] 'Missions', *TP*, June 1873, 61-62.
[112] 'Chat With a Baptist Enthusiast', *SB*, 1 June 1899, 114.
[113] FSBC Deacons Meeting, 3 August 1885.
[114] *Baptist World Congress London July 11-19, 1905*, 86.
[115] *Baptist World Congress London July 11-19, 1905*, 86.
[116] *Global Interaction Guide 2020*, 2. From 1 January 2022 Global Interaction changed its identity to Baptist Mission Australia.

9

Christian Endeavour, Harley College and Travels, 1897-1901

Ken R Manley

Christian Endeavour and travels

As Silas Mead finished his remarkable ministry at FSBC he received impressive tributes from both his church and his denomination but was also greatly moved to be farewelled by the state Christian Endeavourers at Pirie Street Wesleyan Church on Christmas night 1896. As earlier chapters have detailed, Silas was among the first and certainly among the most enthusiastic of Australians to embrace the movement. His daughter Lilian who was leaving with him had given extended service to the state CE as manager of the literature department and was honoured with a presentation of two volumes of Robert Browning's works. As Australasian President of CE, Silas had been appointed representative to the World Convention in San Francisco.[1] He told SA Endeavourers: 'Foreign Missions and Endeavourism were dear to his heart. He believed he was now called to devote himself to these two objects, and to this larger service he would consecrate the remainder of his life'.[2] At that time he had no idea that he would occupy a unique position of mission leadership over the next few years. He also made it clear that he would not be permanently settled in South Australia as he prepared once again for overseas travel, leaving on 16 January 1897 'for a protracted absence'.

---

[1] Silas had presided at the first convention of Australian Christian Endeavour societies held in Adelaide, 30 August – 2 September 1895, where the term 'Australasian' replaced 'Australian' in 'the title of the United Society as to include New Zealand and Tasmania' [*West*, 4 September 1895, 6].
[2] *Southern Baptist (SB)*, 1 January 1897, 1, 4.

The Meads naturally took the opportunity to visit India where they were able to see Cecil and Alice at Orakandi in East Bengal. Soon after his arrival in England Silas shared in discussions at the London Baptist Social Union on the topic, 'Is Spiritual Life Declining in the Churches?'. He spoke on 'the differences between churches now and forty years ago', noting that there had been a great advance in the care of the young.[3] His commitment to the CE movement was, of course, one significant aspect of this change.

Silas certainly loved sharing in large conventions. He had been greatly stimulated in his faith and devotion at the Brighton Holiness Convention in 1875. Here he had met most of the leaders in the holiness and faith mission movements, contacts that later led to an unexpected appointment. Central to his plans for this trip with Lilian in 1897 was to share in two large CE conventions, the British National one in Liverpool at Pentecost and the Sixteenth International Convention at San Francisco from 7–12 July.

The growth in the CE movement had been truly remarkable. Founded in 1881 by Rev. Francis E. Clark within his Congregational church in Portland, Maine, within a decade it grew rapidly from a small group of fifty-eight youth to one million members, divided across 21,080 societies worldwide. At the turn of the twentieth century, the 'Young People's Society of Christian Endeavor' was the largest Protestant youth group in the world. CE continued its impressive growth with global membership climbing to four million by its twenty-fifth anniversary in 1906, and five million by 1914. While the vast majority (at least a third) of its membership was drawn from the United States, it spread across over 60 countries and characterised itself as a 'World Wide Christian Endeavour'. Working under the banner 'For Christ and the Church', CE aimed to build the 'church of the future', training its young members in all methods of religious work while also fostering their religious knowledge and faith. Silas Mead was one of the most enthusiastic leaders of the movement in Australia.

He thought that the Seventh National Convention for Young People's Societies in Liverpool held in June was 'decidedly successful', observing that attendance had been double the number of any former convention in England.[4] Several leading Baptists participated, such as Carey Bonner of Southampton who led the singing.[5] On the way to San Francisco Silas and Lilian sailed for New York. In Chicago Silas preached in two churches and was referred to as Dr Mead, suggesting he had been so

---

[3] *SB*, 3 June 1897, 127.
[4] *SB*, 26 July 1897, 169.
[5] *Liverpool Mercury*, 8 June 1897, 7. Extensive press reports, such as in the *Liverpool Mercury*, make no mention of Silas Mead.

honoured by one of the Baptist universities. He himself later corrected this report in the *Southern Baptist*.[6]

From Chicago they visited Niagara Falls and then on to Toronto in Canada. Finally, they reached San Francisco. Most of the ten thousand who shared in the Sixteenth International Christian Endeavor Convention from 7 to 12 July came by train as reduced fares were offered but when so many arrived together it almost overwhelmed the system. Silas Mead, described as 'a dignified white-haired old gentleman, with a grand young heart', featured quite prominently among the delegates, being the spokesman for visitors in reply to their welcome in the huge Woodwards' Pavilion.[7] He laughingly said he knew why he had been selected: 'I and my fellow delegate, Miss Mead, have travelled only 17,000 miles specifically to attend this Convention'. He added that he represented some 60,000 Christian Endeavourers in Australia and happily recalled the visit of Dr Clark to Australia and also reported on the beginnings of CE in India. 'We want Asia [to be] one of the great corners of Christian Endeavour'. He urged the meeting to think not only of an international convention but of an intercontinental one. Lilian gave an address on 'The World's Prayer Chain' and Silas also underlined the worldwide nature of the movement as constituting 'a world's chain of prayer'.[8] He later spoke 'in honour of American womanhood' urging that they should have citizenship rights 'because they are the best representatives of the people...Let us hope our great Christian Endeavour movement will make us all the citizens of one country'. Silas also advocated the extension of the Senior Endeavour Society, with the object of doing for the mid-week service what had been accomplished for it by the young people's organisation.

This was a rewarding and inspiring convention for both Silas and Lilian. They missed a trip to the Yosemite Valley so that Silas could take up a new position in London.[9]

Principal of Harley College

On 9 June 1897 Silas accepted an invitation to become Principal of the London Institute for Missions Home and Foreign, what came to be called Harley College, beginning on 1 October. Silas insisted that when he arrived in London in April 1897 he had no idea about this.[10] He arranged with James Fowler in Adelaide for over 2,000 of his books to be shipped to London.[11] Later, Lilian's husband Crosbie Charles Brown

---

[6] *SB*, 30 September 1897, 21; 4 November 1897, 242.
[7] *Christian Weekly*, as cited in *SB*, 30 September 1897, 219.
[8] *SB*, 30 September 1897, 219.
[9] Charles Crosbie Brown to Marjory Mead, 21 March 1951 (letter held by R Gooden).
[10] *SB*, 29 July 1897, 169.
[11] S Mead to J Fowler, 10 June 1897 (Fowler papers at Mortlock Library, Adelaide).

recalled, however, that when Silas and Lilian had visited India on the way to England Silas had met with Dr Harry Guinness and he had raised the possibility of Silas being appointed to Harley College.[12]

The Guinness family played a huge role in the evangelical world during their lifetimes. Henry Grattan Guinness (1835–1910), grandson of Arthur Guinness who founded the famous Dublin brewery, was an Irish Protestant evangelist. For fifteen years he travelled and preached in Britain, Europe and North America, with a strong emphasis on biblical prophecy. Henry had a vision for the establishment of an interdenominational missionary training college run on the same faith principle as Hudson Taylor's China Inland Mission. This meant that they did not depend on secure funding and planned budgets but prayed that God would provide for them. The cynic might observe, however, that they were extremely successful in making sure that Christian believers 'overheard' their prayers. In 1895 voluntary contributions were £11,989.

Guinness and his wife Fanny opened their college at 29 Stepney Green in London's East End in 1872 'with a view to increase the number of ambassadors for Christ among the heathen, and in the darker regions of Christendom'. Guinness believed that work among the capital's poorest and most brutalised people was important in the training of prospective missionaries. The East London Missionary Training Institute moved to Harley House, with the renowned Dr Thomas Barnardo (1845–1905) as a co-director, and was known as Harley College. The students were accepted on the basis of their suitability regardless of age, gender, denomination, background, nationality, colour or financial circumstances. They were not expected to pay fees. Cliff House near Cyrbar in Derbyshire was given to the cause in 1873 and this part of the College came to be known as Cliff College. Closely associated with the College was the Regions Beyond Missionary Union which Guinness also founded in 1873. This mission pioneered work in India, Argentina and Peru. The College was remarkably successful, training some 1,330 missionaries for thirty societies of various denominations. Henry's son, Dr Harry Guinness (1861–1915), served on the Harley College Council and assumed responsibility for the College in 1886.[13]

Several Baptists served the College as advisors or were on its council: Archibald Brown, William Cuff and most notably FB Meyer (1847–1929), the popular pastor and Keswick speaker. When he was pastor at Christ Church in Lambeth (1892–1907) Meyer began the South London Missionary Training College in Kennington Park and presided over it from 1893 to 1896. Forty students were trained and took up posts with Guinness's Regions Beyond Missionary Union, CIM and other missions. Meyer soon felt that it would be better to merge with Harley College and Meyer became

---

[12] Charles Crosbie Brown to M Mead, 21 March 1951 (letter in possession of R Gooden).
[13] MJ Dowling, 'Guinness, Howard Wyndham', in *Biographical Dictionary of Evangelicals*, ed. T. Larsen (Leicester: Inter-Varsity Press, 2003), 270-72.

involved in teaching and in supporting Harley.[14] Baptist minister JS Morris served as lecturer and then Principal in 1889. In a report of 1893 Morris refers to forty-eight mission stations in the London area that were served by Harley students. Morris died in August 1895 and the quest for a suitable Principal began.[15]

The instruction was mainly biblical, also with English, New Testament Greek, medical studies, geography, mechanics, cookery, gardening and, where needed, modern languages whilst practical training in preaching and visitation was emphasised.

On 30 October 1896 it was agreed that for the time being Henry Grattan Guinness would be Principal with Harry Guinness as Vice-Principal. Baptist George Downs Hooper (1848–1908), a distant descendant of the Protestant martyr John Hooper (d. 1555), was approached but declined and two others, Walter Hackney and James Douglas, also declined. Meyer and GHC MacGregor helped with tuition. This was the situation into which Silas Mead came.

The extant College minutes, dating from 1896–1910, however, are not quite clear regarding his position.[16] He is first named in the meeting of 28 May 1897 (attended by Meyer, MacGregor, Lucy Guinness [daughter of Henry], Dr Harry and Mrs Annie Guinness) when reference is made to 'the offer of Dr Silas Mead'. Of course, as the position had not been advertised it is evident that some conversations had taken place, confirming the report that Harry Guinness had spoken with Silas in India. It was resolved to approach Alexander MacLaren, who had visited Australia in 1888, regarding Silas and to hear him preach and teach some biblical subjects before a 'definite' invitation could be extended. Silas evidently passed these tests and, as has been noted, he accepted the post on 9 June 1897.

Silas's health was a recurring problem, but he engaged as fully as possible in the demanding College life. After he had been in the post for some two years, a fascinating and lengthy interview with him was published in the English paper *The Baptist* and republished in *The Southern Baptist*.[17] This gives a valuable insight, in his own words, into how Silas regarded his work and his enthusiasm for the task.

Asked about the nature of the College work, Silas replied:

[14] WY Fullerton, *F.B. Meyer A Biography* (London: Marshall, Morgan & Scott, 1929), 125-26; IM Randall, *Spirituality and Social Change. The Contribution of F.B. Meyer (1847-1929)* (Carlisle: Paternoster Press, 2003), 30.

[15] The most useful history of the College and the basis of what follows is APF Sell, 'Harley College and its Congregational Alumni' in his *Commemorations. Studies in Christian Thought and History* (Calgary and Cardiff: University of Calgary Press and University of Wales Press, 1993), 275-300.

[16] Minutes of the Harley College Council (1896-1910) at Centre for the Study of World Christianity, The University of Edinburgh (copy provided by Ms Lauren McKay).

[17] 'Chat with an Enthusiastic Baptist', *SB*, 1 June 1899, 114.

> Well, you know the work is interdenominational; we have Congregationalists, Presbyterians, Baptists, and other denominations represented among our students, who all intend to become foreign missionaries. And our men have gone abroad in connection with thirty different societies.

The international nature of the work appealed to Silas, with 'Armenians, Koreans, Indians, French, German, Jamaicans, Africans, Dutch, and Jews'. Harley and its connected institutions made it 'the largest missionary training college in the world'. There were about a hundred students, Silas added, with one a week leaving, on an average, for the foreign field: 'More than a thousand have gone altogether from the Institute'. Moreover, Silas added, all the students are actively engaged in Home Mission work: 'Benger Hall alone has thirty meetings a week, and then there is the Medical Mission besides, and all sort of evangelistic work in lodging-houses and similar places.'

As to finance, Silas noted that 'to maintain the students and the work, and to meet the expenses of the Congo and South American Missions and the Institute, requires £20,000 a year, or an average of about £50 a day'. They were not in debt and were entirely dependent on 'what the Lord's people send'.

Asked if he liked the work, the light shone in Silas's blue eyes: 'Who could help it?' He explained:

> One is assisting to train men who in a year or at most two, will be away in the neglected parts of the world, preaching Christ's good news to men and women who have never before even heard His name. Think how inspiring it is to face, every morning, thirty or forty men destined for so grand a work! It makes one eager to teach very faithfully and thoroughly the great essential truths. We haven't a man who is not eager to make the best of his Harley days. No one would covet a finer work than to train students as anxious to learn—and so appreciative for work so far reaching and infinitely important.

> No fear that these 'ministers' will fail to 'gather a congregation'. Their congregations wait for them already, under Africa's palm trees, on the Amazon's banks and elsewhere, the only trouble we have with the students is that sometimes they are over-eager to stand before their waiting thousands, and so grudge the time given to preparation. One student said to me this week—'I am too old to be in England still; I am longing to be out in Peru'.

The report concluded, 'It seems to us that a man could desire no nobler, higher life work than has fallen to the lot of the Principal of Harley College'.

Clearly Silas encouraged many students to pursue a missionary calling. After his death JZ Hodge (b. 1872), a missionary and prolific author on India, wrote an article on Silas as 'A Missionary Enthusiast'. Recalling Silas's tenure at Harley, Hodge claimed: 'Many men who have gone to the farthest frontiers of the mission field bearing the impress of his sunny personality, look back on these years as the most memorable in their lives'. He stressed his unwavering optimism 'and Australian sunshine radiated from him even into Butler's Analogy'.[18] Silas's kindness, theological certainty and love of the Greek New Testament won their confidence so that some of them loved to give him the sacred name of 'Father'. His inspiration 'turned some of us to India and largely led to the founding of the Behar Mission'. He recalled that when Silas was on route to England in 1905 he visited Behar (in West Bengal) where 'he made himself perfectly at home amongst us—for at heart he was a Missionary—and charmed Europeans and Indians alike by his sunny disposition and delightful unconventionality'.[19]

But Silas as Principal had been under regular pressure because of his recurring health issues. As the minute of 22 April 1898 records: 'The health of Mr Mead has been so poor that grave doubts were raised as to his permanence'. Silas, now aged 66, continued but on 12 February 1900 it was unanimously felt that 'Mr Mead was too old for the adequate prosecution of the work of the College, more especially in view of the fact that we are hoping to open out evening classes to Christian workers'. They planned, therefore, to relieve him of his duties at the end of the present session. The minutes noted that 'his work had been of more or less of the nature of stop-gap'. It suggested that after the death of Morris, Silas 'happened to be in this country' after resigning his post in Adelaide. Rather presumptuously, the minute added, 'thus in liberating him from his present post, his position is not rendered worse than it was when we invited him to come into our midst. As some members of his family are in Australia, it is exceedingly likely that he may be able to find a home there'.

Silas was not present at any of these College Council meetings but was presumably advised of this situation. The same meeting defined 'the qualifications of a Principal' which perhaps suggests some ways in which Silas had been judged unsuitable:

> In the consideration of a new man for the Principalship, it was felt that not only should he be strong, healthy, and vigorous, but that he should be a spiritual force. He should undoubtedly be a Bible student, and able thoroughly to expound the entire Scriptures. It is of primary importance that he should accept con amore the

---

[18] Joseph Butler (1692-1752), an Anglican divine whose *Analogy of Religion Natural and Revealed* (1736) became a classic Christian argument against unbelief.
[19] JZ Hodge, 'A Missionary Enthusiast. The late Rev. Silas Mead, M.A., LL.B.', unidentified press clipping (Gooden/Mead collection).

Divine authority of the Word of God from Genesis to Revelation.
He should further be missionary hearted and sympathetic, with
a love for teaching and for young men.

But next month, on 26 March, the Council recorded the following minute:

As to the uncertainty of Mr Mead's tenure of the Principalship
of Harley College, owing to advanced age, it was arranged that
as it is likely that new College buildings will be erected in the
near future, it was not advisable to introduce a new Principal into
the work until such were complete, and therefore, that Mr Meyer
and the Secretary should acquaint him with the fact that we are
contemplating a change, on the erection of the new College he
will then be able to make such arrangements as he may deem
suitable under the circumstances.

The next Principal was Rev Forbes Jackson (1858–1913), another Baptist minister, who began in 1901 and served until 1910. Financial problems and the onset of the War meant that the College was eventually closed, and the premises sold in 1918. Proceeds were devoted to the Mission.

Silas's position must have become increasingly uncomfortable almost as soon as he began. Early in 1898 he was reported to be 'winning the hearts and confidence of the trustees of Harley House'.[20] But his bronchitis was severe, and it was feared later that year that he might have to return to Australia. Lilian married Charles Crosbie Brown, a tutor at Harley College, in August 1900. Gertrude had joined Silas at Harley in 1898.[21] Later that year Silas was 'rusticating' in Cornwall where he preached for his friend Rev Alfred Bird whilst he and Lilian participated in another CE Conference.[22]

Silas's appointment to Harley appears to have been rather hastily made and he seems not to have received the full support of the Council. His ebullient interview in 1899 suggests his unfading love of missions and teaching but, as the minutes have shown, his position became increasingly untenable. That he was popular with students is suggested by the fact that after he had announced his intention to finish his term he was petitioned by the whole student body to continue as tutor. At one stage it was thought he might defer his departure for at least another year.[23]

What the College Council thought about this petition is not recorded. But the situation was resolved when Silas's son-in-law AS Wilson was given six months leave of absence from his church in Perth and Silas agreed to supply the pulpit during his

20 *SB*, 17 February 1898, 17.
21 *SB*, 2 June 1898, 122, 131.
22 *SB*, 17 November 1898, 253.
23 *SB*, 3 July 1901, 146, 150.

absence. Accordingly, Silas and Gertrude sailed from London aboard the *Himalaya* on 26 July 1901.[24] The *Southern Baptist* again reported the students' petition but indicated that it was uncertain just where Silas would settle: 'His movements will be guided by the openings for work that may present themselves'.[25]

Thus, one significant stage in Silas Mead's life concluded. When he returned to Perth, he was aged 67. He had made a valuable contribution as teacher and apologist for missions with Harley College as well as reacquainting himself with many aspects of English Baptist life. In April he had presented a memorial address from the Baptists of Australasia to the Council of the Baptist Union of Great Britain.[26] He was English by origin and enjoyed meeting his relatives down in Somerset and always enthusiastically welcomed British visitors to Australia. For example, Dr Harry Guinness, recovering from illness, and his wife had begun a preaching tour of Australia in Tasmania. (FB Meyer and his wife acted as Principal and lived at the College during their absence.) Silas had expressed the best wishes of the students to Guinness.[27] Just as Silas returned to Perth, JG Greenhough, whom Silas had pressed to come to Australia as a pastor in 1875, began an extended preaching/lecturing tour of Australia in Perth.[28]

There was still much for Silas to contribute and Western Australia was to be his final home and sphere of ministry. He made one more trip to England in 1905 to share in the inaugural Baptist World Alliance meetings in London where he was now irrevocably identified as an Australian Baptist.

1-62.

', 208; Manley, *From Woolloomooloo*, 128, 225.

Active to the End in Perth, 1901-09

John Olley

Setting the scene

In 1887 at the Baptist Jubilee meetings in Adelaide Silas 'intimated that he would like to see something done for Western Australia as soon as possible'.[1] The population of the colony, a third of the continental land mass, was then less than 50,000 with no Baptist churches. The next twenty years saw dramatic changes in the colony and in Baptist witness. Silas himself was present and contributed during the latter part of this growth.

While Western Australia was established in 1829, with two towns, Fremantle at the Swan River mouth and Perth 32 km (20 miles) upstream, growth was slow.[2] Great change came in the 1890s with the discovery of gold at Coolgardie and nearby Kalgoorlic, 600 km (375 miles) east of Perth. Travel to Western Australia was by ship, usually to the southern port of Albany, 400 km (250 miles) from Perth.[3] Agricultural development was encouraged from 1886 by the Great Southern Railway line north-

---

[1] *TP*, 1 September 1887, 135.
[2] Self-government was granted in 1890; New South Wales, Victoria, and South Australia in 1856-57.
[3] Since the early 1850s the P&O shipping company had refused to allow its mail-carrying vessels to call at Fremantle due to absence of safe anchorages. Eventually, the limestone rock barring the Swan River entrance was removed and the first P&O mail steamer berthed at Fremantle in 1900 [RT Appleyard, 'Western Australia: Economic and Demographic Growth, 1850-1914' in CT Stannage, ed., *A New History of Western Australia* (Nedlands: University of Western Australia Press, 1981), 222-24].

ward from Albany. The Perth to Kalgoorlie railway followed in 1897. 'In just one decade the small, isolated, rural-based economy saw a fourfold increase in population and a massive increase in capital which lifted infrastructure to a level hitherto thought impossible to achieve.'[4]

The first known moves to form a Baptist church in Perth were in 1893 and 1894—both failed.[5] There were pleas to the eastern colonies for help and in 1893 Silas wrote to England asking 'Dr [Rev James] Spurgeon to send an A1 person at once to Perth' but nothing eventuated.[6] James Cole, a layman from Victoria, saw a need, left his business there, and arranged the formation of the Perth Baptist Church 23 June 1895. He soon moved on to form the Fremantle Baptist Church in October, leaving his colleague, Rev John Hewson, a Spurgeon's College graduate, to pastor. Hewson however did not wish to continue.[7]

Silas's 1895 visit

The Perth church being only five months old and unexpectedly without a pastor was the setting when Silas was first in Perth. He had planned to accompany William Whitley and a group of missionaries travelling to the South Australian mission in India, with a Valedictory Service planned for 18 November before departure from Adelaide two days later. Silas changed his plans so as to visit Perth *en route* and left on 6 November.[8] His visit was full of activity: on Sunday 17 November he preached at both services of the Perth Baptist Church and in the afternoon conducted a Young Men's meeting at the YMCA;[9] Wednesday he spoke at a Women's Christian Temperance Union Demonstration in the Perth Town Hall, in his speech encouraging the women's suffrage campaign in Western Australia;[10] and on Thursday as President of the Australasian Christian Endeavour Society he was welcomed at a specially organ-

---

[4] Appleyard, 'Western Australia', 219; *SB*, 15 April 1897, 86; G Helyar, *A Voice in the City: Perth Baptist Church 1895-1995* (Perth: Perth Baptist Church, 1895), 16-17.
[5] RK Moore, *'All Western Australia is my parish': A Centenary History of the Baptist Denomination in Western Australia 1895-1995* (Perth: Baptist Historical Society of Western Australia, 1996), 13-29.
[6] *TP*, 20 March 1893, 91.
[7] *SB*, 4 April 1895, 81; PBC Minutes, 31 October 1895.
[8] *SB*, 14 November 1895, 252.
[9] *DN*, 16 November 1895, 4.
[10] *West*, 21 November 1895, 6.

ised United Christian Endeavour rally.[11] Finally, on Friday afternoon he left Perth for Albany to join the India group.

On the Thursday the Perth Church met to 'consider the propriety of sending' for AS [Alfred] Wilson to 'supply for the church.' Alfred was Silas's future son-in-law and nearing the end of ministerial studies in Adelaide. A week later the Church meeting 'eventually resolved that Mr. Wilson be asked to come and render his services for a month', soon extended.[12] Later he was called as pastor, commencing on 20 September 1896 and serving for eleven years.[13]

It seems probable that the Perth Church situation had prompted Silas's change of plans and, although not mentioned in the minutes, he had been with the church on Sunday. The brief visit demonstrates both his interest in the West and, as in South Australia, the breadth of his involvement in Christian organisations and societal issues.

One can only imagine Silas's continuing influence, with his son-in-law as pastor and a key leader, George Cargeeg, having come in April 1895 from South Australia where he had been a member of Flinders Street Church.[14] Also active in Perth Church were Frank and Sarah Hann, Sarah (née Staples) being his sister-in-law.[15]

Baptists from 1895 to 1901

Church expansion was rapid. On 2 December 1896 representatives from four churches formed the Baptist Union of Western Australia [BUWA], with Alfred as first President (he himself was absent in Adelaide for his wedding).[16] Growth continued around Perth, in the Great Southern[17] and the Goldfields. In *The W. A. Baptist* July 1907 issue, the last that he edited, Alfred wrote: 'The denomination is but 12 years

---

[11] *DN*, 22 November 1895, 2; *West*, 22 November 1895, 4.

[12] PBC Minutes, 21 November 1895, 28 November 1895, 2 December 1895; *SB,* 12 February 1896, 33.

[13] PBC Minutes, 30 January 1896, 27 February 1896. *SB*, 15 October 1896, 224.

[14] He was Secretary of the Perth Church from its beginning, first Treasurer of the BUWA and six times its President, 1898-99, 1904-05, 1910-12, 1916-17, 1924-25. A prominent businessman, he was a key leader and supporter of the Perth YMCA. Rhoda Walker, 'George Henry Cargeeg JP, a devout man–1851-1925', *WB* 9:2 (1994); Tom Austen, *Something Worth While: A History of the Perth YMCA* (Perth: St George Books, 1992), 22, 28-30, 32, 55-56, 65.

[15] Both were members of the early BUWA Missionary Committee (*WM*, 22 December 1900, 65) and at Silas's funeral they and Gertrude were the 'chief mourners' (*West*, 16 September 1909, 8).

[16] *DN*, 4 December 1896, 2; Helyar, *A Voice in the City*, 19-20.

[17] The Great Southern Railway gave its name to the region.

old, and it is a surprise to many to find that the Baptists of W.A. for eight years erected a building once a quarter. The sweat of toil has flowed freely.'[18]

There were however early tensions into which Silas entered. With most Baptist church members and key people coming from Victoria where churches were mainly 'close' membership or South Australia where most were 'open', understandably differences arose. Alfred was an advocate for 'open' and in November 1900 Perth Church changed its constitution to 'open' and several members left forming another church.[19] The General Baptist Association (formalised 28 January 1901; 'close' membership only) became a rival organisation to the Baptist Union of Western Australia.[20]

A happier situation for Silas's arrival was active interest in Australian missionary endeavours in India. Early in 1896 he wrote to the Perth Church proposing they join with the eastern colonies in supporting work in the Indian field. Alfred chaired the first BUWA Foreign Mission Committee[21] meeting 26 April 1897 which decided to send £15 to Cecil and in 1899 Carrie Brown, daughter of Marie and John Brown, a Perth merchant, went to India at her father's expense to work with the South Australian mission.[22] In October 1901 the BUWA Annual Meetings agreed to its own 'special field', accepting 'responsibility of preaching the Gospel at Goalundo, East Bengal.'[23]

---

[18] *WAB,* July 1907, 116.
[19] PBC Church Minutes, 1 November 1900 [Notice of motion, 30 August 1900]. Perth Baptist Church building was in Museum Street and those who left met in a hall in William Street. The two churches were then known by their meeting addresses. Helyar, *A Voice in the City,* 24-27; Moore, *'All Western Australia',* 49, 283; *SB,* 4 October 1900, 228. Here any reference to Perth Baptist Church is to the Perth (Museum-street) Church.
[20] The controversy, its resolution and aftermath are described in detail in Moore, *'All Western Australia',* 40-56; KR Manley, *From Woolloomooloo to 'Eternity': A History of Australian Baptists,* 2 vols. (Studies in Baptist History and Thought, 16.1, 2; Milton Keynes: Paternoster, 2006), 113-14.
[21] The committee had various names during this period: The Western Australian Baptist Foreign Mission Committee (1897-99) [so minute of 5 July 1897], then combined with Home Mission, WABU Home and Foreign Mission Committee (February 1899 - October 1901), then separated, WA Foreign Mission Committee (December 1901 - February 1903), Goalundo Mission (February 1903 - October 1911). Following the name most common during Silas's time in Perth, 'Goalundo Mission' designates the committee's minutes.
[22] The Brown family continued as enthusiastic supporters of the mission. Marie became a long-term member of the Western Australian committee, along with her daughters Carrie and Grace.
[23] BUWA Minutes (Annual meetings, 21 October 1901), 151-52; RK Moore, ed., *Baptists of Western Australia: The First Ninety Years* (Perth: Baptist Historical Society of Western Australia, 1991), 149-51.

Silas's early months in Perth, 1901

At the age of 67, after a short but very productive time at Harley College,[24] on medical grounds Silas returned to Australia, accompanied by daughter Gertrude. They arrived in Fremantle on the *Himalaya* on 27 August 1901. Silas supplied the pulpit of Perth Church while Alfred, accompanied by Blanche, was in Edinburgh, both being Western Australia delegates to the annual meetings of the Baptist Union of Great Britain and Ireland.[25]

Silas and Cecil, who was returning to India after furlough, were key speakers and participants at the BUWA Annual Meetings in October. One report spoke of 'the ripe wisdom of the elder of those gentlemen and the enthusiastic eloquence of the younger'.[26] At those meetings Silas was elected Vice-President and appointed to the 'Students Curriculum Committee'.[27] He became formally a member of the Perth Church on 28 November.[28] At the 9 December meeting to welcome back Alfred and Blanche, George Cargeeg affirmed Silas's work saying 'he did not think the church could now allow Mr. Mead to leave them. (Applause.)'[29] Perth Church subsequently unanimously called him as 'co-pastor' with Alfred.[30]

A short visit followed to Sydney, Melbourne and Adelaide (arriving there 22 January 1902).[31] In Adelaide at a public reception he spoke to a 'large audience' about his trip through the United States.[32] In a newspaper interview (and no doubt elsewhere) he enthusiastically spoke of the 'alertness and enterprise' of American churches, including their involvement in education through to university level, in contrast to the 'average Englishman' who was 'too conservative in all things.'[33] It foreshadowed his addresses and articles in Western Australia relating to both secondary and university education.

---

[24] *West*, 28 August 1901, 4; *WM*, 31 August 1901, 66. See further in chapter 9.
[25] Silas was initially invited 'to take up the pastor's work during [Alfred's] absence or as much as he can fulfill', but after arrival this was changed to the position of 'acting pastor'; PBC Minutes, 16 May 1901; 5 September 1901.
[26] *Bunbury Herald*, 2 November 1901, 2.
[27] BUWA Minutes (Annual meetings, 21 October 1901), 151; *West*, 19 October 1901, 7; 21 October 1901, 3; 23 October 1901, 3; 24 October 1901, 4.
[28] PBC Minutes, 28 November 1901.
[29] *West*, 10 December 1901, 6.
[30] PBC Minutes: Notice of motion, 30 January 1902, approved 6 March 1902.
[31] *Advertiser*, 24 December 1901, 6; *Register*, 23 January 1902, 9.
[32] *Advertiser*, 28 January 1902, 9.
[33] *Advertiser*, 23 January 1902, 8.

Co-pastor of Perth Baptist Church (1902–07) and continuing ministry (1907–09)

On 20 March 1902 Silas was welcomed back as co-pastor. George Cargeeg 'hoped Mr. Mead would take a large interest in the affairs of the State. The Baptist denomination did not want to monopolise Mr. Mead.'[34] That was to be well-borne out by Silas's subsequent activities.

Unexpected was extra responsibility a year later (28 March 1903) when Alfred left on three-months leave of absence, with his medical adviser ordering 'an extended trip to the Eastern States…for a little relaxation.' Silas was to be assisted by 'lay friends', with 'several of the leading Nonconformist ministers' assisting in the supply of the pulpit.[35] A large gathering welcomed back Alfred on 9 July, with his address 'plainly show[ing] he burned with intense zeal for the future.'[36]

Alfred S. Wilson and Silas Mead

Silas was co-pastor until Alfred concluded his pastorate, moving to New Zealand in August 1907, then continued as 'honorary pastor'.[37] Silas and Gertrude lived in the

---

34 *West*, 21 March 1902, 3; also announced *West*, 20 March 1902, 4.
35 *WAB*, 31 March 1903, 60b; *WM*, 4 April 1903, 58.
36 *WM*, 18 July 1903, 42.
37 Helyar, *A Voice in the City*, 36. PBC Deacons Meeting Minutes, 24 June 1907 refer to his agreeing to do 'editorial work pro tem' for the *WA Baptist* (24 June 1907); finances were not available to 'engage an assistant for Mr. Mead' but a committee would 'arrange for supplies' (6 August 1907). Silas continued to chair deacons and church meetings.

same house as Alfred and Blanche at 'Lyndhurst', in Museum Street across from the church building and then moved to 3 Harvest Terrace, West Perth, opposite the then new Parliament House (completed 1904).[38]

During the four and a half years of 'co-pastoring' Silas was away from Western Australia a few times. The longest was his '15 month holiday trip' (!) to the 1905 Baptist World Congress in London and missionary work in India.[39] He attended national Baptist gatherings in 1902 (Adelaide) and 1903 (Melbourne).[40] At the beginning of 1907 Silas and Gertrude spent several weeks in South Australia, with 'a busy time in the "Queen City of the South"'.[41]

From late 1907 Silas continued various activities as health allowed until his death at Gertrude's residence on 13 September 1909.[42] He self-describes three weeks in May 1908 as his 'first holiday in six years' made possible by 'my kind deacons'. His 'Trip down the G.S.R. Line' included visits to all the churches in the Great Southern region, often speaking. He writes with delight of developments in both churches and the community, 'a most enjoyable time amongst old friends and scenes.'[43]

Silas's eight years in Western Australia involved wide-ranging activities and influence in churches and community, in the state and nation, and in UK and mission in India. He would see all as integrated in the wholeness of a life following Christ.

Serving Western Australian Baptist churches

On the opening day of his first BUWA Annual Meetings in October 1901, two months after arrival in Perth, Silas preached the 'annual sermon,… an inspiring discourse on the passage, "Be ye sure of this, that the Kingdom of God is come nigh to you" ', outlining the principles and characteristics of the kingdom.[44] Thereafter he regularly preached at Baptist churches throughout the state, including public occasions such as laying of foundation stones and opening of buildings.

---

[38] Australian Electoral Rolls; Western Australia PO Directories; addresses given by Alfred and Silas when they edited *WA Baptist (WAB)*.
[39] *WAB*, 30 November 1904, 260b; *West*, 22 November 1904, 5; the 'holiday' description is in *DN*, 5 February 1906, 7.
[40] See below, 'An Australian Baptist'.
[41] *WAB*, 15 February 1907, 4d; 15 March 1907, 20.
[42] *West*, 14 September 1909, 5.
[43] 'A Trip Down the G.S.R. Line: Impressions by the Way (By a Pastor)', *WAB*, 15 April 1908, 74. Republished in *DN*, 30 May 1908, 6 where Silas is identified.
[44] *WM*, 26 October 1901, 70.

His impact was broad as he spoke with evident integrity and enthusiasm. In his 1902 BUWA Presidential sermon on 'The Sensational in Our Religious Life' he spoke of how:

> emotion plays the decidedly radical part in the grand educative teaching of Sinai...It becomes us to set to work to see how more feeling may get into the pulpit and into the pew–into the family and into the business of life...We owe everything to the fiery feeling of some of God's saints, who through the centuries have been moved by strong emotion to let their light–the light glowing in their emotions–so shine they have in deed and truth glorified God by their words and deeds.[45]

His was an emotion consistent with a keen intellect and interest and openness to new developments. At that same Annual Meeting, he donated 100 books as 'the nucleus of a denominational library' and the following month was appointed by the BUWA Council as 'theological professor to the Baptist denomination in Western Australia.'[46]

He continued as a member of the BUWA Council till his death and throughout was active in the Goalundo Mission Committee.

Reconciliation

Moves seeking arbitration during the existence of two Baptist bodies took place mainly before Silas's arrival and it had been pre-arranged that reunion take place at the BUWA Half-Yearly Meetings, 30–31 May 1902. In the absence of the President, as Vice-President Silas took the chair. After unanimous approval, 'Rev Silas Mead (representing the Baptist Union) and Rev Edward Dybing (representing the Baptist Association) joined hands in a symbolic gesture of reunion.'[47] Silas gave further endorsement and encouragement of unity in his presidential address at the Annual Meeting:

> I remember our recent half-yearly meetings and recall Mr. Dybing's appearance on the platform and his grip on my hand on behalf of the churches that sent him to this platform ... What since then? ... I do not recall, even in the many years of Council

45 Quote from report of a 'layman' in *Register*, 20 December 1902, 10. Full text is in *SB*, 17 December 1902, 279-80.
46 *West*, 1 November 1902, 2; BUWA Minute (Council), 8 December 1902, 57; *WAB*, December 1902, 40; in Western Australian Baptist circles he was often referred to as 'Professor Mead'.
47 Moore, *'All Western Australia'*, 53-54.

meetings in fair South Australia, a year of more general accord in Council than we have had this year in our West Australian Union Council meetings.[48]

This did not prevent arguments for 'open' or 'close' membership being presented from time-to-time. When he was briefly editor of the *W.A. Baptist News* after Alfred left Perth, Silas included in full (four pages) the presidential address of the Victorian President, Westmore G Stephens, which had 'not been allowed to be printed in [that state's] denominational paper, owing to the nature of the subject'—it was a stirring appeal for all Victorian churches to adopt open membership, linked with the unity of all Christians![49] Three months later he included at length 'Principles contained in Romans xiv' as applying 'to the observance of the Lord's Supper and to Open Membership.'[50] He was able to write in a clear and irenic manner.

Always teaching

Wherever Silas was involved he was active in teaching, broadening people's knowledge, equipping for ministry and life, encouraging informed approaches to issues, and exhorting Christian involvement and witness in all areas of society and overseas.

From BUWA's beginning, structures for ministerial training had been implemented. Soon after arrival Silas was appointed to the 'Students Curriculum Committee', tasked to prepare 'second year course of study', and the following year was appointed 'Professor'. Teaching was through textbooks and notes, with examinations which he generally conducted.[51] Silas encouraged two home missionaries to further their studies at Harley College in London: in 1905 Walter F White[52] and 1906 James S Nelson.[53] Fittingly Silas preached at Nelson's ordination service at what would turn

---

[48] *SB*, 17 December 1902, 280.

[49] *WAB*, 15 January 1908, [276a-d]; the address was given 19 November 1907 and the full text Silas published was from *The Australasian* (Melbourne) 14 December 1907, 51; also in Melbourne in *The Age*, 14 December 1907, 5 and *The Leader*, 14 December 1907, 36. Silas later announced that the address was available in large numbers in 'pamphlet form'; *WAB*, 15 March 1908, 18.

[50] *WAB*, 15 April 1908, 42.

[51] BUWA Minutes (Council, 8 December 1902); 'General News: Professor Mead', *WAB*, 31 December 1902, [n.p.]; *West*, 20 December 1902, 9.

[52] *West*, 14 November 1905, 4; White returned in 1907 and joined the Goalundo Mission in India, *WAB*, 15 November 1907, 210.

[53] *West*, 20 August 1906, 4. Nelson returned in 1908 and continued to minister in the Great Southern, Moore, 'All Western Australia', 282.

out to be his last BUWA Annual Meetings. He 'based his address upon Paul's advice to the youthful Timothy, "Give attention to the reading".'[54]

Study by ministers and laypeople was to be ongoing. Similarly to his sermon at James Nelson's ordination, a previous ordination message had spoken of 'the absolute necessity of study, especially of the Scriptures, by the Christian minister in order to fit him for his calling.'[55] At that same 1906 BUWA Annual Meetings 'Professor Mead constructed a Bible Class for delegates at 6 p.m....each day...These were full of strong meat, and it was clear that our Theological Professor does not consider the weak intellects or unthinking minds to be in the country.'[56]

George Menzies who had pastored in Western Australia since 1904 wrote after Silas's death that:

> He was a great reader, and kept himself abreast of the latest publications of the theological and literary world. One of the questions he was sure to ask any visiting minister was, What have you been reading lately? and the question itself was of educational force, for one felt it was no good going to see him unless one could justify the use he had been making of his time in that direction.[57]

The 1909 BUWA Annual Meetings discussed 'some permanent memorial' for Silas's work. It was noted that 'The extensive theological library of the late clergyman had been bequeathed to the Union, and arrangements were being made for its accommodation at the Perth Church.'[58] He continues to teach!

The Perth Church Christian Endeavour Society (including a Junior Department) was an important responsibility, as was the equipping of Sunday School teachers, both at Perth Church and more widely through the Sunday School Union of W.A.[59] At the BUWA Half-Yearly meetings in May 1902 he 'read a carefully-prepared and highly-instructive paper, bristling with points.' He said 'Sunday schools would

---

54 *WAB*, 15 November 1908, 242.
55 *WAB*, 15 December 1906, 252e; ordination of Reuben Bailey.
56 *WAB*, 15 December 1906, 252c.
57 *DN*, 9 October 1909, 3.
58 'Baptist Union of W.A. Annual Meetings', *WAB*, 15 December 1909, [n.p.]. Some books in the present Morling College Heather and Noel Vose Library, Perth 'carry a printed bookplate "presented to the Baptist Union of West Australia as the nucleus of a denominational library by Rev Silas Mead, MA LLB, September 1909".' Nathan Hobby, 'A History of Vose Library' in *Vose Seminary at Fifty*, edited by Nathan Hobby, John Olley and Michael O'Neil (Preston, Victoria: Mosaic, 2013), 141.
59 *West*, 31 March 1909, 5.

improve only as the training of those engaged in it improved.'[60] Silas's influence (he was the incoming President) may be seen in the addition in the 1902 revised BUWA constitution statement of 'Objects': 'to promote the efficiency of Christian Endeavour Societies and Sunday Schools.'[61]

The scope of his vision is seen in his 1904 address on laying the foundation stone of the North Perth Baptist Church. 'The Church, as the stone was inscribed, should be dedicated to the glory of God' and so the first great purpose was 'proclaiming God's message'. Next was 'the fostering of the Christian life' and so 'one half at least of the services to be held there would have the developing and maturing of the Christian thought distinctly in view.' His broad perspective on Christian service in all of society is clear in his third purpose, 'the training of Christian recruits for service in the kingdom of God, for the busy life of the city, of the State, and of the Commonwealth.'

With such a vision the content of 'teaching' was unlimited, for example, he spoke at Perth Church's Young Men's Class on 'Milton's Philosophy'[62] and to the Museum Street Literary Society on 'Thibet and the Thibetans'.[63] All were welcome to 'Professor Mead's Missionary Study Class'.[64]

Another venture at Perth Church was a fortnightly 'theological class', to study 'theology, Christian evidences and church history' with Silas as tutor. While 'all testify to the value of the instruction received' it was regretted that 'more of our young men and women have not availed themselves of the opportunity.'[65] This was additional to the weekly Young Men's and Young Women's Bible Classes, sometimes combined, for which participants often prepared papers, and the pastors responded.

In visits to churches, as well as services there were meetings where he spoke on wider topics. Even late in his life, in October 1908, he was able to be at Brookton[66] for the church's anniversary and to address 'crowded meetings, morning, afternoon, and evening … On the Monday evening Mr. Mead gave a lantern lecture on "Ancient Ephesis" [sic], which was listened to and appreciated by all who were present, the

---

[60] *West*, 31 May 1902, 9. He presented a paper on Sunday School work at the BUWA 1906 Annual Meetings; *WAB*, 15 December 1906, 252-53.
[61] BUWA Minutes (Annual meetings, October 1902), 43.
[62] *WAB*, 31 January 1903, [n.p.].
[63] *WAB*, 30 April 1904, 71/(5).
[64] *WAB*, 15 June 1907, 92; also, *WAB*, 15 September 1908, 162; held in Guild Room of Trinity Church, with 'tutors Revs. W. Kench [Trinity Congregational Church] and Silas Mead.'
[65] *WAB*, 31 October 1904, 215.
[66] 135 km ESE of Perth; James Nelson had been appointed pastor on his return from Harley College.

lecturer having visited that place made the narrative very interesting with personal comments.'[67]

The early 1900s saw talks between Baptists and Churches of Christ, Silas and Alfred being amongst the six Baptist representatives.[68] Silas wrote at length a response to an article in *The Australian Christian*,[69] methodically quoting from that article and 'compar[ing] with the teaching of Baptists'. He argued from the New Testament against the 'sacramentarian' view of the Churches of Christ and affirmed the faith of paedo-baptists as leading to salvation.[70] Readers were treated as partners in the discussions.

Call to prayer–and action

Gold yield declined after 1904 and farming conditions were very harsh, although farm mechanisation began to improve.[71] Churches were scattered and small and particularly in rural areas pastors often had subsistence level salaries.[72] By the middle of the 1900s, following the enthusiastic expansion of the previous seven years, BUWA and some churches faced financial debt and obtaining pastors was difficult. Victoria and South Australia were experiencing long-term financial downturn and so churches there were unable to help Western Australia. During his time as President, Silas was 'requested to do his utmost to secure the more active interest of the churches in the funds of the union.'[73] In a context of continuing need, in 1906 Silas called for a 'Week of Prayer for all Baptists' and in July 1909 urged Council to have 'special prayer and effort to raise required amounts.'[74]

Silas had not been able to attend the July 1909 Council meeting (he sent a letter) and the next month's Council meeting, which also minuted his apology, recorded that a prayer meeting at Silas's house resolved to establish an 'Out of Debt Fund' and 'hold

---

[67] *Great Southern Leader*, 23 October 1908, 3; *WAB*, 15 December 1908, 236. Silas also chaired and spoke at a 'sumptuous tea' the following evening. Following were the BUWA Annual Meetings he attended, but the December issue of *WAB* includes the comment that Silas 'has been seriously ill … but is recovering' (268).

[68] BUWA Minutes (Half-yearly meetings, 1-4 April 1904), 157, 161; (Council, 4 July 1904), 175.

[69] E.g., correspondence in *West*, 17 August 1904, 7; 18 August 1904, 7; *Australian Christian* [published by Churches of Christ in Australia], 13 October 1904, 564-66.

[70] *WAB*, 15 February 1905, ii-iii.

[71] Appleyard, 'Economic and Demographic Growth', 227-30.

[72] Moore, ed., *Baptists of Western Australia*, 222-23.

[73] *WAB*, 30 November 1903, 238. A subsequent visit to the Great Southern by Alfred 'has been highly successful thus far… should wipe off the deficiency'; *WAB*, 30 January 1904, (3).

[74] BUWA Minutes (Council, 15 June 1906), 74; (Council 19 July 1909), 104.

periodical prayer meetings at the various churches, the next at Claremont.'[75] These are the last official records of Silas's input before his death, appropriately a call to prayer followed by prayer together. This can be placed alongside a comment of the Goalundo Committee in October which eulogised Silas including 'above all his constant ministry of intercession.'[76]

He saw the need for more ministers than were being trained and proposed recruiting unmarried ministers from England, stating that 'an anonymous friend was willing to pay the expense of bringing out not only three, but up to six ministers, if they could be found.'[77] In the event, the BUWA Council made no financial proposal for ongoing support and the scheme failed to attract anyone. Silas was aware of financial practicalities and of the need for prayer—but what is the focus of prayer? We sense his pleas in a 1907 editorial: he observed that amongst the churches he had

> many, many times heard the petition offered for the minister that he be this or that; but seldom, very seldom have I listened to the prayer that church members may be found generous in their giving. I am familiar with the prayer that God would send along an able minister. I am unfamiliar with the request that the members may be first taught and then constrained to send into the treasury of the church the several amounts they ought to give. The minister is left frequently to practice all the self-denial and the members enjoy the benefits.[78]

He wrote strongly to Council in 1908 of the need for 'a positive, self-denying and personal share in the business of extinguishing debt and of securing the £200 to sustain home missioners for this single year' and repeatedly moved in Council that 'properties not be sold or work closed.'[79] One can only surmise Silas's own financial situation, but he was known to be generous. He was living at his daughter's residence and in 1907 the Baptist Union of South Australia had agreed to a committee 'if it thinks fit, to raise money for the purchase of an annuity, or to raise the sum of £100 per annum in some other way' for payment to Silas.[80] *The W.A. Baptist* regularly listed donors and amounts to BUWA funds, including the Goalundo Mission and Silas is

[75] BUWA Minutes (Council 16 August 1909), 108.
[76] Goalundo Minutes, 24 October 1909.
[77] *WAB*, September 1906, 163.
[78] *WAB*, November 1907, 209.
[79] Letter of 10 January 1908 in BUWA archives; BU Minutes (Council 20 January 1908), 250; (16 March 1908), 262; (13 April 1908), 267; Moore, ed., *Baptists of Western Australia*, 41.
[80] *DN*, 5 October 1907, 3.

generally amongst the higher amounts. When he died, probate was granted with his estate valued at £330.2s.11d.[81]

Beyond Western Australia

England and India visit, 1904-06

On 20 November 1904 he left to visit England, one of three Western Australian delegates to the first Baptists' World Congress which led to formation of the Baptist World Alliance.[82] The Congress, held 11–19 July 1905 in London, was attended by around 3,000 delegates.

Prior to the Congress he was the Australian representative and one of the speakers at the British Christian Endeavour Convention held in Birmingham.[83] After the Congress 'he spent some time in the country with Judge Wilson, President of the Baptist Union of Great Britain and Ireland.' One interest was seeing the Welsh Revival.[84] While in England, before and after the Congress, he preached at many churches. Widely reported was his slipping in wet turf and breaking his arm near his wrist on his way to preach at Tunbridge Wells—but he 'pluckily kept his engagement, and with his arm in a sling delivered his sermon.'[85] The Western Australian Emigration Commissioner in London reported 'a series of lectures in connection with a number of agricultural and other institutions', mentioning Silas as one of those who 'have been rendering good services by their lectures and addresses on Western Australia.'[86]

---

[81] *DN*, 30 September 1909. 5.
[82] *WAB*, 30 November 1904, 260b, 268, describes his farewells at Perth and Fremantle. BUWA Half-Yearly Meetings, 1905; *West*, 1 May 1905, 3; John HY Briggs, 'From 1905 to the End of the First World War', in *Baptists Together in Christ 1905-2005: A Hundred-Year History of the Baptist World Alliance*, edited by RV Pierard (Falls Church, VA: Baptist World Alliance, 2005), 20-46. As he left, the church agreed to his request that he continue as 'co-pastor' while overseas [PBC Minutes, 1 December 1904].
[83] *Advertiser*, 5 August 1905, 11.
[84] *WAB*, 15 March 1906, 50.
[85] *DN*, 28 October 1905, 15; *WAB*, 15 November 1905, 214. His persistence despite pain is seen later in Perth when he 'fell headlong' down steps of Trinity Church Buildings. 'Any other man would then probably have gone home in an ambulance. Silas walked [1.6 km uphill] ... Although no bones broken he was so shaken and bruised as to be obliged to keep to his room for a few days' [*WAB*, 15 July 1908, 116].
[86] *West*, 3 August 1905, 3.

In October Silas left for an extensive visit to India, in company with Carrie Brown, her mother Marie and Annie Oliver.[87] He returned to Perth on 2 February 1906 with a 'welcome home' at Museum Street five days later.[88]

Immediately he was informing people in the community of both the education debate in England and Wales and the 'Swadeshi' movement, 'which practically means "India for the Indians"' and which had effect on the education of children'. What he had seen overseas was relevant to Western Australia.[89] At the BUWA Half-Yearly Meetings in Katanning he spoke with 'fire as well as pathos' about the 'suffering of those who embrace Christianity [in India].'[90] The July 1906 issue of *The W.A. Baptist* focused on the work in Goalundo, with Silas writing the opening article, followed by a report from Silas and the other West Australian visitors of a day visit to Rajbari. Exemplifying Silas's own attitudes, intertwined were letters received from both nationals and missionaries and 'Our Goalundo Staff' lists without distinction two missionaries and three 'native preachers'.[91] A year later, for his first lead article as *W.A. Baptist* editor he returned to 'The Swadeshi Movement in India'.[92]

An Australian Baptist

On 1 January 1901 Australia became a 'Commonwealth', with the separate colonies becoming federated states. Baptist churches also looked at national identity. The path was tortuous, from initial proposals in 1868 to the formation of the Baptist Union of Australia as a federation of state unions in 1926.[93] As in Great Britain the first national Baptist body was a missionary society, the Australian Baptist Foreign Mission formed in 1913.[94] Silas was a key promoter of both Australian cooperation and missionary endeavour.

---

[87] Annie Oliver, a former hotel proprietor, had been converted in 1899 through Alfred's open-air ministry. She became a member of PBC and a generous benefactor to many Baptist churches, the Goalundo mission (she was an active committee member) and YMCA. Ann Harding, 'In Search of Annie Oliver', *WB* 8.1 (1993); *WAB*, 15 February 1907, 26; Dec 1921, 15; Austen, *Something Worth While*, 34, 55-56.
[88] *DN*, 5 February 1906, 7; *WAB*, 15 February 1906, 1d.
[89] 'The Bible in Public Schools' and 'India for the Indians. The "Swadeshi Movement"', *West*, 6 February 1906, 4, 6.
[90] *WAB*, 15 May 1906, 69.
[91] *WAB*, 15 July 1906, 113-20.
[92] *WAB*, 15 September 1907, 161-62.
[93] Manley, *From Woolloomooloo*, 182-93, 459; Basil S. Brown, *Baptised into One Body: A Short History of the Baptist Union of Australia* (Hawthorn, Vic.; Baptist Union of Australia, [1987]), 5-15.
[94] Tony Cupit, Ros Gooden and Ken Manley, eds., *From Five Barley Loaves: Australian Baptists in Global Mission 1864-2010* (Preston, VIC: Mosaic, 2013), 179-80. Similarly, in USA the first national body was the American Baptist Foreign Mission Society (1814).

Twenty months after Federation Silas was a Western Australian representative and chaired the Interstate Baptist Federal Conference in Adelaide.[95] The Conference deliberated *inter alia* on 'A College for the whole States, a Federal Baptist Newspaper, and a Federal status for ministry', the first and third being matters for which Silas had long argued.[96] These continued as ongoing issues in subsequent federal meetings.[97] Silas was the BUWA delegate for the following year's Federal Council meeting in Melbourne, but interest waned.[98] Reports of the 1905 Baptist World Congress became an incentive for the 'First Australasian Baptist Congress', 22–28 September 1908. There were seventy-seven delegates, but only two from Western Australia: Carrie Brown and Miss Briggs. Silas was unwell but Carrie Brown read his paper on 'Home Problems in relation to Indian Baptist Missions'.[99] The next Australasian Congress was after Silas's death, in Melbourne 1911.[100]

'Father of Baptist Missions in Australasia'[101]

Such was Silas's passion, background, expertise and drive, as early as October 1901 he chaired the BUWA Foreign Mission Committee and continued leadership throughout.[102] Silas's deep emotional commitment to the Indian mission was evident in presenting the Goalundo Mission report at the 1904 BUWA Annual Meetings: 'As he came to the part in the report referring to Miss Edith King going out to India to join Miss [Grace] Brown, [he] was so overcome with emotion that someone else had to continue the reading.'[103]

---

95 The other Western Australian representative was George Cargeeg [*WAB* 31 July 1902 (n.p.)].
96 *DN*, 25 June 1902, 5. Silas in 1884 had proposed an inter-colonial ministerial training college in Melbourne and in 1885 an inter-colonial council to determine status of ministers seeking pastoral settlement; *TP*, 1 May 1885, 59; 1 October 1887, 155.
97 *SB*, 17 September 1902, 210.
98 Brown, *Baptised into One Body*, 7–13; Manley, *From Woolloomooloo*, 182–93; *WAB*, 31 October 1903, (10); 30 November 1903, 270.
99 Manley, *From Woolloomooloo*, 189–90; *WAB*, 15 September 1908, 198; 15 November 1908, 211. A report by 'a Delegate' (Carrie Brown?) regretted that 'this State ... was not represented by one of our strongest men.' [*WAB*, 15 January 1909, 292].
100 Manley, *From Woolloomooloo*, 191.
101 So described in *Advertiser*, 28 January 1902, 9, during his brief visit to Adelaide.
102 Goalundo Minutes, 7 October 1901. After the committee's integration with the BUWA in 1907, the Union President was ex-officio President of the committee, but Silas was Vice-President until his death (*WAB*, 15 November 1907, 214; 15 November 1908, 211, announcing the committee for the following year). He had also served as Secretary when Alfred chaired in 1904; Goalundo Minutes, 5 August 1904.
103 *WAB*, 31 October 1904, 214. Grace Brown, sister of Carrie: Goalundo Minutes, 18 May 1903; *WAB*, 31 December 1904, 262; Edith King: Goalundo Minutes, 15 April 1904.

Promotion of mission in India by both Silas and Alfred is evident in the many articles and reports in each issue of the *W.A. Baptist*[104] and at State Christian Endeavour conventions, with Carrie Brown active on committee and as a speaker.[105]

At the 1905 Baptist World Congress Silas was able to present his mature thinking on mission. He was always forward-looking: methods of previous decades may have been 'the most wise' at that time but now be 'quite out of date'. His arguments and proposals are detailed and practical, and with informed fervour.[106]

There is little documentation of Silas's involvement with work amongst indigenous Australians in the state. The 1905 BUWA Annual Meeting formed 'a new committee to foster our interest in the evangelisation of the Aborigines of Australia' with Alfred speaking strongly about the current neglect, as he had earlier.[107] In 1908 Silas himself was appointed one of the two Vice-Presidents of the newly formed Western Australian Council for the Australian Aborigines Mission.[108] A year later, the Mission had to report his death: 'In the midst of his busy life he did not forget the Australian Aborigines.'[109]

The last public meeting for which a record has been found of Silas attending was a Goalundo Mission occasion. Due to health issues Edith King had to return to Perth early 1908 but ten months later Silas (as Vice-President of the Goalundo Mission) would have been pleased to be on the platform when she was farewelled to return to India. Present also was 'Miss [Marie] Gilbert, ... who has spent over 25 years in Mission work, almost without a furlough until now and who is even now eager to be back on the field.' Here was an unexpected gathering with two women spanning the years of Silas's encouraging and sending out of missionaries to India.[110]

---

[104] As Alfred was editor during his Perth ministry, and Silas editor during Alfred's absence, both were involved in what news items and reports to include. Silas also edited from August 1907 to May 1908 [*WAB* July 1907, 116].

[105] Katanning 1901: *WM*, 4 May 1901, 71; Coolgardie, 1902: *Coolgardie Miner*, 29 March 1902, 4; a director, *West*, 12 Apr 1904, 4.

[106] Silas Mead, 'Missionary Methods–Australian', in *The Baptist World Congress. London, July 11-19, 1905. Authorised Record of Proceedings* (London: Baptist Union Publication Department, 1905), 86-92; David Bebbington, 'Foreword', in *Five Barley Loaves*, ix-x. See further in the 'Conclusion' chapter.

[107] BUWA Annual Meeting Minutes, 1905, 18; *WAB*, 15 October 1905, 189; Moore, ed., *Baptists of Western Australia*, 43-44.

[108] *West*, 29 August 1908, 14.

[109] *Australian Aborigines Advocate*, No. 102, 31 December 1909.

[110] *WAB*, 15 February 1909, [4]; Cupit, Gooden and Manley, *From Five Barley Loaves*, 11-12.

Beyond Baptists

'Father of the Australian Christian Endeavour Society'[111]

Silas had been a key promoter of Christian Endeavour, becoming the first President of the South Australian CE Union, and then of the Australian United Society, and this continued in the West, in both the Perth Church and throughout the state. The Western Australian annual convention Silas attended two months after his arrival in 1901 was its seventh.[112] As in South Australia he served as President.[113]

A profile in August 1902 quotes Silas, 'I thoroughly and unreservedly believe in the Christian Endeavour movement, when the model constitution is followed.'[114] As noted earlier, the BUWA 1902 revised constitution statement of 'Objects' included 'to promote the efficiency of Christian Endeavour Societies and Sunday Schools.'[115] At the 1902 Convention in Kalgoorlie, after being elected as President, Silas 'referred to the grand work that Endeavour societies were doing for the unification of the churches and the breaking down of barriers by which they have been separated in the past.'[116]

A highlight was the 1904 nine-day visit to Western Australia of Dr Francis E Clark, the Founder of Christian Endeavour, arriving on Easter Monday, and including meetings in Fremantle, Perth, Kalgoorlie and Narrogin. Silas as President of the W.A. CE Union led the welcome.[117]

Silas saw the societies as training in leadership, witness, bible knowledge, Christian character and missionary participation (whether preparing to serve as a missionary, praying, giving, sharing news, or being generally informed). The link between Christian Endeavour. and missionary endeavour is reflected in the obituary in *The West Australian*: 'His greatest work might almost be said to have been the founding of the Christian Endeavour movement in Australia, which, it is stated, led to the discovery of many missionaries for foreign countries.'[118]

[111] Title of the death notice in *West*, 14 September 1909, 5; reproduced in *WM*, 18 September 1909, 45.
[112] *West*, 31 October 1901, 4; *WM*, 9 November 1901, 76.
[113] *West*, 3 Apr 1902, 5; 9 Apr 1903, 4; 9 Apr 1904, 7.
[114] *WAB*, 23 August 1902, 14.
[115] Brown, *Baptised into One Body*, 7-13; Manley, *From Woolloomooloo*, 182-93; *WAB*, 31 Oct 1903, (10); 30 November 1903, 270.
[116] *Kalgoorlie Miner*, 1 April 1902, 4; see also 1903 Western Australian Convention report of denominational growth, *WAB*, 31 April 1903, (1).
[117] *WAB*, 30 April 1904, 67 (1) and 'Great Southern Department' supplement (1); *The Mail* (Fremantle), 5 April 1904, 3.
[118] *West*, 14 September 1909, 5.

The latest article by Silas that has been found is in *The Westralian Endeavourer*, 'One of the talks of Christ'. His desire to communicate a personal vital faith amongst young people is evident as he writes of the conversation between Christ and Nicodemus and concludes: 'We can to-day, though Christ is visibly only present on the Throne of Heaven, talk to him personally and receive from Him a beautiful, pure and white life that will qualify us one by one for everlasting friendship with Him in glory.'[119]

Contributing to community issues

Education: secondary and tertiary

Government involvement in education was a live community issue. Silas wrote at length to *The West Australian* Editor in response to an address the Colonial Secretary and Minister for Education, Walter Kingsmill had given at the 1903 annual dinner of local alumni of the Adelaide colleges, Prince Alfred (Methodist) and St. Peter's (Anglican).[120] Silas commended the work of those colleges with which he was familiar and the 'zeal' of the Methodists and Anglicans, followed by

> But I do very much object to the idea that in this State we should allow secondary education to become a denominational affair ... The tremendous injustice lately enacted in England by the unjust Education Bill[121] ... ought to be a sufficient beacon to us here never to allow any trace of denominationalism to prevail, either in our primary or secondary education ... Mr. Kingsmill tells us it is the duty of the Government to provide for the primary education of our boys and girls.[122] Will he tell us why it is not equally the duty of Government to provide for the secondary education of our brilliant youths?

---

[119] Reprinted in *DN*, 17 July 1909, 3.
[120] *West*, 26 March 1903, 7. I have been unable to find Kingsmill's speech. Alfred sent a letter supporting Mead, written 30 March from 'S.S. Wollowra, Albany' while on his unexpected sick leave [*West*, 2 April 1903, 6.]
[121] With Alfred's visit to and news from England, Western Australian Baptists were regularly informed of developments there, with frequent reports and articles in the *WA Baptist* (e.g., *WAB*, 23 August 1902, 103).
[122] Since the latter half of the nineteenth century the Western Australian government had provided public primary schools and limited aid to Catholic schools. Secondary level education was limited to independent schools [Laadan Fletcher, 'Education of the people' in Stannage, ed., *A New History of Western Australia*, 551-74].

To support his argument, he noted the 'poor education given in Britain' causing it to 'fall into the rear in the industrial race of the world', the inability of 'any one denominational institution to afford to bring all the fullest up-to-date apparatus … in order to be absolutely abreast of the times and continue so.' He commended the 'very first rank' of Western Australia's primary education under one regime and contended for 'a single system' for secondary education (which no other State had at that time). While costly, provision of secondary education 'will be among the money most economically spent by the Government in the interest of the people.'

'Secondary Education', the lead article in the July 1903 *W.A. Baptist Monthly*, was by Silas. Noting that the subject 'found a decided place in the Premier's speech the other day', after referring to the limits of existing denominational schools, Silas holds 'that every boy and girl in Western Australia should have the chance, if possessed of capacity, inclination, and available opportunity, of advancing to the top of the ladder of knowledge. We plead for Government facilities for secondary education, in the use of which no insurmountable barrier is placed in the way of the poorest.' Again the argument is that 'no private corporation' can keep up-to-date: 'the education of yesterday must give way to the advanced methods of to-day.'

While 'there should be no religious bias to interfere with the freedom of communication of knowledge', this does not mean 'irreligious education.' There is to be 'recognition both in school and Parliament, as well as in business, of the living God, and of the eternal principles of righteousness, whether seemingly expedient from a money point of view or not.' Not to be introduced are 'denominational religious tenets and peculiarities.' On his later return from England Silas reported on debates there on the place of the Bible.[123]

While the argument commonly related to use of State money (i.e., publicly paid taxes) to support denominational teaching,[124] Silas noteworthily extends the argument to the overall cost of education that is to provide for all in society and keep abreast of future developments.[125]

The forward-looking, community-wide vision saw him fully supporting the campaign for a State university led by the editor of *The West Australian*, John (later

---

[123] *West*, 6 February 1906, 4.
[124] E.g., the lead article by Alfred, *WAB*, 31 December 1902.
[125] Eventually in 1911 Perth Modern School opened, the first secondary school fully supported and run by the State.

Sir John) Winthrop Hackett.[126] In 1903, the same period as he is arguing for state provision of secondary education, Silas wrote supporting an editorial arguing for a university.[127] He affirmed 'it is not a day too soon to set about the establishing of an University for this State.' An overview of the United States scene led to negative comparison with England. His flexibility and forward looking is seen as he continues:

> Now, I heartily adopt your warning that in our instituting an University for West Australians we should avoid making our University 'a pale reflection' of the old Universities of Cambridge, Oxford, Dublin, and Edinburgh. The belated shadows of Oxford and Cambridge lie far too deeply on the Adelaide University. I can bear witness to this, as I took part in the establishment of the Adelaide University ... What is wanted here ... is present adaptation to the existing requirements of this young nation's life ... I hold that the fields of science should occupy a most prominent place.

Again, as he had said regarding secondary education, 'The money however it is found, will be the cheapest money laid out by this people, and, if not returning actual coin value, in the early years, will infallibly benefit and enrich the people of this country beyond any arithmetical estimate.'

Progress was slow, but various steps were taken.[128] Silas clearly maintained an interest, together with Gertrude.[129] He noted a report in *The West Australian* of the gift by Andrew Carnegie to a library in New Zealand, and asked: 'Now, as Mr. Carnegie is so lavish with his money [giving to a library], is it not possible—nay, likely—he might be ready to aid us here in Perth if properly approached?' He ended with a comment that a private donation had started the Adelaide University.[130] No mention is made of this being acted upon.

His vision for education and church involvement was broad, far beyond anything then happening in Australia. In an interview in Adelaide, Silas commented that

---

[126] When the University came into being 1911-13, Hackett was the first chancellor, and later benefactor after his death in 1916 [Fletcher, 'Education of the People', 572-73]. Gertrude was appointed a member of the first Senate.
[127] *West*, 27 July 1903, 6.
[128] A lengthy report of a 1905 presentation of diplomas for Western Australian candidates for Adelaide University examination gives most space to 'the need for a local university' (Gertrude was present) [*West*, 17 March 1905, 2]. A meeting of key community leaders held 7 September 1906 reviewed actions hitherto and planned ahead; Silas is noted as having tendered his apology [*West*, 8 September 1906, 12].
[129] See chapter 13.
[130] *West*, 30 May 1906, 4 (with a correction re the Adelaide donor, 31 May 1906, 3).

since he had left South Australia and, following his visit to USA and seeing the vigour of universities there, 'he has come to the conclusion that the churches should take a more active part in the instruction of the people in secular subjects than they are doing in Australia or England.'[131]

Other community issues and activity

Soon after arriving in Perth, in common with ministers and leading laypeople of other denominations, Silas shared in public debate relating to gambling,[132] and a proposed Federal Divorce Bill.[133] As in South Australia, he was involved in the YMCA.[134] He actively encouraged and supported local missions that involved the 'Free Churches' cooperatively, often chairing meetings.[135]

As editor of *W.A. Church Monthly* during Alfred's absence in 1903, he was responsible for the lead article on 'Today's Secular Newspaper' in the English-speaking world. The article stated that 'every cause, good, bad, indifferent, sustains its newspapers' and spoke critically of the amount of attention given to horse racing and athletics in Australia and of how 'the voice of the newspaper…has become the bible of huge multitudes of people.'[136] The following month saw a careful article on 'majority rule'.[137]

One community issue where Silas, Gertrude and Alfred demonstrate together their varied expertise and influence, concerned the proper provision of care of 'waifs', including method and funding. A public meeting held 25 April 1907 at the Perth

---

[131] *Advertiser*, 23 January 1902, 8.

[132] *West*, 17 September 1901, 2 (reprinted in *WM*, 21 September 1901, 65) had summaries of sermons by the ministers of Wesley (Methodist) Church and Trinity Congregational Church and by Silas at Perth Baptist, as requested by the Council of Churches. Also announced were similar sermons at other churches (Baptist, Presbyterian, and Methodist) [*West*, 14 September 1901, 2; 21 September 1901, 7]. At some stage he wrote 'a very able article on "Sports, Athletics, and Gambling"' [*WAB*, 31 January 1903].

[133] *West*, 16 October 1901, 6. Meetings to circulate petitions, *WM*, 26 October 1901, 70.

[134] *WM*, 26 September 1908, 22; 25 September 1909, 18. Silas was appointed to the first Board of Management of the re-established YMCA in October 1908; Austen, *Something Worth While*, 32.

[135] E.g., a major mission with interstate speakers, 'Mr. Giel, accompanied by Mr JJ Virgo of Melbourne YMCA', to conduct meetings at Perth, Fremantle and the Goldfields (*West*, 9 May 1902, 5; 31 May 1902, 3); a local 'non-sectarian mission' held in the Public Hall, Midland Junction, and in Guildford Methodist Church, at which Silas was one of the 'visiting ministers' (*Swan Express*, 19 July 1902, 2); and a '16 days mission' in Perth conducted by 'Mrs. [Emilia] Baeyertz, the Jewish evangelist', invited by the 'Ministers' Union', with Silas amongst those who gave 'appreciative testimony' (*West*, 10 August 1904, 3; 30 August 1904, 6).

[136] *WAB*, 30 May 1903, [1].

[137] *WAB*, 30 June 1903, [1].

Town Hall under the presidency of the Mayor of Perth[138] was followed by a chain of correspondence in *The West Australian* to which Silas contributed.[139] The Anglican Dean and Roman Catholic spokespeople proposed Government aid for denominational institutions while Silas argued against aid for 'church institutions' and their 'religious work'. Rather than the state running a foundling institution, he propounded the 'boarding-out' approach with stringent controls. Silas's arguments and proposals evidence both (a) Baptist views on issues of the State aiding specific denominations and on the role of family life and (b) a policy which reflected practice in South Australia which Silas would have known and that of the Children's Protection Society in which Gertrude was active.[140] Alfred in a *W.A. Baptist* article presented the history and proposal at length, including details of the South Australian experience. He mentions Gertrude's advice that a consignment be obtained of a book by CH Spence, *State Children in Australia*, and the intention of the Child Protection Society to 'send a copy to every legislator in the State.'[141] Silas, his daughter, and his son-in-law are acting together.

One further contribution to the State has little detail beyond that in a tribute by the Rev George Menzies, pastor at Fremantle, Northam and then Narrogin: 'It may not be generally known that Mr. Mead held a farm of about 1,500 acres in Western Australia [Boundain, 11km (7 miles) from Narrogin], and did good service in that capacity, also as a member of the State, helping to reduce the wilderness, and bring smiling plenty, where erstwhile there was nought but dreary bush.'[142]

Breadth of concerns continued. Late 1908 Silas was still on the Church Council of Western Australia, and a member of its 'Vigilance Committee' whose duties included 'to promote legislation in the interests of public morals...to consider the best means of dealing with social evils...to promote intercourse and a better understanding between the Churches and the workers.'[143]

---

[138] *West*, 25 April 1907, 2; Editorial report by Alfred, *WAB*, 15 May 1907, 65-66.
[139] His letters: *West*, 29 April 1907, 2; 3 May 1907, 3; response from the Anglican Dean, 1 May 1907, 4.
[140] Letters from Dr Roberta Jull, *West*, 29 April 1907, 2, and Edith Cowan, and decisions of the Society's General Meetings, *WM*, 11 May 1907, 42; 25 May 1907, 22; also *West* 25 April 1907, 2.
[141] *WAB*, 15 June 1907, 89-90, 92.
[142] *DN*, 9 October 1909, 3. (He also had a farm in South Australia, *West*, 14 September 1909, 5.) The Narrogin property was put up for lease or sale by Gertrude in January 1910 [*Great Southern Leader*, 7 January 1910, 2]. An advertisement stated that '1300 acres are conditional purchase, three years' rent paid; 160 acres freehold; 1,000 acres have been cleared ... Last year 375 acres were under crop', *Sunday Times*, 13 March 1910, 6. The sale was reported in a summary, *WM* 25 June 1910, 4.
[143] *West*, 12 August 1908, 9.

His funeral and tributes

Though he had been ailing,[144] Silas's death on Monday morning, 13 September 1909 at Gertrude's home was from an unexpected heart failure. Aged 75 he had been looking forward to the expected arrival from India on 23 October of Cecil, accompanied by his wife and daughters, but that meeting was not to be.[145] Blanche and Alfred were in New Zealand and Lilian in England, so at the burial the chief mourners were Gertrude and Sarah and Frank Hann.[146]

His burial was on 15 September at the Baptist Cemetery, Karrakatta, conducted by Rev Grimshaw Binns, minister of the Perth Church, assisted by Rev ASC (Adolphus) James, minister of St Andrews Presbyterian Church, Perth, with ministers of various denominations present.[147] The following Sunday the Perth Church held a Memorial Service where Grimshaw Binns was the main speaker, along with Rev Frank Radford of Albany Baptist who had been a student of Silas in South Australia, with members of the YMCA, BUWA and CE Union present.[148] That same day, 'in a prelude to his sermon', Adolphus James at the Presbyterian Church gave a heartfelt eulogy.[149]

His obituary in *WAB* briefly mentions some formal roles, but extols at length his character:

> He was the devoted servant of all the smaller churches for Jesus' sake...Our friend was a strong man of deep convictions; and yet withal so genial and affable, so generous and kind-hearted, that by a rare combination of firmness and kindness, decision and prudence, he wielded an unusual power over his fellow men...A Christian scholar, whose gifts, consecrated to the highest and noblest ends, were even less conspicuous than his grace of character, whose strength was allied with a gentleness of spirit, and unaffected humility, and a generous and unselfish demeanour.[150]

[144] His 'indisposition' was reported in July [*WAB*, 15 July 1909, (7)].
[145] *West*, 14 September 1909, 5.
[146] *West*, 16 September 1909, 8.
[147] *West*, 16 September 1909, 8. Coming from English ministry, Grimshaw Binns was pastor of Claremont Baptist Church from May 1908, then of Perth Church from April 1909.
[148] *West*, 20 September 1909, 4, includes section of words by Binns and Radford.
[149] *West*, 20 September 1909, 4. Other reports and eulogies include *WAB*, 15 September 1909: 'In Memoriam'; 15 October 1909: 'In Memoriam Rev. S. Mead'–a poem by 'Student'; 15 November 1909: Goalundo Mission report includes letter from 'Miss Edith King, Mission House, Rajbari, September 29, 1909'; *SB*, 28 September 1909, 229-30.
[150] *WAB*, 15 September 1909, [n.p.].

The Next Generations

Mead family, FSBC, 1889

'This is Silas Mead continued. How he would have rejoiced to see this effort being carried forward.'

(CS Mead, 1914)

11

Lilian: An 'Awakened Woman'

Rebecca Hilton

Childhood

Lilian Staple Brown, née Mead, was the eldest child of Ann Staple and the FSBC minister, Silas Mead. She was born in Adelaide on 30 June 1865. Over the following eight years, four siblings were added to the family: Cecil, Gertrude, Annie Blanche (always called Blanche), and Flora. In addition John Angel Mead was born and died on 12 October 1871.[1] The family lived in Franklin Street until 1870 and then in Wakefield Street, as the manse, adjacent to FSBC, was not built until 1877. In 1874 when Lilian was nine years old, her mother died. Lilian attended the service at the grave, along with Cecil, Gertrude, and Blanche.[2] However, Lilian and her siblings were fortunate that their mother's sister, Sarah Hann, was living in Adelaide and looked after the Mead children.[3] One month after their mother's death, Silas departed Adelaide for England and was away for eighteen months. Probably by this stage Lilian was attending boarding school and so was not living at home: although details of Lilian's early education are unknown, from the age of thirteen Lilian attended the newly

---

[1] 'Family Notices', *Evening Journal* (Adelaide) *(EJ)*, 12 October 1871, 2.
[2] 'The Late Mrs Mead', *EJ*, 18 June 1874, 2.
[3] Walter Barry, *There was a Man: The Life of Cecil Silas Mead: Missionary-Doctor* (Melbourne: Australian Baptist Foreign Mission, 1952), 13.

opened Advanced School for Girls in Franklin Street.[4] In any case, all the siblings retained a loving friendship that continued throughout their lives.[5]

In 1877 the Mead family moved into the FSBC manse, next to the church. The following year Lilian and her siblings gained a stepmother, when Silas Mead married Mary, née Pitty. Mary's obituary noted that she 'practically adopted' two nephews, yet she does not appear to have been a maternal figure, nor a significant influence on Lilian, or indeed Lilian's siblings.[6] Possibly this was because Mary appears to have focused on work supporting people in the FSBC congregation, such as visits and providing hospitality, rather than building maternal bonds with Lilian and her siblings.[7] The lack of a relationship further supports the assumption that Lilian attended boarding school.

Lilian attended FSBC with her family, and her strong Christian faith as a teenager was evident from an article she wrote for the *Christian Colonist* when she was fifteen. Her article, published in the Children's Inquiry column, was titled 'Our Father' and contained Lilian's consideration of the meaning of the phrase from the point of view of an earthly father, a father who inflicts punishment, a loving father, and an 'elder brother' who can be relied upon.[8] Her intent was clear, although her arguments reflected that she was still a teenager. She summed up her argument by concluding:

> Let us hope that we may, in the future: yield more hearty obedience to our Father; appreciate more fully the pleasures He provides for His children; bow more submissively under His punishments; realise more fully the Father's love, and the sympathy of our Elder Brother; and be all united at last in the home which He is still preparing for us, where some of His children are now enjoying the sunlight of the Father's loving smile.[9]

Lilian received a good education: indeed Silas was committed to giving his children a good education. In the early 1880s the University of Adelaide was considering the issue of offering women the opportunity to earn degrees. This discussion was prag-

[4] 'Educational', *Register*, 3 November 1879, 4.
[5] For example, see: Lilian Brown, Letter to Gertrude Mead, 13 October 1909, Gooden/Mead collection. Other letters indicate warm friendships.
[6] 'In Memoriam: The Late Mrs Mead', *TP*, 1 April 1886, 50.
[7] 'In Memoriam: The Late Mrs Mead', *TP*, 1 April 1886, 50.
[8] Lilian S Mead, 'Our Father', *Colonist*, 25 March 1881, 6. A woman using the pen name 'Thalia Curtis' managed the column, and the aim was to 'assist young people in the study of the Bible and their efforts at Christian service.' The identity of 'Thalia Curtis' is unknown.
[9] Mead, 'Our Father', *Colonist*, 25 March 1881, 6.

matic rather than a call for equality: the University wanted to increase their student numbers. Silas become involved with the consideration of the issue.[10] One impediment to university admission for women was that at the time there was no school in Adelaide that offered women all the subjects required for matriculation, which was needed for entrance into the University. In 1882 Prince Alfred College in Adelaide decided to allow women to be enrolled who wanted to matriculate. Lilian took advantage of the change in policy and duly, in mid-1883, she commenced studying at the College. She was the only woman to take up this opportunity and she remains the only woman to have ever been a student at Prince Alfred College.[11] The school reversed its policy after Lilian probably because other schools in Adelaide commenced offering women the courses required for matriculation. Lilian was enrolled at the College in 1883 and 1884. Her results were not exceptional, yet gave her entry into University. She was nineteen years old at matriculation. Lilian's brother, Cecil, who was one year younger than her, was already a student at the University of Adelaide, presumably as he was able to access the necessary matriculation earlier than her in order to qualify for University. Women were admitted to the University of Adelaide from 1883, and a letter written in 1885 from Dr Laura Hope suggested that 'Lily [Lilian] is studying for a degree'.[12] Yet although she was possibly a student at the University, Lilian did not complete a degree and she does not appear to have lamented her lack of a degree. In 1927 she wrote a letter to 'a friend' that was published in the *Register* in Adelaide, in which she explains in detail the PhD graduation ceremony of her friend Dr Eleanor Allen from the University of London, with no discernible hint of regret.[13]

ɔn, *The New Women: Adelaide's Early Women Graduates* (Netley, South
d Press, 1986), 21.
ɘn Staple Mead PAC 1883-1884', *Prince Alfred College*, 30 October, 2019.
ɤa Hope to her brother James Fowler, in Mackinnon, *The New Women*, 45.
Eleanor Allen: Graduate of London University', *Register*, 1927, 17. Eleanor
desmaid.

Lilian Staple Mead

One reason Lilian may not have enrolled at the University of Adelaide is that she had decided to travel to England. On 12 February 1886 Lilian, then age twenty-one, and Gertrude, nineteen, departed Adelaide for England, where they spent most of the year with relatives. While away, their step-mother Mary died, and then later in 1886 their siblings, Cecil, Blanche and Flora, all contracted typhoid. On 9 September their youngest sister Flora, who was nearly fourteen years old, died. Lilian and Gertrude were informed of Flora's death through a letter from Silas.[14]

Assistant to Silas Mead

On returning to Australia at the end of 1886 Lilian did not commence university study, she instead became her father's assistant, albeit unpaid. She managed her father's house—the FSBC manse—and sometimes she travelled with him, for example in late 1896 together they visited New South Wales and Queensland.[15] This was a role

[14] 'In Memoriam: Flora Beatrice Mead', *TP*, 1 October 1886, 146.
[15] 'South Australian items', *SB*, 17 December 1896, 268.

that she undertook for fifteen years during which time she demonstrated her organisational skills and commitment to various Christian causes.

Lilian was fond of her father and wrote loving memories about him. In her 1881 article on 'Our Father' she reminisced: 'How many remember with delight the miniature farms which were given them by a loving father in childhood and when in after years they see them in a toy-shop window are tempted to say, "I almost wish I could play with one again, I did so enjoy mine."'[16] In addition, her printed booklet, 'The Awakened Woman', was 'lovingly and gratefully dedicated to [her] father'.[17] A letter she wrote after Silas's death in 1909 reinforces their deep and warm relationship. She wrote: 'I always have been proud of him for many, many years; more and more proud as I realised, not only his fine powers, but his constant endeavour to do what he believed to be right…And one knew his love and interest were constant as well.'[18]

Lilian was closely involved in several different organisations, some of which clearly show the influence that Silas had in her life, including her involvement in Christian Endeavour (CE), temperance and mission organisations, and groups established within FSBC, such as the Sunday School.[19]

Activist for temperance and women's rights

Lilian supported temperance and besides being one of the coordinators of the Band of Hope group at FSBC, she also attended meetings of the Woman's Christian Temperance Union (WCTU). The WCTU commenced in the United States of America in the 1870s when Christian women sought alcohol restrictions. During the 1880s local WCTU Societies were formed throughout the Australian colonies, along with colonial Unions culminating in an Australian Union being established in 1891.[20]

[16] Mead, 'Our Father', *Colonist*, 25 March 1881, 6.
[17] Lilian S Mead, *The Awakened Woman: Paper read at Seventh Annual Convention of Woman's Christian Temperance Union of South Australia* (Adelaide: Woman's Christian Temperance Union, 1895).
[18] Lilian Brown, Letter to Gertrude Mead, 13 October 1909, Gooden/Mead collection.
[19] For example: 'Church Intelligence', *ET*, 16 September 1891, 4.
[20] Judith Pargeter, *'For God, Home and Humanity': National Woman's Christian Temperance Union of Australia: Centenary history: 1891-1991* (Geelong, Victoria: National Woman's Christian Temperance Union of Australia, 1995), 1.

Through the WCTU, Lilian was actively engaged in an influential, active and trans-national Christian organisation.[21]

While WCTU sought temperance, it was also involved in various social reforms, particularly the right of women to vote. At least two of Lilian's papers were printed on women's suffrage and gender equality: 'Ought Women to Vote' and 'The Awakened Woman', although there are no extant copies of the former paper. The paper 'The Awakened Woman,' was presented by Lilian in 1895 at the Seventh Annual Convention of the SA WCTU after SA women had gained the right to vote. Lilian 'claim[ed] that man and woman, husband and wife, were intended to be essentially equal and relatively different.'[22] She used Scripture to justify this conclusion, stressing the 'promise' in Galatians 3:28 'that there can no longer "be male and female, bond or free".'[23] She also stated that 'enlightened women' knew that women should not be restricted to home life, and 'Why … if an intellectually accomplished man is not unmanly, is an intellectually accomplished woman unwomanly?'[24] Lilian also discussed the importance of unmarried women having a means to paid work, which was an interesting viewpoint given that she was unmarried and reliant on her father Silas. However, her approach indicates that she was aware of issues faced by women who were uneducated and poor. Indeed, she wrote about this theme in her book *Patsie's Bricks* discussed below.

Lilian's engagement with women's groups such as the WCTU meant that she would have frequently heard, and been personally acquainted with, prominent women older than herself who were involved in SA politics, suffrage and social reform, most particularly Catherine Spence and Rosetta Birks.[25]

Christian Endeavour

Arguably Lilian's work in CE most demonstrates the influence of her father, while highlighting Lilian's writing and speaking abilities. In 1888 the introduction of CE to FSBC was an important milestone for the congregation, but also provided Lilian

---

[21] Geoffrey R. Treloar, *The Disruption of Evangelicalism: The Age of Torrey, Mott, McPherson and Hammond*, vol. 4, *A History of Evangelicalism*, ed. David Bebbington and Mark Noll, 5 vols. (Downers Grove, Illinois: IVP Academic, 2017), 56.

[22] LS Mead, *The Awakened Woman*, 2.

[23] LS Mead, *The Awakened Woman*, 6.

[24] LS Mead, *The Awakened Woman*, 24.

[25] Catherine Spence was on many of the same committees as Lilian; and Rosetta Birks was a prominent Baptist and member of FSBC.

with a mainstream structure through which she could exhibit her skills. The FSBC CE Society was the third Australian society established, largely because of the enthusiasm and support of Silas.[26] CE commenced in the United States in the early 1880s and became one of the largest world-wide evangelical organisations. Importantly CE provided a mechanism for women to contribute to Australian religious activities, although its significance in this area is generally ignored.[27] Baptist congregations, such as FSBC, saw CE as an integral part of the church because it targeted young people. Yet, clearly women were attracted to CE. The FSBC CE Society quickly became part of a larger SA CE Union. CE had an egalitarian attitude and allowed women to be in leadership roles through involvement in regional and state CE unions. In the early 1890s Lilian and her sister Blanche were on the executive committee of the SA CE Union. Lilian appears to have been an effective member of the executive. She actively worked to expand the scope and membership of CE, through visiting other congregations and speaking about the benefits of CE.[28] Indeed, she performed 'invaluable services . . . to the [SA CE] Union.'[29] Lilian spoke at the second SA CE Convention in 1892 on 'The Christian Endeavour Society, its work and obligations.' In addition, she spoke at various CE meetings, and wrote articles about CE: an example in 1894 was in *The Golden Link*, the CE national publication, on 'Helpful suggestions for carrying on our Junior Societies' where she stressed the need for prayer: 'pray much about the society, and be not wearying in well-doing.'[30]

In 1896 Lilian was one of the few women who presented a paper at the Australian CE Convention in Sydney. Her paper was on 'Literature', and she said that 'She had a hobby, and she had been asked to speak of her hobby, which was Christian Endeavour literature'.[31]

---

[26] Murray Chambers, *Centenary of Christian Endeavour in Australia* ([s.l.]: Australian Christian Endeavour Union, 1983), 48. In 1883 the first CE Society was established by the young women at the Hope Street Church of Christ in Geelong. In 1888 the second Society was established at the Wharf Street Baptist Church in Brisbane, some weeks before FSBC.
[27] For examples of women's activities, see: 'Christian Endeavour Convention: Stirring Addresses', *SMH*, 18 September 1896, 5; 'Christian Endeavour: The Junior Demonstration', *West*, 15 October 1928, 15. Chambers, *Centenary of Christian Endeavour in Australia*, 7.
[28] See, for example: 'South Australian Union Young People's Societies of Christian Endeavour', *Colonist*, 27 November 1891, 3; 'Rally of Christian Endeavourers', *Register*, 28 December 1896, 6.
[29] 'Christian Endeavour: Farewell to the Rev Silas Mead and Miss Mead', *AO*, 2 January 1897, 18.
[30] Lilian S Mead, 'Helpful suggestions for carrying on our junior societies', *The Golden Link* (Melbourne), 1 August 1894, 6.
[31] 'Christian Endeavour Convention: Stirring Addresses', *SMH*, 18 September 1896, 5.

In 1897, following Silas's resignation from FSBC, she travelled with him to his job at the East London Institute for Home and Foreign Missions, Harley College, travelling via the Australian Baptist missions in East Bengal and the World CE Conference in San Francisco.[32] At the CE farewell for Silas and Lilian, the then President of the SA CE Union, Methodist minister the Rev. Joseph Barry, was reported as saying that:

> Miss Mead had rendered good service, partly in taking care of her father—(Laughter, and applause)—and partly in serving the Endeavour movement in many respects; but mainly in having taken charge of the Literature Department, which she was now handing over in a splendid state of organisation.[33]

Lilian spoke at the World CE Convention in San Francisco on 'The world's prayer chain'.[34] Francis Clarke, the founder of CE, claimed that the prayer chain was an 'important feature of CE societies'.[35] The prayer chain allowed all members of the society to participate in prayer, members are considered part of a 'chain'. The prayer chain was a mechanism through which women were involved in the meetings, as all members were invited—expected—to pray, and accordingly women's voices were heard. Speaking at the conference would have been a wonderful experience. There were over twenty thousand attendees, at a time that the population of Adelaide was only forty thousand. She wrote that her 'number' was 4834 which helped with both catering and accommodation for the attendees.[36] While Lilian loved the social aspect of meeting other CE members, she knew that the friendships she made at the conference would be fleeting. She wrote:

> a brief sweet song service, a few earnest loving words, a dozen individual conversations meantime with the miners and ranchmen who assembled in crowds to see the great process of trains pass, a parting song, a parting cheer, and the paths that crossed for so brief a time, diverged perhaps for ever.[37]

Perhaps she was speaking more generally about her own circumstances in this statement, as she was embarking on a new path that changed her life.

---

[32] Chapter 9 discussed the Convention.
[33] 'Christian Endeavour: Farewell to the Rev Silas Mead and Miss Mead', *AO*, 2 January 1897, 18.
[34] 'Church Intelligence', *ET*, 17 September 1897, 2.
[35] Francis Edward Clark, *The Christian Endeavor Manual* (Boston, Mass.: United Society of Christian Endeavor, 1903), 74.
[36] Lilian S Mead, 'Convention Impressions: 'Frisco, 1897', *The Golden Link* (Melbourne), 1 September 1897, 16.
[37] LS Mead, 'Convention Impressions: 'Frisco, 1897', 16.

Marriage and motherhood

In London Lilian met Crosbie Charles Brown, who was a tutor at Harley College. Crosbie was the eldest child of Elizabeth and Charles Brown, a Congregational minister. Thus, both Lilian and Crosbie were children of ministers. Crosbie was born in 1867, in Tunbridge Wells, Kent, about seventy kilometres south of London. He had a younger brother, Rennie Jameson, who also became a Congregational minister, and a sister, Emily Ada. Crosbie's family moved soon after Rennie's birth from Tunbridge Wells to Nottingham, where Emily was born in 1872. The family then moved to various locations in the East Midlands region of England. In the early 1890s Crosbie relocated to London and in 1895 he obtained a Bachelor of Arts from the University of London and presumably following his graduation he commenced work at Harley College. Crosbie's father died in 1886 and his mother died in 1897.

Marriage of Lilian Mead to Crosbie Brown, 1900.
Gertrude Mead is on Lilian's left.

At the age of thirty-five Lilian married Crosbie on 16 August 1900 in the Baptist Bethesda Chapel in the small town of Isle Abbots, in Somerset, 230 kilometres west of London. This location was chosen because of its link to Lilian's parents. Various members of Lilian's family lived in the district including the siblings of both her mother and father, along with various cousins. Lilian's sister Gertrude attended the wedding, but her other siblings, Cecil and Blanche, were not in attendance, being in East Bengal and Australia respectively. Both of Crosbie's siblings were at the wedding. The reception was held at nearby Swell Court, the fifteenth century farmhouse inhabited by her cousin, Elizabeth Hallett (née Mead) and Christopher Hallett. An article of the event described her wedding dress as:

> a cream liberty silk, made with a long train, the bodice trimmed in gathered chiffon and Maltese lace, and a veil fastened with sprays of orange blossom. She carried a beautiful bouquet of white lilies and fern . . . The bride's going-away dress was a pale grey coat and skirt, a pink front covered with cream chiffon, and a cream hat.[38]

Lilian had five bridesmaids: her sister Gertrude; Bessie Uttermare and Ada Drayton, two cousins (daughters of her father's sister and her mother's sister respectively); Eleanor Allen, a friend from Adelaide; and 'Miss Aitken,' whose identity and connection to Lilian is unknown. Lilian and Crosbie went to Switzerland for their honeymoon.[39]

After their marriage the couple lived with Silas, until he left Harley College and returned to Australia in mid-1901. Lilian and Crosbie's only child, Roger Crosbie Brown, was born on 26 August 1902 in Bourneville, Birmingham, 180 kilometres north-west of London. Bourneville was created in 1861 as a 'model' town for Cadbury chocolate factory employees and the sale of alcohol was forbidden for many years. Given Lilian's view on temperance, such a location seems appropriate although there is no information about why Roger was born in this location.

Published books

Throughout her life Lilian was interested in literature. Possibly she became interested in literature through the influence of her aunt Sarah Hann who was involved in literary societies in Adelaide and Perth.[40] Nonetheless in Adelaide Lilian was a member of the FSBC Girls' Literary Society, which had about forty members, and she actively participated in the group, for example in 1887 she presented 'an excellent essay ... [on] Australian Girlhood—its Possibilities'.[41] She was also a member of the

---

38 'Personal Notes from England', *Register*, 7 November 1900, 5.
39 'Personal Notes from England', *Register*, 7 November 1900, 5.
40 See 'News of the Week', *West*, 5 December 1885, 6.
41 'Girls' Literary Society Social', *Register*, 28 December 1887, 5.

SA Girls' Literary Society and was Secretary in 1890. In 1884 her essay on 'Girls' Education' won first place in the Society's annual awards.[42]

From 1903 to 1912 Lilian published three books under her birth surname. The reason for using 'Mead' is unknown. Potentially she believed that she and her father were well-known, particularly within the Baptist denomination and CE, plus Brown is a common surname. The books were published in England, and they do not appear to have been widely distributed within Australia.[43] Despite the exponential growth of publishing in the early twentieth century, only a small percentage of women were able to be published writers. From 1900 to 1940 just over one hundred Australian writers had books published in the United Kingdom when they lived in England.[44]

Lilian's first book was a fictional story titled *A Brother's Need* and was published in 1903. The story promoted foreign mission and it drew heavily on Lilian's visit to the Australian Baptist missions. Indeed, in 1897 when she was in East Bengal, she wrote an article for *Our Bond,* the Baptist Australasian Mission paper, containing some impressions of East Bengal and she included the same story in *A Brother's Need.* In the 1897 article Lilian wrote: 'I noticed more than one boy shielding his slate from the view of his next door neighbour.'[45] In *A Brother's Need* Lilian wrote that the protagonist, Roger, said to his fellow missionary: 'Did you see that boy shielding his slate with his brown arm so that the next boy should not copy from him?'[46] Lilian thought that such behaviour showed that children in East Bengal behaved in the same way as children in Australia. While explicit in its support of foreign mission, essentially Lilian's book was a love story. The main character was Roger Hurst who had been accepted for missionary work in India. He was engaged to be married, although his fiancée broke their engagement because she wanted a comfortable life. While upset, Roger quickly realised that he was in love with one of his friends, Christie Cardew. Meanwhile, Christie wrestled with the idea of being a missionary and wanted to volunteer, but she did not want Roger to feel that 'she was longing for him to invite her

---

[42] 'Girls' Literary Association', *EJ*, 9 February 1884, 4.
[43] The books were not published in Australia, despite the trend of 'colonial editions' at the turn of the century. The National Library of Australia (NLA) does not have copies of her books in its collection. Only *Patsie's Bricks* is available in any Australian collections (the State Library of SA and the Newcastle Library). In addition, in 2019 no second-hand copies were available for purchase within Australia. Copies of the books were obtained from England.
[44] Helen Bones, *Expatriate Myth: New Zealand writers and the colonial world* (Dunedin, NZ: Otago University Press, 2018), 13.
[45] Lilian S Mead, 'Faridpur', *Our Bond* (Calcutta, India), March 1897, 2.
[46] Lilian Staple Mead, *A Brother's Need* (London: S. W. Partridge & Co, [1903]), 103.

to be his companion.'[47] Roger went to India and wrote to Christie declaring his love. She travelled to India, where they married.

Lilian demonstrated elements of her evangelical beliefs in the story through the commitment to actively convert non-Christian people and her use of Biblical references to explain why foreign mission was so important. The book finished with a conversation between Christie and Roger that is a paraphrase of Luke 17:20: 'The Kingdom of God cometh not with observation. …But it comes, … it comes.'[48]

The book also demonstrated features shared by other expatriate writers in that it is written by an Australian, set in England, and has an obvious link to Australia.[49] The positive review by the Rev John Price, an Australian Baptist minister, noted: 'The objective of the tale is evidently our Australasian Bengali Mission, and it is written (as might be expected of one of the Mead family) with a full knowledge of that branch of the Master's service.'[50]

Lilian's second and third publications were children's books. Writing children's books was not particularly unusual: they became very common at the turn of the twentieth century, especially as literacy rates improved. Lilian's children's books followed patterns often used in early twentieth-century children's literature in that they contained moral lessons, encouraged brave acts, promoted Christian values and children made decisions sometimes without adult help.[51]

Lilian's second book, published in 1905, certainly followed this format. *Patsie's Bricks* was about a young, destitute child named Patsie Hereford, who lived on the streets of Edinburgh with her older brother, Tim, and their friend, Blossom. Initially her mother earned a shilling a day which was enough to pay for food and access to a lodging hall at night, which provided wooden boxes for herself and Patsie to sleep on, while Tim slept on the streets.[52] After Patsie's mother died a young woman called Pearl Collison gave the children directions to the 'Father's House', which was an orphanage. There was not enough room for Blossom to live at the orphanage with Patsie, although Blossom was later accepted by another orphanage. Patsie decided to sell paper

47 Mead, *A Brother's Need*, 74.
48 Mead, *A Brother's Need*, 132.
49 Bones, *Expatriate Myth*, 13.
50 John Price, 'Missionary News: A Brother's Need', *SB*, 15 December 1903, 281.
51 Susan Broomhall, Joanne McEwan, and Stephanie Tarbin, 'Once Upon a Time: a Brief History of Children's Literature', *The Conversation* (30 March 2017), https://theconversation.com/once-upon-a-time-a-brief-history-of-childrens-literature-75205.
52 The wooden boxes were called 'coffins' and used to help homeless and destitute people, particularly those in crowded cities such as Edinburgh.

building bricks to raise money for another orphanage. Patsie, Tim, and Blossom raised seventeen pounds before Patsie was diagnosed with tuberculosis ('consumption') and died. Pearl decided to raise the money on behalf of Patsie.

> But even for Pearl Collison, it was no easy matter to secure three thousand pounds for one object, in these days of manifold charities and philanthropies, and the girl bent her whole energies to its accomplishment.[53]

Thus, Patsie's initial idea was realised through the work of Pearl. Potentially Lilian wrote the book to raise awareness of the plight of poor and orphaned children, and to encourage philanthropy to organisations such as Dr Barnardo's Homes, which supported orphans. Despite the sadness of the plot, the story finishes with hope and the opening of another orphanage.

In 1912 Lilian Brown published her third book titled *Daring and Doing!: true stories of brave deeds*, which contained eighteen different stories about young people doing 'brave deeds.' The book is dedicated to 'Our boy—Roger, in the hope that he may some day do noble deeds.'[54] As the title notes, the stories are about young people who perform acts of bravery to rescue others, mainly children. In the eighteen stories, three involve the death of the young person undertaking the brave deed. Investigations of some of the stories reveals that Lilian has amended the details of the 'true stories' to illustrate that young people undertook these brave deeds. One example is the story of Alice Ayres in chapter 9, titled 'Three to save'.

The story of Alice Ayres was well known in London when she died in April 1885. Lilian writes that Ayres 'was scarcely more than a child herself, though she was in service', and she saved the three children in the home she worked at after the house caught on fire, but she had suffered smoke inhalation and spinal injuries in escaping the home, and died.[55] In reality Ayres was twenty-six at the time of her death and the children she saved were her nieces, rather than an unrelated family as the story implies. In addition, one of the children Ayres rescued later died along with the children's parents and an older son. After the death of Ayres a public subscription raised money for a relatively grand tombstone. However, she might have preferred that the

[53] Lilian Staple Mead, *Patsie's Bricks* (London: S. W. Partridge & Co, [1905]), 159.
[54] Lilian Staple Mead, *Daring and Doing!: True stories of brave deeds* (London: SW Partridge & Co, [1912]), 4. Copies of her books contain inscriptions indicating they were gifts to Band of Hope members.
[55] Mead, *Daring and Doing!*, 50.

money had been spent on her two surviving nieces who instead were placed in an orphanage and trained for domestic service.

Nonetheless Lilian's account of this story included a beautiful piece about memorials. Lilian wrote:

> London delights to honour brave deeds, and the statues and monuments of the men who performed them meet you everywhere.
>
> The great cathedral of St. Paul's is full of memorials of those who have greatly served their country, and when you are in the church, you may often see a fresh wreath of laurel laid on the tomb of such men as General Gordon, to shew they are not forgotten.
>
> Westminster Abbey is even more full, and Nelson's column is only one of the many monuments, built to show honour to those who have possessed great courage and devotion to duty. Even in quite unexpected places, you may read the record of many a brave deed, and if ever you go down to Aldersgate Street, spare a little while to go and see the memorial of Alice Ayres. It is a tablet, fastened to a wall, and on each side of the inscription, is a crown of flames.
>
> There have been many heroes and heroines in this brave land of ours, but never was a braver deed done than by this little servant-maid, who, in the face of death and danger, showed a coolness and self-sacrifice, a splendid courage, that would have done honour to any name in any age.[56]

This is a particularly eloquent sentiment and justification about the importance of honouring people who are not considered 'great men': those who are poor and marginalised—and women.

---

[56] Mead, *Daring and Doing!*, 54. A facsimile of the memorial was included in Lilian's book. Incidentally Alice Ayres' memorial also does not mention her age, but it does emphasise that she was 'the daughter of a brick-layer's labourer'.

Life after 1912

Lilian was Australian by birth although she lived just over half of her life in England. In 1897 on her arrival in England she:

> declared that if she lived in England for twenty years she would always have 'of Australia' printed after her name, because English Endeavourers gave such generous greetings to their kinsfolk from over the sea.[57]

Lilian lived in England for nearly forty years. There is no evidence that she ever returned to Australia after her marriage, although at some point a suggestion was made that she and Crosbie would come to Australia if there was a suitable position available. Lilian and Crosbie also debated emigrating to Canada, although this did not occur.[58] Crosbie continued in his role as a teacher. Various members of Lilian's family travelled to England to see her, including Silas, who spent most of 1905 in England. Lilian's letter to her sister Gertrude following the death of Silas shows the love that she had for her father, which was shared by Crosbie and Roger Brown. She wrote that Roger 'cried as if his heart would break' when he was told that his grandfather had died.[59]

Lilian and Crosbie Brown

[57] 'Christian Endeavour Notes', *EJ*, 19 October 1898, 3.
[58] 'Personal notes England', *Register*, 25 August 1903, 5.
[59] Lilian Brown, Letter to Gertrude Mead. Gooden/Mead collection, 1909.

Lilian did not lose her desire to assist the mission enterprise. In 1916 her brother Cecil wrote an article about the student hostel that was run by Crosbie, presumably with significant input from Lilian. The hostel provided accommodation for students from the 'east and west' who live together.[60] Cecil acknowledged their family's mission heritage, writing: 'This is Silas Mead continued. How he would have rejoiced to see this effort being carried forward.'[61]

Given Lilian's interest in literature and writing, it is almost inconceivable that Lilian would not have continued to write, but no additional published works have been identified.

Lilian died on 27 November 1936 in Newton Abbot, Devon, aged 71. Crosbie died nearly twenty years after Lilian, on 16 January 1956 in Kent.[62]

Lilian (Mead) Brown

---

[60] Cecil Silas Mead, 'An interesting missionary experience', *AB*, 19 May 1914, 11-12.
[61] CS Mead, 'An interesting missionary experience', *AB*, 19 May 1914, 11.
[62] Chapter 16 includes a brief account of her son Roger Brown's story.

Cecil: 'The Missionary Who Happened to Be a Medical Man'

Pauline Tudball[1]

Dr Cecil Silas Mead, BA, MB, BS (1866–1940) was welcomed into the world by Silas Mead and Ann ('Annie') Mead (née Staple) on October 18, 1866. A delighted Ann was heard to exclaim, 'Our missionary son!' As he grew up, Cecil was profoundly influenced by his father's enthusiasm for overseas mission and felt strongly called to share the gospel with people as yet unreached by the good news. Cecil's academic prowess, love of music, combined with devotion and unswerving determination to serve the poor and fight for their rights, made a lasting impression on all who knew him. When he died, *Our Indian Field*, 6 July 1940, was devoted to his memory.[2] Published biographies include *There Was a Man*, written by his friend, Walter Barry,[3] and Elva Schroeder's book *Doctor Sahib*.[4] Unpublished family papers also reveal much about Cecil Mead, the man.[5]

---

[1] The author sincerely appreciates Dr Rosalind M Gooden's encouragement, experience, and expertise.
[2] *Our Indian Field* was the official organ of the Australian Baptist Foreign Mission at that time.
[3] Walter Barry, *There Was a Man* (Melbourne: Jenkin Buxton & Co. Pty. Ltd., 1953).
[4] Elva Schroeder, *Doctor Sahib* (Tooperang, SA: Rowett Print, 2006), 14. A book for young people based on Dorothy Mead's memories of family traditions.
[5] Baptist Mission Australia archive, Moore Potter House, Melbourne, Cecil Silas Mead files, Boxes #1–#5.

Silas Mead with son Cecil, c.1867

Cecil excelled at school. He attended Prince Alfred College and the University of Adelaide (B.A., 1887; MB, BS, 1891). Cecil was baptised by his father at FSBC at the age of eleven and maintained his membership there for the remaining sixty-three years of his life.[6] As an honoured and beloved member of FSBC, Cecil rendered outstanding service in practically every department of the church's activities, holding the office of elder, deacon, Sunday School teacher, Christian Endeavour leader, church organist and choirmaster. After serving as a medical missionary in Bengal for twenty-nine years, he returned to teach Anatomy at the University in Adelaide (1923–39). He died in Adelaide, June 1940.

The Mead family collection includes several letters to Silas, including one from eight year old Cecil, just months before the death of his mother:

---

[6] Stow Smith, 'Cecil Silas Mead, A Missionary Statesman', *Our Indian Field*, 6 July 1940, 2; *The Baptist Record of South Australia*, 18 July 1940, 17, Baptist Mission Australia archive, CS Mead Box #4.

Dear Papa, I have hoard about a Gentleman who used to go out every night and get Children to come to his house for street Children. Mrs Beeby[7] told us in the little chapel. And papa when I grow up to be about 20 years of age I have made up my mind to be a missionary and teach little children to come to Jesus. If you take me to England. I am trying for the prize a day and Sunday School. I am getting up in sums I am up to compound [interest]. / Your loving Son, Cecil Silas Mead.[8]

Cecil Mead in 1875, aged 9

Cecil had unqualified respect for his beloved father's wisdom as a preacher and teacher. Silas's library was stocked with books and magazines written by the great preachers and theologians of the day. The atmosphere of this missionary-oriented home strongly influenced Cecil in his choice of the life-work he believed God had prepared for him in India. Cecil offered himself for medical missionary work in Bengal in response to an appeal at a Christian Endeavour Convention consecration meeting in 1892 at the Adelaide Town Hall. A delighted Silas was overheard saying, 'Look! My son! My son!'[9]

---

[7] Mrs Beeby was one of the founding members of FSBC.
[8] Cecil to Silas, 8 May 1874, Baptist Mission Australia archive, CS Mead Box #4.
[9] Rev J Arthur Lewis, 'In memory of Dr CS Mead, BA, MB, BS', *The Baptist Record of South Australia* 17:1, 18 July 1940, 1. Baptist Mission Australia archive, CS Mead Box #3.

Dr Cecil Silas Mead, 1892

But the 1893 typhus epidemic found Cecil as a patient in Guy's Hospital, London, while furthering his medical training, writing a prayer:[10]

'LO, I AM WITH YOU ALWAY'
I may not seek Thy face to worship Thee
Within Thy temple-gates, where I would be;
But I may seek it here,
For Thou art here.

I may not see the Table of the Lord,
But still may know the grace it doth afford;
And here remember Thee
For Thou art here.

---

[10] 19 March 1893. Baptist Mission Australia archive, CS Mead Box #4.

> And so, while public worship 'may not' be,
> Thy glory, and Thyself, I still MAY see;
> For Thou, my Lord, art mine,
> And Thou art here.

Later in 1893, Cecil was on his way to India, expressing his excitement as he neared the coast in a letter to a support group in England:[11]

> It was a lovely morning and the coast of India was just in sight as I sat in a corner of the quarterdeck reading Isaiah VI. In my mind I could read verse 1, 'In the year that I came to India, I saw the Lord high and lifted up (over India)' and in v.3 'The whole of India is full of His glory.' That is true, although God is not worshipped, for His glory does fill the whole earth and He is the Ruler here though the land is full of idols. Opposite v.8 'Who will go' there is written in the margin of my Bible 'I will 6.9.92, C.S.M.'[12]

Annotations in the margin of his Bible are characteristic of Cecil, who often viewed the text as a message that spoke directly into his present situation and was heard to say 'My Bible spoke to me'. This use of Scripture sometimes puzzled his hearers:

> 'And when they were come to Gumeracha,[13] they were received of the Church, and they rehearsed all things that God had done with them' (Acts 15.4). One of the Gumeracha lassies wanted to know if missionaries used just the same Bible as other people. Some doubt had arisen in her mind through hearing me read in the service the eleventh chapter of John, substituting the name of India for the name of Lazarus: 'He whom thou lovest (India) is sick'; 'Thy brother (India) shall rise again.' Her doubts were removed, and she was assured that we all had the same Scriptures. ...We told her it was only missionaries who saw missionary meanings and missionary messages in many places in the Bible, as they read with missionary spectacles.[14]

An accomplished musician, Cecil had filled the position of choir leader and organist in his father's church, FSBC, following installation of the pipe organ in 1886.

---

[11] Cecil arrived in India 5 November 1893.
[12] Letters from Dr Cecil Mead 14 November 1893 to 1899, 2, Baptist Mission Australia archive, CS Mead Box #2.
[13] Gumeracha is a town in the Adelaide Hills.
[14] Rev R Taylor, ed. *Salem Messenger*, 1 October 1910. The *Salem Messenger*, published quarterly at Gumeracha (1891-1913).

When Cecil finally arrived in India with his precious violin, his fellow Australians living in the Faridpur house welcomed him enthusiastically with an unplanned 'music festival'. Music remained a memorable feature of occasions involving Cecil, with the newly-published *Baptist Church Hymnal* a quarry of inspiring music.

> Dr. Mead, I remember, particularly in those days, because of his leadership in the music of convention, both in the meetings and in between. It was a sheer delight, and also an education in church music, to gather round the small organ when Dr. Mead played and sang.[15]

Cecil playing home organ in Bengal with family

When Cecil arrived in Pabna in 1893, he lived with Drs Charles and Laura Hope, fellow students from his university days.[16] He revelled in touring local villages, learning as much as he could about the culture. His experiences at that time are graphically described in letters to his English supporters as well as in articles published in the *Our Bond* mission magazine and his 'Journal of a River Trip'.[17]

[15] Rev PC Nall, 'Some Memories of Dr. C.S. Mead', *Our Indian Field,* 6 July, 1940, 8, Baptist Mission Australia archive, CS Mead Box #4.
[16] Laura Hope, née Fowler, was the sister of Cecil's school friend James. The Hopes were independent doctors who chose to work alongside SABMS staff.
[17] Cecil Mead, *Letters to Elsie*. Letters addressed to his cousin Elsie who forwarded them on to supporting churches. Baptist Mission Australia archive, CS Mead Box #2; 'Journal of a River Trip', Baptist Mission Australia archive, CS Mead Box #3.

Faridpur had been supported by the South Australian Baptist Missionary Society (SABMS) since 1865.[18] It had been home base for the first five young women, studying language, well-known as 'The Five Barley Loaves'.[19] What they saw in the secluded women's quarters there convinced them of the appalling need for medical help. One of these, Alice Green Mead (née Pappin) (6 May 1861 – 12 September 1935), not only undertook a three-month midwifery course in Calcutta, but she also regularly offered lessons to low caste children.[20] With her excellent command of the local language, Alice became highly respected in the community, being competent to dispense medicines and assist both patient and doctor with her accurate translations.

Since mission work required mastery of the local language, cross-cultural workers were expected to spend their first two years in the field mastering the language before commencing work. But soon after Cecil's arrival, the Drs Hope were called away unexpectedly and his medical skills were immediately needed to continue the medical service. Cecil was fortunate to have Alice available to assist him. As well as the usual complaints, Cecil found himself dealing with malaria, rife in Bengal at that time, as well as severe skin and eye diseases and the fatal biennial cholera epidemics. With medical services continually in demand, Cecil struggled to understand where his responsibilities lay: providing an essential medical service or preaching Jesus as Lord? 'If we go from Pubna [Pabna] men will go on dying while we are away, without hearing about Jesus.'[21]

Cecil was instructed to go to Faridpur to concentrate on language, but in the absence of suitable accommodation, he was permitted to stay in Pabna but required to limit his medical work. In November 1896, with his language studies completed, Cecil headed for the mission house in Faridpur, his base until 1908.[22]

Cecil and Alice became engaged on 17 October 1894, but mission rules required completion of language studies before marriage. Cecil finished his exams just before

---

18 Rosalind M Gooden, ' "Mothers in the Lord": Australasian women missionaries at the intersection of cultural contexts 1882-1931', (PhD (Theology) thesis, Tabor College of Higher Education, Adelaide, 2016), 61.
19 Tony Cupit, Ros Gooden and Ken Manley, ed., *From Five Barley Loaves* (Preston: Mosaic Press, 2013), xvii.
20 Marjory Mead, *A Daughter of Missionaries Remembers*. Marjory Mead to Mr Lindsay Smith, March 1981, Baptist Mission Australia archive, CS Mead Box #2; Gooden, 'Mothers in the Lord', 170-71, 247-48.
21 Cecil Mead, *Letters to Elsie*, 1894.
22 Arrived Faridpur November 1896.

Silas and William T Whitley arrived from Australia as an official delegation.[23] Silas decided he wanted to witness his son's wedding and Cecil and Alice were married on 24 February 1896 at the American Baptist Mission in Nellore. At the ceremony, Silas offered:

> a prayer that none on earth but he could have offered. It was his son, his only son, whom God had called from his birth, anointed and commissioned and had honoured with great gifts of service. And now with the gift of a gifted and consecrated wife 'to work out a destiny that shall make heaven and earth richer'.[24]

Cecil was not an advocate of translating hymns into local languages. The imagery in hymns from western cultures were often quite foreign to the local culture. The symbolic phrase, 'whiter than the snow,' for example, conveyed nothing to Bengalis, who, with rare exceptions, had never seen snow. Cecil did find one hymn, however, translated by an educated young Hindu convert that captured the spirit of the original beautifully: 'Just as I am, without one plea' became a treasured Bengali Christian hymn.[25]

Cecil fully endorsed the SABMS philosophy that medical work, dispensing and nursing, should always be subsidiary to mission work. He was determined to learn to speak Bengali vernacular competently, but because the locals were hesitant about correcting the 'Sahib's' language for fear of offending him, he constantly found himself making absurd mistakes. The mission was fortunate, therefore, to have an excellent Bengali speaker in Alice. In time, Cecil's language improved and he trained himself to speak in several local dialects.

Having settled down to routine work in public, Cecil was confronted with the fact that seventy-five per cent of the population being Muslim did not speak and could not understand the pure Bengali language he had toiled for two years to learn. School students, lawyers and merchants were mostly Hindus, speaking Bengali. But Cecil quickly recognised his limited ability to communicate with the Muslim village people. He faced the inevitable, and wrote:

---

[23] Silas Mead and WT Whitley, *Our Indian Trip: Notes and Impressions of a Visit to Several Mission Stations from November 1895 to March 1896* (Melbourne: Bible and Tract Repository, 1896), Baptist Mission Australia archive, CS Mead Box #4.

[24] Mead and Whitley, *Our Indian Trip*.

[25] Barry, *There Was a Man*, 127. Composed by Charlotte Elliott (1789-1871), the hymn was published in *The Invalid's Hymn Book* in 1836 and was included in many subsequent Baptist hymnals, e.g. No 442 in *The Baptist Hymn Book with Music* (Psalms and Hymns Trust: London, 1978).

> Now that my two years of preliminary study are over, I am free to throw myself into the work more fully...This year...I address myself to the language of the Mohammedans whose language, especially on religious subjects, varies a great deal from the pure Bengali spoken by Hindus...We preach to the Hindus, 'God is love', and say: 'Iswar prem'. Mohammedans who may be listening are immediately disinterested. 'It is for the Hindus,' they say, until we give utterance to the same glorious little phrase in the Muslim tongue and say: 'Khoda piar'.[26]

In order to hold the interest and understanding of a crowd, a preacher had to explain and alternate between both dialects.[27] Cecil met the challenge, achieving mastery not only of the local Muslim dialect, but also their religious history and traditions.[28] Cecil's approach to Muslims was to inform and enlighten. Cecil was always keen to learn the local way of saying things, he would put up a picture of some spiritual incident and get his servants to sit down on the floor and describe the details of the picture in their own colloquial Bengali. In that way they would get interested and when they heard a sermon preached using their own idioms and expressions, interest became personal as they heard their own words with a big meaning. In contrast with the Islamic idea that God's word was a *book* in only one language for one people, Cecil taught that God spoke in a *person*, his son Jesus Christ. Christ was God in action among men, moving, loving, speaking, doing, and dying and living to reveal himself.

> Doctor Mead's first lesson in nautical phraseology was a "thriller." He was initiated by means of one of his own pictures displayed as the subject of a sermon. One of his boat men surrendered completely to the coloured picture of Christ in a boat with his disciples and the great draught of fish. The vocabulary that Mead got written down from this Mohammedan's vivid and detailed description was his Bengali nautical dictionary for many days. What the unconscious teacher learned was the other side of the story–the *inner side*. His comment was only two words: 'Wonderful man.'[29]

Both as lifelong student and great teacher, Cecil's adaptations of Bible characters to Indian life were always original and arresting. As a linguist in the Bengali language, Dr Mead was the hero of many a missionary. He would gloat over the discovery of

[26] Barry, *There Was a Man,* 71
[27] Barry, *There Was a Man,* 71.
[28] Barry, *There Was a Man,* 71.
[29] Barry, *There Was a Man,* 73-74.

a village idiom as if it were a gold nugget if it fitted to point the Gospel message to the 'common people,' both Hindu and Muslim. In the market place in Faridpur, his pulpit was a glorified soap-box, and it was respected, never removed.[30]

On one occasion, when Cecil and his two Indian preachers had been in conversation for nearly four hours, some of the Muslims in the group hurried off to say their sundown prayer. Having explained the inwardness of religion, Cecil made a suggestion: 'You have heard what we have said about prayer; now listen to our prayers.'

> A hush came over all, and not a sound was heard as Upen Akshoy[31] and I squatting among them simply bowed our heads and each in turn pleaded for the Enlightenment of the village, and especially for those sitting with us,...Our hearts went out in our prayers that night...The quiet continued for some time. No one spoke. The men seemed subdued and astonished to hear us pleading with God for them, and especially in their own mother tongue, instead of an unknown Arabic language. The silence was broken at length by an old man asking: 'Is that prayer?'[32]

Silas corresponded regularly with Cecil, encouraging and organising much needed supplies including cheap copies of Bibles for distribution in the markets. During his visit in 1897, Silas took the opportunity to spend time with Cecil discussing options for the development of the mission:

> Dr. Mead did not go to India as a medical man who happened to be a Christian. He went there as a missionary who happened to be a medical man...Ever ready to use his medical knowledge as a means to an end, the healing of men's bodies was never, for him, the main end he had in view. His medical skill was the door through which he entered seeking men's souls, and often it caused him deep concern lest his missionary activity be swamped by the demands upon his professional services...We called him 'The Doctor' because he had earned the right to that

[30] Rev W Barry, 'The Missionary Passion of Dr Mead', *Our Indian Field*, 6 July 1940, 4, Baptist Mission Australia archive, CS Mead Box #4.
[31] Upen Akshoy [Rev Akshoy K Krista Das] was Cecil's language tutor, colleague and lifelong friend.
[32] Cecil S Mead, *Journal of a River Trip* (Melbourne: Watt & Co. Printers, 1896), 10–11, Baptist Mission Australia archive, CS Mead Box #4. Barry, *There Was a Man*, 74.

title. But it is not as a medical man that he will be treasured in our memories.[33]

Nevertheless, Cecil had the gift of expressing his love of God by way of his medical skills.

As physician and surgeon, Dr. Mead was 'touched with a feeling' that shared the sufferer's suffering. It was a privilege to watch him in his dispensary. His skill and kindness diagnosed so much as he groped patiently among the flood of words, words, words. And it was good and unforgettable to watch him take hold of a half-terrified Mohammedan woman to feel her pulse. His touch seemed to project confidence and calm. And who could forget his prayer as a patient was laid out and ready for a major operation, when the Bengali doctor giving the anaesthetic stood by, and the missionary surgeon said 'Let us pray'?[34]

Because Cecil's medical skills were intrinsic to his service to God, he was heartbroken when things did not go well. In his journal, he records

we had to look up for a little extra supply of Rejoicingness the other day when I had to turn to a boy's father and say, "It is all over". He was the son of one of the leading men of the town. 6 native doctors were in attendance when I first saw him. For 20 days he had been suffering from a very severe attack of tetanus (lock jaw). I consulted with these 6 gentlemen and then dismissed them, undertaking the case alone.[35]

Aware that the eyes of the whole town were on them, Cecil prayed and selected a treatment. The boy began to improve and Cecil was able to discuss faith in Christ with his father. But then:

The 50th day was reached- for 30 days I had visited him three times a day and sat up whole nights nursing him. I was hoping he was practically cured—the wound which I had had to treat so severely was healed. I used to sit on the bed and amuse the

---

[33] Extract from a sermon preached by Rev J Arthur Lewis at the thanksgiving service for the life of the late Dr Cecil Silas Mead, FSBC, 23 June 1940: 'In memory of Dr CS Mead, BA, MB, BS', *The Baptist Record of South Australia* 17:1, 18 July 1940, 1. Baptist Mission Australia archive, CS Mead Box #3.
[34] Barry, 'Missionary Passion', *Our Indian Field*, 6 July 1940, 4.
[35] Cecil Mead, *Letters to Elsie* (Letter II vol III, 14 April 1895), Baptist Mission Australia archive, CS Mead Box #2.

children, who played in their brothers' room, by teaching them English.[36]

Cecil had hoped that a 'triumph of the medical school' in a prominent wealthy home would encourage spread of the gospel. But it was not to be. The boy died in Cecil's arms.

> ...the father's eyes eagerly sought mine. Can I ever forget what they looked; when I laid him gently down and said, "It is all over"? or that awful cry that came from the zenana? We walked home praying in our hearts, but saying little. I wrote only these words to my dearest friend—"He must increase, but I must decrease". My name...was now down in the mud and I thought that His dear name was there too. We thought that for His glory's sake it was necessary that that life should be spared to us. Oh how little we know his plans! and what really is necessary to fill out his purposes.[37]

Cecil's daughter Marjory recorded some vivid glimpses of her early life in Orakandi where the Dr. Sahib's preaching box was a fixture in the local bazaar:

> Preaching, it was Dad's passion, almost his life, anywhere, anytime, to anyone. He had soaked himself in Hindu and Mahommedan [sic] lore, so was ready with the appropriate words to a cultured gentleman, a crowd of students, an argumentative priest or a wayside contact. On river steamers, on trains, in bazaars, once a month to a group of Anglican English folk at Goalundo, as well as to his church members, he would pour out his soul if haply 'the seed might fall on good ground'.[38]

> He had a free railway pass and would join a train anywhere, preaching in a crowded carriage as far as the next station, then do the same on a returning train. It was exhausting, almost terrible work, but he exulted in it.[39]

Before their furlough in 1910, the big decision was made to move to Orakandi. Some Nama Sudras had sent a deputation to the Faridpur mission house with a document.[40]

---

[36] Cecil Mead, *Letters to Elsie* (14 April 1895), 2.
[37] Cecil Mead, Letters to Elsie, 2.
[38] Marjory Mead, *A Daughter Remembers*.
[39] Marjory Mead, *A Daughter Remembers*.
[40] The Nama Sudras lived outside the four-tier ritual caste system and were viewed as outcasts.

> We come as representatives of a great, sad class—hated, despised, downtrodden, treated for centuries like dogs. We have at last wakened to the fact that we too are men; that same great God who made the proud Brahmin, made us too, and now we have it in our hearts to rise to a better and bigger life. Will you help us?[41]

Cecil was deeply moved by their pleas. They had been praying about the work and asking God to show them to what extent their strength and time should go to the rich and educated — and how much should be given to the illiterate and poor villagers. For Cecil this was a 'Macedonian call'.[42] Home on furlough, Cecil's enthusiasm for work with the Nama Sudras convinced Australian Baptists that it was time to redirect their mission activities.

Moving from Faridpur was a major venture and entailed a heavy sacrifice, both for himself and the members of his family, because the hot humid atmosphere of Orakandi aggravated Cecil's chronic asthma.

> But they said good-bye to the comfortable mission house and much-loved dispensary, and joined the station at Orakandi serving the needy, low-caste Nama Sudras who lived in the low-lying flood country. The Nama Sudras were not aware of any spiritual need; they were clamouring for education and a better social life. The village leaders were eager for their local school to be raised to High School standard, and Cecil helped them. Many of his students became village leaders and some who followed Christ came to serve their people as teachers and preachers.[43]

Cecil was in India when it was part of the British empire, indeed 'the jewel in the crown'. He was able to bring pressing issues to the attention of the authorities. When the early missionaries landed in India, it was natural for them to meet the keen, intellectual and influential high caste men and they believed that the way to win India for Christ would be by winning the higher caste men. They argued that these educated men would make 'Apostles and Evangelists by whose ministry the Church

---

[41] CS Mead, *The Nama Sudras and other Addresses* (South Australian Baptist Furreedpore Mission Inc. Adelaide: Hussey & Gillingham, 1911), 7, Baptist Mission Australia archive, CS Mead Box #4.

[42] A reference to Paul's vision of a man of Macedonia pleading with him, saying, 'Come over to Macedonia and help us.' (Acts 16:9 NRSV).

[43] Arrived Orakandi 9 January 1911. C Williams, 'Orakandi–A Living Monument', *Our Indian Field* (6 July 1940): 11.

will be gathered and built up'.[44] Directing efforts to men who could understand was their inspiring vision for many years. They held lectures, they preached in temples, at festivals and in halls. They concentrated on the colleges and high schools, gathering high-class youths, and instructing them daily in the Scriptures. They laboured to win the high castes for Christ. But it was

> like knocking at a fast-closed door. Some few converts have been won, some splendid men who have given up all and have shown what Christ's power can do. But they have been like a few stones dug out of a thick solid wall of a fortress which is still left standing, great and grim, and with scarcely a flaw.
>
> The education given in our mission colleges has proved to the high castes that Christianity cannot be despised, and that it teaches a morality superior to anything they know. Christianity, by this means, has helped to create a new moral tone throughout India, nevertheless the high castes do not receive it. It was a great and splendid conception to seek India's conversion through the intellectual high caste men…BUT it does not seem to be 'God's way for India'.[45]

Cecil's 'Macedonian call' led him to believe that God's way for India was by working with the lower castes, a radical shift in mission thinking at the time. The term Nama Sudra was a derogatory one in the Hindu community. Nama Sudras lived outside the four-tier ritual caste system and were traditionally engaged in cultivation and as boatmen. Yet it was to work with the Nama Sudras that the family undertook the upheaval of moving from Pabna to Orakandi, from the known to the unknown.

On one occasion as guest of the Commissioner of the District at an official dinner, Cecil even had the opportunity to raise the issue of Nama Sudras in Orakandi. The 'irrepressible Doctor and the representative of the Government sat together on a table, swinging their legs and talking about the destiny of the depressed classes from the mission-angle'.[46] The British–Indian Government officially recognised Dr Cecil S Mead's service to the Nama Sudras by awarding him the Kaisar-i-Hind Medal for

[44] CS Mead, *The Nama Sudras*, 28.
[45] CS Mead, *The Nama Sudras*, 28.
[46] Barry, 'Missionary Passion', 12.

Public Service to India.[47] Embarrassed by ceremony and officialdom, he took off his clerical collar as soon as he got out of the gate.[48] His service was neither for the government of India nor even the people, but 'for the Master I serve'.

After the move to Orakandi, Cecil's daughters enjoyed coming home in the holidays to see the building programme progress and watch 'the mission islands' grow. All the homes were on artificial islands, laboriously built up with earth cut from the fields. The Silas Mead Memorial House, Zenana House, Health Welfare Centre and the House of Light for widows were established.[49] Alice chivvied the workmen along, patient, joking, wheedling, thus taking the burden off Cecil's shoulders, leaving him more time for medical work and Bible classes. In the holidays, Marjory's pre-breakfast job was as personal assistant to her father:

> Pink Mahommedan and blue Hindu papers on the Dr.'s table—one side for medical notes, the other with simple Christian teaching. Maybe somebody in the family could read! Patients, mostly men, numbered from one to three hundred daily (The record? 935!) Each carried a bottle for every sick family member, could be six or more. Prescriptions cost a penny. Mother would help to dispense and it was my special holiday highlight to be there too....'But, Sahib, that one is my wife's, not my aunt's'. 'No, it is for your wife; she must take it twice in the day and once at night'. Strange words! Why not all at once? Did he say TWICE in the night?'[50]

Cecil thoroughly enjoyed teaching English Bible lessons and several senior pupils 'witnessed a good confession'. Many widows were baptised and the little flock grew. The first bungalow became the church. Land was raised ready for the real church building although Cecil never saw it. His health finally failed after twenty-eight years of overwork, strain, passionate self-giving and asthma. 'How many pillows tonight? Seven? That meant sitting up, little sleep.'[51] Only Alice's unflagging care kept him going.

---

[47] Barry, *There Was a Man*, 144. The Kaisar-i-Hind Medal for Public Service in India was a medal awarded by the Emperor/Empress of India between 1900 and 1947, to 'any person without distinction of race, occupation, position, or sex...who shall have distinguished himself (or herself) by important and useful service in the advancement of the public interest in India'. London Gazette, 11 May 1900, 2996. https://www.thegazette.co.uk/London/issue/27191/page/2996.
[48] Cecil possessed no clerical collar so Alice had created one for the occasion.
[49] C Williams, 'Orakandi—A Living Monument', *Our Indian Field*, 6 July 1940, 11.
[50] Marjory Mead, *A Daughter Remembers*.
[51] Marjory Mead, *A Daughter Remembers*.

Marjory recalled life with her father in Orakandi with pleasure:

> How did he find time to play with us? But he did, and to keep
> up medical and theological reading, to cope with endless
> land troubles and job-seekers, accounts and correspondence,
> Convention Bible studies, sermons and white-hot missionary
> articles? But he did, 'the Lord working with him.'[52]

Cecil and Alice Mead with Dorothy and baby Marjory

Cecil was optimistic that a Christian movement would start to spread across India, but India was changing with the social reforms following the Bengali Renaissance. As soon as the people found that the mission would not provide free support for any converts or give free education, interest began to wane.[53]

Marjory recalls that family life invariably began with Scripture reading and prayer, later published in a booklet.[54]

> Habakkuk 3:17. 'Though the fig-tree shall not blossom, neither
> shall fruit be in the vines...yet I will rejoice in the Lord.'
>
> Prepare us, Lord, for the loss of things and for the passing away
> of the companionships Thou hast granted for us for happy years
> to be the strength of our life. Though, in the days to come, we

[52] Marjory Mead, *A Daughter Remembers*.
[53] Gerald B Ball, 'India–Bengali Disappointments', in Cupit, Gooden and Manley (eds), *From Five Barley Loaves*, 49-61.
[54] CS Mead, 'LORD, TODAY: Family Prayers of Dr Cecil Silas Mead', Baptist Mission Australia archive, CS Mead Box #2.

look into the trees, and find no fruit of the old time comfort, YET let us not fail Thee, as Thou wilt not fail us.[55]

Close colleagues also remembered Cecil as a man of prayer:

The most precious memory I have of Dr. Mead is of him as a man of prayer. ...In the days of his virility, in his long bouts of sickness, before the house servants, in his interviewing of government officials, preaching on the roadside and in the market-places, or in teaching the little flocks of converts in Faridpur and Orakandi, he was eminently a man called by God.[56]

Rev Percy C Nall, who worked with Cecil for over thirty years, first met Cecil at an Australian and New Zealand Baptist missionary convention, in Faridpur, 1897.

Some thought Dr. Mead to be austere. Not so some of us, who knew him intimately. One of our ladies used to call him 'Two-Strokes' because of the decisive way he had of making his opinion known. Yet he was most thoughtful and kind. When my wife was attacked by fever in far-away Birisiri, I wrote to him for advice, not thinking that he himself would come along. The ordinary three-day journey he did in two days, having walked eleven miles along the sandy bank of a river in order to make an earlier steamer connection, and that with his asthma. How welcome he was in our stricken home. He examined the patient, then had an interview with the local Bengali doctor who had been treating Mrs. Nall. [57]

Then Dr. Mead said to me: 'He has something in the bottle for this and that, something else for something else, but not a drop to cure your wife's fever. If such treatment had been continued for a few more days, [she] would have died.' Then he took the bottle and poured the medicine out of the window. By his own injections of quinine he soon broke the fever and the patient recovered. His skill as a medical man he did not lose; but he esteemed his missionary calling before his medical one.[58]

---

[55] Mead, 'LORD, TODAY', 3.
[56] PC Nall, 'Some Memories of Dr C. S. Mead', *Our Indian Field*, July 1940, 8.
[57] Nall, 'Memories', *Our Indian Field*, July 1940, 8.
[58] Nall, 'Memories', *Our Indian Field*, July 1940, 8.

Cecil's constant motto was 'My work to learn – live – give Christ'. His work among the low caste Hindus in the southern swamps at Orakandi is mission history; his breakdown in health and subsequent retirement to Adelaide in 1922 was a regret to all on the field.

After a period of rest and skilful treatment, Cecil was strong enough to accept a position at Adelaide University as Demonstrator in Anatomy in 1923, and later as Lecturer in Anatomy, a position he filled with distinction. Not content with studying the best English texts he also read German works and persuaded his devoted daughters to read French textbooks. He retired in 1938.

> On my last visit to him we had our usual intimate talk on affairs, both at home and on the field. Some-thing I said about an old war-horse desiring to be in the battle led him to remark on his work as tutor in Anatomy in Adelaide University. He wanted to be preaching the Gospel, but instead, as he put it, had to spend his time 'teaching youngsters *bones*!'[59]

One of Silas's visions had been to amalgamate all the Australian Baptist missions, an idea which was generally greeted without much enthusiasm at the time. Cecil, with experience of actually working in the field, strongly supported this concept and it was gradually accepted. In 1913, the missionary societies of the six Australian states merged into 'The Australian Baptist Foreign Mission Incorporated', later the Australian Baptist Missionary Society, then Global Interaction until 2021, and from 2022 Baptist Mission Australia.

Cecil was not only convinced of the importance of cross-cultural work spreading the gospel, he was well aware of the urgent need for support from the Australian churches. When home on furlough he spent the time enthusiastically visiting churches, speaking with young people and created a sensation at an annual meeting of the Baptist Union with his 'surgeon's probe to the core of the cause of all the faintheartedness in and paucity of funds for mission activity'.[60] Age did not diminish Cecil's passion for mission. His news bulletins to the Foreign Missionary Department were thrilling to listen to: 'He has left behind…a memory that will be treasured…but more than a memory—a challenge and an inspiration.'[61]

---

[59] Nall, 'Memories', *Our Indian Field*, July 1940, 8.
[60] Barry, *There Was a Man*, 116.
[61] J Arthur Lewis, 'Dr Mead as Flinders Street Church knew Him', *Our Indian Field*, 6 July 1894, 9.

Dr Cecil S Mead, c.1929

In his last nineteen years, Cecil conducted a rich ministry of the pen, writing hundreds of letters, birthday cheer and appreciation for the talents and efforts of others. His aim was encouragement to all in service for the Master with a special word to those who in fearful nervousness had undertaken a task for which they felt inadequate. 'A kind hand on the shoulder…helped the beginner to return and try again. He was Big Brother to his fellow ministers, to whom he lent books, wise counsellor to all…a good friend especially to lonely souls.'[62]

[62] Special Minute of the Foreign Mission Department, FSBC, *The Baptist Record of South Australia*, 18 July 1940, 8.

Gertrude: 'Beloved Physician'

Stefanie C Pearce

In a suburb of the Australian capital, Canberra, is a street named Mead Street. It is not named after Silas Mead despite his pioneering contribution to the Australian Baptist denomination. Neither is it named after Silas's great medical missionary son, Dr Cecil Mead. In fact, Canberra bears no streets named after them (as yet). The roads in the suburb of Chisholm, Australian Capital Territory, are named to commemorate 'notable women' of Australia, and Mead Street in Chisholm is named after Dr Gertrude Ella Mead, Silas's third child, in recognition of her outstanding contribution to Australia.

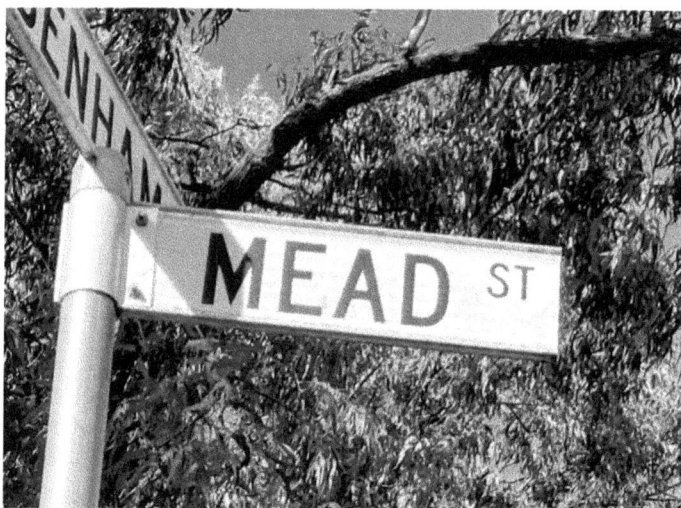

Mead Street, Canberra

Birth and early years: 1867–1901

Gertrude's story begins in Adelaide where, on New Year's Eve 1867, Ann Mead gave birth to her third child and second daughter, whom she and Silas called Gertrude Ella. They already had two children, Lilian, two and half years old, and Cecil, a toddler of 14 months.[1] Ann herself, now 28, had lived in Adelaide for three years having arrived to marry Silas, now 33.[2] Ann's sister Sarah had recently joined them when she married Frank Hann at FSBC.[3]

It would appear that Gertrude's early life was stable and supportive. Her father was a busy and successful minister at FSBC although his many activities frequently kept him from home attending meetings and visiting outlying new churches and rural communities. Her mother Ann is described as 'ever ready with a kind look, a cheering word, or a helping hand' including in 'the sacred relations of the home' and, although 'naturally diffident and retiring', Ann's 'self-sacrificing disposition, patience, faith and perseverance' contributed to a stable home life and empowered Silas in his work.[4]

A week after Gertrude's second birthday, the family welcomed another baby girl, always known as Blanche, to whom Gertrude would become very close.[5] Less than two years later, shortly before Gertrude turned four, John Angel was born but died the same day (12 October 1871). Gertrude's youngest sister, Flora, was born three weeks after Gertrude's fifth birthday.[6]

Tragedy struck the young family when Gertrude was six years old. Her mother Ann caught typhoid and died on 15 June 1874. The four older children (Lilian, Cecil, Gertrude and Blanche) attended the funeral and burial, accompanied by their father, aunt Sarah (Ann's sister), uncle Frank, and a large crowd of church friends and associates.[7] For the six-year-old Gertrude, this must have been a drawn-out and traumatic event.

---

[1] Lilian Staple (30 June 1865 – 27 November 1936); Cecil Silas (18 October 1866 – 17 June 1940)
[2] *Truth and Progress* (*TP*), June 1874, 76–79.
[3] Sarah Staple arrived on *The City of Adelaide*, 11 October 1866 ('Shipping News', *The Adelaide Express*, 12 October 1866, 2). Wedding Notice: 'Hann–Staple–On 15th November [1866], at Flinders Street Baptist Chapel by the Rev S Mead, AM LLB, Mr Frank Hann, to Miss Sarah Staple, late of East Stoke, Somersetshire, England'. In 'Family Notices', *Register*, 16 November 1866, 2.
[4] *Evening Journal* (Adelaide, SA: 1869-1912) (*EJ*), 18 June 1874, 2.
[5] Annie Blanche (8 January 1870 – 29 June 1961)
[6] Flora Beatrice (20 January 1873 – 9 September 1886)
[7] *EJ*, 18 June 1874, 2.

Gertrude Ella Mead as a small child

Silas and Ann had been planning a lengthy trip to England, to begin in December 1874. Now the church assisted Silas to bring forward these plans, and Silas left for prolonged recuperative travel on 16 July 1874. His five young children were left behind in the care of their aunt Sarah and uncle Frank Hann. The children would not see their father again for sixteen months, when he finally returned in November the following year (1875).[8] The bereaved family were a tight-knit, interdependent and mutually supportive unit who remained close to each other throughout their lives.

In 1878, the widow Mrs Mary Leighton arrived in the colony to care for her aunt and uncle. She attended FSBC, was baptised by Silas Mead, and the two became friends. They were married on 22 October 1878, when Gertrude was ten years old.[9] Her step-mother seems to have been capable:

> [The new] Mrs Mead at once entered upon a very busy life, both in presiding over the household, and in the various relations which a pastor's wife is expected to sustain...The manse at Flinders Street has always been the scene of warm and extensive hospitality. [Many visitors] experienced the kindness and care of

---

[8] For a full discussion on Silas Mead's journey, see Chapter 4 elsewhere in this volume
[9] 'In Memoriam: The Late Mrs Mead', *TP*, 1 April 1886, 50.

> Mrs Mead's hospitable services...[and were] cordially welcomed and unostentatiously entertained.[10]

However, sadly, twelve months later, Mary Mead suffered a stroke, which left her partially disabled on one side. Again, increased responsibilities would have naturally devolved to the older girls.

Towards the end of 1880, FSBC and the South Australian Baptist ministers hosted the visit of 'a kind of City Missionary', Emilia Baeyertz.[11] During her three-week campaign, Mrs Baeyertz achieved 'over a hundred' conversions, particularly among young teenage girls.[12] Lilian (then 14) and Gertrude (12, almost 13) together with Cecil (13) certainly attended one or more of the dynamic and moving presentations as the opening and closing services of the campaign were held at FSBC.[13] A further campaign the following year was similarly successful in encouraging commitments, and December alone saw thirty-eight baptisms 'as the direct fruits of Mrs Bayertz' ministry among us'. 'Two of these were daughters of the pastor': Gertrude and her younger sister Blanche were baptised by immersion on 4 December 1881 by their father.[14]

In her final address before leaving, two days before the baptism service, Mrs Baeyertz addressed the young people:

> Some of you are going to be baptised on Sunday. And oh, I've been praying so today that all of you who are going down into the water, may be consecrated to God...I pray that every dear one who is baptized, may be able to say—'Lord, I am consecrated to thee; from this time forward I cut myself adrift from everything that is not of Christ.'...And I say to you young converts now listening to me, do not notice what others may be doing; take Christ as your example.[15]

---

[10] 'In Memoriam: The Late Mrs Mead', *TP*, 1 April 1886, 51. The youngest daughter, Flora, noted that 'there is one thing I sometimes long for and that is a mother' (*TP*, 1 October 1886, 147), suggesting that the second Mrs Mead did not succeed as a mother figure.

[11] 'Letter to Mrs Baeyertz from Committee', and 'Mrs Baeyertz in Adelaide', *TP*, 1 January 1881, 8. See chapter 5 for discussion on Emilia Baeyertz's visits to SA. Walker, JS, 'The Baptists in South Australia, 1863 to 1914', BTh thesis, Flinders University, 1990; 'Baeyertz, Emilia Louise', Brian Dickey, *Australian Dictionary of Evangelical Biography* (Sydney: Evangelical History Association), 1994.

[12] 'Mrs Baeyertz in Adelaide—Farewell Meeting', *TP*, 1 January 1881, 8.

[13] 'Mrs Baeyertz in Adelaide—Farewell Meeting', *TP*, 1 January 1881, 8.

[14] 'Denominational News—Flinders-Street', *TP*, 1 January 1882, 4; 'Dr Gertrude Mead', *AB*, 25 November 1919, 5.

[15] 'Mrs Baeyertz's Final Meeting for Converts at Flinders Street', *TP*, 1 January 1882, 2-4, 4.

Whether these specific exhortations were taken to heart by Gertrude is not known; however, her subsequent life and work demonstrate that she did indeed consecrate her life to God. Many years later she was described as evincing 'the deepest devotion to the Master whom she loved and served. She realised that the external life of power must rest on the hidden life of devotion to her Lord and Master.'[16] She began a lifelong habit of donating to Baptist association funds and other causes.[17] As a mature woman of independent means, she said 'I do not want a large practice, just enough for a living. I want time to help others.'[18] Gertrude trod the difficult path of a pioneering professional woman and was often confronted by criticism and opposition; however, she demonstrated a determination and single-minded focus on fulfilling her calling.

While exploring her spiritual nature, Gertrude was also extending her intellectual horizons, attending, with Lilian, the newly opened Advanced School for Girls in Franklin Street.[19] The first intake of students was in late 1879, when Gertrude was eleven and her elder sister Lilian was thirteen. Although this coincided with their stepmother Mary's illness, they attended Advanced School from the earliest opportunity. The Advanced School was overtly aimed at a more academic education for young women, offering the potential for matriculation to university. It contrasted with a traditional model of training girls in 'accomplishments', such as art, languages, and music.[20] This was consistent with her family's views on advancing women.[21] Gertrude excelled at study, and in December 1881, Gertrude passed the 'Primary Examination' as a student of Advanced School, with extra subjects in Physical Geography, and cred-

---

[16] 'The Late Dr Gertrude Mead', *Western Mail*, 8 June 1922, 22. http://nla.gov.au/nla.news-article4169262.

[17] *Truth and Progress* began listing Gertrude as a donor to Baptist causes from 1884 until well after she left Adelaide.

[18] 'Dr Gertrude Mead: Beloved Physician', *AB*, 25 November 1919, 5.

[19] The Advanced School for Girls was the first State school in SA and was designed to prepare girls for entry to the University of Adelaide. It opened in October 1879 with thirty students aged around 12 years and above (Alison Mackinnon, *One Foot on the Ladder: Origins and outcomes of girls' secondary schooling in South Australia.* (St Lucia: University of Queensland Press, 1984), 56). Its outstanding results quickly made it a very popular choice with more than 100 students ('Advanced School for Girls', *Register*, 27 April 1882, 4. http://nla.gov.au/nla.news-article47109173). The School merged with the Adelaide High School in 1907. See also Alison Mackinnon, 'Advanced School for Girls', in *Worth Her Salt: Women at Work in Australia*, ed. M Bevege, M James and C Shute (Sydney: Hale & Ironmonger, 1982), 62-71.

[20] Mackinnon, *One Foot on the Ladder*, 60.

[21] Alison Mackinnon, *The New Women: Adelaide's early women graduates* (Netley, SA: Wakefield Press, 1986), 21; and see discussion of Lilian Mead's pamphlet on 'The Awakened Woman', chapter 12.

its in French and English.[22] Six months later, Gertrude was admitted 'as a student of the University' by special dispensation of the Vice-Chancellor because she was 'under sixteen years of age'.[23] She vindicated this decision by winning equal first prize of £20 in an Education Department Exhibition in December 1883 as a student of Advanced School,[24] and matriculating twice: in December 1884 as Class 2,[25] and in March 1885 coming third in the State in Class 1.[26] She also won first prize of thirty shillings in the South Australian Sunday School Union Senior Division in 1884.[27] She and her sister Lilian were also active members of a girls' Literary Society, which met weekly to present and discuss essays they had each written.[28]

Blanche and Flora with Gertrude (seated on right)

[22] *Express and Telegraph* (Adelaide), 15 December 1881, 3. http://nla.gov.au/nla.news-article208198201

[23] 'The University of Adelaide', *Register*, 29 May 1882, 6. http://nla.gov.au/nla.news-article47102026.

[24] *Register*, 27 December 1883, 4ff. http://nla.gov.au/nla.news-article43609499.

[25] Gertrude matriculated equal first place in Second Class, with German, English (credit), Animal Physiology (credit) and Botany. 'Matriculation Examination', *Register*, 13 December 1884, 7. http://nla.gov.au/nla.news-article43807347.

[26] Gertrude passed the March Matriculation examinations in third place of First Class, with German, English, Animal Physiology (credit) and Botany (credit). 'Educational', *Register*, 28 March 1885, 2. http://nla.gov.au/nla.news-article44550192. 'The compulsory subjects...were English, Arithmetic, Geography, Mathematics, Latin, except in the case of female students who might substitute French [as Gertrude did]. The Optional Subjects in which she passed were German, English, Physiology, Botany and she got a credit in Physiology and Botany.' (Letter from Silas Mead, Flinders Street Adelaide, to The University Education Committee, dated 2 December 1891. Gooden/Mead collection.)

[27] 'General News', *ET*, 11 September 1884, 2. http://nla.gov.au/nla.news-article208281945.

[28] Mackinnon, *The New Women*, 47.

Changes and challenges 1886–1901

Perhaps as a reward for this scholastic achievement, Lilian (20) and Gertrude (18) left Adelaide together on 12 February 1886 for a visit to England. They were to broaden their horizons and visit relatives in England. At the time of their departure, their stepmother, Mary Mead, was already in deteriorating health, and five weeks later, Mary died at the manse on 21 March 1886. The black-lined letter that carried this news was not the last that the girls would open while they were away.

Tragically, within days of the church's 25th Anniversary on the first weekend of August, all three Mead children at home were seriously ill with typhoid fever. The youngest sibling, Flora, died on 9 September. Silas wrote to Lilian and Gertrude in England to convey the sad news.[29]

Lilian and Gertrude returned to Adelaide the following year, and it was Gertrude's turn to battle with typhoid. For five weeks she was desperately ill, so 'that life appears as though it would ebb away'.[30] She recovered, but remained frail throughout her life. She herself believed she 'suffered from mitral [valve] disease [but was] very philosophical about it'.[31]

Perhaps inspired by her family's experiences of ill health and wishing to be useful, Gertrude began nursing at the Adelaide Children's Hospital.[32] She and her sisters were also called on to continue supporting their widowed father in providing manse hospitality: 'thanks was accorded to the reverend host [Silas], who generously passed it on to his daughters who he said had most to do in preparing the repast.'[33]

---

[29] See chapter 15 for more on the brief life of Flora Mead.
[30] 'News and Notes: That Scourge of Australia', *TP*, 1 May 1889, 69.
[31] Prue Joske, 'Mead, Gertrude Ella (1867–1919)', *Australian Dictionary of Biography*, National Centre of Biography, Australian National University. https://adb.anu.edu.au/biography/mead-gertrude-ella-7544/text13161, published first in hardcopy 1986. Cardiac involvement in typhoid is well documented; see LM Baddour, WR Wilson et al, 'Infective Endocarditis in Adults: Diagnosis, Antimicrobial Therapy, and Management of Complications: A Scientific Statement for Healthcare Professionals from the American Heart Association', *Circulation*. 132:15 (13 Oct 2015), 1435–86.
[32] Gavan J. McCarthy, 'Mead, Gertrude Ella (1867–1919)', in *Where are the Women in Australian Science?*, ed. G McCarthy, H Morgan, A Smith, A van den Bosch (Canberra: Australian Science and Technology Heritage Centre, 2003): http://www.austehc.unimelb.edu.au/wisa/wisa.html.
[33] 'Luncheon at Mr Mead's', *TP*, November 1890, 180.

Gertrude Ella Mead, c1889

After a couple of years of nursing, Gertrude had won the support of her father to attempt to study medicine and qualify as a doctor, just as her brother Cecil had done. Silas wrote to the Education Committee of the University of Adelaide on 2 December 1891:

> I am desirous that my daughter Gertrude E. Mead should in the term commencing with March 1892 enter as a Student on the Medical Course. She passed First Class in the Matriculation Exam. in March 1885...I write to ask whether the fact of her having passed the Matriculation Exam. First Class according to the Regulations then in force does not entitle her to enter now as a Medical Student. If this be impracticable, can she be allowed to enter as a Medical Student in March next and present herself for Examination in Latin at the Senior Public in December 1892? I am anxious that she should not lose another year before beginning her medical course. Hoping you will be able to accept my daughter as a Medical Student for the March Term.[34]

---

[34] Letter from Silas Mead, Flinders Street Adelaide, to The University Education Committee, 2 December 1891. Gooden/Mead collection.

In March 1892, Gertrude passed the requisite Latin at a Special Senior Public Examination, with private tuition.[35] Despite this and Silas's entreaty, Gertrude was not permitted to begin studying for the Bachelor of Medicine until 1893; she then came second in her first-year class of nine students.[36] Second and third years were challenging, then in fourth and fifth years, Gertrude and her two fellow female medical students—Violet Plummer[37] and Christina Goode[38]—were inadvertently embroiled in the prolonged controversy that became known as the 'Hospital Row'. Gertrude led the response of the female students on the propriety of their conduct, writing letters to the editors of the major newspapers:

> Sir---In reference to the statements made at the meeting of the Board of the Adelaide Hospital, we the undersigned women students wish to state that we have on no occasion examined any patient after 5 p.m. There are no women students beside ourselves working in the Hospital. We are, Sir, etc.., Gertrude E. Mead / Violet M. Plummer / Christina L. Goode[39]

Simultaneously, Silas had come to the realisation that it was time to retire from the pulpit at FSBC, which he had established and held for thirty-five years. He and Lilian decided to travel to England, Silas 'convinced of a call to new and larger service'.[40] They left on 13 January 1897, and almost simultaneously Gertrude and her cohort of senior Adelaide medical students departed for Melbourne to complete their

[35] 'The University of Adelaide', *EJ*, 16 March 1892, 4. http://nla.news-article204474157.
[36] 'Ordinary Examination for the Degrees of M.B. and Ch.B., November 1893', *Register*, 5 December 1893, 5.
[37] Violet May Plummer (1873-1962) became known as Adelaide's 'pioneer woman doctor, the first woman to practise medicine in Adelaide'. She retired in 1929. *Register News-Pictorial* (Adelaide), 31 August 1929, 26.
[38] Christina Love Goode (1874–1951) married Dr Alexander Krakowsky in 1914 in the United Kingdom. 'Marriages', *Advertiser*, 10 December 1914, 6.
[39] 'The Hospital Students and the Board', *EJ*, 19 October 1896, 2. Also in *Register*, 19 October, and *Advertiser*, 20 October 1896.
[40] 'Notes and Comments', *SB*, 14 January 1897, 1.

degrees.[41] Cecil was in Bengal; and Blanche had just married Rev. Alfred S. Wilson, and arrived at his new ministry at Perth Baptist Church, Western Australia. Gertrude completed all the requirements for her degrees of M.B. and B.S. at the December examination at Melbourne University, and had her degrees conferred at last on 23 December 1897. 'Dr G.E. Mead' set sail the following day for a four-month break in Perth to catch up with her sister Blanche and brother-in-law Alfred Wilson, then London.[42]

Gertrude at graduation, 1897

[41] The protracted 'Hospital Row' began in earnest in 1896 and was not resolved until 1901. Due to staffing disputes between the Medical School and the Hospital, the senior medical students were unable to attend lectures at Adelaide Hospital. They therefore opted en masse to complete their degrees at Melbourne or Sydney universities. The Melbourne University Dean of Medicine negotiated their transference. Gertrude in her fifth and final year, Violet Plummer (5th year) and Christina Goode (4th year) moved to Trinity College, Melbourne, as part of a contingent of 16 Adelaide students. Others moved to Sydney. Rebecca Martin, 'Adelaide Medical School: 1885-1919', Adelaide Connect. (2020) https://connect.adelaide.edu.au/nodes/view/7390; 'The Departure of Medical Students', Register, 1 February 1897, 4. http://nla.gov.au/nla.news-article54483262; 'Adelaide Medical Students in Melbourne', Register, 5 February 1897, 7. http://nla.gov.au/nla.news-article54475614; The Age (Melbourne), 25 December 1897, 8. http://nla.gov.au/nla.news-article188148868; Donald Simpson, 'The Adelaide Medical School 1885-1914: A study of Anglo-Australian synergies in medical education' (MD thesis, University of Adelaide, 2000), 147, 177.
[42] 'News and Notes', West, 30 December 1897, 4; SB, 17 February 1898, 1.

Gertrude left Perth on RMS *Rome* for London in mid-May 1898, planning to spend time with her father at Harley College, and to seek 'special London experience with children's complaints', before returning to Australia to practise medicine.[43] She worked first at Belgrave Hospital, London,[44] then took up a six-month *locum tenens* as 'one of the six house surgeons—three of them men and three women—at Leith Hospital, Scotland',[45] and later at Dublin Hospital.[46] Gertrude's eldest sister Lilian, living with their father at Harley College, became engaged to Charles Crosbie Brown at Harley, and Gertrude was able to attend their wedding and be a bridesmaid to her sister.

As Silas's health began to falter with recurring asthma, he and Gertrude planned to return to the sunnier and healthier climes of Western Australia, where Blanche now lived. By June 1901 it was arranged that Silas would quit Harley College on 30 June and he and Gertrude would sail for Perth on 26 July, while Blanche and Alfred Wilson left Perth for UK on 13 June as delegates to the Baptist Union meetings. Silas would supply the pulpit for Alfred Wilson in his absence.[47]

Professional life 1901–1919

Arriving in Perth on 27 August 1901, Gertrude promptly registered to practise 'as a duly qualified medical practitioner'. By November she could advertise that she was consulting in Queen's Hall Building, William Street, and at Museum Street.[48] Thus at the age of 33, Gertrude was an independent professional woman with the ex-

[43] 'News and Notes', *West*, 16 May 1898, 4. http://nla.gov.au/nla.news-article3221375. Also on board the *Rome* to England was fellow Baptist medical doctor Charles North of New Zealand, 'his ultimate destination being the Foreign Mission field'. 'Notes and Comments', *SB*, 2 June 1898, 1.
[44] 'News and Notes', *West*, 18 January 1900, 4. http://nla.gov.au/nla.news-article3242609.
[45] 'Personal', *EJ*, 21 August 1900, 2; 'Personal Notes from England', *Register*, 9 April 1901, 5. http://nla.gov.au/nla.news-article56075394.
[46] 'Baptist: Rev. Silas Mead', *WM*, 31 August 1901, 66. http://nla.gov.au/nla.news-article33214109. Previous female medical graduates from Adelaide had also worked at these hospitals, which were open to female doctors and offered more obstetric and paediatric experience than was possible in the Australian medical scene. Simpson, 'The Adelaide Medical School 1885-1914'.
[47] 'Personal', *Advertiser*, 1 June 1901, 7. http://nla.gov.au/nla.news-article4841492.
[48] A series of advertisements over three months, such as in *West*, 22 November 1901, 8. http://nla.gov.au/nla.news-article24763840. The Museum street consulting room was the PBC manse, 'Lyndhurst', opposite the church, where Silas and Gertrude took up residence, later joined by Blanche and Alfred Wilson, the minister, when they returned.

perience and skills to offer substantial service to others. She was the third 'lady doctor' in Perth and the first unmarried.[49]

She had discerned her calling to specialise in health work for children and women. She had learned to combat prejudice and discriminatory policies with factual information and firm resolve. She had worked alongside capable female medical practitioners in the UK. As her father's daughter, she had the moral courage of her convictions on the rights of women to work equally with men, and for better healthcare, welfare and support for women and children. Her early experiences at Adelaide Medical School and overseas had given her self-confidence and assurance, self-discipline and an extraordinary work ethic. She had learned the value of female networks. Often described as physically frail and petite, she 'did not know her own energy and worked far too hard' with a characteristic thoroughness. Her intellect was keen, her sympathies broad, and her soul generous.[50]

From Silas she had learned how to organise: throughout his ministry Silas gathered together groups of people, inspired them with a need, and encouraged the group to act collaboratively. He saw that a committee or group had inherent sustainability, better ideas, wider access to resources, and higher reach for influence than acting alone. Within the Baptist church sphere in Adelaide, Silas had set up associations and organisations, repeatedly seeding churches and groups, then uniting them into mutually supportive associations. Now, in a new city, knowing few people, Gertrude quietly began to develop her own networks and to uncover the needs of the city and where she could best contribute her support.

Silas was enthusiastically adopted by Perth Baptist Church as honorary co-pastor to his son-in-law Alfred Wilson, and likewise Gertrude was admitted into membership on 2 January 1902.[51] Both Silas and Gertrude lived in the manse with Blanche and Alfred and their young son, Colin.[52] There must have been many benefits of this household arrangement to each of them. In particular, Gertrude became very fond of

---

[49] Her predecessors were Dr Margaret Corlis of Menzies, and Dr Roberta Jull, the first woman to establish a medical practice in WA. 'Our Public Women: Dr Roberta Jull', The Australasian, 5 May 1928, 19; 'Glimpses of the Past: Karrakatta Club Jubilee', WM, 30 November 1944, 30. http://nla.gov.au/nla.news-article38558708. Roberta Jull became a lifelong friend and through the Karrakatta Club they 'masterminded' many social welfare projects together.
[50] 'The Late Dr Gertrude Mead', WM, 8 June 1922, 22. http://nla.gov.au/nla.news-article41692652.
[51] Perth Baptist Church Minute, 2 January 1902, by visitation of two members.
[52] Albion Staple Colin ('Colin') Wilson (1899-1918).

her nephews Colin and Bernard (born 1904), with daily interaction until the Wilsons moved to New Zealand in 1907.[53]

Gertrude was an early and active member of both the influential Karrakatta Club for women and the newly formed Women's Australian Natives Association (WANA).[54] WANA was a group of around fifty women who met fortnightly for lively debate and discussion on contemporary topics.

> A feeling was very strong among the young girl members that they would like to have a woman doctor as well as a doctor of the sterner sex, and Dr Gertrude Mead consenting to act...[she was] appointed medical officer...to the Association...[and]...kindly consented to give a paper.[55]

The subject of her paper to the WANA was 'Organisation amongst Women Workers',[56] and was based on the congress of the National Council of Women held in London. She 'applied herself to the possibilities of organised women in Australia in relation to home life, education, legislation, and the public welfare generally.' Like her father, Gertrude had an ambitious global vision: she challenged the WANA members to act in society and become 'a power for good throughout Australia and subsequently for humanity as a whole.'[57] In this paper she was in fact setting out her own life's agenda: to inspire networks of women to work collaboratively for social welfare policy change, using both discrete and overt political pressure as well as personal direct intervention.

There were some particular advantages to being an independent female medical practitioner in a heavily male-dominated profession. Gertrude was free to pursue her interests in paediatrics and gynaecology, and in the social constructs of health. In addition to her role at WANA, Gertrude accepted a role as medical adviser to the 'Ministering Children's League Convalescent Home', where she could recommend structural reforms. She also took on a role as nurse educator for the St John Am-

---

[53] Bernard Mead Wilson (1904-1981). For more on the lives of Colin and Bernard, see chapter 16.
[54] The Karrakatta Club was the first women's club in Australia. It was founded in Perth by a small group of intellectual women in 1894 and sought to widen women's horizons beyond the home sphere. It supported its members to make significant contributions to the social and political development of Western Australia. 'Glimpses of the Past: Karrakatta Club Jubilee', *WM*, 30 November 1944, 30.
[55] 'Social Notes', *West*, 16 August 1902, 2. http://nla.gov.au/nla.news-article24841313.
[56] Classified Advertisements, *West*, 23 September 1902, 1. http://nla.gov.au/nla.news-article24844170.
[57] 'Social Items: Notes', *WM*, 4 October 1902, 41. http://nla.gov.au/nla.news-article37540334.

bulance Association, which—like WANA—gave her personal access to prominent figures, both male and female, in Perth's social and political sphere through contact with the board of management, as well as the opportunity to educate nurses directly in practical nursing.[58] She quickly gained a reputation for combining medical skill and knowledge with 'womanliness, gentleness and freedom from all that does not bespeak the utmost refinement'.[59] Her modest demeanour counteracted criticism from 'men who had long been accustomed to see women performing the most arduous and trying work for the sick as nurses, [yet] suddenly found it amazingly indelicate of them to wish to practise medicine'.[60]

However, although some fellow professional women, such as the *West Australian*'s 'Adrienne',[61] asserted that 'a lady doctor takes her place as a matter of course and creates no sensation as an extraordinary type of being', some of the male medical fraternity were strongly opposed. When public protests by two male doctors arose over the appointment of Dr Ethel Ambrose to the staff of Perth Public Hospital,[62] Gertrude immediately wrote a 'thoughtful and courteously-worded letter' to various newspaper editors, stating: 'One lady doctor surely, is not an anomaly in a hospital existing for men, women and children'.[63] She listed statistics about the many 'lady doctors' already working in interstate hospitals (some like Dr Violet Plummer were friends), and wrote in frustration:

> May I remind the medical gentleman...that though these two ladies [from Melbourne Hospital] were elected amidst a storm of protests from both friends and foes, at the completion of the year's work the board formally expressed their entire satisfaction with the way in which their duties had been performed. ...the difficulties are more imaginary than real...Would it not therefore

58 'MCL Convalescent Home: Annual Meeting', *West*, 1 June 1903, 3. http://nla.gov.au/nla.news-article24825055.
59 'Of Interest to Women–by "Adrienne"', *West*, 13 June 1903, 10. http://nla.gov.au/nla.news-article24826060.
60 'Adelaide's Pioneer Woman Doctor', *Register News-Pictorial* (Adelaide), 31 August 1929, 26. http://nla.gov.au/nla.news-article53483779.
61 Muriel Jean Eliot Chase, née Cooper (1880–1936), journalist and philanthropist; see fn82.
62 Dr Ethel Ambrose (1874–1934) became the first female doctor at Perth Hospital. Like Gertrude, she was also South Australian, Baptist and a graduate of Adelaide's medical school. She subsequently spent most of her life as a missionary doctor in India, and died in Poona ('Pioneer Medical Missionary', *West*, 16 February 1937, 6. https://trove.nla.gov.au/newspaper/article/41277675); Mrs WH [Louisa] Hinton, *Ethel Ambrose: pioneer medical missionary, Poona and Indian Village Mission, Bombay Presidency, India* (London: Marshall, Morgan & Scott, [1937]), 77–81.
63 Editorial, *West*, 18 August 1903, 4. http://nla.gov.au/nla.news-article24831343.

have been more fair...to allow Dr Ambrose to prove her ability to perform the duties allotted to her, before the honorary medical staff protested against the appointment?[64]

Gertrude's letter was promptly supported by Reah Cumming, the President of WANA: 'it is well known that it is no uncommon thing to have a woman attached to a hospital staff...I am glad to say that the Association of which I am president was fortunate in securing the services of Dr Gertrude Mead, another qualified woman,'[65] and by *The West Australian* Editorial,[66] and *The Sunday Press*:

> It would be hard to imagine anything in worse taste than the protest raised by the medical staff after the appointment of Doctor Ambrose to the Perth Public Hospital. And the objections put forward were about as ridiculous as they can well be...The action of Dr Gertrude Mead in taking up the cudgels on Dr Ambrose's side was, at least, generous, and contrasted favourably with the action of other doctors.[67]

As *The Southern Baptist* reported on the 'newspaper discussion': 'Dr Gertrude Mead figures prominently. Judging from the leading article and letters in the *West Australian* so far, the ladies have much the best of it.'[68]

In recognition of her services to the St John Ambulance Association, as nursing educator and other consulting services,[69] Gertrude was soon made a life member of the Association.[70] In this role, she was even called upon to provide first-aid instruction to 'a party of ladies who met at Government House'. Gertrude's forthright approach earned her a caution not to mention the word 'haemorrhage' in front of the Governor's wife, 'as it might offend sensibilities'![71]

---

[64] 'The Lady Doctor', *West*, 17 August 1903, 9. http://nla.gov.au/nla.news-article24831229.

[65] 'Lady Doctors–To the Editor', Letter by Reah Cumming, *West*, 19 August 1903, 4. http://nla.gov.au/nla.news-article24831430.

[66] 'Editorial', *West*, 18 August 1903, 4. http://nla.gov.au/nla.news article24831343

[67] 'When Women's Tongues Wag', *The Sunday Press* (Perth), 23 August 1903, 6. http://nla.gov.au/nla.news-article257709945.

[68] 'West Australian: Lady House Surgeons', *SB*, 1 September 1903, 195. At the conclusion of her term, Dr Ambrose was highly commended for her 'invariably careful, skilful and humane' work, and the Perth Hospital Committee asked her to remain, noting with 'sincere regret the mistake they had made in their earlier opposition' (Hinton, *Ethel Ambrose*, 78-79).

[69] 'Classified Advertisements–St John Ambulance Association, *West*, 26 August 1903, 5. http://nla.gov.au/nla.news-article24831951.

[70] 'News and Notes', *West*, 22 December 1904, 6 (2). http://nla.gov.au/nla.news-article25369868.

[71] *Sporting Life: Dryblowers Journal* (Kalgoorlie), 15 April 1905, 3 (2). http://nla.gov.au/nla.news-article260595163.

By now Dr Gertrude Mead was a name featured often in invitation lists to premier social events and vice-regal occasions. Through the Karrakatta Club she had developed valuable and supportive networks with influential female professionals and the wives of prominent and wealthy men.[72] She forged a firm, long-standing friendship with fellow medical professional Dr Roberta Jull.[73]

Gertrude and Roberta Jull together initiated another policy organisation, the West Australian Health Society, to address 'the alarming mortality among infants'. Gertrude joined a deputation from the Society to meet with the WA Colonial Secretary to suggest improvements for educating mothers on infant feeding, and sanitation in milk dairies.[74]

The year 1907 was particularly busy. Gertrude was active on many fronts. She and Silas paid a short visit to South Australia in January, and Gertrude stayed with her former classmate from medical school, now Dr Violet Plummer.

In March, back in Western Australia, she provided a paper on 'Medical Missions' for the Baptist Union of W.A. annual meeting at Pingelly.[75] The paper was read by Rev Norman L Beurle in Gertrude's absence,[76] most probably because she was moving house from the Perth Baptist Church manse to 55 Harvest Terrace.[77] She continued to consult at Queen's Buildings, William Street. Her discussion paper on 'Medical Missions' described the health and spiritual impact of Christian doctors working on the mission field and is clearly influenced by her brother Cecil's experiences. However, it is written in Gertrude's distinctive style of logical order, laced with factual and statistical information, yet so direct and practical that it is far from dry. The overarching theme, reflecting closely the vision of both Silas and Cecil, was that 'Our Medical Missions exist primarily to win souls for Christ'.[78] Those who heard it described it as 'a revelation', that 'touched all our hearts', and was 'remarkable for the high ground it

[72] Dr Roberta Jull (1872-1961), first general practitioner in Perth and social reformer, and Dame Edith Cowan (1861-1932), first female Member of Parliament and social reformer, were early members of the Karrakatta Club. http://nla.gov.au/nla.news-article38558708.

[73] 'Mainly about People', Daily News (Perth), 7 May 1906, 4. http://nla.gov.au/nla.news-article82874815.

[74] 'Infant Mortality: Cause and Cure: Deputation of Doctors', Daily News (Perth), 25 September 1903, 8. http://nla.gov.au/nla.news-article82016381.

[75] 'Medical Missions', WAB, 15 April 1907, 75-80.

[76] 'Baptist Union of WA–Half Yearly Meetings', SB, 30 April 1907, 108. Rev NL Beurle (1877-1931), former student of Silas in SA, was minister of South Perth Baptist Church, 1902-09.

[77] Classified Advertisements: Miss Gertrude Mead', Mirror (Perth), 13 April 1907, 6 (2). http://nla.gov.au/nla.news-article257351003.

[78] 'Medical Missions', WAB, 15 April 1907, 79.

took' and 'delighted those who listened'.[79] By popular request, it was printed in full in the next issue of the WA Baptist newsletter.

Gertrude's incisive analysis of the value of trained medical professionals on the mission field begs the question of why Gertrude herself did not pursue a career as a foreign missionary. The existing records do not provide a definitive answer. Conjecture suggests a combination of awareness of her own fragile state of health, commitment to caring for her widowed father and to be available for her sisters, and perhaps a reluctance to be parted from them, and above all, no sense of call to serve overseas, but a clear call to serve 'at home'. At the start of the twentieth century, Western Australia had the highest infant mortality rate in the country and no children's hospital. Gertrude was aware of new movements in sanitation, maternal education, the benefits of breastfeeding, and preventative medicine; there was much that could be achieved 'at home'.[80]

Gertrude 'took up the cudgels' again as honorary medical consultant to the House of Mercy, which provided residential accommodation for single mothers. The House of Mercy became embroiled in public controversy over the rate of infant mortality. As before, Gertrude did not hesitate to put pen to paper and provide factual information on exact figures to the news media.[81] She had also decided that Perth needed a district nurse to assist poorly educated mothers who struggled to care effectively for their children. She had seen a district nursing system in Adelaide and wanted to implement a similar scheme in Perth. She enlisted the help of the Silver Chain League and its founder, the journalist and philanthropist Mrs Muriel Chase, who wrote a children's column in the *Western Mail* newspaper.[82] The young readers were encouraged to donate small sums, and select a worthy project. Gertrude seized

[79] 'Goalundo Column: Home Notes', *WAB*, 15 April 1907, 45; 'The Pingelly Meetings', *WAB*, 15 April 1907, 41.
[80] Gertrude's estate included a library of the latest medical books, particularly on child and maternal health.
[81] 'The House of Mercy–To the Editor', *West*, 27 April 1907, 12. http://nla.gov.au/nla.news-article25701964.
[82] Muriel Jean Eliot Chase, née Cooper (1880-1936), journalist and philanthropist, founder of Silver Chain Nursing Association, foundation member of Karrakatta Club, wrote under pseudonyms 'Adrienne' in the *West Australian (West)*, and 'Aunt Mary' in *Western Mail (WM)*, and advocated social reforms. Through the work of the Silver Chain district nurses, she encouraged building a maternity hospital, infant health clinics, cottage homes for the aged and bush nursing services. Noël Stewart, 'Chase, Muriel Jean Eliot (1880-1936)', *Australian Dictionary of Biography*, National Centre of Biography, Australian National University, https://adb.anu.edu.au/biography/chase-muriel-jean-eliot-5565/text9489, published first in hardcopy 1979.

the opportunity and wrote a letter to these young 'Silver Links' encouraging them to support the employment of a district nurse, rather than endow a cot in the Children's Hospital:

> Dear Silver Links…with a district nurse, an Immense Want will be partly supplied…there are so many mothers who cannot leave their homes when ill, unless absolutely urgent, who now have no help, leave alone skilled help. There are sick children who fret their little hearts out at the idea of a hospital. There are babies who die, in spite of ignorant devotion, who might live were a nurse daily instilling cleanliness, and regularity into the mothers' minds…a God-fearing, trained, conscientious woman would do infinitely more good than an ornate cot with an inscribed brass plate…I am your friend, Gertrude Mead.[83]

Sir Winthrop Hackett[84] 'touched by the baby visioning of a real community need, supplemented the few pounds by many hundreds, and thus made possible the Silver Chain service'.[85] This service developed into the Silver Chain District Nursing Association. Subsequently, Muriel Chase, the long-serving district nurse Sister Frances Cherry (Mrs Drew)[86] and Gertrude established through the Silver Chain organisation some independent living units (cottage homes) for the elderly. One of them was posthumously named the 'Dr Gertrude Mead Cottage' in honour of Gertrude's commitment.[87]

A district nursing service was a practical solution to a pressing social need, but Gertrude was also aware of 'the urgent need for legislation for the protection of child life' following some horrific, well-publicised cases of baby farming.[88] Gertrude was one of the honorary physicians to the newly formed Children's Protection Society of

---

[83] 'About the District Nurse. Letter from Dr Gertrude Mead', *WM*, 8 June 1907, 42. http://nla.gov.au/nla.news-article37399720.

[84] Sir John Winthrop Hackett (1848-1916), editor/owner of *West Australian* newspaper; MLC WA Parliament 1894-1916, Chancellor of University of Western Australia (1913-16).

[85] 'The Silver Chain Homes. How a Child's Idea Developed', *West*, 2 March 1936, 4.

[86] Nurse Frances Cherry (1872-1941), WA district nurse from 1908-41. Deborah Burrows, *Nurses of Australia: The Illustrated Story* (Canberra: NLA Publishing, 2018), 99.

[87] 'Silver Chain Nursing Association' (*InHerit*, Heritage Council, Government of Western Australia, City of Vincent, updated 2018), http://inherit.stateheritage.wa.gov.au/Public/Inventory/Details/3e9772c7-54d1-464e-8cdb-ef9a1ad58897.

[88] Alice Mitchell is arguably Australia's worst serial killer. She was arrested in Perth in 1907 for the death of baby Ethel Booth, whose mother was paying Mitchell for fulltime care for the baby. It was discovered at trial that at least 37 babies had died of want and gross neglect while boarding with Mitchell who was operating a 'baby farm', i.e. taking in babies for money and not necessarily caring for them. See Stella Budrikis, *The Edward Street Baby Farm* (Fremantle: Fremantle Press, 2020).

Western Australia (CPS).[89] She was a member of the delegation from the CPS that met with the Colonial Secretary to discuss the draft Bill (eventually the State Children Act 1907) for the protection of children.[90] Again she put pen to paper to defend the CPS and protest the wording of the proposed legislation, and enlisted the support of her brother-in-law Alfred Wilson. She presented a keynote address to the Interstate Children's Congress in 1909 on the plight of aboriginal mission children, some of whom she treated.[91] She remained actively involved in the CPS and its work to improve the lives of children.

Sorrows and loss

Blanche and Alfred Wilson and their two boys moved to New Zealand in 1907, so Gertrude had sole care of her father Silas at the Harvest Terrace house. At the age of seventy-five, Silas was still active; however, his health began to deteriorate over the winter months of 1909. He contracted pneumonia, and on Monday 13 September Silas died of heart failure. The tributes poured in, and Gertrude herself wrote to Flinders Street Baptist Church that in the years since Silas left FSBC he 'had laboured with characteristic energy...Illness brought him low but it never quenched his dauntless spirit.' She included her father's last message, clearly precious to her: 'I leave to all my children, in equal shares, a father's unbounded love'.[92] Cecil, his wife Alice and their daughters, Marjory and Dorothy, already *en route* from Bengal on furlough, reached Perth six weeks after Silas's death. They spent three months recuperating with Gertrude before heading to South Australia.[93]

After nine years of medical consulting and vigorous campaigning to improve the lives of women and children in Western Australia, Gertrude too needed recuperation. A year after her father's death, in October 1910 she embarked for England to stay with her sister Lilian in Torquay; she did not return to Perth until August 1911.

---

[89] Leanne Rowe, 'The Children's Protection Society: Child Protection in Western Australia, 1906–1930: Towards a Medical Welfare Model', *Studies in Western Australian History*, 25 (2007), 118.
[90] 'Annual Meeting of the Children's Protection Society', *West*, 24 July 1907, 3. http://nla.gov.au/nla.news-article25708526; 'Child Protection: Colonial Secretary Interviewed', *Evening Mail* (Fremantle), 7 June 1907, 1. http://nla.gov.au/nla.news-article256595332.
[91] 'Aborigines and Half-Castes: How should they be treated?', *Advertiser*, 22 May 1909, 12. http://nla.gov.au/nla.news-article5726606; 'The Work in the West', *The Australian Aborigines' Advocate*, 31 July 1909, 6. I am indebted to John Olley for this research.
[92] 'The Late Rev. Silas Mead, MA, LLB', *SB*, 12 October 1909, 249.
[93] *SB*, 2 November 1909, 1; 1 January 1910, 8.

She resumed her medical practice and honorary consultancies; and in 1913 was appointed to the first Senate of the new University of Western Australia as the Medical Representative. She won election in 1915 against four male candidates when the University introduced preferential voting for its Senate.[94] She also continued to work energetically with Muriel Chase in developing supported accommodation for the elderly, and became directly involved in the purchase and detailed planning of the cottage homes as the project progressed.

The Wilsons returned to Perth in 1912, bringing their sons Colin, now thirteen, and eight-year-old Bernard, with them. Gertrude had known her nephews since they were small children when they lived together in the Perth church manse, and she felt very close to them both. Colin's tragic death in 1918 of 'pneumonic influenza' (1918 Influenza A (H1N1) or 'Spanish flu') was devastating to her. It was later written that 'Dr Mead had a very great sorrow [when] she lost her young nephew Colin Wilson, as splendid a young fellow [as] it would be possible to see anywhere in the world. ...the sorrow was a terribly heavy one for his parents and for Dr Mead, because...she loved Colin and his brother Bernie as if they were her own children'.[95]

Winter of the following year, 1919, left her often struggling with her own health. Now aged 51, she felt run down and she dreaded the imminent re-location of the Wilsons from Perth back to New Zealand. In October, Gertrude visited Adelaide to stay with her brother Cecil and his family who were again on furlough. She was characteristically busy, attending a missionary fair with her sister-in-law, visiting friends, and touring cottage homes in Adelaide to gain information for the work in Perth. She attended two church services on Sunday 2 November at which her brother preached, including the evening service at FSBC. The next day she felt:

> weary [and] kept to her bed. On Tuesday morning she was found in a state of unconsciousness, and medical aid was sought. [The doctors] agreed that cerebral haemorrhage had taken place in the night...Everything that was possible was done, but the beloved patient did not regain consciousness [and] she passed away peacefully and painlessly on Thursday [6 November, at

---

[94] 'University of WA: New Senate Members: Mr Hancock and Dr Mead Elected', *Kalgoorlie Miner*, 2 April 1915, 6. http://nla.news-article92574156.

[95] 'Aunt Mary's Letter', *WM*, 13 November 1919, 37. http://nla.gov.au/nla.news-article37458266. More on Colin and Bernard in chapters 14 and 16.

'Orakandi', Daphne-street, Prospect, the home of her brother Cecil].[96]

Her brother-in-law Alfred Wilson, on his way to New Zealand, detoured immediately from Sydney to Adelaide by train to join Cecil, although he arrived the day after Gertrude was buried on Friday 7 November at the West Terrace Cemetery, in the family plot beside her mother, youngest sister and baby brother.[97] Memorial services were held at FSBC on 9 November, and at Perth Baptist Church the following Sunday. Other tributes followed, expressing shock and grief at the sudden and untimely death. All mentioned her character of kindness, generosity and determination to serve others.

'Held in the highest esteem'

Three years after her death, Gertrude was remembered at an impressive event held in her honour at the Silver Chain Cottage Homes in Wright Street that she had laboured so long and hard to bring to fruition: 'she it was who very largely determined their purpose, she it was who had the last word in designing the buildings, and as honorary physician had endeared herself to the inmates of those cottages'.[98] A brass tablet inscribed with a memorial was unveiled by the Anglican Archbishop of Perth,[99] and one of the cottages was named 'The Dr Gertrude Mead Cottage Home'. Tributes were laid before the memorial by the chairman of the Silver Chain League, the minister of Perth Baptist Church, the Archbishop on behalf of the Senate of the University of Western Australia, and representatives of the St John Ambulance Association, the Children's Protection Society, and the City of Perth. The Silver Chain

[96] 'Dr Gertrude Mead: Beloved Physician', *AB*, 25 November 1919, 4-5; 'The Late Dr Gertrude Mead: An Appreciation', *West*, 10 November 1919, 6. http://nla.gov.au/nla.news-article27667286.
[97] 'Funeral Notices', *Register*, 7 November 1919, 2; 'Personal', *West*, 10 November 1919, 7; 'Dr Gertrude Mead: Beloved Physician', *AB*, 25 November 1919, 5.
[98] 'The late Dr Gertrude Mead/Silver Chain Memorial', *WM*, 8 June 1922, 22. The cottage homes themselves were opened on 3 October 1920. Cecil and Alice Mead, *en route* from Adelaide to India, visited the new cottages the next day, 'to see what a memorial it is to the memory of Dr Gertrude Mead….the friend who had done so much to help forward the work and strengthen it in every direction by her wisdom and skill and love.' (*WM*, 7 October 1920, 29).
[99] Archbishop Charles Owen Leaver Riley (1854-1929) was the first Anglican Archbishop of Perth. He was instrumental in establishing the University of WA with his friend Sir Winthrop Hackett and was Chancellor 1916-22. He knew Gertrude well. Peter Boyce, 'Riley, Charles Owen Leaver (1854-1929)', *Australian Dictionary of Biography*, National Centre of Biography, Australian National University, https://adb.anu.edu.au/biography/riley-charles-owen-leaver-8213/text14371, published first in hardcopy 1988.

Nursing Association Inc complex continues to honour Gertrude's name through the rebuilt 'Mead House', Wright Street, Perth, and the Heritage Council has allocated a heritage listing.[100]

The Canberra suburb of Chisholm, gazetted in 1975, is named after Caroline Chisholm (1808–1877) who provided support services for migrant women and championed reforms for women and families. The streets in the suburb, gazetted in 1987, are all named for 'notable women', many in medical professions, social reformers or scientists. Mead Street links Benham and Proctor Streets.[101] The lengthy citation lists Gertrude's many significant achievements and impressive roles. It fails to capture the essence of this woman who worked so hard in these positions. The *Medical Journal of Australia* tribute did her greater justice:

> Her life was spent for the advantage of others. In her practice she proved herself especially skilful with children, who were irresistibly drawn toward their kind and capable physician. In her sociological work the aged learned to love her, and never looked in vain for sympathetic aid or material assistance. In a quiet, unassuming manner she contributed towards the firm establishment of women's proper place in medicine. Her colleagues, as well as her patients and friends, held her in the highest esteem, and deplore a fate that robbed them of her all too soon.[102]

---

[100] 'Silver Chain Nursing Association', *InHerit*, Heritage Council, Government of Western Australia, City of Vincent, Place Number 11451, 1998. Gertrude's grave is also included in the Adelaide Cemeteries Authority 'Trailblazing Women Interpretive Trail–West Terrace Cemetery', Adelaide.

[101] Ellen Ida Benham (1871-1917), SA educationist; first female academic University of Adelaide 1901. Alethea Mary ('Thea') Proctor (1879-1966), artist; contributed to modernism in Australia through her work as a painter, printmaker, designer and teacher. *Commonwealth of Australia Gazette*, No P-11, 'Schedule A: Street Nomenclature' (Canberra: Australian Government Publishing Service, 15 May 1987), 4.

[102] 'Concerning People', *Register*, 5 January 1920, 6. http://nla.gov.au/nla.news-article65020610.

Blanche: Daughter, Sister, Wife and Mother

Rebecca Hilton

> Mrs Annie Blanche Wilson, widow of the late Rev. A. S. Wilson, died on June 29 at the age of 91. Mrs. Wilson, mother of Rev. Bernard Wilson, and sister of the late Dr. Cecil Mead, Dr. Gertrude Mead and Mrs. Crosby [sic] Brown, was the last remaining child of Rev. Silas Mead. Rev. and Mrs. A. S. Wilson began their ministry at the Perth Central Church, where they are still remembered with gratitude.[1]

As this notice shows, the life of Blanche Wilson—she was always known as Blanche—can effectively be described through her relationships to others, and particularly others in the Australian Baptist denomination: a Baptist minister's daughter; a sister—including of two doctors, one of whom was a Baptist missionary; Baptist minister's wife; and Baptist minister's mother.

Perhaps this type of description is appropriate and accurate for a woman living in the first half of the twentieth century: an identity through relationships.

Blanche's adult life was the most traditional of Silas Mead's children. Unlike her older siblings it does not appear that Blanche Mead ever considered attending university, nor did she undertake significant public speaking or produce written works. She married, had children, and lived largely within conventional boundaries. Because of this her activities are less visible than her siblings. However, as a minister's daughter,

---

[1] 'South Australia: passing of daughter of Silas Mead', *AB*, 9 August 1961, 11.

missionary's sister, doctor's sister, minister's wife, and minister's mother, Blanche Wilson's life-story can be discerned.

Blanche travelled quite extensively, both before and after her marriage. She travelled to the United Kingdom twice, once with her brother and once with her husband. She moved cities with her husband Alfred's employment: living in Adelaide and Perth in Australia and Wanganui and Auckland in New Zealand (NZ). She attended various conferences and meetings throughout Australia, NZ and overseas.

Blanche made a significant contribution to the Baptist congregations of which she was a member: FSBC; PBC; Wanganui; the Tabernacle in Auckland; Grange Road, Auckland; and St Albans, Christchurch. Her Christian views were never articulated in print, as far as can be discerned, as she has only three extant written works and one of these is the minutes to the first women's committee of the WABMS, that is, a report of the views of a group of women. Yet her beliefs can be seen in the *actions* that she undertook, even when those actions are viewed through her relationship with others—particularly her father, Silas.

Baptist minister's daughter

Blanche Wilson was the fourth child of Ann and Silas Mead. She was born on 8 January 1870 in Adelaide. Her older siblings were Lilian, who was four at the time of Blanche's birth, Cecil, three, and Gertrude, two. A younger brother John was born and died on 12 October 1871 and a younger sister Flora was born when Blanche was three. Blanche's childhood was bookended by the death of her mother in 1874 when she was four years old and the deaths in 1886 of her stepmother, Mary, née Pitty, and her younger sister, Flora, when Blanche was sixteen.

Presumably Blanche had few memories of her mother's death and the subsequent arrangements made for her and her siblings. Ann died suddenly from typhoid on 15 June and four-year-old Blanche went to the gravesite service along with her father and older siblings. On 16 July Silas left Adelaide for England: Ann and Silas had already organised to return to England to visit family, instead Silas went on his own.[2] The Mead children did not harbour feelings of abandonment by their father, in fact all the Mead children were extremely fond of their father. During the time Silas was away Blanche and her siblings were cared for by Sarah Hann, née Staple. Sarah was the sister of Blanche's mother Ann and almost certainly had already agreed to the caring

---

[2] 'Notes of the month', *TP*, 1 July 1875, 85.

arrangement before Ann's death.[3] In October 1866 Sarah arrived in Adelaide and she married Francis (Frank) Hann in November 1866. They had no children. Probably Sarah continued her involvement in the young lives of Blanche and her siblings on Silas's return, although this may have changed from 1878 when Silas remarried.

Blanche's stepmother Mary does not appear to have been a significant influence in Blanche's life. Mary married Silas when Blanche was eight, but Mary had poor health, and Mary's obituary did not mention a close relationship with the Mead children. Mary died on 21 March 1886.[4]

Conversely the death of Blanche's younger sister Flora was a significant event in Blanche's life.[5] On 9 September 1886 Flora died of typhoid fever, which Blanche and her brother Cecil had also contracted. Blanche's other siblings, Lilian and Gertrude, were visiting family in England and so avoided the illness. Blanche recalled that Silas would spend time daily with each of his three children, visiting them in their bedrooms. Blanche and Cecil could talk to each other through their bedroom walls and they discussed between themselves that their father was no longer visiting Flora's room: neither had been told that Flora had died.[6]

From the age of about ten Blanche was educated at Tsong Gyiaou, a girls' boarding school in McLaren Vale, located about forty kilometres south of Adelaide. Tsong Gyiaou School was established by two sisters, Eliza and Mary Ann Aldersey, who inherited a house, with spacious grounds, that had belonged to their aunt, Mary Ann Aldersey, a former missionary in China. She had named the house after her favourite place in China, and her nieces kept the name for their school. It was common in the late nineteenth century for girls' schools to be in converted residences. The school had about twenty-five students at any one time with most students being boarders.[7] Records of the school have been lost, but it was tailored to the middle class, and students included the daughters of several ministers and prominent Christians.[8] Indeed the students who remained at the school over the weekend, which probably included

[3] Cecil Mead. Letter to Silas Mead. Gooden/Mead collection. 1874. The letter indicates that Cecil was aware of arrangements for himself and his siblings to be cared for in Adelaide while their parents were in England.
[4] 'In memoriam: the late Mrs Mead', *TP*, 1 April 1886, 50.
[5] Walter Barry, *There Was a Man: the Life of Cecil Silas Mead: Missionary-Doctor* (Melbourne: Australian Baptist Foreign Mission, [1952]), 13. Barry notes that the stories of Cecil's childhood were relayed to him by Blanche Mead.
[6] Barry, *The Life of Cecil Silas Mead*, 13.
[7] Ira Nesdale, *The Third Bridge: Tsong Gyiaou, McLaren Vale* (Hawthorndene, South Australia: Investigator Press, 1980), 57.
[8] Nesdale, *The Third Bridge: Tsong Gyiaou, McLaren Vale*, 63,103.

Blanche, attended the local Congregational church services. The school curriculum was broad, and teachers followed various Australian textbooks.[9]

In 1882 Blanche sent a letter to the editor of the *Christian Colonist* about a school trip:

> We went for a holiday last Monday to the Onkaparinga Beach, which is about six miles from McLaren Vale. It is a very pretty beach indeed, and about a mile from the jetty is the mouth of the Onkaparinga River. We spent a very pleasant day, but our feet were rather sore the next day, as we had been running about on the beach with our boots off.[10]

These school trips occurred once per quarter in 'the middle Monday' of the school term and enabled the students to have a break from their studies.[11]

When in Adelaide Blanche attended FSBC with her father and siblings. She was baptised and became a member of the congregation in late 1881. She made her Christian commitment as a result of a campaign undertaken by Emilia Baeyertz, an Australian woman evangelist.[12] Her subsequent interest in various Christian activities, specifically Christian Endeavour (CE), foreign mission, and the Woman's Christian Temperance Union, were almost certainly attributable to the influence of her father, and potentially her older siblings.

With respect to CE, Silas had established the first CE branch in South Australia (SA) and from the 1890s CE was a major activity in Blanche's life. She was active in the FSBC CE Society until she left Adelaide, and she was the assistant secretary of the SA CE in 1891.[13] In 1900 she spoke at the WA CE Union conference, her subject being 'How', which was the third speech in a 'Why, When, and How' session.[14] Later, when living in NZ, she also spoke at CE events.[15] Unfortunately none of the relevant reporting makes mention of the content of Blanche's speeches.

---

[9] Nesdale, *The Third Bridge: Tsong Gyiaou, McLaren Vale*, 51.

[10] Blanche Mead, 'Letter to the Editor: Children's Column', *Colonist*, 22 September 1882, 920.

[11] Nesdale, *The Third Bridge: Tsong Gyiaou, McLaren Vale*, 66.

[12] 'Mrs Baeyertz in Adelaide–Farewell Meeting', *TP*, 1 January 1881, 8.

[13] 'South Australian Union Young People's Societies of Christian Endeavour', *Colonist*, 27 November 1891, 3.

[14] 'Western Australian Christian Endeavour Union', *Inquirer and Commercial News* (Perth), 16 November 1900, 2.

[15] See, for example: 'Ecclesiastical', *Auckland Star* (Auckland), 20 September 1924, 10.

Blanche

Like her father and siblings, Blanche was interested in foreign mission. In 1906, when Silas chaired the first meeting of the WA Baptist Women's Goalundo Auxiliary at PBC, nineteen women attended including Blanche. Blanche was elected the minute secretary and her aunt Sarah Hann was secretary.[16] Blanche's interest and support of mission continued throughout her life. For example, in NZ she was the President of the Wanganui Baptist Women's Missionary Union (BWMU) and the Grange Road BWMU.[17]

---

[16] Baptist Women's Goalundo Auxiliary, Minute Book, 1906-1909, Baptist Union of Western Australia Archives, Perth, Western Australia.
[17] 'Grange Road Baptists: Annual Meeting Held', *New Zealand Herald* (Auckland), 22 August 1925, 9.

Baptist missionary's sister

Blanche's first visit to Great Britain was with her brother Cecil. They departed Adelaide on 4 January 1893. Blanche later told Walter Barry that she and Cecil 'when half-way through [their] teens, became great mates, and so [they] continued until he left for India.'[18] This trip—undertaken with a 'great mate'—would have been a wonderful experience for Blanche. Cecil was going to England to undertake further medical studies before he planned to go to East Bengal as a missionary, and Blanche accompanied him.[19] They attended various meetings and targeted church services featuring high profile preachers—presumably they knew of most of these men from their father or as visitors in their home. Most importantly, they visited family members, aunts, uncles, and cousins, who lived predominantly in Somerset, but ranged from Yorkshire to Dorset.[20] This travel mirrored a similar journey that had been undertaken six years earlier by their sisters Lilian and Gertrude.

Blanche and Cecil spent a significant amount of time together in England, although initially Cecil worked in London, while Blanche stayed with relatives in Somerset.[21] When travelling Blanche managed their daily itinerary as 'Cecil was interested only in hospitals'.[22] The two most significant conferences that Blanche and Cecil attended were the English CE Convention and the Keswick Convention.[23] Unfortunately, Blanche's memories of the two Conventions are not extant, but Cecil's surviving comments concerned the Keswick Convention.[24] Cecil wrote that he 'remember[ed] so well those happy days with Blanche at the Convention.'[25]

[18] Barry, *The Life of Cecil Silas Mead*, 12.
[19] 'Endeavour Farewell to Dr Mead', *Register*, 4 January 1893, 6.
[20] Blanche Mead, 'A Family Affair', *TP*, 12 April 1894, 125.
[21] 'News and Notes', *TP*, 4 May 1893, 131.
[22] Barry, *The Life of Cecil Silas Mead*, 25.
[23] Barry, *The Life of Cecil Silas Mead*, 27.
[24] The Keswick Convention is discussion further in chapter 4.
[25] Barry, *The Life of Cecil Silas Mead*, 26.

Blanche and Cecil

Cecil left England for the Australian Baptist missions in East Bengal in late 1893, and Blanche, together with other family members established a 'missionary circle' to provide support to him from his English relatives.[26] Blanche's article about the circle was written while she was in England and then published in *Truth and Progress*. The four 'rules' of the circle were: to pray daily for foreign missionaries, including Cecil; to read Cecil's letters and pass them on quickly to other members; to write to Cecil once a year; and to donate goods for a 'box' to be sent to Cecil every October.[27] The support provided through the missionary circle continued once Blanche returned to Australia. Blanche ultimately wanted this model to be adopted by congregations in Australia, writing:

---

[26] Mead, 'A Family Affair', *TP*, 12 April 1894, 125.
[27] Mead, 'A Family Affair', *TP*, 12 April 1894, 125.

Will not a little group of churches take a personal interest in one of our missionary workers, not to divert or limit finances to that one, but to write to her regularly, to copy and pass on her letters, to be familiar with her photo and her special needs and desires, to send her a special box once a year, and in any other way that occurs to us to know her and her work as intimately as if she were a relation? For are we not all brothers and sisters in Christ Jesus?[28]

Essentially this missionary circle reflected the aims and activities of missionary organisations in the Baptist denomination, particularly those established by women.[29] It is noteworthy that she commented on the missionary as 'she': at that time the Australian Baptist missions supported twenty-three missionaries, twenty of whom were women.[30]

Blanche was away for eighteen months and returned to Australia in mid-July 1894. The FSBC CE groups organised an event to welcome her home. At this event Blanche Mead is reported as 'urging all to do whatever good they could without saying anything about it, or wishing to be praised for it.'[31] This is a lovely, simple sentiment, and one of the few occasions that any spoken words by Blanche were reported. The lack of speeches or writing by Blanche, particularly in comparison to her siblings, means that one cannot make assessments about her intelligence. However, Silas was described as having 'three gifted daughters'.[32] Perhaps Blanche's gifts were expressed through her commitment to Baptist mission and CE, along with her friendly personality, as Blanche was described as 'an exceedingly popular lady'.[33]

Baptist minister's wife

On 7 December 1896 Blanche Mead married Alfred Samuel Wilson in Flinders Street Baptist Church, Adelaide. Alfred Wilson was born in 1867 in Charleston, in the Adelaide Hills near Nairne, SA, 40 km east of Adelaide. He was the fifth of seven children of Wemyss and William Wilson, and he grew up on his parents' farm. He had worked as a banker and stockbroker but decided to train for the Baptist ministry in

---

28 Mead, 'A Family Affair', *TP*, 12 April 1894, 125.
29 Baptist Women's Goalundo Auxiliary, Minute Book. The aims of this Auxiliary, written in Blanche's neat handwriting, reflect the missionary circle.
30 'Roll-call of missionaries', *Our Bond* (Calcutta), Jubilee Issue 1932, 31.
31 'Miss Blanche Mead', *Advertiser*, 19 July 1894, 6.
32 'South Australian notes', *AB*, 1938, 15.
33 'South Australian notes', *AB* 1938, 15.

Way College, SA, and was ordained in September 1896 in Perth.[34] He attended FSBC and was involved in many of the activities of the church. In particular, he had been secretary of the CE group with Blanche.

At an age of 26 Blanche Wilson was slightly older than the average SA bride.[35] Alfred Wilson had been appointed the first permanent minister of the newly formed PBC, after spending a few months as interim minister prior to completion of his ministry training. During his interim in Perth he had lived with Sarah and Frank Hann, Blanche's aunt and her husband. Thus, immediately after their wedding, Blanche and Alfred Wilson moved to Perth. As a 'child of the manse' Blanche Wilson would have known the demands that accompanied living with a Baptist minister. Perth was remote, with a small population, and the fledgling Baptist Union of WA had only just been formed with four churches—as Adelaide had been when Blanche's parents commenced work there thirty years earlier. Did Blanche ever consider the parallels in her life in this period with her mother's life? Ultimately Blanche and her mother had very different life experiences, but the early years of their marriages had significant similarities. Likewise, there were parallels between the early ministries of Alfred and Silas. Like Silas, Alfred started ministry in a new church and, soon after, commenced publishing and editing a church paper. Alfred shared several key theological views with Silas. In particular, Alfred argued for open membership throughout his ministries in Perth and NZ, whereby any Christian could become a member of the congregation regardless of whether they had undertaken believer's baptism.

Blanche knew people already living in Perth, as other SA Baptists had moved to Perth. Her aunt, Sarah, had moved to Perth in the mid-1880s, and Jean Wilson, the younger sister of Alfred Wilson, also moved to Perth, possibly at the same time as Blanche. Sarah, Frank and Jean attended PBC. Alfred and Blanche initially lived in a house in Colin Street, which was about 2km from the block obtained for the building of the church. In early 1900 they moved to a house named 'Lyndhurst' in Museum Street, across from the church building, which had opened in 1899.

Blanche and Alfred regularly travelled from Perth to eastern Australia. In 1897, for example, they represented WA at the Hobart CE Convention in October, and

---

[34] Richard K. Moore, *'All Western Australia is My Parish': A Centenary History of the Baptist Denomination in Western Australia, 1895-1995* ([Perth]: The Baptist Historical Society of Western Australia, 1996), 304.
[35] 'Vital Statistics', *Advertiser*, 10 September 1902, 6. Most women were aged between 20 and 25 when they married.

then the Baptist Union of Victoria in Melbourne in November.[36] Alfred presented a paper on 'Denomination extension in the country districts'.[37]

Blanche and Alfred Wilson

From 14 June to 6 December 1901 Blanche, Alfred, and their infant son Colin travelled to the United Kingdom. Blanche's father Silas and sister Gertrude had been living in London and they met up briefly before Silas and Gertrude returned to Australia. Indeed, before Blanche and Alfred departed Perth, PBC had announced that Silas was to take on Wilson's pastorate during his absence—noting that the PBC pastor was absent from June through August.[38] Blanche's eldest sister Lilian had permanently relocated to England. Blanche and Alfred visited Edinburgh where they attended the Baptist Union's General Assembly as official delegates of the BUWA. Alfred delivered a paper at the Ecumenical Session of these meetings. They had planned to return to Perth via the WABMS work at Goalundo, but this did not occur.[39] Cecil, his wife Alice, and daughter Dorothy were not in East Bengal at the time, as they had spent most of 1901 in Adelaide on furlough. While Blanche was interested in the work of the Australian Baptist mission, quite apart from Cecil's involvement, Blanche and Alfred may not have had the time or money to visit the mission.

[36] 'Notes and comments', *TSB*, 4 November 1897, 241. These meetings were the first time that all colonies, including NZ, were represented at a conference of the Baptist Union of Victoria.
[37] 'Baptist Union of Victoria', *The Age* (Melbourne), 20 November 1897, 14.
[38] 'Personal', *Advertiser*, 1 June 1901, 7; Geoffrey Helyar, *A Voice in the City: Perth Baptist Church: 1895-1995* (Perth, WA: Perth Baptist Church, 1995), 33.
[39] 'Baptist Union of Western Australia', *West*, 20 May 1901, 3.

In early 1902 PBC affirmed Silas as co-pastor, and he and Gertrude lived in 'Lyndhurst' with Blanche, Alfred and Colin. A second son, Bernard, was born to Blanche and Alfred in 1904. Thus Blanche was living with her father, sister, husband and sons. Blanche managed the house, although she was fortunate to be in a position where she could hire domestic help.[40] Her household management raises issues about women's contribution to the achievements of others. One cannot surmise about the workings of the Wilson household, but the contributions of Alfred to the Baptist denomination—and also of Silas during this period—rarely mention the work Blanche undertook to maintain their household. In addition, Gertrude, as an unmarried doctor, effectively had a 'wife', as Blanche's work in the home enabled Gertrude to fully focus on her medical work.

Throughout Alfred's ministries there were several instances where disagreements arose between Alfred and members of the church, or other congregations, that obviously created stress for Alfred, who is sometimes described as being unwell and requiring a break from his work. For example, the 1901 trip to England was to enable Alfred to have a break so he could be 'invigorated physically and mentally by his rest from active ministerial work.'[41] During the first part of 1903 Alfred was again unwell, and his doctor ordered him 'to take a complete rest …on a health recruiting trip.'[42]

In 1905 Alfred had a disagreement with Frank Hann, Blanche's uncle by marriage, and as a result Frank resigned from the diaconate and left PBC.[43] Blanche must have been distressed about the argument given her close relationship with her aunt Sarah. When Sarah died in 1915 Alfred wrote her obituary for *The Australian Baptist*—possibly at Blanche's request. The obituary is significant in that Frank was merely mentioned as Sarah's husband, and Sarah's life and activities were hers alone. Most women's obituaries from this time include information about their husband's position or achievements.[44]

From 1907 to 1912 the Wilson family moved to Wanganui as Alfred accepted the position of minister at Wanganui Baptist Church in NZ, and Blanche continued in her role as minister's wife and the mother of two children. However, in 1912 the Wilson family returned to Perth. Alfred had accepted the position of the General Sec-

---

[40] 'Advertising', *West*, 11 November 1902, 8.
[41] 'Baptist Union: farewell to Rev A.S. and Mrs Wilson', *West*, 11 June 1901, 6.
[42] 'Local and general news', *Great Southern Herald* (Katanning, WA), 4 April 1903, 2.
[43] Helyar, *A Voice in the City*, 28.
[44] Analysis of over 250 obituaries written about Baptist women around this time reveals that there are very few obituaries of married women where there is no mention of the work of a woman's husband.

retary of the Young Men's Christian Association (YMCA) in Perth. With Alfred out of the Baptist ministry, Blanche was no longer a minister's wife, nor indeed a minister's daughter, as they returned to Perth after the death of Silas. Alfred and Blanche were known, respected and liked by Baptists in Perth. The deacons of PBC wanted to host a welcome to the Wilson family, but the then Minister of the Church, the Rev. Grimshaw Binns, was uncomfortable with this prospect for reasons that were not recorded, and the subsequent discussions led to Grimshaw Binns resigning as minister.[45] The fact that Alfred chaired the welcome meeting for the new minister, the Rev Frederick Harry and his family, points to the respect that PBC had for Alfred. Certainly over the following eight years Alfred and Blanche were involved in the life of PBC. Blanche was involved in various activities with the women of the church, and Alfred often preached or assisted in memorial services.[46]

Baptist minister's mother

Blanche gave birth to three children and, given her Baptist heritage, it is reasonable to assume that she would have wished for all her children to be involved in the Baptist denomination. Yet only one son became a Baptist minister. Her first child was born in April 1898 and was named Cecil Silas Mead Wilson, and thus his name was a tribute to Blanche's brother and father. On 24 November 1898 Cecil Wilson died at the age of seven months, from infant enteritis.[47] At the time infant enteritis accounted for about 10 per cent of infant deaths; thankfully less than a century later it could be treated through intravenous fluids and in the twenty-first century it is rarely fatal.[48] In 1899 Blanche gave birth to her second son Albion Colin Staple Mead, who was known as Colin, and in 1904 to a third son Bernard Mead. Colin and Bernard became committed Christians and joined their parents in various Baptist activities, particularly once the family returned to Perth from 1912.[49]

---

[45] Helyar, *A Voice in the City*, 43.

[46] Helyar, *A Voice in the City*, 45.

[47] 'Family Notices: Deaths', *West*, 25 November 1898, 4.

[48] NM Mann, Sheila Ross and WH Patterson, 'Gasto-enteritis in infancy', Archives of Disease in Childhood, 1 October 1952, 457; Australian Institute of Health and Welfare, Mortality over the twentieth century in Australia: Trends and patterns in major causes of death. Mortality Surveillance Series no. 4. Cat. no. PHE73. Canberra, 2005.

[49] Moore, *All Western Australia is My Parish*, 80.

Blanche with her sons Colin and Bernard

In 1914 war was declared, and as General Secretary of the YMCA, Alfred was actively involved in the war effort. On 27 June 1918 Blanche and Alfred's eighteen-year-old son, Colin, enlisted for service. Colin left Australia on 29 October 1918 on the HMAT *Boonah*, which then returned to Australia once peace was declared on 11 November 1918. Blanche and Alfred would have been relieved that their son was spared from seeing active duty, but their relief would have quickly turned to dismay when WA health officials stopped the *Boonah* from docking in Fremantle on its return to Australia. Troops on the *Boonah* had contracted the 1918 influenza when the boat had docked in South Africa, and health officials wanted to ensure that the influenza did not enter WA. Alfred, as a father and as General Secretary of the YMCA, publicly expressed his anger about the way in which the Government dealt with the situation.[50] The sickest soldiers were eventually moved to a quarantine facility so they could receive better care, but sadly Colin was one of those who died.[51]

Blanche's experiences of the death of her first two sons are very difficult to analyse from a twenty-first century perspective. Many women lost children during that period: child mortality was high, as was the toll of Australian soldiers during the First World War and during the influenza pandemic. Yet it is still likely that Blanche car-

---

[50] Ian Darroch, *The Boonah Tragedy* (Bassendean, WA: Access Press, 2004), 211.
[51] Darroch, *The Boonah Tragedy*, 83, 88.

ried the losses experienced in the deaths of her sons throughout her life: one a seven-month-old and the other an eighteen-year-old. She may have felt the loss expressed by Lilian Wooster Greaves, a Western Australian Baptist poet, who wrote: 'The pain and the parting, the grief and the tears. Our human inheritance, down the long years.'[52] Despite these sad events, Blanche would have been delighted that Bernard, her youngest son, followed in the path set by his father and grandfather and became a Baptist minister. She would have been proud that her grandson also became a Baptist minister.[53]

Rev AS Wilson and Blanche Wilson with their sons Colin and Bernard, Perth, c.1915

A 'shining saint'?

1919 was a momentous year for Blanche. She and Alfred decided to move with Bernard to NZ. One wonders whether they needed to leave the city that held reminders of Colin's death, such as the boats in the harbour, or the organ being played in PBC. Perhaps Alfred found his job difficult, as he would have dealt with some of the people whom he felt were responsible for Colin's death. Sadly, in mid-1919 Blanche's sister Gertrude, who lived with the family, died while on holidays in Adelaide. Gertrude's death meant that Blanche's last family link to Perth was gone. Indeed, her death may have made it easier for Blanche to leave Perth.

In NZ Alfred took up the position of General Secretary of the Auckland YMCA. In 1921 he joined Rev. Kemp as associate minister of the Baptist Tabernacle in Auckland for a short period, before becoming the minister at Grange Road Baptist Church,

---

[52] Lilian Wooster Greaves, *The Road to Glory* (Perth: ST Upham, 1915), 2.
[53] Chapters 16 and 18 discuss Blanche's son Bernard and grandson Torrey respectively.

also in Auckland. Blanche was once again a minister's wife. Another move was made to St Albans in Christchurch from 1930–31, but they returned to Auckland after this pastorate. Alfred did not take up further full-time ministerial roles: he occasionally preached and he wrote a number of booklets on Christian living.

Blanche was a model minister's wife. Officials in the BUWA wrote that she was 'an able helpmeet and indefatigable co-worker with [Alfred].'[54] Likewise Alfred was almost certainly thinking about Blanche's contribution when he wrote: 'Truly Baptist ministers' wives are large contributors to the work, a fact generally insufficiently recognised.'[55] The *New Zealand Baptist* called her a 'shining saint'.[56] Yet, the attendance of Blanche at various events was often ignored by the writers of reports; for example in 1938 even Alfred was guilty of neglecting to reference Blanche in a letter he wrote about a visit to Perth.[57] Such omission was common for ministers' wives.[58]

Blanche (Mead) Wilson, Perth

[54] 'The Rev. A. S. Wilson', *West*, 13 June 1901, 2.
[55] Alfred S. Wilson, 'Notes on travel', *TSB*, 13 July 1901, 171.
[56] 'South Australia: passing of daughter of Silas Mead', 11. The term 'shining saint' was not used in other Baptist women's obituaries.
[57] Alfred S. Wilson, 'Letter to the editor', *West Australian* (Perth), 9 April 1938, 15. There was no mention of Blanche, yet she was clearly with Alfred during this visit (although an earlier article in the *West* referred to her as 'Dr Gertrude Mead').
[58] David Balfour, 'When it's your wife', in *Opening the Cage: Stories of Church and Gender*, ed. Margaret Ann Franklin and Ruth Sturmey Jones (Sydney: Allen & Unwin, 1987), 21. David Balfour, a man whose wife was an Anglican minister in NZ in the late twentieth century, wrote of his experience of being overlooked.

Alfred Wilson died on 17 October 1954, in Auckland, NZ. Blanche's son, then a Baptist minister in Tasmania, was not able to attend the funeral, but Blanche's daughter-in-law Winifred travelled to be with her. A large group of 'friends and loved ones' attended his memorial service at the Auckland Tabernacle.[59] With no family ties in NZ, 84-year-old Blanche returned to Australia.

Blanche and Alfred Wilson had spent almost forty years in NZ, nearly half of Blanche's life. Family folklore states that she initially went to Launceston with Bernard, Winifred and their children, and in 1956 they all moved 'back' to Adelaide, the city of Blanche's birth. Initially she lived with Bernard's family until she went to the Carinya Nursing Home in Adelaide where she died on 29 June 1961 at the age of 91. Blanche was present with the Mead family for the opening of Mead Hall prior to the centenary of FSBC, but had died before the Anniversary service August 1961. Blanche outlived all her siblings and their partners. She was buried in the family plot in West Terrace Cemetery, Adelaide, with her mother, step-mother, two sisters (Gertrude and Flora), and her brother (John Angel who was born and died on 12 October 1871). The unique obituary description of Blanche as a 'shining saint' was overly effusive, yet perhaps appropriate for a woman who was a dependable, faithful and committed Baptist woman, and a loving daughter, sister, wife, mother and grandmother.

---

[59] 'To higher service', *New Zealand Baptist* (Auckland), December 1954, 286.

15

Flora: 'Happy and Bright'

Rebecca Hilton

Flora Mead was the youngest child of Ann and Silas Mead. There are no extant writings from her, merely a few quotes from letters or conversations that she had with other people who recounted them at the time of her death. Except for Blanche, her siblings never mentioned her in their extant writings.[1] Little is known about her life experiences, such as her education or hobbies. She remains a mystery, like so many other young people who died in the nineteenth century from diseases that are now preventable.[2]

Flora as a baby

---

[1] Walter Barry, *There was a Man: The Life of Cecil Silas Mead: Missionary-Doctor* (Melbourne: Australian Baptist Foreign Mission, 1952), 13. Blanche recounted the story of Flora's death to Barry for the book.
[2] Fiona Stanley, 'Child health since Federation', Australian Bureau of Statistics, 1301.0 Year Book Australia, 2001, updated 5 October 2007. https://www.abs.gov.au/ausstats/ABS@.nsf/Previousproducts/1301.0Feature%20Article212001.

She was born on 20 January 1873 in Adelaide. In 1874 a photo was taken of her four older siblings, but she was not included. The obvious reason was that she was too young to sit. However, Ann and Silas were planning a trip to England to see relatives and it is likely that they were taking Flora with them, and accordingly she would not need to be in the photo with the older children who were staying in Adelaide. Ann's death of typhoid interrupted these plans. Instead, Silas went to England alone, and was away for sixteen months. Flora and her siblings were cared for by Sarah Hann, née Staple, who was Ann's younger sister. When Silas returned to Adelaide, Flora was three, and would not have remembered her father. Presumably Flora and her siblings returned to live with her father at this time.[3] In 1878 Silas remarried but Flora's new stepmother Mary does not appear to have been a significant figure in the life of the Mead children. Flora is the child who was most likely to have spent time with Mary, but she was described as saying: 'there is one thing I sometimes long for and that is a mother'.[4] Despite this longing, Flora was 'beloved for her bright, happy, innocent, and affectionate character'.[5]

Flora Mead

---

[3] Given Flora's age it is possible that she stayed with her aunt.
[4] 'In Memoriam: Flora Beatrice Mead', TP, 1 October 1886, 146.
[5] 'In Memoriam: Flora Beatrice Mead', TP, 1 October 1886, 146.

While Flora attended FSBC with the rest of her family, she had not yet been baptised. In early 1886, when asked whether she 'had given herself to her Saviour,' she was reported as responding:

> I can answer firmly and truly 'Yes' to your question. I have been His for some time, and although I fail many times yet I know He is the same, yesterday, today and forever.[6]

In August 1886 Flora and her older siblings Cecil and Blanche contracted typhoid. This would have created significant stress on Silas: three children sick with the disease that killed their mother. Flora died on 9 September 1886. Flora's death notice said:

> MEAD—On the 9th September, at the Flinders-Street Baptist Manse, Flora Beatrice, the beloved daughter of Rev. S. Mead, age nearly 14.[7]

However, the Baptist denominational paper *Truth and Progress* included a lengthy obituary for Flora.[8]

Naturally Silas was upset about Flora's death, but his faith was such that he believed that his wife and daughter would be together in eternal life. He wrote to his two children who were visiting relatives in England: 'We must rejoice that my darling Flora has had the privilege of being the first of our family to join her noble mother in glory.'[9] Some of the sympathy letters received by Silas reiterated this belief and her memorial service included the hymn 'For ever with the Lord'.[10] On 25 September 1886, two weeks after her death, the results of the SA Sunday School Union examinations were published, and Flora passed in the Senior Division.[11]

Silas wanted to see something positive from her death and wrote to the FSBC deacons suggesting arranging an evangelistic campaign led by the well-known English Congregationalist evangelist the Rev James Mountain:

> It would be a joy to me as my precious Flora's removal to the Saviour's Home may be used by God for the arousing of thoughtful solicitude and practical decision for Christ in the case of many of our young people. I feel a fresh and deeper interest in

[6] 'In Memoriam: Flora Beatrice Mead', *TP*, 1 October 1886, 146.
[7] 'Family notices', *Advertiser*, 10 September 1886, 4.
[8] 'In Memoriam: Flora Beatrice Mead', *TP*, 1 October 1886, 146.
[9] 'In Memoriam: Flora Beatrice Mead', *TP*, 1 October 1886, 146.
[10] 'In Memoriam: Flora Beatrice Mead', *TP*, 1 October 1886, 146.
[11] 'South Australian Sunday School Union', *Evening Journal* (Adelaide), 25 September 1886, 4.

the early salvation of the young in our families and in the school. I feel appalled at the thought of my position now were it not for the solid conviction that my child went last Thursday to her Lord and to her Mother up into the School above.[12]

Despite Silas's enthusiasm, Mountain's visit does not appear to have occurred due to his ill health.

[12] Silas Mead, Letter to Flinders Street Baptist Members meeting, in Flinders Street Baptist Members meeting minutes, 15 September 1886, 365.

16

Colin, Roger, Bernard: Silas's Grandsons

Rosalind Gooden

Silas Mead had six grandchildren: Cecil Silas Mead Wilson (born 1898 in WA), Dorothy Mead (1899 in India), Albion Staple Colin Wilson (1899 in WA), Roger Crosbie Brown (1902 in England), Marjory Mead (1903 in India) and Bernard Mead Wilson (in WA in 1904).[1] His first grandson Cecil Silas Mead Wilson, his namesake, only lived seven months, dying of enteritis,[2] yet another tragedy in the life of this family. Silas was in London at that time, isolated from the grieving family. While Silas was still in London Dorothy was born in Faridpur, India and Colin in Perth. But Roger was born in England, after Silas left; a year later Marjory was born in India. The only occasion when Silas was in the same city at the birth of a grandchild was with his last, Bernard Wilson in 1904 and then that family moved to New Zealand just three years later in 1907, where AS Wilson served as pastor of the Wanganui Baptist church. The Wilson family returned to WA late in 1912 with AS Wilson becoming the General Secretary of the YMCA, but by then Silas had died at the home of his daughter Dr Gertrude Mead on 13 September 1909. The Cecil Meads arrived from India six weeks later on 23 October 1909. Clearly, a price of ministry for Silas was very limited time with his grandchildren, and the price for the grandchildren was little time with

---

[1] Lilian and Crosbie Brown had Roger (1902); Cecil and Alice Mead had Dorothy (1899) and Marjory (1903); Blanche and Alfred Wilson had Cecil (1898), Colin (1899) and Bernard (1904).
[2] 'Family Notices: Deaths', *The West Australian (West)*, 25 November 1898, 4. An alternative cause of death as 'bubonic plague' is given by GS Freeman, 'Rev A S Wilson First Permanent Minister of Perth Baptist Church', *Westralian Baptist (WB)*, 3:3, 13 September 1988, 4.

Silas. Even so Silas left his mark on their lives. This chapter considers Silas's grandsons and the next chapter his granddaughters.

Colin Wilson–son of Silas's daughter Blanche

When Silas arrived back in Australia in 1902 Colin's parents (with him) were away representing WA Baptists at the Baptist Union meetings in Edinburgh. For the next five years Colin was to be in the church where his father was the pastor and his grandfather was co-pastor. In fact, the Wilsons lived in the one household with Silas and Aunty Gertrude until the Wilsons moved to New Zealand. There Colin continued as a 'PK' ('pastor's kid') while his father pastored churches between 1907 and 1912.

Silas with Bernard and Colin

From New Zealand in 1912 Colin's father, Alfred S Wilson, accepted the secretaryship of the Perth YMCA and was to be deeply involved in the establishing of a credible program for the all-round development of young men. Alfred was ably supported by several Baptist laymen, particularly Hann and Cargeeg. At the Perth Modern School, Colin was both an excellent student and a significant member of both tennis and cricket teams.[3] On finishing school he worked as a bank clerk.

---

[3] 'The Late Private ASC Wilson', *West,* 16 December 1918, 6.

Over the years the Perth YMCA had made several attempts to establish programs.[4] In 1907 they enlisted sponsors, including George Cargeeg (a significant Baptist from FSBC and PBC).[5] They did commence a magazine, *Perth Young Men.* One of their targets was to acquire their own premises. In the process Mrs Annie Oliver, the converted hotelier, donated a site of land in Murray Street,[6] between the *Westralia* (which she owned) and the *Bon Marche* store, where Cargeeg conducted his business with her son.[7] She nominated Silas Mead as her representative on the YMCA Board, which he served until his death.

The two main influences on teenage Colin were church and YMCA. He was appointed the organist at the Church, only resigning as he embarked for the First World War Front. He conducted the Sunday school choir, a competent musician, like his Uncle Cecil, working often with Gwen Harry, the pastor's daughter.

Perth (Museum Street) Baptist Church was being constantly impacted by the events of the war. Their roll of honour contains seventy-seven names, including one woman, Nurse M Ashton. There are twelve who gave their lives 'for God and humanity' as the roll claims. News of the war was part of Baptist church life; the women formed a Comfort Society to prepare packages for their soldiers; the pastor's wife, Helen Harry, wrote numerous letters to their soldiers.

Perth Baptist Church Roll of Honour

[4] Tom Austen, *Something Worthwhile: A History of the Perth YMCA* (West Perth: St Georges Books, 1992).
[5] Rhonda Walker, 'George Henry Cargeeg JP a devout man 1851-1925', *WB* 9:2, 1994.
[6] Ann Harding, 'In Search of Annie Oliver', *WB* 8:1, 2005, 15.
[7] Austen, *Something Worthwhile*, 34.

Initially in 1912 the YMCA under Wilson was serving young men but as the war intensified the YMCA developed more and more programs to care for embarking and serving soldiers. The Perth YMCA with its facilities at Blackboy Hill training camp 'had the largest Social Hall in any military camp in the world able to seat 4,000 men'.[8] Colin was a cadet for four years before enlisting as a Private on 27 June 1918 and then trained at Blackboy Hill until he embarked on the *Boonah* on 29 October, just a week over 19 years of age.

Colin as a Private in Army uniform

The *Boonah* with more than 1,000 soldiers was the last troopship to leave Australia during the First World War.[9] Colin wrote cheerfully to his brother Bernard describing life on board:

> It's quite interesting to take a midnight stroll on deck this weather. It's pitch dark and you are bound to tumble over quelquechose [something] (no lights on board of course after 9pm) and if you have any luck over comes the sea and washes your pyjamas for you.

---

[8] Ann Harding, 'World War 1 and the Effect on the Baptist Churches of Western Australia on the Century of the Armistice to end World War 1', *WB* 24.1, 2019, 3.
[9] Ian Darroch, *The Boonah Tragedy* (Bassenden: Access Press, 2004).

Thinking of home, Colin imagined his brother playing the church organ for the service, Bernard's geometry lessons and a new cricket bat: 'hope…the windows of the house are intact'.

They had not even reached Cape Town when armistice was declared on 11 November 1918. They were instructed to refuel in Cape Town, their troops mingled with wharf labourers, and the ship became infected with Spanish flu that during the return voyage to Perth spread rapidly. Colin was one of the victims. The story of the handling of the situation in the light of the COVID-19 pandemic makes interesting reading.[10] There were bureaucratic delays in responding to the outbreak and caring for those who were ill.[11] Eventually, Colin was taken off the ship to the Quarantine Station at Woodman Point that was ill equipped to handle the situation. Appeals were made for volunteer nurses and twenty were recruited, including one Baptist woman, Hilda Wilson, who also died at Woodman Point.[12]

Colin died two days after his transfer to the station and was buried there by his minister Rev FE Harry. The following was shared with the Baptist family:

> Colin Wilson was a manly and beautiful youth, clean of heart and life, and the very soul of honour. A promising speaker, with a charming manner and a gracious personality, his pastor hoped that he would soon be preaching the Gospel; whilst his musical instructor, Mr Leckie, Mus Bac, predicted for him a splendid musical career…In the church and Sunday School there is much sorrow: for Colin was not only church organist, but conductor of the Sunday School choir.[13]

As Rebecca Hilton sums it up:

> The story of the *Boonah* was very quickly driven from public attention. Firstly, the Western Australian Government did not want a formal investigation into how badly the soldiers…had been treated and secondly, Spanish Influenza found its way into every state and became a much wider issue. But a large number of people were pushing for a formal investigation…Colin's family

[10] See Glenn Davies, '1918 HMAT Boonah flu tragedy echoes cruise ship COVID-19 debacle'; independentaustralia.net, 12 April 2020.
[11] Henry Weston, Letter to editor, 'The Boonah Tragedy', *West*, 12 March 1919, 8.
[12] Daughter of William Wilson, lay pastor at Claremont and Louisa, who had already had their son Arthur killed in action. Hilda was a civilian nurse, and her grave is still at Woodman Point, while those of military personnel were moved.
[13] *AB*, 31 December 1918, 7.

was devastated. His father wrote a very comprehensive letter including the line 'I believe my son was murdered between his berth and his bed at Woodman's (sic) Point'.[14]

Roger Crosbie Brown—son of Silas's daughter Lilian

Crosbie Charles Brown had married Silas's daughter Lilian and later wrote to his niece Marjory Mead in 1951:

> During my honeymoon Lilian told me that her father would leave Harley College at the end of June 1901 when the college year ended. So in 1901 Mr Mead left for Australia. About 1905 he came again to England and stayed with us at Clarence School, Weston Super Mare for a short time. You may know [the] photo of him and Roger (who was born 26 Aug 1902).[15]

Silas Mead with Roger Crosbie Brown, c. 1905

Roger was an only son. We know less of this grandson, for despite Mead suggesting that the Crosbie Browns would happily come to live in Australia if there was suitable employment, they never did so. Roger lived with his parents, alongside the

---

[14] 'The Boonah Tragedy Reply to Dr Cox', *West*, 10 March 1919, 5. Email Rebecca Hilton to Rosalind Gooden, 7 April 2021.
[15] Personal Letter Crosbie Brown to Marjory Mead, 21 March 1951 in Gooden/Mead collection.

international boarding home they ran for overseas tertiary students, while his father taught in various schools. He gained London Matriculation in September 1919, and enrolled as a student at St Thomas' Hospital. On 1 October 1927 he qualified as a MRCS (Member of the Royal College of Surgeons) and LRCP (Licentiate of Physicians). In 1932 he returned to live in the family home. In 1938, the year he married Emily Lloyd, he was working at HM Prison, Hornby Road, Walton Park, Liverpool, and between 1939 and 1946 he was deputy superintendent of Crowthorne Asylum, Berkshire. He was a qualified instructor for the Air Raid Precautions in the Second World War. Roger and Emily had three children: Avril who was born in 1941 (and died at three), son Robin in 1943 and then Audrey in 1945. Roger died in Rye, East Sussex 26 August 1991. Roger certainly carried on a Mead tradition of humanitarian medical service.[16]

Roger Crosbie Brown with his children Robin and Audrey

[16] Unfortunately, nothing is known about his church connections. They are not mentioned in his father's surviving correspondence with Dorothy or Marjory Mead.

Bernard Mead Wilson—son of Silas's daughter Blanche

Bernard Wilson (left) with his older brother Colin and father Rev Alfred S Wilson

The third son of Blanche and Alfred Wilson was Bernard, born in Perth on 1 September 1904, five years after Colin. In 1907 the family moved to New Zealand and did not return until 1912. The family then remained in Perth until after the end of the First World War and Colin's tragic death. Much of Bernard's nurture was in the PBC, in the shadow of his brother Colin, and in the YMCA where his father was General Secretary. He attended Guildford Grammar School. The family returned to New Zealand in 1921 where his father was the Assistant Minister at the Auckland Tabernacle for a short time before moving to Grange Road Baptist Church in suburban Auckland. By this time, Bernard was 26.

Bernard (left) with his mother Blanche and father Alfred in New Zealand

On 3 March 1926 Bernard was one of the students of the Baptist College of New Zealand as it moved to a new property at the Tabernacle in Auckland. That day Rev Lionel Fletcher led in prayer, 'asking that many would come from the College on fire to win sons for Christ and so set New Zealand ablaze for him'.[17] Lionel Fletcher became Bernard's mentor, someone he respected deeply, and Bernard's son, Torrey, writes:

> A name which was heard with almost tiresome regularity down through the years in the Wilson household. The family all knew who Lionel Fletcher was. In his day he had been called the Empire Evangelist.

Torrey also adds of his father:

> While in his room in [the NZ Baptist Theological College] in Mount Hobson, he knew the power of God come upon him, assuring of salvation full and free. In a moment of dedication he promised the Lord that if given the chance, he would 'belt' the globe with the Gospel.[18]

[17] EF Sherburd and AL Silcock, *Eighteen Thousand Yesterdays. The Story of The NZ Baptist Theological College* (Auckland: Institute Press, 1976).
[18] Torrey Wilson, 'A Brief Survey of the Life and Ministry of Baptist Minister Rev Bernard Wilson: with particular reference to his call to evangelism during the years 1930-1939' (Essay submitted to Burleigh College, 4 November 1983).

The newly ordained Bernard Wilson went from College to Opawa in Christ-church with 'the fire of the Spirit lit in his heart'. It was to be a time of rapid growth and vitality. Three years later he decided to accept a persistent call from the Sema-phore Baptist church in SA, much to the regret of the NZBU who had trained him. They felt he should serve in New Zealand for at least another two years.

South Australia meant family associations. His uncle, Dr Cecil Mead, led in prayer at his induction to the pastorate. Bernard's ministry was a time when many responded to the gospel message. He was dedicated at a rally in FSBC in April 1934 for a Discipleship Campaign held in Gawler, Port Pirie, Goodwood and Broken Hill.

Lionel Fletcher and Mildmay Centre invited Bernard to participate in its London Campaign. He left Outer Harbour on 8 January 1936 and preached in Baptist churches including Spurgeon's Tabernacle until September. From September to March 1937 he worked with affirming success in the Great London Evangelistic Campaign. The *Australian Baptist* carried regular news of his ministries.[19] He then travelled north and attended Keswick Convention in July. He returned to Australia in order to join the World Christian Endeavour Convention in Melbourne as a sessional speaker. While there he discovered his bride-to-be, Win Hughes, among the New Zealand delegates.

Bernard on board ship for London in 1936

In 1939, Bernard made a hurried trip to New Zealand between missions to marry and bring back his bride to NSW to be the pastor's wife at East Chatswood, followed by a time at the Manly Baptist church, where their daughter Colleen was

19 *AB*, July 1935, 4; January 1936, 4; February 1936, 7; January 1937, 4.

born. The family returned to New Zealand in 1941 to the Free Methodist Church in Auckland, then Royal Oak Church and a ministry at the Grange Road Baptist Church from where he had entered the ministry during his father's ministry there. While in New Zealand young Colleen saw much of her grandparents but could not manage to say 'grandfather', so shortened the name to 'Farr', which became Alfred's family name.

From New Zealand the family returned to Australia and the pastorate of the Ballarat Central church in Victoria. After four years in Victoria calls were accepted from Nundah church in Brisbane and then Punchbowl in New South Wales. At the historic Henry Reed Memorial Baptist Church, Launceston, Tasmania, in 1955 the family was joined by the widowed Blanche. They returned to South Australia. One of the guiding factors was Bernard's desire that his mother return to the place of her father, Silas, and the friends of her youth.

Win and Bernard Wilson, with Torrey, Raewyn, Colleen

Opportunities for ministry in South Australia were accepted at Mount Barker, Colonel Light Gardens and Finsbury Park (later named Woodville North) churches. On retirement, Bernard accepted interim ministries at Peterhead, then returned to his loved Semaphore, where he was interim until his son Torrey was inducted into that pastorate.

> Brief ministries characterised [Bernard's] style, despite on numerous occasions pleadings for him to stay longer. Yet he would always move on, almost as though he could never be content until he had 'belted' the world with the gospel. To this end, he lived and died and was laid to rest on November 17th 1981...Somehow God in His grace used the restless, urgent nature of one such as Bernard Mead Wilson to bring many to the crisis moment of decision for Christ and into the Kingdom of God.[20]

Bernard had grandfather Silas's commitment to the Gospel, counting himself privileged to declare the 'unsearchable riches of Christ'.[21] He accompanied his mother to the dedication of the renamed Mead Hall on 30 March 1958.[22]

---

[20] Torrey Wilson, 'A Brief Survey', 10.
[21] Ephesians 3:8b.
[22] *AB*, 9 April 1958, 28.

Dorothy, Marjory: Silas's Granddaughters

Rosalind Gooden

Torrey Wilson gave me a fine collection of old photos of the Mead family: Silas with his first wife, then with his second wife, with his children at various ages, and with his grandsons Colin, Bernard and Roger. But there are no photographs of Silas with his granddaughters, sisters Dorothy and Marjory.[1] Why? Did they ever meet? What did it mean to be the granddaughters of Silas and Ann, and daughters of Silas's son Cecil and Alice Mead? Did Silas's granddaughters carry on the enthusiasms and gifts of their grandfather? Their parents were missionaries of that colonial era, where education and travel were more valued than family togetherness; the children were what today would be called 'MKs' ('Missionary Kids') or 'Third Culture Kids'.[2] Silas did in fact meet his granddaughters in Bengal, India, over Christmas 1905, when Marjory was almost two and Dorothy was six, but no photograph seems to have survived, which is ironic when we owe so much to both Dorothy and Marjory for so many Mead family treasures.

Missionary parents

Alice Pappin, their mother, went to Bengal in 1885. Their father, Dr Cecil Mead, arrived eight years later in 1893. Alice and Cecil's engagement was announced on 17 October 1894, but mission rules demanded no marriage until Cecil passed language

---

[1] Dorothy (26 August 1899 – 9 May 1988), Marjory (29 March 1903 – 10 May 1973)
[2] In today's post-colonial world Missionary Children (MKs) are becoming an increased focus of study and care.

exams. Silas, while visiting Bengal, finally decided he wanted to witness his son's wedding. Alice promptly joined them in Nellore, South India and she and Cecil married on 24 February 1896.[3]

Alice was 38 when Dorothy was born in Faridpur on 26 August 1899, presumably delivered by her father. Cecil feared for Alice's life for several weeks, but the baby was healthy. Almost immediately, the family planned leave in Australia. Before they left, Cecil chaired the Missionary Convention for 1899 at Comilla:

> ...our President received one of those horrid yellow-labelled telegrams. Poor little Dorothy had taken a bad turn and needed her father's skill. It was wise therefore...that Dr. Mead should leave...[W]e...prayed, remembering specially that the doctor would soon be homeward [Australia] bound. [4]

Alice Mead with Dorothy

When the family reached Adelaide, Silas was in England so there were no photo shoots with him while the family recuperated in the home of George Swan Fowler.[5] In November 1901 the family travelled through Perth to Faridpur, just after Silas and

---

[3] For further details on the parents see Chapter 12.
[4] *OB*, December 1899, 4.
[5] Elva Schroeder, *Doctor Sahib: The Story of Dr Cecil Silas Mead* (Capalaba, Qld: Even Before Publishing, 2013), 67.

Gertrude arrived back from London. A photo shows Silas and Cecil at a Goalundo Mission meeting (see chapter 8) but no photo of Silas and Dorothy are in our collection. But at least they met (and again in 1905 in India). The family arrived back in Bengal for December 1901 to join the Convention at Mymensingh, where there were other MKs. The missionary children were recorded as attendees:

> the two little Nevilles—Ernest and David, Dorothy Mead, and Baby Takle...[The President] also gave Dr and Mrs Mead a hearty welcome back from Australia and did not forget a word for 'the two new little zenana missionaries'—Miss Dorothy Mead and the little one from Brahmanbaria.[6]

But although there were other Australasian missionary children in Bengal, the families were isolated and only met annually at Convention or at boarding school.

Marjory arrived on 29 March 1903 at Faridpur. *Our Bond* referred to it as 'DO-MESTIC OCCURRENCE'!![7] This was another home birth.

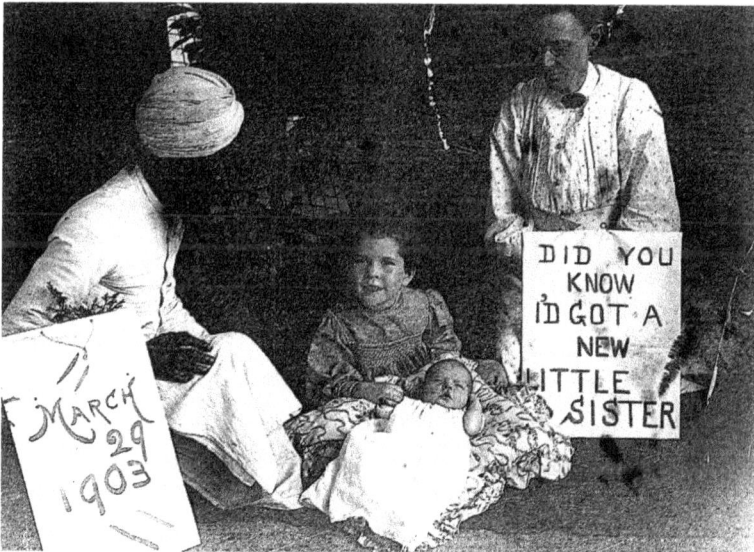

Dorothy announces the arrival of Marjory lovingly watched by Ellen Arnold

[6] *OB*, December 1901, 3.
[7] *OB*, April 1903, 8.

Life of MKs in India

Mid-year 1905, Alice went to Darjeeling with the girls to leave Dorothy in school, returning to the plains with two-year-old Marjory. Boarding school for a six-year-old! Dorothy herself writes: 'We both went to boarding school, Queen's Hill School in Darjeeling. I went aged 5 and Marjory at 6. Mother usually took us all the way to Darjeeling.'[8] This involved about thirty-six hours of travel. Dorothy adds more details of the challenges of travel:

> Missionaries usually travelled Intermediate class—not at all comfortable. Robbers were common and skilful. On one such trip to school one got into our carriage. Mother woke to see some luggage disappearing but managed to grab it and foiled the thief. Their poverty makes you judge them less harshly—but missionaries couldn't afford to lose meagre possessions.[9]

Alice wrote of a mother's feelings about the schooling experiences of 1908:

> After over three-and-a-half month's exile in Darjeeling it is very pleasant to be at home again…Out of fifteen weeks about twelve were spent in quarantine, for first one child and then another. But we feel we have much to be thankful for, in that Marjory's diphtheria was not a very severe type. However it left her a good deal pulled down and immediately on the top of it she got whooping cough…As there was no prospect of her re-entering school I had to bring her home, and I also brought Dorothy as friend and companion. Life for one child is far too lonely here.[10]

Cecil was known to say, 'Only the kettle stood between us and cholera'.[11] All drinking water had to be boiled and food cooked. There were snakes, mad dogs and earthquakes. The expectation that mothers would stay in the hills for several months while fathers remained working on the plains became the norm as the separate Australian Baptist Societies federated. By this time there were reputable schools for expatri-

---

[8] Arcadia, Queen's Hill School founded in 1895 was later known as Mount Hermon School. In 1918 the total enrolment was 163 students.
[9] Personal letter, Dorothy Mead to Elva Schroeder. Gooden/Mead collection.
[10] *OB*, September 1908, 3.
[11] Personal letter from Dorothy Mead to Elva Schroeder, 3 May 1982 discussing *Doctor Sahib*. Gooden/Mead collection.

ates in the Himalayas, and their students studied an English curriculum. Good news of schooling was shared with home supporters and missionary 'aunts and uncles'.[12]

> Our readers, and supporters will rejoice with Dr and Mrs Mead in the success of their 'girlies' in the Cambridge exams...The long-looked-for results arrived the other day...The first batch of results was evidently lost and another set had to be sent. But they were worth waiting for. Dorothy passed FIRST in the Senior and Marjory FIRST in the Preliminary *with honours.* Marjory is justly proud to be the only 'Honours' girl in the School. She writes, 'My back absolutely aches from the congratulatory thumps I have had to bear.'[13]

Schooling was always suspended at Christmas, the cool season. They returned to the plains and Marjory later wrote of her childhood memories of going out to the villages on boats and living in the district headquarters of Faridpur:

> Mother and Dad often made long itinerating trips together. Sometimes we would be left in charge of kindly missionaries, once at least we went too. Mother could tell of...cyclonic storms, when it seemed that the next gust <u>must</u> turn the boat over. At home while storms crashed overhead making mother nervous, Dad would always spend the time at the organ with all the stops out. We heard of the earthquake that cracked every arch in the Faridpur house...That house and compound are the background of our memories of childhood. There was the big tank behind where baptisms were sometimes held. The dispensary nearby where in delicious horror we might watch minor operations; the Christian homes where we played with Nirmolla, Kirti, lame Binodhini and the rest. We would stand in the road on bazaar days, begging bits of sugar cane from passers-by...Convention times were exciting, the house full of guests and the over flow occupying tents. Redoubtable 'Aunty Nell' (Miss Arnold) would be there of course. The Nalls with Doris and Cliff, the Barrys, the Ings and many more.[14]

---

[12] In mission circles all the colleagues were called 'Uncle' or 'Aunt' by the MKs. The single women often had a special relationship with these surrogate nieces and nephews. This was particularly so for Ellen Arnold and Dorothy Mead.
[13] *OB,* May 1916, 10.
[14] Marjory Mead, 'A daughter of missionaries remembers', undated manuscript, Baptist Mission Australia archives.

Alice with Marjory (holding pot), Dorothy and an unidentified playmate at Faridpur

'Aunty Nell' was special in the lives of the girls. She had been God's instrument in Dorothy's early spiritual decisions and wrote of Dorothy's baptism in Faridpur at the age of eleven. 'Aunty' Ellen ('Nell') Arnold wrote:

> [I] reached Goalundo...to catch the night mail to Rajbari, and camp in the Faridpur train, for had not the Mead family arrived, and Auntie had not seen the bairns for two years...Dorothy soon confided that she was to be baptized on Sunday. How Auntie's heart rejoiced! Father and mother kindly arranged for the baptism to be on Thursday afternoon, January 5th, my dear father's birthday...we all repaired to the tank to witness three young girls being buried with Christ. First came Nirmola, then Dorothy, and her father had to make a visible pause before speaking to her and baptizing her in Bengali manner, she clothed in a sari, for oh what unspeakable thanksgiving was in his heart... Last came the paralysed Binodini.[15]

Life was also interrupted by lengthy visits to Australia. In 1909–10 while the missionary women established work at Orakandi the family was in Australia with Cecil travelling widely. But they did not make it in time to see Silas before his death.

15 *OB*, February 1911, 7.

On their return to Bengal in 1911 the girls visited their new home in Orakandi, staying in temporary rooms until time for school in March.

Marjory chose to be baptised in Orakandi by her father in 1914.

Late in 1918 another trip to Australia was due. The whole family was suffering from (Spanish?) influenza. There was no available shipping until April 1919, so Marjory was unable to start schooling in Adelaide until later that year, another stress for MKs. There was additional strain:

> ...[Cecil's] health is very poor and the [welcome home] reception proved almost overwhelming. He has been ill since arrival but is showing signs of recovery. We shall have to exercise self-denial...He needs the completest rest possible, and all public meetings must be cut out.[16]

Their Aunt Gertrude, Cecil's sister, came to visit the family in Adelaide and died unexpectedly while with them.

The girls remained in Adelaide when their parents left again on 1 October 1920. Dorothy was enrolled in medical studies at the University of Adelaide and Marjory completed her matriculation at Methodist Ladies' College.

Cecil, Dorothy, Alice and Marjory, Orakandi, 1919

---

16 *OB*, 24 May 1919, 6.

Professional life

Unexpectedly, at the end of 1921, their parents again returned to Australia with Cecil's health wrecked. The reunited family found a home in North Adelaide, which they named 'Orakandi'.[17] At the end of her second-year medical course Dorothy withdrew. She holidayed with the Wilson family in 1926 and Alice wrote thanking Blanche for 'spendidly young[ing] her up'.[18] While in New Zealand Dorothy was described in the Auckland press social notes as a guest of her aunt, Mrs AS Wilson of Mt Eden, and as a native of Eastern Bengal on a first visit to Auckland during the university vacation.[19]

Marjory Mead, Crosbie and Lilian Brown, Switzerland, 1926.

Dorothy re-enrolled at Adelaide University in Arts, clearly a brilliant student, and was granted BA (Honours) in English. She taught English and French at Creveen School in North Adelaide. After its closure she was appointed Medical Librarian at the University of Adelaide in 1938, where she worked until retirement. Dorothy commissioned Elva Schroeder to write the story of her father's life as a book for children,

---

17 The property is still called 'Orakandi' in Melbourne Street, North Adelaide.
18 Alice Mead to Blanche Wilson, 6 February 1926, handwritten letter. Gooden/Mead collection.
19 'Women's World', Auckland Star, 15 January 1926.

published as *Doctor Sahib: The Story of Dr Cecil Silas Mead*. Dorothy corresponded extensively with the author in 1982.

Marjory took her matriculation in 1921 (just as her parents arrived home) and joined the Education Department, training for infant teaching. She eventually completed her Bachelor of Arts degree on 13 December 1932. She progressed to Inspector in 1952 and was later appointed as Assistant Superintendent of Infant Departments. She published *The Teaching of Reading in Grades I and II* in 1957. It was noted that she was the first woman in South Australia to attain a post above that of an Inspector.

On her retirement in 1973 'her' retired infant mistresses gave annual gifts for an educational scholarship for Bangladeshi women, augmented in Marjory's honour by the SA Senior Girls Missionary Union (SGMU). The first recipient was Sunita Ritchil, a teacher at the Oxford Mission at Haluaghat in 1973 and the final grant was to Supti Diba in 2003.[20]

Marjory Mead, 1973

Passion for missions

Both Marjory and Dorothy shared the Mead passion for mission. Like their grandfather Silas and their parents, Dorothy and Marjory believed in evangelism and

---

[20] G Dodge letter and notes to Marjorie Gooden, 1992; GL Johnson letter to ML Gooden, 26 April 1992, Gooden/Mead collection. The list of the recipients is in the Gooden/Senior Girls Missionary Union collection (Gooden/SGMU collection.).

the significance of prayer. I still remember Marjory telling me that every time she participated in a communion service she prayed specifically for Orakandi. Marjory herself considered missionary service, but a medical clearance was felt unlikely. She came to the opinion 'that God wanted her *to be willing* to be obedient to His call.' [21]

Their interest was particularly focused through the SGMU. A handwritten document headed SA SGMU records the initiative of Faridpur missionary Dr Alice Barber (known as 'Aunty Alice' to Dorothy and Marjory):

> In 1922 while in Melbourne on furlough from India [Dr Alice] Barber was invited to address the ladies of many churches...The idea came to her of what a fine thing it would be if the elder girls of our churches could be similarly banded together—The idea grew into a reality and in several of the churches groups were formed 'of girls whose...interest in Foreign Missions became burning as they learned more of our Mission activities'...*To study—To pray—To give*, might well be taken as the 'motto'... These separate groups soon formed themselves into a Union which became known as the [SGMU].[22]

The first SGMU group in South Australia was formed in FSBC in July 1923. By August 1925 ten branches formed the South Australian Missionary Union.[23] Dorothy was their first treasurer.[24] As they planned their first camp she was appointed convenor of the Recreation Committee, and after camp she took on the role of editor of the *Camp Chronicle*. She was very active as the SA SGMU decided to support the Widows' Home at Orakandi. She challenged the branches to have targets for their giving, showing Silas-like skills of organisation and fund raising. By 1928 Marjory, too, was a regular member of the State committee, and song leader for camp. She was to go on to lead the local, state and federal Union.[25] Her role was foundational.

In 1906 Alice Mead started to collect saleable items to raise funds for orphans from Faridpur whom she had sent to school at Mymensingh. She borrowed £10 to make a capital of £50. She bought jewellery, handicrafts and handmade cards. Her daughters assisted her and then carried on this tradition after Alice's death in 1935,

[21] In handwritten notes made by Mrs Marjorie Gooden of an SGMU Leaders meeting at Lobethal in 1946 or 1947 where Marjory spoke on her indecision and its results, in Gooden/SGMU collection..
[22] Handwritten account 'A Broad and Illuminating Survey of the SA SGMU' by Miss Nancy Waddy, in Gooden/SGMU collection.
[23] Notes in front of the Central Executive Minute Book, Gooden/SGMU collection.
[24] SA SGMU Executive Meeting, 25 September 1925, Gooden/SGMU collection.
[25] There is no definitive history of the Australian SGMU from 1922 to the 1990s.

as did Dorothy after Marjory's death in 1973. Every year, payments were made to ABMS. In addition, the major beneficiary of Dorothy's will in 1988 was the ABMS with the instructions that funds be used as the organisation may see fit in the mission field overseas and she expressed the wish—but without creating an obligation so to do—to give preference to its work in Bangladesh.

Dorothy Mead, 1982

Both Dorothy and Marjory are buried in the Mitcham Cemetery with their parents.

Conclusion

Both women were passionate about family history, visiting Somerset in England on many occasions, accumulating notes of gravestones, letters of relatives, articles and photos. There is a delightful record of one such family visit by Marjory to the home of her aunt Lilian in England:

> It was a coincidence that the *Bhagabati* who was a little boy when we went to Orakandi not knowing a word of English should meet the...formerly 'little teacher Marjory', who in holidays loved to marshal the kindergarten boys and give them lessons.... Orakandi was a great subject of conversation that Sunday

evening at Mrs Brown's tea table. Most truly some of the *Bara Karta's* dreams of his family and his caste rising in the social scale were coming true. Whether *Bhagabati* is allowing himself to be influenced towards actually becoming a Christian we have not a hint.[26]

When FSBC renovated its property in preparation for its centenary on 30 March 1958, the sisters turned the key into the newly decorated Mead Hall supported by their aunt Blanche Wilson and her son Rev. Bernard Wilson.

Their collections of memorabilia and personal records have been carefully deposited in places like Flinders Street and North Adelaide Baptist churches, Baptist Mission Australia archives, the State Library of South Australia, and with the family. The editors of this volume are indebted to the family for making this collection available for research.

---

[26] July 1928, 3. *Bhagabati* was a son of the *Bara Kata*, leader of the Nama Sudras at Orakandi. He was studying in London, and had made a good name at the Scottish Church College.

18

Torrey: Reflections of a Great-Grandson of Silas Mead

Torrey Wilson

I grew up from my earliest years knowing three significant things of importance to our family: Silas Mead, Flinders Street Baptist Church and the Bible.

My mother, Lucy Winifred ('Win') Jackson Wilson (née Hughes) of New Zealand, instilled in us the family history, although my father, Rev. Bernard Mead Wilson, was really the direct descendant of Silas Mead. He once recounted to me about sitting on the knee of Silas Mead, his grandfather—which would have been a lasting memory for 'Barney'—surely a boy no older than four years of age at the time.

From time to time, dad visited his cousins in North Adelaide, Dorothy and Marjory Mead, the unmarried daughters of my great-uncle, Dr Cecil Mead, the only son of Silas; and I, too, was able to meet them during my years at Teachers' College. At that time, Marjory had retired as the SA Education Department inspector of infant schools and Dorothy had retired as the librarian in charge of the Adelaide University Medical School Library.

My father's mother, one of Silas Mead's daughters, Annie Blanche ('Blanche') Wilson was brought over in 1954 from New Zealand to Tasmania to live with our family following the death of her husband, and my grandfather, Rev. Alfred Samuel Wilson of Auckland, New Zealand. At that time, my father, Bernard Wilson, was the minister of the historic Henry Reed Memorial Baptist Church in the heart of Launceston, Tasmania.

My boyhood memory of 'Grandma (Blanche) Wilson' living with us in Tasmania was of someone austere and forthright in her opinions, albeit she was an elderly lady even then—which, being interpreted, probably means I had to be as well-behaved as I could and reduce any noise I made around the house!

Three generations: Bernard Wilson (left), his mother Blanche ('Grandma') and son Torrey (centre)

Whilst in previous years I had received correspondence and books of encouragement in Christian living mailed over from New Zealand by my grandfather AS Wilson ('Farr', as we called him), I deeply regret not knowing him personally. So, the experience of knowing Grandma Wilson was indeed special, even if not fully recognised at the time. She was, in fact, the only grandparent I was fortunate to know.

Recognising that his mother was in the latter years of her life, my father felt bringing Grandma Wilson back to her roots in South Australia would be a meaningful thing to do. With Grandma Wilson now as part of the family, we left Tasmania to settle in South Australia. I remember the eager anticipation when our immediate family walked from the North Terrace Grosvenor Hotel (where we were staying temporarily) for my first visit to the historic family church in Flinders Street during the ministry of the late Rev. LJ Gomm. In 1958, as a boy of twelve years of age, it was all a big experience—a big church building, big family connections, and a big welcome to South Australia.

Soon after arriving in Adelaide, we went to live at Mount Barker where dad commenced ministry in the Baptist Church. It was certainly a contrast to the grand Memorial Church he had left and other previous pastorates in the eastern states. However, he gave of his best and in his four years there he built up the diminished congregation which, in hindsight, provided a good foundation for the thriving Mount Barker Baptist Church of today.

As Grandma Wilson advanced in years, with a greater dependency on family support due to age and infirmity, it became more difficult for my parents to meet her needs in addition to caring for Colleen and Raewyn, my two older sisters, and me. (Raewyn was initially named 'Raewyn Cecil' but she later changed her name to 'Raewyn Christine'.)

Eventually, reluctantly, a place was found for Grandma Wilson in the then 'Carinya' nursing home, Fisher Street, Fullarton.[1] My father would visit her at least once or twice a week, and as often as his work allowed him to travel from the manse in Mount Barker to see her, to take her for the usual drive to Brown Hill Creek and back.

At the age of 91, Annie Blanche Mead, my Grandma Wilson, died and, following her funeral in Mead Hall of the Flinders Street Baptist Church (as the renovations for the Church Centenary were in progress), she was buried in a family plot in West Terrace Cemetery, Adelaide.

From Mt Barker, we moved to the city where dad took up pastorates at Colonel Light Gardens (now Trinity Baptist), Finsbury Park (later named Woodville North) and other interim ministries during his retirement.

My late father had had significant ministries in New Zealand, and in most states of Australia. Amongst those were Manly (New South Wales), Semaphore (South Australia), Ballarat Baptist Tabernacle (Victoria) where I was born and blessed with the name Torrey Alfred Mead Wilson, Nundah Baptist (Queensland), Memorial Baptist Church, Launceston (Tasmania) and then further pastorates in South Australia, including a brief ministry at Semaphore from which he had left forty years earlier to join Rev. Lionel Fletcher's evangelistic team in England. Following his interim ministry at Semaphore in 1975, I commenced a six-year ministry there in 1976.

---

[1] Now known as Carinya Aged Care, 39 Fisher Street, Myrtle Bank, SA.

Some years later, as a theological student in Burleigh College, Adelaide, I chose to write a brief summary of the early ministry of my father as an evangelist and church builder in New Zealand, New South Wales, South Australia (State Evangelist) and the wider Evangelistic Mildmay Campaign in England in the 1930s.[2]

These were his gifts which may well have been in the DNA of Silas Mead, his grandfather, and AS Wilson, his father. In any case, he would have been reminded of his heritage through his mother, Silas Mead's daughter.

What did it mean for me to live in the shadow of the great Silas Mead, the re- nowned Dr Cecil Mead, the Rev. AS Wilson, who ministered with Silas Mead, his fa- ther-in-law, at Perth Baptist Church in Western Australia, and then, for me, to follow in my father's footsteps into ministry?

On becoming a fourth-generation ordained minister of the Baptist churches of South Australia in 1984, following my six years as a teacher and further ten years of pastoral ministry prior to ordination, I have sometimes mused as to where some of the early influences of my call to the ministry may have come. From an early age, I felt my course was set by family history, conditioning and probably the expectation of my mother's prayers. I trust the guiding hand of God was also present, although God has also guided me into other concurrent careers in human services.

Whilst I would have chosen to have been ordained in the Flinders Street Baptist Church because of family and historic links, my ordination took place in the former Norwood Baptist Church, on The Parade, which, nevertheless, was one of the many churches in Adelaide which had the early marks of the Rev. Silas Mead's influence being indelibly part of its history.

I doubt that there will be a fifth generation Baptist minister of the Mead line, albeit my two sons and daughter have achieved success in their chosen careers, as have the other great-great-grandchildren of my older sisters, Colleen Page and Raewyn Corey. However, my niece, Vanessa Corey and my nephew, Greg Mead Corey, have been in Japan teaching English in a Christian school for many years. So, it was a joyous occasion for my wife Elizabeth and me to attend the baptism of Silas Mead's great-great-great-grandson, Jack Corey, in Tokyo in 2017.

---

[2] Torrey AM Wilson, 'A Brief Survey of the Life and Ministry of Baptist Minister Rev Bernard Mead Wilson, with particular reference to his call to evangelism during the years 1930-1939' (Research paper, Burleigh College, 1983). This paper was used by Ros Gooden in research for chapter 16 of this book.

Torrey Wilson

It has therefore been interesting and humbling to be linked with family history over the years in different ways. Playing the small pipe organ for services at Semaphore Baptist, my father's much beloved former church in Adelaide, was always a great joy for me. I might have wished to have inherited the greater musical skills of Cecil Mead, who was the organist at FSBC, or of my uncle Colin Wilson (my father's elder brother), who was church organist at Perth Baptist before his untimely death in 1918 at the age of nineteen.

Finally, the invitation in 2013 for me to become the Associate Minister at Flinders Street Baptist Church was a great personal honour—to serve in the church where my great-grandfather had ministered for thirty-six years from its inception. Occasionally my imagination would see Silas Mead in the pulpit, although every Sunday I was reminded of him as we entered Mead Hall for morning tea and beheld the larger-than-life portrait of the great man hanging on the wall.

It was disappointing, therefore, for me to conclude my ministry at FSBC after five years (and two years in the pew prior to my appointment) just as I was feeling my way in a new role of focusing on ministry to the city centre itself. That opportunity, as I sought to find inroads for the Gospel into the heart of Adelaide, certainly stirred in me the vision of Silas for inclusive missionary outreach to the world, the compassion and care of Drs Cecil and Gertrude Mead for the sick, disadvantaged and downtrodden, and the evangelistic fervour of my father in reaching people for Christ in many cities. At the time of writing, my on-going activity with the Carrington Cottages homeless men's project in the city continues to 'fan into flame' (2 Tim 1:6) what may have been passed down and inspired by those who have gone before. Since retirement, I have become an Associate Minister of Trinity Baptist Church, formerly Colonel Light Gardens Baptist Church, Adelaide, where my father ministered from 1960 and where both my sister Raewyn and I were baptised.

What I took away from FSBC was a 'Mead-like' vision, inspired by Christ's love, of reaching peoples from around the world, especially the many overseas students who still attend English classes at this city church. It was, of course, from FSBC that the first Australian Baptist missionaries were commissioned to service for Christ in India, and my great-uncle, Dr Cecil Mead, followed them later as a medical missionary when he travelled to Bengal, India—now Bangladesh.

In the course of his medical and Christian witness there, Cecil Mead set up a school for the downtrodden Nama Sudra community at a remote village called Orakandi, in the Gopalganj Province. The school opened its doors to Hindus, Muslims and Christians seeking education and seeking truth, and has continued to do so ever since.

So, I am indebted to Dr Rosalind Gooden (of Flinders Street Baptist Church) for encouraging me to consider going to Bangladesh in 2016 to bring a greeting and a message at the Celebration Handover of the Australian Baptist Mission work to the local churches after 130 years.

Such was my delight whilst there, to make the long trip from Dhaka to Orakandi (in south-west Bangladesh) to visit the Mead Memorial High School, still surviving after more than 100 years. I was quite overwhelmed by the welcome given by the school staff to our party (including my daughter, Carmen) from those who revered the Mead name and memory from long ago. I even met a very old man from the Hindu community whose family well remembered 'Dr Sahib' (Cecil Mead) and I was so touched by their gracious hospitality that day.

Sadly, in the course of a century, the buildings of the Mead School had deteriorated to a great extent of disrepair. On returning to Adelaide after my trip, I shared with Flinders Street Church my despair at the state of the buildings. The Church Missionary Committee magnificently took up the challenge and organised a Mead Memorial Concert which raised sufficient funds to repair and renew the school buildings for generations to come.

To stand inside the small Christian chapel nearby, to see the well-worn lectern from which Cecil Mead preached or gave daily devotions, to look out through the shutters to see the serene water lilies growing peacefully upon the little lakes, was truly a memorable experience that I hold dear.

Indeed, I thank God for my forebears and for those who have chosen to celebrate and write this story of their Christian faith and witness to Christ in the world. I thank the contributors to this book for their interest, hard work and contribution to preserving the life-story of Silas Mead, a man who literally and figuratively stands tall in Baptist history.

I trust they would join with me in echoing the words of the hymn:[3]

> For all the love that from our earliest days
> Has gladdened life and guarded all our ways,
> We bring Thee, Lord, our song of grateful praise:
> Hallelujah! Hallelujah!

---

[3] LJ Egerton-Smith (1879-1958), 'For All the Love' (c.1921-1953).

PART 3

Conclusion

Mead family, FSBC manse, 1889

*'[The Mead name] will go down to the future as one of the great names
in the religious history of South Australia...'
(Peter Fleming)*

Conclusion

Rosalind Gooden and Ken Manley

Speaking at the unveiling of the memorial brass tablet for Silas Mead in the Flinders Street Church on 6 October 1912, Peter Fleming, pastor at the church, recalled that Congregational Principal AB Fairbairn (1838–1912) had once declared that the greatest moment in history was when Paul chose Silas because that was the beginning of the enterprise that became worldwide, and carried the gospel not only to the Gentiles but into Europe. The eloquent preacher declared that the supreme moment in the history of the Baptist movement in South Australia was when Silas Mead was chosen for Adelaide.[1] As John Walker has argued in this volume, 'apostolic' remains an excellent description of the mission of Silas in South Australia.

Certainly, that sense of a special calling for Silas Mead was a common theme at the several memorial services held after his death. Tributes at his funeral in Perth came from across denominational boundaries but from within his own Baptist family around the nation one word recurs in numerous tributes and memorials: Silas was honoured as one of the 'fathers' of Baptists in Australia. As their long-serving founding pastor, he was the 'father' of FSBC, the leading Baptist church in the state; 'father' of the South Australian Baptist Association and most especially the 'father' of Australian Baptist 'foreign' missionary work.

But unlike the biblical apostles, the memory of these later 'apostles' has often been quickly forgotten or only partially recalled. Memorial tablets can all too easily become tarnished or ignored. This book has sought to recall at least one of our Australian Baptist pioneer 'apostles' by tracing the significance of Silas Mead and of his descendants for the Baptist movement. On any reckoning theirs is a remarkable con-

---

[1] *SB*, 17 October 1912, 667.

tribution. At the same time, studies on his wider influence have also revealed his contribution not only to the cross-denominational evangelical movement to which he was deeply committed but also to the general cause of Christianity and civic morality in his adopted country

The memorial tablet at FSBC reads:

> In memory of the noble and inspiring life of Rev. Silas Mead, M.A., LL.B. who filled the pastorate of this church from the date of its formation on 5th August 1861, till 18th February 1897. Born 16th August 1834. Fell on sleep 13th September 1909. 'For he was a good man, full of the Holy Ghost, and of faith, and much people was added unto the Lord'. (Acts 11:23). 'Found faithful'

FSBC Tablet to Silas Mead

There were also hundreds for whom Silas Mead was 'father' in that he had guided them to faith in Christ. In a more intimate sense, he was father to his own children. Indeed, his youngest surviving daughter Blanche (Wilson) unveiled the memorial in FSBC on that special Sunday.[2] How his descendants sought to continue the work of the gospel in the tradition of Silas is also a part of his and our story.

---

[2] *SB*, October 1912, 677.

From Somerset to Adelaide

From his earliest days working on the family farm in rural Somerset, Silas was nurtured in the Baptist faith and soon committed himself to the work of the gospel. His first hope, that of being a 'foreign' missionary to India, was denied him but by his deep faith, excellent academic accomplishments and unfailing willingness to serve wherever God led him, he found his true calling in Flinders Street and in Australia more generally. Evident abilities, strength of character and deep faith marked his ministry across the many fruitful years that followed. Courage in venturing to the other side of the world was not unique for the times but for him it was obedience to a divine call.

Mead's achievements as pastor of Flinders Street have been described in earlier chapters. He began as he intended to proceed. Sensitive to criticism of the cost of the erection of the impressive Flinders Street chapel in 1863, Mead let it be known at the opening service that he would refuse to be paid for preaching for as long as a debt remained on the property.[3] This was a strategy that Mead often practised.[4] For most denominations, but perhaps especially for Dissenter churches, the reputation and fame of a leader rested supremely on his or her work as a minister of a local church. Of course, when Silas arrived in Adelaide there was a desperate need for a strong pastor who could not only command the support of the men of wealth and influence in the colony but also foster personal faith in ordinary people. This Mead achieved by an unfailing proclamation of the gospel which invited an intensely personal and immediate response. While he could plan and dream of a bigger place for Baptists in that 'Paradise of Dissent', Mead's most constant method of growing the church was that Sunday by Sunday and in every possible place, he made a passionate plea for his hearers to receive Christ as Saviour and to be baptised by immersion as the biblical way of confessing that faith. He encouraged children and young people to receive this gift of new life and church membership in a way that was unusual in many Baptist churches where cautious attitudes to any expressions of a youthful faith were common. One early observer suggested it was more like a Salvation Army meeting than a traditional Baptist chapel.[5]

---

[3] *Australian Evangelist*, volume 4, 1863, 152-53.
[4] *TP*, September 1886, 138.
[5] *TP*, September 1886, 137.

Mead kept careful records and could always quote the number of baptisms and church members in his church. He rejoiced when he baptised the 1,000th person.[6]

Any criticism of the Baptist understanding of baptism met a vigorous response. Whilst genuine in his acceptance of Christians in other denominations he did not hesitate to defend the baptismal beliefs of Baptists. Early in his time in Adelaide he published a scholarly booklet in which he carefully argued for immersion as the only way to translate the Greek word *baptizo* in the New Testament.[7] Yet he was sufficiently ecumenical later to endorse the idea of forming 'Congregational Baptist' churches although this was not endorsed by his fellow Baptists.[8]

Mead encouraged women, not only to have faith and be baptised, but to exercise their ministry in the life of the church. The role of deaconesses and a general recognition of the place of women within the communities of faith was something that Mead had learned from Angus at his College back in London. He certainly encouraged this in his Australian ministry. Deaconesses were appointed to have 'spiritual oversight of the sisterhood', these deaconesses in Flinders Street came before any males became elders.[9] This theology and practice later led to women being encouraged as pioneers in the overseas mission work of Australian Baptists in India. His own daughters, as seen in their chapters also demonstrated powerful examples of this influence.

In those early years, Mead found great encouragement and a steady response to his ministry. He had not adopted the more extreme revivalist methods emerging in the USA but his preaching was always biblical and Christocentric. From 1864 his wife Ann made her own special contribution to his life and to the church.

Mead's vision was always for unity and for expansion. Unity in his own congregation was maintained by his gracious but firm leadership, whilst within the association of churches he brought inspiration and stimulation for growth. Gradually there came a greater sense of *esprit de corps* within the Baptist Association. A denominational paper called *Truth and Progress* of which he was a pioneering editor was commenced, its name represented Mead's hopes for the Baptist churches. He led as President on three occasions and served as secretary on others. A wide range of initiatives were undertaken under his inspiration. As John Walker has suggested, Mead 'gave exactly

---

[6] *TP*, July 1885, 82.
[7] S Mead, *Scripture Immersion*, 1867.
[8] *Australian Evangelist*, volume 6, 1865, 318.
[9] *TP*, September 1868, 185.

the type of leadership that the hitherto divided Baptists of South Australia needed'.[10] Members of his own congregation were repeatedly dismissed to form new churches with the same spirit as he had helped engender in Flinders Street. When the Norwood church was formed in 1868 Mead spoke about both his pain and pleasure: he felt the loss from Flinders Street of several key people but found great joy in the expansion of Baptist witness into that growing suburb.[11]

Inevitably, this helped foster a strong sense of identity and purpose within the shared life of many churches. Other ministers were caught up in his enthusiasms. Gradually he came to be thought of as their 'Baptist bishop', one to whom pastors and churches looked for guidance and encouragement.[12] He stimulated every effort to form new churches and would most commonly preach about Baptist ideals at the opening of church buildings around the colony.

At the same time his theology of the church was impressed upon his denomination as a whole. What was termed 'open' membership came to be accepted uniformly within the colony, unlike New South Wales where only those baptised by immersion could become members. Tension over this issue had also led to a major schism in Western Australia.

In almost every aspect of denominational life in both South Australia and Western Australia Mead led the way and made his own unique contribution. In both places he began such theological education as he could provide for young men and this led not only to Baptists being prepared for ministry but the establishment of the remarkable Union College in Adelaide when students from two other traditions joined with Baptists. This work led directly to the foundation of the University of Adelaide. Mead tutored South Australian ministerial students for some further fourteen years.

Mead was always open to new methods of propagating the gospel within the worldwide Christian movement. He read widely in overseas journals and significant books, especially on religious themes. He, however, did not embrace new theological trends such as questioning the Bible's inspiration and resisted emphases such as the social gospel teachers advocated. The Christian Endeavour movement captured his mind with its structures designed to train young people to serve 'Christ and the Church'. His family embraced this movement with an enthusiasm that must have

---

[10] J Walker, 'Mead, Silas' in B Dickey (ed), *The Australian Dictionary of Evangelical Biography* (Sydney: Evangelical History Association, 1994), 259.
[11] *TP*, January 1868, 23.
[12] For examples, see *TP*, July 1890, 109; November 1891, 187f.

delighted Silas, whilst his own considerable fervour for CE remained a marked feature of his later days. When Francis Clark the American founder of CE visited Adelaide in 1893 he described Flinders Street as 'not only a church but a missionary headquarters, a tract repository, a theological seminary and a CE office all in one'.[13]

On a different level of commitment was the zeal with which Silas together with his wife Ann embraced the holiness movement. He came to this through reading the works of key figures such as Robert Pearsall Smith. It obviously spoke to his own deep spiritual needs. Indeed, Silas had to speak openly to his congregation about this new experience. He had discovered 'the missing stone of the arch of God's truth' and needed to inform his people openly that his preaching and teaching would now be different. Some accepted these beliefs for themselves and the congregation continued with him as pastor.

This conviction led Silas to an involvement in some of the large conventions such as at Brighton in 1875 that promoted the movement. If in his later years this was not quite as prominent in his teaching, it remained the secret of his spirituality and ministry across those years. It also welcomed him into a world-wide evangelical community committed to faith-holiness which undoubtedly led him to be offered a position at Harley College in London.

Decades after Mead's death, Principal GH Morling of Sydney wrote about how Mead and two other Australian Baptist 'fathers' (Samuel Chapman and Thomas Porter) had left a great legacy and example.[14] He described how Silas and later Ann had come to embrace the holiness movement and of how Silas became such an earnest and enthusiastic teacher in the movement. All three Baptist 'fathers' shared this experience and teaching in common.[15]

As Adelaide and the whole colony developed, the influence of leading clergy like Mead became increasingly important as community leaders. Although he believed in the separation of church and state, Mead did not hesitate to bring a Christian response to civic matters such as education and public morality but he was always more concerned with providing a Christian perspective than with promoting a narrow

[13] *TP*, 16 February 1893, 53.
[14] Rev Samuel Chapman (1831–1899), minister at Collins Street Baptist Church, Melbourne (1877–1899); Rev Dr Thomas Porter (1838–1926), Baptist minister for sixty years in several States, principally NSW. See Ken R Manley, *From Woolloomooloo to 'Eternity': A History of Australian Baptists, Volume 1: Growing an Australian Church (1831-1914)* (Milton Keynes: Paternoster, 2006).
[15] *AB*, 25 July 1939, 1.

sectarianism. This was in part his motivation for his enthusiastic endorsing of the YMCA movement in both Adelaide and Perth and for his involvement with the place of Scripture in public education.

Inevitably, as the years passed a new generation arose who did not always understand or appreciate what Mead had given to Flinders Street or the denomination. Tensions developed. The memory of the early days, although regularly rehearsed, gradually faded. Mead's ambitions persisted but with less acceptance. Few ministers can sustain a ministry for as long as Silas did at FSBC. Numbers declined, services were thought by some to have become rather dreary and unattractive to a younger generation. Those problems are significant for an accurate account of Mead's whole life. His fierce determination, once admired, now seemed to be the stubbornness of an aging man. His theology was now seemingly outdated. Mead could not embrace a liberal theology with its focus on a social gospel such as swept the eloquent Charles Bright to popularity at Norwood. There were disagreements, even in the life of Flinders Street so that when Silas eventually did resign it was accompanied by his public declaration that he would not stay in South Australia. This may well have been a concern not to impose his personal views on a church or denomination in which he had played such a determinative role, but the general impression is rather of a more petulant and disappointed man. Of course, he now had no family members living in South Australia.

In fact, at his last service in Flinders Street Silas articulated some of his disappointments: he wished that the 'higher life' teaching had been more widely received; regretted that there were so few conversions in his later years as pastor; the weakness of church discipline; less interest in prayer and in the life of the 'institutional' church. But, of course, the positives were far more significant: these centred in the great joy he had found in proclaiming the central gospel themes of justification by faith, personal regeneration and the atonement with, of course, the glad tidings of the fuller and holier life.[16]

Peter Fleming, pastor at FSBC (1908–1921) stated, a decade after Silas's death:

> The rising generation holds [the Mead] name in reverence and it will go down to the future as one of the great names in the religious history of South Australia, and as the very greatest of the first generation, or perhaps of any generation of the Baptist ministers in this State.[17]

[16] *SB*, 14 January 1897, 17.
[17] *AB*, 25 November 1919, 4.

Silas Mead undoubtedly exerted a profound influence in his adopted colony, but his vision and impact extended far beyond that one area.

Beyond Adelaide

Although his main ministry was in Adelaide and South Australia, Mead's interest and support ranged across the whole of Australia, especially to Victoria where he was often a welcome visitor as preacher and friend. Every move for a greater union of Baptists across the colonies found his encouragement. Whether it was the establishment of a denominational paper across three states as in *The Southern Baptist* from 1895, the possibility of a federal theological college or other ways of cooperation, the wise and genial support of Mead was assured. When he moved to Western Australia, his enthusiasm and commitment to unity and expansion among Baptists were powerful.

Even before he became a student at Regent's Park College Silas Mead had cast his eye of pity on the plight of those from many nations who had no real knowledge of Jesus Christ. He took literally and personally the call of Christ to 'go into all the world' with the gospel. Joseph Angus, his College Principal, had served for many years in the administration of the Baptist Missionary Society and encouraged students like Mead and his friend Rouse to contemplate missionary work in India. Mead came with that missionary spirit to Adelaide and, it seems, thought and prayed every day about the needy peoples of India, China and everywhere else. Some in his congregation lamented that he was so predictable in his earnest prayers for this mission work that they hesitantly whispered it had almost become tiresome.

That Mead was honoured as the 'Father' of Australian Baptist 'foreign' mission work has been clearly demonstrated in this book. He prayed, worked and encouraged his denomination and indeed all believers to support this cause. Faridpur was a name that all South Australian Baptists came to love. To anyone, woman or man, who sensed a personal call he was always sensitive and supportive. Most remarkably, the pioneers and the iconic 'five barley loaves' led the way, but many others followed. Late in life, he spent many hours teaching and encouraging missionary students at Harley College. That his own son Cecil became a leading medical missionary in Bengal was a cause of great pride, but he treated all missionaries who were supported by Australian Baptists with a fatherly concern. Once he left South Australia, his urging of West Australian Baptists to mission work was similarly unceasing and productive.

Reflections on the lives of Silas Mead's offspring have added an extra dimension to the Mead story. Mead's love of Scripture, his verbal and written proclamation of the gospel, and his guidance of others to understand and teach it were all characteristics that are traced in the lives of his children, grandchildren and great-grandson. The same zeal to evangelise and develop discipled followers of Christ are found in his descendants. His ability with words, and his exceptional business skills can be traced through the family. Organisations that he enthusiastically endorsed (Keswick Convention and Christian Endeavour, for example) became significant for his children. His commitment to spend his life in 'full time' service of Christ continued in the lives of his children although somewhat varied in the spheres of service. Silas believed in the corporate life of the church, the committed community. He spent significant time in prayer, worship (including music) and writing and he gave financially. So did they. His bias towards missions was crowned by Cecil's nineteen years in Bengal but was also emulated by others. Finally, he was sensitive to social issues in the developing South Australian, London and Western Australian communities. Their stories have enhanced this story of Silas.

London, July 1905

A suitable conclusion to the story of Silas Mead may be found in an afternoon meeting in London of the first Baptist World Congress on 13 July 1905 when Silas gave an address on 'Missionary Methods—Australian'. That he had been asked to do this was itself eloquent witness to his status as a missionary statesman. He had spoken to large gatherings before, at the Brighton Holiness Convention in 1875 and at the huge Christian Endeavour convention in San Francisco in 1897, but this London meeting was different. This was his world family. Baptists from some 26 countries came together to form the Baptist World Alliance. Silas was a delegate from Western Australia. Three thousand delegates registered, including JG Raws and E Bungey from South Australia. Most of the meetings were held in the impressive Exeter Hall in the Strand, the place where the Anti-Slavery Society meetings had been held with such powerful effect and where many evangelical and missionary gatherings had been held.

Silas knew many of the British leaders, men like Alexander McLaren, JH Shakespeare and most likely saw the newly unveiled statue of CH Spurgeon. John Clifford became the first BWA President. Mead bowed with all the delegates to repeat 'slowly and deliberately' the words of the Apostles' Creed as McLaren led them. His friend

Dr WT Whitley was one of the chief organisers. Mead was appointed the Australian representative on the BWA committee.

Silas must have known that this was almost certainly his last visit back to England. He still had his West Country accent but he was without doubt a representative of his adopted nation which had become a Commonwealth only a few years before. He had a distinguished presence with his white tie matching his head of white hair and trimmed white beard.[18] Talking with missionary enthusiasts was what he loved to do, and one suspects never more so than on this international Baptist stage.

His address was long (almost seven pages of close print in the official report of the Congress) but full of insights and inspiration.[19] He began by noting that it was over a century since William Carey had ventured to India and that after a century of mission work in which Baptists and all churches had taken part there were still 'a thousand million of people now living to whom the Gospel has not been preached with any degree of fulness'. This was, he insisted 'the problem of problems for all the churches'. He cautioned against the use of the term 'heathen' to describe those with whom the church was working, preferring the term 'Nations'.

Mead's particular charge was to outline the methods needed for mission as Australians understood them. The following speakers, on what was a rather long afternoon, drew on their Canadian and American experiences. Mead spoke, as he acknowledged, not as an actual missionary but as a leader in the home churches. His address was not so much descriptive of what Australians had done but rather his own thoughtful reflections on the nature of the task.

He felt that too much had been expected of missionaries on furlough when rest was their greatest need and that much else could be done to educate churches about mission work. In Australia, laymen and women had been encouraged to visit India and had subsequently proved excellent deputationists and committee members. With the increased possibilities of faster travel much more should be done in this regard.

Mead also argued that an even greater number of women was needed and that women could influence children in Eastern households. Indeed, he pleaded for 'at least a fourfold' increase in women workers throughout East Asia. He believed that 'thousands' of young women teachers would be delighted 'to take steamers to those far-off lands'.

---

[18] See the photo of Mead in *The Baptist World Congress…Authorised Record of Proceedings* (London: Baptist Union, 1905) opposite p. 4.
[19] *Baptist World Congress*, 86–92.

Another significant policy he advocated was that decisions about evangelism and the use of resources should be taken by those who were on the fields and not from the home base. This had in fact already largely happened in the Australian Baptist mission work. He deprecated the notion of putting one method of mission service against some other—educational, industrial, medical or what is termed 'evangelistic'. This was 'the greatest occasion for missionary enterprise since the Reformation' and every opportunity must be taken.

Missions must also be prepared to exert even greater pressure on governments to abolish evils such as female foot-binding in China and unduly early marriages in India which had led to great numbers of young women becoming widows with serious social degradation.

Silas Mead's speech was almost done. But he concluded with characteristic vigour, optimism and challenge calling Christ the true Conqueror of all nations. Here was revealed, as clearly as anywhere, precisely what motivated Silas and more of what had made him such a powerful and long-lasting 'father' of missions and church life in Australia and far beyond:

> [Christ] is the great Destroyer of error and evil, whether it exists north or south of the Himalayan mountains; whether the errors date back to half a millennium B.C. or are of more recent date; whether indigenous to the east or imported from the West. It is He who will extract from Buddhism whatsoever of good there is in it; He will gather out from Mohammedanism [sic] what is just and true in its teachings; it is He who will dissolve out of Confucianism what in that system is worthy. Yes, He will deduce from idolatry itself the principle of worship and sacrifice which is wrapped up in its contortions; He will deduce from all true science and philosophies and from all Nature's forces what will contribute to make His Kingdom come and which will constrain the whole earth to join in one gladsome Hallelujah of adoring praise. So will Christ weave into a glorious triumph, worthy of the Father God, all the kingdoms of this world as the nations will bow the knee in loving homage before the King of Kings and Lord of lords.[20]

---

[20] *Baptist World Congress*, 92.

Family trees

Prepared by Eric Kopittke

The following family trees were designed by Eric Kopittke from family records compiled by the extended Mead family, particularly by grand-daughters Dorothy and Marjory Mead, and grand-daughter-in-law Win Wilson.

Some of the dates in the family records differ from dates derived from external sources and recorded elsewhere in this volume. The information in the family trees reflects the results of the family's research.

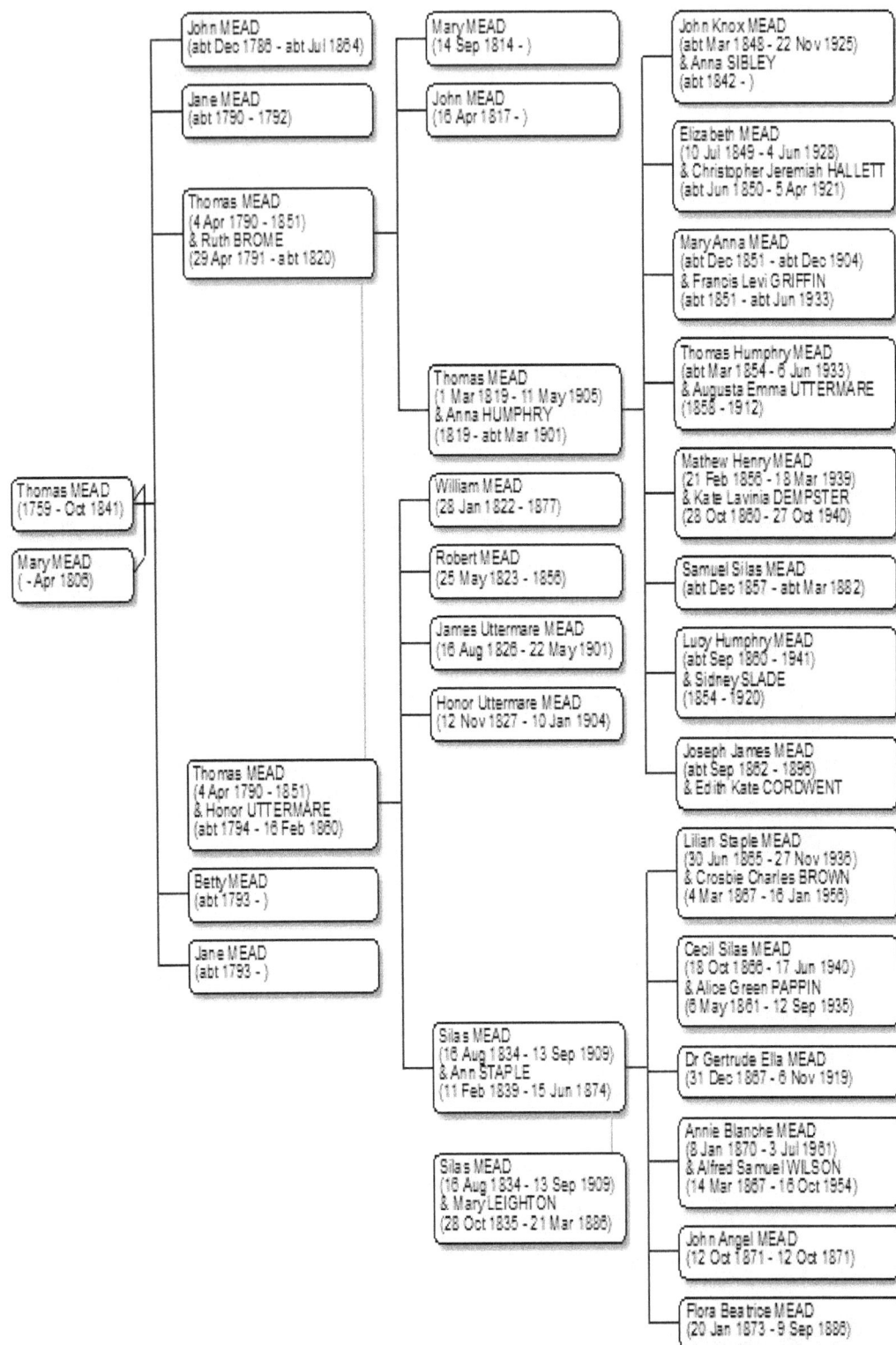

Thomas MEAD
(1759 - Oct 1841)

Mary MEAD
(- Apr 1806)

John MEAD
(abt Dec 1786 - abt Jul 1864)

Jane MEAD
(abt 1790 - 1792)

Thomas MEAD
(4 Apr 1790 - 1851)
& Ruth BROME
(29 Apr 1791 - abt 1820)

Thomas MEAD
(4 Apr 1790 - 1851)
& Honor UTTERMARE
(abt 1794 - 16 Feb 1860)

Betty MEAD
(abt 1793 -)

Jane MEAD
(abt 1793 -)

Mary MEAD
(14 Sep 1814 -)

John MEAD
(16 Apr 1817 -)

Thomas MEAD
(1 Mar 1819 - 11 May 1905)
& Anna HUMPHRY
(1819 - abt Mar 1901)

William MEAD
(28 Jan 1822 - 1877)

Robert MEAD
(25 May 1823 - 1856)

James Uttermare MEAD
(16 Aug 1826 - 22 May 1901)

Honor Uttermare MEAD
(12 Nov 1827 - 10 Jan 1904)

Silas MEAD
(16 Aug 1834 - 13 Sep 1909)
& Ann STAPLE
(11 Feb 1839 - 15 Jun 1874)

Silas MEAD
(16 Aug 1834 - 13 Sep 1909)
& Mary LEIGHTON
(28 Oct 1835 - 21 Mar 1886)

John Knox MEAD
(abt Mar 1848 - 22 Nov 1925)
& Anna SIBLEY
(abt 1842 -)

Elizabeth MEAD
(10 Jul 1849 - 4 Jun 1928)
& Christopher Jeremiah HALLETT
(abt Jun 1850 - 5 Apr 1921)

Mary Anna MEAD
(abt Dec 1851 - abt Dec 1904)
& Francis Levi GRIFFIN
(abt 1851 - abt Jun 1933)

Thomas Humphry MEAD
(abt Mar 1854 - 6 Jun 1933)
& Augusta Emma UTTERMARE
(1856 - 1912)

Mathew Henry MEAD
(21 Feb 1856 - 18 Mar 1939)
& Kate Lavinia DEMPSTER
(28 Oct 1860 - 27 Oct 1940)

Samuel Silas MEAD
(abt Dec 1857 - abt Mar 1882)

Lucy Humphry MEAD
(abt Sep 1860 - 1941)
& Sidney SLADE
(1854 - 1920)

Joseph James MEAD
(abt Sep 1862 - 1896)
& Edith Kate CORDWENT

Lilian Staple MEAD
(30 Jun 1865 - 27 Nov 1936)
& Crosbie Charles BROWN
(4 Mar 1867 - 16 Jan 1956)

Cecil Silas MEAD
(18 Oct 1866 - 17 Jun 1940)
& Alice Green PAPPIN
(6 May 1861 - 12 Sep 1935)

Dr Gertrude Ella MEAD
(31 Dec 1867 - 6 Nov 1919)

Annie Blanche MEAD
(8 Jan 1870 - 3 Jul 1961)
& Alfred Samuel WILSON
(14 Mar 1867 - 16 Oct 1954)

John Angel MEAD
(12 Oct 1871 - 12 Oct 1871)

Flora Beatrice MEAD
(20 Jan 1873 - 9 Sep 1886)

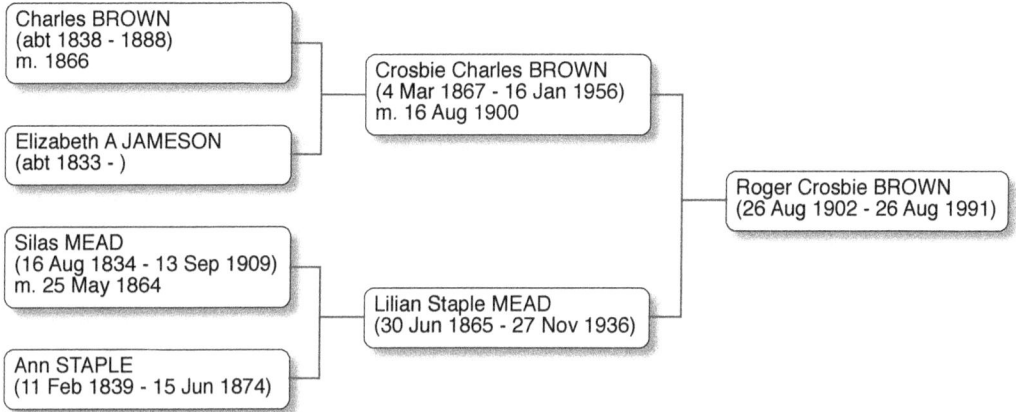

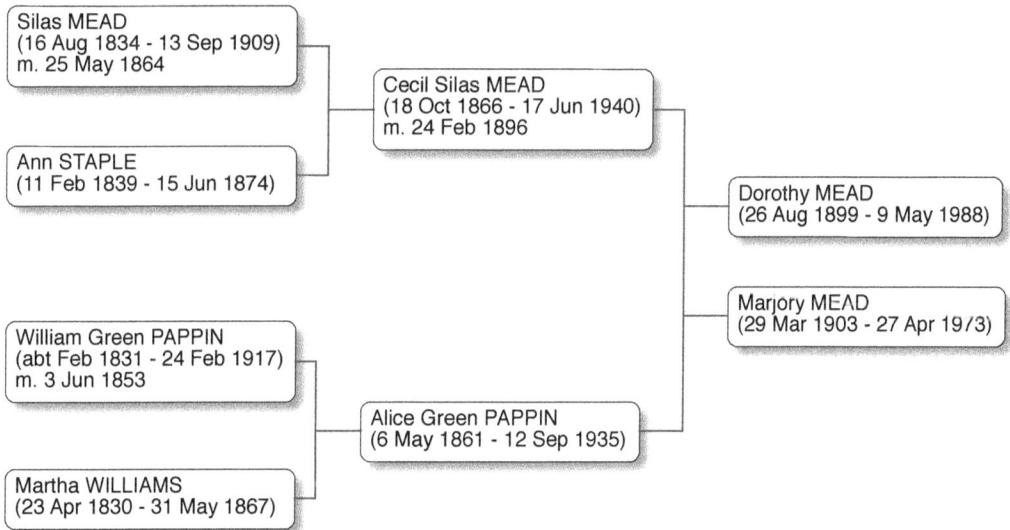

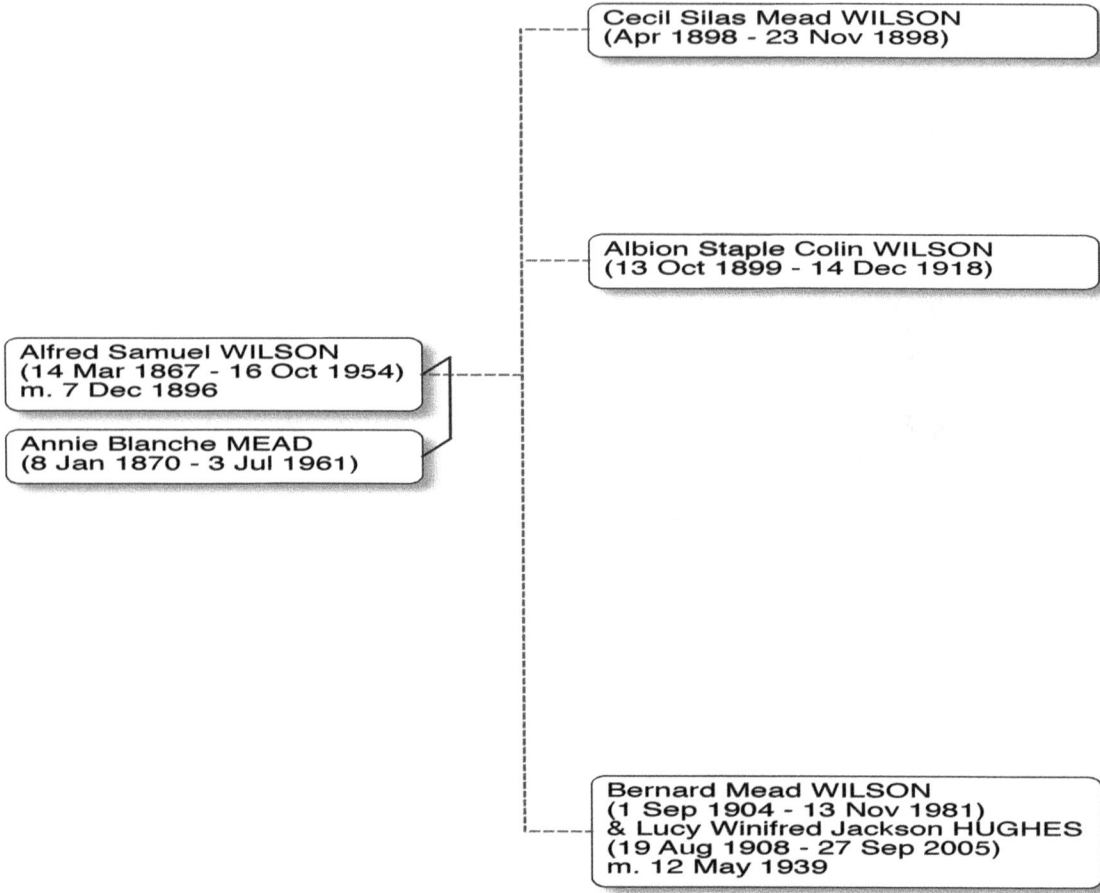

Cecil Silas Mead WILSON
(Apr 1898 - 23 Nov 1898)

Albion Staple Colin WILSON
(13 Oct 1899 - 14 Dec 1918)

Alfred Samuel WILSON
(14 Mar 1867 - 16 Oct 1954)
m. 7 Dec 1896

Annie Blanche MEAD
(8 Jan 1870 - 3 Jul 1961)

Bernard Mead WILSON
(1 Sep 1904 - 13 Nov 1981)
& Lucy Winifred Jackson HUGHES
(19 Aug 1908 - 27 Sep 2005)
m. 12 May 1939

Natalie Dawn PAGE
(26 Jan 1960 -)
& John Leslie COOPER
(28 Dec 1959 -)
m. 1979

Kathryn Marie PAGE
(22 Apr 1961 -)
& Andrew Robert KNISPEL
(6 Jul 1959 -)
m. 1980

Kathryn Marie PAGE
(22 Apr 1961 -)
& Graeme John NICOL
(10 Jan 1952 -)
m. 2005

Colleen Elizabeth Mead WILSON
(17 May 1940 -)
& Malcolm Roy PAGE
(8 Nov 1936 - 14 Jun 2014)
m. 26 Mar 1959

Lisa Karen PAGE
(4 Feb 1964 -)
& Kerry John FORWARD
(24 Oct 1956 -)
m. 1982

Rodney Malcolm PAGE
(1 Mar 1966 -)
& Kathleen Ann RILEY
(16 May 1967 -)
m. 1995

Darren Malcolm PAGE
(11 Aug 1974 -)
& Tanya Lee GHERBESI
(15 Apr 1980 -)
m. 2006

Vanessa Joyce COREY
(25 Feb 1973 -)

Gregory Warren Mead COREY
(26 Sep 1974 -)
& Yukiko OTSUKA
(28 Aug 1973 -)
m. 2004

Raewyn Christine WILSON
(31 May 1943 -)
& Peter Warren COREY
(4 Sep 1938 -)
m. 5 Feb 1972

Matthew Peter Cheyne COREY
(8 Jan 1979 -)
& Kristy NAGY
(26 Oct 1982 -)
m. 2014

Carmen Elizabeth WILSON
(3 Mar 1973 -)

Marcus Bernard WILSON
(19 Sep 1975 -)
& Catherine Marie EHLERS
(6 May 1977 -)

Torrey Alfred Mead WILSON
(15 Jan 1946 -)
& Elizabeth Ralph HANN
(15 Oct 1945 -)
m. 6 Sep 1969

Benjamin Simon WILSON
(8 Jun 1978 -)
& Melanie Jane ROBERTS
(27 Nov 1978 -)
m. 2001

Abbreviations and shortened forms

AB	*The Australian Baptist* (1913–1991)
ABFM	Australian Baptist Foreign Mission (1913–1959) (see Baptist Mission Australia)
ABMS	Australian Baptist Missionary Society (1959–2003) (see Baptist Mission Australia)
ADEB	*The Australian Dictionary of Evangelical Biography*, ed. Brian Dickey. Sydney: Evangelical History Association, 1994.
Advertiser	*The Advertiser* (Adelaide, SA)
AFA	Aborigines' Friends' Association
AO	*Adelaide Observer* (Adelaide, SA: 1843–1904)
BMA	Baptist Mission Australia (2022–), formerly Global Interaction (2003–2021), Australian Baptist Missionary Society (1959–2003), Australian Baptist Foreign Mission (1913–1959)
BMS	Baptist Missionary Society (British)
BUWA	Baptist Union of Western Australia
Colonist	*Christian Colonist* (Adelaide, SA: 1879–1894)
CE	Christian Endeavour/Endeavor: Young People's Society of Christian Endeavor
Chronicle	*SA Weekly Chronicle,* also known as *SA Chronicle & Weekly Mail, SA Chronicle, The Chronicle* (Adelaide, SA: 1858–1954)
CIM	China Inland Mission
DN	*Daily News* (Perth, WA)
ET	*The Express and Telegraph* (Adelaide, SA : 1867–1922)
EJ	*Evening Journal* (Adelaide, SA: 1869–1912)
FSBC	Flinders Street Baptist Church
Gooden/Mead collection	Rosalind Gooden/Mead Family private collection. Mead family documents and photographs held by Rosalind M Gooden, Myrtle Bank, SA, rgooden5@bigpond.com.
Goalundo Minutes	Goalundo Mission Committee minutes. The committee went under various names from 1897–1959. Goalundo Mission was the name most common during Silas Mead's time in WA.

Gooden/ SGMU collection	Gooden/Senior Girls Missionary Union collection, held by Rosalind M Gooden, Myrtle Bank, South Australia, rgooden5@bigpond.com
LMS	London Missionary Society
MK	Missionary Kid, also 'Miss Kid' (i.e. child of missionary parents)
NSW	New South Wales
NZ	New Zealand
OB	*Our Bond* (Calcutta, India)
PA	*The Pictorial Australian* (Adelaide, SA: 1885–1895)
PBC	Perth Baptist Church (sometimes known as 'Museum Street Church', Perth)
PK	'Pastor's kid', child of a church/Baptist minister, 'child of the manse'
Register	*The Register*, later the *South Australian Register* (Adelaide, SA: 1836–1931)
SA	South Australia/Australian (e.g. SA Company)
SABA	South Australian Baptist Association, formed in 1863, changed to South Australian Baptist Union in 1895
SABMS	South Australian Baptist Missionary Society
SABU	South Australian Baptist Union (1895–)
SB	*The Southern Baptist* (1895–1912)
SLSA	State Library of South Australia
SMH	*Sydney Morning Herald* (Sydney, New South Wales)
TP	*Truth and Progress* (Adelaide, SA) (1868–1894)
UK	United Kingdom
USA	United States of America
WA	Western Australia
WAB	*WA Church Monthly* (Perth, WA), July 1902 – June 1903; *WA Baptist Monthly*, July 1903 – June 1905; *The WA Baptist* (August 1905 – December 1909) [An initiative of the Perth Baptist Church until late 1909].
WABMS	West Australian Baptist Missionary Society (see Goalundo Mission)
WB	*Westralian Baptist* (Perth: Baptist Historical Society of Western Australia), occasional papers
West	*The West Australian* (Perth, WA)
WM	*Western Mail* (Perth, WA)

Bibliography

Manuscripts and Other Sources

Baptist Union of Western Australia. Minutes.

Bristol Education Society. Papers. Bristol Baptist College, UK.

Flinders Street Baptist Church. Deacons meeting minutes; members meeting minutes. Flinders Street Baptist Church, Adelaide, SA

Fowler, JR. Fowler Papers. State Library of South Australia.

Goalundo Mission Committee minutes (Goalundo Minutes). The committee went under various names: The Western Australian Baptist Union Foreign Mission Committee (1897–99) [so minute of 5 July 1897], combined with Home Mission, WABU Home and Foreign Mission Committee (February 1899 – October 1901), thereafter separate, WA Foreign Mission Committee (December 1901 – February 1903), Goalundo Mission (February 1903 – October 1911), W.A.B.M.S. Committee (December 1911 – April 1912; so minutes heading), Foreign Mission Committee (July 1912–1959). Goalundo Mission is used following the name most common during Mead's time in Perth.

Harley College Council Minutes (1896–1910). Centre for the Study of World Christianity, University of Edinburgh.

Mead family papers. Baptist Mission Australia archive, Moore Potter House, Melbourne.

Mead family papers. Gooden/Mead Family private collection. Rosalind M Gooden, Myrtle Bank, South Australia.

Perth Baptist Church. Minutes

Regent's Park College Minutes. Regent's Park College, Oxford.

Registry of Dissenter Births. Dr Williams's Library, London.

Short, Bishop Augustus. Letters to the Society for the Propagation of the Gospel. United Society for the Propagation of the Gospel Papers, Oxford, Bodleian Libraries.

The Report of the Committee of the Baptist College of Stepney for MDCCLIV (London, 1854)

Wigfield, WM. 'A Short History of the Baptist Churches at Isle Abbots (1808–1968) and Fivehead (1868–1968)', typescript, 1968. https://fiveheadbaptist.co.uk

Journals and Magazines and Newspapers

Adelaide Observer (Adelaide, SA) *(AO)*

Auckland Star (Auckland, NZ)

Australian Baptist (1913–1991) *(AB)*

Australian Evangelist

Baptist Magazine (UK)

*Christian Colonist (*Adelaide*) (Colonist*)

Christian Weekly

Daily News (Perth, WA) (*DN*)

Evening Journal (Adelaide, SA) (*EJ*)

Express and Telegraph (Adelaide, SA)

Freeman (UK)

Great Southern Herald (Katanning, Western Australia)

Inquirer and Commercial News (Perth, WA)

Kalgoorlie Miner (Kalgoorlie, WA)

Liverpool Mercury

Mirror (Perth, WA)

New Zealand Baptist (Auckland, NZ)

New Zealand Herald (Auckland, NZ)

Our Bond (Calcutta, India) *(OB)*

Our Indian Field

Quiz and Lantern

Register News-Pictorial (Adelaide, SA)

South Australian Chronicle and Weekly Mail (Adelaide, SA) (*Chronicle*)

South Australian Register also *The Register* (Adelaide, SA) (*Register*)

Southern Baptist (1895–1912) *(SB)*

Sporting Life: Dryblowers Journal (Kalgoorlie, WA)

The Advertiser (Adelaide, SA) (*Advertiser*)

The Age (Melbourne, Victoria)

The Australasian (Melbourne, Victoria)

The Express and Telegraph (Adelaide, SA) (*ET*)

The Golden Link (Melbourne, Victoria)

The Pictorial Australian (Adelaide, SA) *(PA)*

*The Sydney Morning Herald (*Sydney, NSW*)*

The Weekly Chronicle (Adelaide, SA) (*Chronicle*)

The West Australian (Perth, WA) (*West*)

Truth and Progress (Adelaide, SA, 1868–94) *(TP)*

Victorian Baptist

WA Church Monthly (Perth, WA), July 1902 – June 1903; *WA Baptist Monthly*, July 1903 – June 1905; *The WA Baptist* (August 1905 – December 1909). (*WAB*) [An initiative of the Perth Baptist Church, until late 1909].

Western Mail (Perth, WA) (*WM*)

Westralian Baptist (WB). (Perth: Baptist Historical Society of Western Australia), occasional papers.

Books and Articles

'An Epitomized Report of the South Australian Baptist Missionary Society', 1865. Baptist Mission Australia archive.

'Angas, George Fife (1789–1879)'. In *Australian Dictionary of Biography*, National Centre of Biography, Australian National University. https://adb.anu.edu.au/biography/angas-george-fife-1707/text1855, published first in hardcopy 1966.

Angus, J. *The Bible Handbook*. London: Religious Tract Society, 1853.

Austen, Tom. *Something Worth While: A History of the Perth YMCA*. Perth, WA: St George Books, 1992.

Australian Baptist Foreign Mission. *The Missionary Heritage of Australian Baptists*. Sydney: Australian Baptist Publishing House, 1937.

Australian Institute of Health and Welfare. *Mortality over the twentieth century in Australia: Trends and patterns in major causes of death*. Mortality Surveillance Series no. 4. Cat. no. PHE73. Canberra, 2005.

Baddour LM, WR Wilson, AS Bayer, VG Fowler Jr, IM Tleyjeh, MJ Rybak, B Barsic, et al, American Heart Association Committee on Rheumatic Fever, Endocarditis, and Kawasaki Disease of the Council on Cardiovascular Disease in the Young, Council on Clinical Cardiology, Council on Cardiovascular Surgery and Anesthesia, and Stroke Council. 'Infective Endocarditis in Adults: Diagnosis, Antimicrobial Therapy, and Management of Complications: A Scientific Statement for Healthcare Professionals From the American Heart Association'. *Circulation*. 132 (15) (13 October 2015): 1435–86.

Ball, Gerald B. 'The Australian Baptist Mission and its Impact in Bengal 1864–1954'. MA Thesis, Flinders University, SA, 1979.

Baptist Women's Goalundo Auxiliary. Minute Book. 1906–1909. Baptist Union of Western Australia Archives, Perth, Western Australia.

Barry, Walter. *There Was a Man: The Life of Cecil Silas Mead: Missionary-Doctor*. Melbourne: Australian Baptist Foreign Mission, 1952.

Baruch, Betty and Amanda Coverdale. *This is My Beloved: The Story of Emilia Baeyertz, Jewish Christian Lady Evangelist*. Melbourne: Emilia Baeyertz Society, 2017.

Bebbington, David. 'The Baptist Colleges in the mid-Nineteenth Century'. *Baptist Quarterly* 46.2 (2015), 49–68.

Bebbington, David. *Evangelicalism in Modern Britain: A History from the 1730s to the 1980s*. London: Unwin Hyman, 1989.

Bebbington, David. *Holiness in Nineteenth Century England.* Carlisle: Paternoster Press, 2000.

Bebbington, David. *Victorian Religious Revivals. Culture and Piety in Local and Global Contexts.* Oxford: Oxford University Press, 2012.

Bebbington, David. 'Foreword'. In *From Five Barley Loaves: Australian Baptists in Global Mission 1864–2010*, edited by Tony Cupit, Ros Gooden and Ken Manley, ix–x. Preston, Victoria: Mosaic, 2013.

Bebbington, David. *The Dominance of Evangelicalism: The Age of Spurgeon and Moody.* Volume 3 in *A History of Evangelicalism*, edited by David Bebbington and Mark Noll. 5 volumes. Leicester: Intervarsity Press, 2005.

Boardman, WE. *The Higher Christian Life.* Boston: Henry Hoyt, 1858. (A facsimile edition was published in 1984 by Garland Publishing.)

Bollen, JD. *Australian Baptists: A Religious Minority.* London: Baptist Historical Society, 1975.

Bones, Helen. *Expatriate Myth: New Zealand Writers and the Colonial World.* Dunedin, NZ: Otago University Press, 2018.

Boyce, Peter. 'Riley, Charles Owen Leaver (1854–1929)'. In *Australian Dictionary of Biography*. Canberra, National Centre of Biography, Australian National University, 1988. https://adb.anu.edu.au/biography/riley-charles-owen-leaver-8213/text14371, published online 2006.

Bradley, J, JM Dupree, and A Durie. 'Taking the Water-Cure: The Hydropathic Movement in Scotland, 1840–1940'. *Business and Economic History*, 26.2 (1997), 426–37.

Briggs, JHY. 'Baptists and Higher Education in England'. In *Faith, Life and Witness: The Papers of the Study and Research Division of the Baptist World Alliance 1986–1990*, edited by WH Brackney and RJ Burke, 92–114. Birmingham, AL: Samford University Press, 1990.

Briggs, JHY. *The English Baptists of the Nineteenth Century.* Didcot: Baptist Historical Society, 1994.

Briggs, JHY. 'From 1905 to the End of the First World War'. In *Baptists Together in Christ 1905–2005: A Hundred-Year History of the Baptist World Alliance*, edited by RV Pierard, 20–46. Falls Church, VA: Baptist World Alliance, 2005.

Brock, P and Tom Gara, eds. *Colonialism and its Aftermath: A History of Aboriginal South Australia.* Adelaide: Wakefield Press, 2017.

Broomhall, Susan, Joanne McEwan, and Stephanie Tarbin. 'Once Upon a Time: A Brief History of Children's Literature'. *The Conversation* (30 March 2017). https://theconversation.com/once-upon-a-time-a-brief-history-of-childrens-literature-75205.

Brown, Basil S. 'A Century of Australian Baptist Overseas Missions'. *Foundations* (1964).

Brown, Basil S. 'The Australian Japanese Mission'. *The Baptist Quarterly* 19.7 (1962).

Brown, Basil S. *Members One of Another: The Baptist Union of Victoria 1862–1962.* Melbourne: The Baptist Union of Victoria, 1962.

Brown, Basil S. *Baptised into One Body: A Short History of the Baptist Union of Australia.* Hawthorn, VIC; Baptist Union of Australia, [1987].

Budrikis, Stella. *The Edward Street Baby Farm.* Fremantle, WA: Fremantle Press, 2020.

Burrows, Deborah. *Nurses of Australia: The Illustrated Story.* Canberra: NLA Publishing, 2018.

Butler, J. *The Analogy of Religion, Natural and Revealed, to the Constitution and Course of Nature.* London, 1736.

Chambers, Murray. *Centenary of Christian Endeavour in Australia.* [s.l.]: Australian Christian Endeavour Union, 1983.

Clark, AJ and PS Fiddes. *Dissenting Spirit. A History of Regent's Park College 1752–2017.* Oxford: Regent's Park College, 2017.

Clark, Francis Edward. *The Christian Endeavor Manual.* Boston, Mass.: United Society of Christian Endeavor, 1903.

Clifford, J Ayson. *A Handful of Grain. The Centenary History of the Baptist Union of NZ. Vol 2 1882–1914.* Wellington, NZ: NZ Baptist Historical Society, 1982.

Condon, Brian. 'Dissent in Paradise: Religious Education, 1840–1940: An Historical Outline'. In *Dissent in Paradise: Religious Education Controversies in South Australia,* 2nd. ed. Edited by PC Almond and PG Woolcock, 3–18. Magill, SA: Murray Park College of Advanced Education, 1978.

Cooper, RE. *From Stepney to St. Giles': The Story of Regent's Park College 1810–1960.* London: Carey Kingsgate Press, 1960.

Cross, Anthony R. *Useful Learning: Neglected Means of Grace in the Reception of the Evangelical Revival among English Particular Baptists.* Eugene, Oregon: Wipf and Stock, 2017.

Cross, AR. 'Baptists, Peace, and War: The Seventeenth Century British Foundations'. In *Baptists and War. Essays on Baptists and Military Conflict, 1640s–1990s,* edited by GL Heath and MAG Haykin, 24–25. Eugene, Oregon: Wipf and Stock, 2015.

Cupit, Tony, Ros Gooden and Ken Manley, eds. *From Five Barley Loaves: Australian Baptists in Global Mission 1864–2010.* Preston, Victoria: Mosaic, 2013. Re-printed Northcote, Victoria: Morning Star Publishing, 2014.

Darroch, Ian. *The Boonah Tragedy.* Bassendean, WA: Access Press, 2004.

Dickey, Brian. 'Baeyertz, Emilia Louise (1842–1926)'. In *Australian Dictionary of Evangelical Biography.* Sydney: Evangelical History Association, 1994.

Dover, Irene. *Pathway to India: The Life of Amy Parsons—Pioneer.* London: Poona and Indian Village Mission, 1958.

Dzubinski, Leanne M and Anneke H Stasson. *Women in the Mission of the Church: Their Opportunities and Obstacles throughout Christian History.* Grand Rapids, Mich: Baker Academic, 2021.

Edgar, SL and MJ Eade. *Towards the Sunrise: The Centenary History of the New Zealand Baptist Missionary Society.* Wellington, NZ: New Zealand Baptist Historical Society, 1985.

Fisher, GL. 'Hussey Henry (1825–1903)'. In *Australian Dictionary of Biography,* National Centre of Biography, Australian National University, Vol 44 (MUP) 1972, https://adb.anu.edu.biography/hussey henry 3829/text6077.

Fisher, W. 'The Baptists of Hatch Beauchamp'. *Baptist Quarterly* 12:1–2 (1946), 34–40.

Franklin, Margaret Ann and Ruth Sturmey Jones, eds. *Opening the Cage: Stories of Church and Gender.* Sydney: Allen & Unwin, 1987.

Freeman, GS. 'Rev AS Wilson: First Permanent Minister of Perth Baptist Church'. *Westralian Baptist,* 3:3. Perth: The Baptist Historical Society of Western Australia, 1988.

Fullerton, WY. *FB Meyer A Biography.* London: Marshall, Morgan & Scott, 1929.

Gibbs, RM. *Under the Burning Sun: A History of Colonial South Australia, 1836–1900.* Adelaide: Southern Heritage, 2013.

Gooden, Rosalind M. 'Silas Mead: Baptist Missions Motivator', *Our Yesterdays* 2 1994, 47–95.

Gooden, Rosalind M. 'The First Australasian Baptist Missionary: Ellen Arnold and the Bengalis, 1882–1931'. In *Interfaces. Baptists and Others,* edited by DW Bebbington and M Sutherland, 311–22. Milton Keynes: Paternoster, 2013.

Gooden, Rosalind M. ' "Mothers in the Lord": Australasian Women Missionaries at the Intersection of Cultural Contexts 1882–1931'. PhD (Theology) thesis, Tabor College of Higher Education, Adelaide, 2016.

Gooden, Rosalind M. 'Awakened Women: Initial Formative Influences on Australasian Baptist Women in Overseas Mission 1864–1913'. Master of Theology thesis, Melbourne College of Divinity, 1997.

Gooden, Rosalind M. ' "In the City But Not of the City": Reflections of 150 Years of Baptists in Adelaide', 22 May 2011. Gooden/Mead collection.

Harding, Ann. 'In Search of Annie Oliver'. *Westralian Baptist* 8:1. Perth: The Baptist Historical Society of Western Australia, 2005.

Harding, Ann. 'World War 1 and the Effect on the Baptist Churches of Western Australia on the Centenary of the Armistice to end World War 1'. *Westralian Baptist* 24.1. Perth: The Baptist Historical Society of Western Australia, 2019.

Harris, John. *One Blood: Years of Aboriginal Encounter with Christianity: A Story of Hope.* 2nd ed. Sutherland: Albatross Books, 1994.

Helyar, Geoffrey. *A Voice in the City: Perth Baptist Church: 1895–1995.* Perth, WA: Perth Baptist Church, 1995.

Heyn, Mark and Mandy Paul. 'Aborigines' Friends' Association'. South Australian Museum Archive, 2021. https://www.samuseum.sa.gov.au/collection/archives/provenances/aa1.

Hinton, (Mrs) WH [Louisa]. *Ethel Ambrose: Pioneer Medical Missionary, Poona and Indian Village Mission, Bombay Presidency, India.* London : Marshall, Morgan & Scott [1937].

Hobby, Nathan. 'A History of Vose Library'. In *Vose Seminary at Fifty,* edited by Nathan Hobby, John Olley and Michael O'Neil, 140–58. Preston, Victoria: Mosaic, 2013.

Hodder, E. *George Fife Angas, Father and Founder of South Australia.* London: Hodder and Stoughton, 1891.

Hodge, JZ. 'A Missionary Enthusiast. The Late Rev. Silas Mead, M.A., LL.B.', unidentified press clipping. Gooden/Mead collection.

Hughes, H Estcourt. *Our First Hundred Years: The Baptist Churches of South Australia*. Adelaide: South Australian Baptist Union, 1937.

Jenkin, Graham. *The Conquest of the Narrindjeri*. Adelaide: Rigby, 1979.

Jones, Helen. 'Hope, Charles Henry Standish (1861–1942)'. In *Australian Dictionary of Biography*, Volume 14. Carlton, Victoria: Melbourne University Press, 1996.

Joske, Prue. 'Mead, Gertrude Ella (1867–1919)'. In *Australian Dictionary of Biography*. Canberra: National Centre of Biography, Australian National University, 1986. https://adb.anu.edu.au/biography/mead-gertrude-ella-7544/text13161.

Kember, I. *Taunton Silver Street: A Baptist Chapel and Its Town: The Early Years 1814–51*. Taunton: privately published, 1988.

Kent, J. *Holding the Fort: Studies in Victorian Revivalism*. London: Epworth Press, 1978.

Kerry, George. 'In Memoriam—the Late Rev James Smith of Delhi'. *Missionary Herald,* January 1899.

Laird, MA. *Missionaries and Education in Bengal 1793–1837*. Oxford: Oxford University Press, 1972.

Lanker, Jason. 'Francis Edward Clark'. In 'Christian Educators of the 20th Century', Talbot School of Theology, Biola University. Accessed at www.biola.edu/talbot/ce20/database/francis-edward-clark.

Larsen, T, ed. *Biographical Dictionary of Evangelicals*. Leicester: Inter-Varsity Press, 2003.

Latham, RG. *The English Language*. London, 1841.

Mackinnon, Alison. 'Advanced School for Girls'. In *Worth Her Salt: Women at Work in Australia*, edited by M Bevege, M James and C Shute, 62–71. Sydney: Hale & Ironmonger, 1982.

Mackinnon, Alison. *One Foot on the Ladder: Origins and Outcomes of Girls' Secondary Schooling in South Australia*. St Lucia: University of Queensland Press, 1984.

Mackinnon, Alison. *The New Women: Adelaide's Early Women Graduates*. Netley, South Australia: Wakefield Press, 1986.

Manley, Ken R. *From Woolloomooloo to 'Eternity': A History of Australian Baptists*, 2 volumes. Studies in Baptist History and Thought, volume 16.1, 2. Milton Keynes, UK: Paternoster, 2006.

Manley, Ken R. *'Redeeming Love Proclaim': John Rippon and the Baptists*. Carlisle: Paternoster, 2004.

Mann, NM, Sheila Ross and WH Patterson. 'Gastro-enteritis in Infancy'. *Archives of Disease in Childhood*, 1 October 1952, 457–467.

Martin, Rebecca. 'Adelaide Medical School: 1885–1919'. In *Adelaide Connect*. 2020. https://connect.adelaide.edu.au/nodes/view/7390.

Martin, RH. *Evangelicals United: Ecumenical Stirrings in Pre-Victorian Britain 1795–1830*. New Jersey: Scarecrow Press, 1983.

Massey, Jack, ed. *At Milestone 50: A Brief History of the Y.M.C.A. in Adelaide from 1850 to 1930, including the Fiftieth Annual Report*. Adelaide: YMCA, 1930.

McCarthy, Gavan J. 'Mead, Gertrude Ella (1867–1919)'. In *Where are the Women in Australian Science?,* edited by G McCarthy, H Morgan, A Smith, A van den Bosch. Canberra: Australian

Science and Technology Heritage Centre, 2003. http://www.austehc.unimelb.edu.au/wisa/wisa.html.

Mead, Cecil S. *Letters to Elsie, 1893–1899*. Baptist Mission Australia archive, Moore Potter House, Melbourne.

Mead, Cecil S. *LORD, TODAY: Family Prayers of Dr Cecil Silas Mead*. Baptist Mission Australia archive, Moore Potter House, Melbourne.

Mead, Cecil S. *The Nama Sudras and Other Addresses*. South Australian Baptist Furreedpore Mission Inc. Adelaide: Hussey & Gillingham, 1911.

Mead, Lilian S. *A Brother's Need*. London: SW Partridge & Co, [1903].

Mead, Lilian S. *Daring and Doing!: True Stories of Brave Deeds*. London: SW Partridge & Co, [1912].

Mead, Lilian S. *Patsie's Bricks*. London: SW Partridge & Co, [1905].

Mead, Lilian S. *The Awakened Woman: Paper Read at Seventh Annual Convention of Woman's Christian Temperance Union of South Australia*. Adelaide: Woman's Christian Temperance Union, 1895.

Mead, Marjory. 'Rev Silas Mead', *Australian Baptist*, 22 April 1959, 11.

Mead, Marjory. *Our Building*. Adelaide: Flinders Street Baptist Church, 1961.

Mead, Silas. 'Missionary Methods—Australian.' In *The Baptist World Congress: London, July 11–19, 1905*, 86–92. London: Baptist Union Publication, 1905.

Mead, Silas. *Scripture Immersion: Or Arguments Showing Infant Baptism to be Unscriptural, and Believers' Immersion to be Exclusively Scriptural and Obligatory, Intended as a Reply to the Rev. John Hannah's Book entitled 'Infant Baptism Scriptural and Immersion Unnecessary' and Issued at the Wesleyan Conference, London*. Adelaide, SA: Andrews, Thomas and Clarke, 1867.

Mead, Silas and WT Whitley, *Our Indian Trip: Notes and Impressions of a Visit to Several Mission Stations from November 1895 to March 1896*. Melbourne: Bible and Tract Repository, 1896. Copy held in Baptist Mission Australia collection of Mead files, Moore Potter House, Melbourne.

Milner, T. *The History of England*. London: The Religious Tract Society, 1853.

Moon, NS. *Education for Ministry. Bristol Baptist College 1679–1979*. Bristol: Bristol Baptist College, 1979.

Moore, Richard K. *'All Western Australia is My Parish': A Centenary History of the Baptist Denomination in Western Australia, 1895–1995*. [Perth]: Baptist Historical Society of Western Australia, 1996.

Moore, Richard K., ed. *Baptists of Western Australia: The First Ninety Years*. Perth, WA: Baptist Historical Society of Western Australia, 1991.

Nesdale, Ira. *The Third Bridge: Tsong Gyiaou, Mclaren Vale*. Hawthorndene, South Australia: Investigator Press, 1980.

Neville, Abia. *White unto Harvest: An Account of the Mission in Mymensing, East Bengal*. Geelong: Victorian Baptist Foreign Mission, 1898.

Official Report of the Sixteenth International Christian Endeavor Convention held in Mechanics', Woodward's Pavilions and in many churches. San Francisco, July 7–12, 1897.

Orr, J. Edwin. *The Light of the Nations: Progress and Achievement in the Nineteenth Century.* The Paternoster Church History, vol 8. Exeter: Paternoster Press, 1965.

Pargeter, Judith. *'For God, Home and Humanity': National Woman's Christian Temperance Union of Australia: Centenary History: 1891–1991.* Geelong, Victoria: National Woman's Christian Temperance Union of Australia, 1995.

Payne, EA. 'The Development of Nonconformist Theological Education in the Nineteenth Century with Special Reference to Regent's Park College'. In EA Payne, *Studies in History and Religion,* 229–53. London: Lutterworth Press, 1942.

Petersen, RC. 'Zion Chapel', SA History Hub, History Trust of South Australia, https://sahistoryhub. history.sa.gov.au/organisations/zion-chapel.

Phillips, Walter. 'Studies: Union College Adelaide, 1872–1886: A Brief Experiment in United Theological Education'. In *The 'Furtherance of Religious Beliefs': Essays on the History of Theological Education in Australia,* edited by Geoffrey R Treloar, 59–71. The Centre for the Study of Australian Christianity, Macquarie University, NSW, 1997.

Pierson, Arthur Tappan. *George Müller of Bristol and His Witness to a Prayer Hearing God.* London: Pickering & Inglis, 1899.

Pierson, Paul E. *The Dynamics of Christian Mission: History Through a Missiological Perspective.* Pasadena: William Carey International University Press, 2009.

Piggin, Stuart and Robert D Linder. *The Fountain of Public Prosperity: Evangelical Christians in Australian History 1740–1914.* Clayton: Monash University Publishing, 2019.

Pike, Douglas. *Paradise of Dissent, South Australia 1829–1857.* Melbourne: Melbourne University Press, 1957.

Pollock, JC. *The Keswick Story: The Authorized History of the Keswick Convention.* London: Hodder and Stoughton, 1964.

Price, John, Silas Mead and Samuel Vincent. *The Centenary Volume 1792–1892 The South Australian and Tasmanian Baptist Missions of Furreedpore and Pabna.* Adelaide: WK Thomas & Co, 1892.

Price, John. *Memoir of George Swan Fowler: Christian Merchant.* Adelaide: ES Wigg & Sons, 1897.

Prior, Alan C. *Some Fell on Good Ground: A History of the Beginnings and Developments of the Baptist Church in New South Wales, Australia, 1831–1965.* Sydney: Baptist Union of NSW, 1966.

Pulford, Kate, 'Lilian Staple Mead, PAC 1883–1884'. *Prince Alfred College,* 30 October 2019.

Randall, IM. *Spirituality and Social Change: The Contribution of FB Meyer (1847–1929).* Carlisle: Paternoster Press, 2003.

Record of the Convention for the Promotion of Scripture Holiness at Brighton 29 May to 7 June 1875. London: 1875.

'Religion: Education.' SA Memory, State Library, South Australia. https://www.samemory.sa.gov.au/site/page.cfm?u=1456.

Rowe, Leanne. 'The Children's Protection Society: Child Protection in Western Australia, 1906–1930: Towards a Medical Welfare Model'. *Studies in Western Australian History*, 25 (2007): 116–131.

Rowston, Laurie. 'One Hundred Years of Partnership in Foreign Missions Part 1: Serajgunge for Christ'. *Tasmanian Baptist Advance* (May 1991).

'SA Newspapers: Early History,' SA Memory, State Library, South Australia. https://www.samemory.sa.gov.au/site/page.cfm?u=1473.

Schroeder, Elva. *Doctor Sahib: The Story of Dr Cecil Silas Mead*. Tooperang, S Aust: Rowett Print, 2006.

Schroeder, Elva. *Doctor Sahib: The Story of Dr Cecil Silas Mead*. 2nd ed. Capalaba, Qld: Even Before Publishing, 2013.

Sell, APF. *Commemorations. Studies in Christian Thought and History*. Calgary and Cardiff: University of Calgary Press and University of Wales Press, 1993.

Sherburd, EF and AL Silcock. *Eighteen Thousand Yesterdays. The Story of The NZ Baptist Theological College*. Auckland: Institute Press, 1976.

'Silver Chain Nursing Association'. *InHerit*, Heritage Council, Government of Western Australia. City of Vincent, Place Number 11451, 1998. http://inherit.stateheritage.wa.gov.au/Public/Inventory/Details/3e9772c7-54d1-464e-8cdb-ef9a1ad58897.

Simpson, Donald. 'The Adelaide Medical School 1885–1914: A Study of Anglo-Australian Synergies in Medical Education'. MD thesis, University of Adelaide, 2000.

Skinner, Craig. *Lamplighter and Son*. Nashville: Broadman Press, 1984.

Slee, Ronald George. 'The Politics of Religious Education in South Australia.' MA Dissertation, University of Adelaide, 1979.

Souvenir Brochure Flinders Street Baptist Church (Incorporated). Adelaide: Hussey & Gillham Ltd, 1911.

Stanley, Brian. *The History of the Baptist Missionary Society 1792–1992*. Edinburgh: T & T Clark, 1992.

Stanley, Fiona, 'Child Health since Federation'. Canberra: Australian Bureau of Statistics, 1301.0 Year Book Australia, 2001, updated 5 October 2007. https://www.abs.gov.au/ausstats/ABS@.nsf/Previousproducts/1301.0Feature%20Article212001

Stannage, CT, ed. *A New History of Western Australia*. Nedlands, WA: University of Western Australia Press, 1981.

Stewart, Noël. 'Chase, Muriel Jean Eliot (1880–1936)'. In *Australian Dictionary of Biography*. Canberra, National Centre of Biography, Australian National University, 1979. https://adb.anu.edu.au/biography/chase-muriel-jean-eliot-5565/text9489.Telfer, EJ. *Amongst Australian Aborigines: Forty Years of Missionary Work: The Story of the United Aborigines' Mission*. Sydney: printed for E.J. Telfer by Fraser & Morphet, 1939.

The Adelaide University Calendar for the Academical Year 1887. Adelaide: WK Thomas & Co, 1887.

The Baptist World Congress. Authorised Record of Proceedings. London, July 11–19, 1905. London: Baptist Union Publication Department, 1905.

The Handbook of Flinders Street Baptist Church, Adelaide 1865. Adelaide: Andrew, Thomas and Fisher, 1865.

The Keswick Week. Independently published, 1893. Reprinted 2019.

Treloar, Geoffrey R. *The Disruption of Evangelicalism: The Age of Torrey, Mott, Mcpherson and Hammond.* Volume 4 in *A History of Evangelicalism,* edited by David Bebbington and Mark Noll. 5 volumes. Downers Grove, Illinois: IVP Academic, 2017.

Tucker, Ruth. *From Jerusalem to Irian Jaya: A Biographical History of Christian Missions.* Grand Rapids, MI: Academie Books, Zondervan Publishing House, 1983.

Vamplew, W, E Richards, D Jaensch, J Hancock, eds. *South Australian Historical Statistics.* Kensington, NSW: History Project Incorporated, University of New South Wales, 1988.

Walker, John S. 'The Baptists in South Australia, 1863 to 1914'. Thesis for Honours degree in Theology, Flinders University, South Australia, 31 October 1990.

Walker, John S. 'Mead, Silas'. In *The Australian Dictionary of Evangelical Biography*, edited by B Dickey, Sydney: Evangelical History Association, 1994.

Walker, John S. 'The Baptists in South Australia, circa 1900 to 1939'. PhD dissertation, Flinders University, 2006.

Walker, Rhonda. 'George Henry Cargeeg JP: A Devout Man, 1851–1925'. *Westralian Baptist* 9:2. Perth: The Baptist Historical Society of Western Australia, 1994.

Wallace, Anthony FC. 'Revitalization Movements'. *American Anthropologist,* 58:2 (April 1956): 264–281. https://anthrosource.onlinelibrary.wiley.com/doi/pdf/10.1525/aa.1956.58.2.02a00040.

Wardin, AW, ed. *Baptists Around the World.* Nashville: Broadman & Holman, 1995.

Watts, Michael R. *The Dissenters.* Oxford: Oxford University Press, 1978.

Whately, Richard. *The Elements of Logic.* London: 1825.

White, BR. *The English Baptists of the Seventeenth Century.* Didcot: Baptist Historical Society, 1996.

White, John E. *A Fellowship of Service: A History of the Baptist Union of Queensland 1877–1977.* Brisbane: Baptist Union of Queensland, 1977.

Wilson, AS. *What is a Baptist Church?* Perth: 1906.

Wilson, Torrey. 'A Brief Survey of the Life and Ministry of Baptist Minister Rev Bernard Wilson: With Particular Reference to His Call to Evangelism During the Years 1930–1939'. Essay submitted to Burleigh College, 4 November 1983.

World's Christian Endeavor Union. 'The Christian Endeavor Pledge'. Accessed at www.worldsceunion.org/files/the_christian_endeavor_pledge.pdf.

Contributors

ROSALIND M GOODEN: Ros completed her doctorate *'Mothers in the Lord': Australasian Baptist Women Missionaries at the Intersection of Cultural Contexts 1882–1931* in 2017 bringing both academic discipline and the personal experience of four decades with ABMS/Global Interaction (now Baptist Mission Australia) in East Pakistan/Bangladesh and Melbourne. She was co-editor of the definitive study of Australian Baptist missions—*From Five Barley Loaves: Australian Baptists in Global Mission 1864–2010* (2013). She became a member of Flinders Street Baptist Church, Adelaide, in her teens. Her early training was in science and education at The University of Adelaide and she has been concerned to develop competency-based training/cultural intelligence for those working interculturally. Now retired in Adelaide and again a member of Flinders Street Baptist Church, Ros has been honoured with the inaugural 'Mead Emeritus Scholar' award by the South Australian Baptist churches in 2017. She realised that a biography of Silas Mead was long overdue, yet could not undertake it alone, and so very enthusiastically initiated this collaborative project

REBECCA HILTON is researching the history of Australian Baptist women for a PhD at Charles Sturt University. Her research focuses on the roles, contribution, and identity of Baptist women from 1882 to 1945. She undertook research on Australian Baptist missionary women's history as part of her Master of Theology. Rebecca has an interest in social justice and equity issues, and worked in the Commonwealth Public Service in areas of employment for disadvantaged Australians, remote housing, and family programmes. She is the daughter, wife, mother, and friend of Baptists. Rebecca would like to thank her parents, Gary and Helen Hilton, and the History and Gender group at the Australian National University for comments on her chapters.

KEN R MANLEY, former Principal of Whitley College, University of Melbourne and author of *From Woolloomooloo to 'Eternity': A History of Australian Baptists* (2006), the definitive 2-volume history of Baptists in Australia. Scholar and educator at three Australian theological colleges, as well as church pastor and preacher, he co-authored the centenary history of the Baptist World Alliance. His most recent publications include biographies of John Saunders (2014), Samuel Pearce Carey (2016), TE Ruth (2021) and as co-editor of From Five Barley Loaves: Australian Baptists in Global Mission 1864–2010 (2013).

JOHN OLLEY is a Research Fellow of Morling College, and formerly Principal of the Baptist Theological College of Western Australia (now Morling College Vose Campus) where he lectured in Old Testament and Missiology. He has published articles and commentaries in biblical studies and missiology—and family history. After completing a PhD in Physics at Sydney University, John studied at Morling College and was ordained in 1966. He and Elaine served as ABMS (now Baptist Mission Australia) intercultural workers in Hong Kong where John lectured in the Divinity School of Chung Chi College, The Chinese University of Hong Kong. After 'retirement' they served briefly in the Silk Road area. They are actively involved in the wide-ranging ministries of Carey Baptist Church, Perth.

STEFANIE PEARCE has had a long career in research, writing, publishing, and editing for government and in the private sector. Born in Adelaide, a great-great-great-granddaughter of George Fife Angas, Stefanie now lives in Melbourne after years based in Canberra and on overseas postings. She has an MA in Communications, and her Master of Theological Studies research paper on the 150-year history of Melbourne's inter-denominational Gospel Hall Trust was published in Our Yesterdays in 2020. She was production editor of Baptist Identity into the 21st Century (2016). For many years a member of the Canberra Society of Editors and The Society of Editors (Victoria), she has won national print and design awards for books she edited. She was awarded the 2018 HJ Jenkins Award for Academic Excellence at Whitley College, University of Divinity, Melbourne, on completion of her Master of Theological Studies.

FRANK TUCKER grew up in rural South Australia. He studied agriculture at the University of Adelaide and theology at the Bible College of South Australia. He and his wife, Ann, served as missionaries in Indonesia where they worked with the Evangelical Church of Indonesia. Frank taught community development in the Theological and Vocational Training School of Indonesia in Sentani in Papua, Indonesia. While there he also advised various Christian-based community development programs. This experience was capped by a Masters in Missiology at Fuller Seminary. After returning to Australia, he became the pastor of two (consecutive) Baptist churches in Adelaide. Overlapping that time he has been an adjunct lecturer in missiology at the Bible College of South Australia, and an adjunct lecturer in Intercultural Studies at Tabor Adelaide. In that capacity he has written several books on missions and contributed to journals. His passion is to honour Christ in life and work. He and Ann attend the Lighthouse Community Church (Baptist) in South Australia. They have three adult children.

PAULINE TUDBALL: Pauline's published papers include early research experience in biochemistry and later with eucalypts. She has teaching experience at secondary and tertiary levels in science and IT. She developed an interest in local history and, while teaching Indigenous students, she published an Index of the Papers of William Thomas: an 'Assistant Protector of the Aborigines' from 1839 until 1867. She has a number of postgraduate degrees including a PhD in eucalypt disease and a Master of Biblical Studies. With her husband, Bruce, she served with Global Interaction (now Baptist Mission Australia) in the Silk Road Area and with the South Asia team. She enjoys delving into the Baptist Mission Australia archives to prepare memorial minutes for cross-cultural workers. She is committed to cross-cultural mission and empowering communities to develop their own distinctive ways of following Jesus.

JOHN WALKER is a Baptist pastor who has served in South Australia and Queensland since 1986. In the 1990s, he lectured in church history as an adjunct staff member of Burleigh College and the Bible College of South Australia. John, with his wife Karen, also served in Cambodia as Christian cross-cultural workers with Global Interaction (now Baptist Mission Australia) between 2008 and 2014, mainly working with post-graduate students. The focus of John's Bachelor of Theology honours thesis was on nineteenth and early twentieth century South Australian Baptists, while his 2006 Flinders University doctoral thesis was on South Australian Baptists, circa 1900 to 1939. John has had several journal articles and book chapters published based on his research. John coordinates the South Australian Baptist History Project and at the time of the writing of this book he was about to retire. He hopes to be able to give much more time to historical research and writing on South Australian Baptists.

TORREY WILSON: A fourth generation Baptist Minister, beginning with his great grandfather, Rev Silas Mead, Torrey Alfred Mead Wilson was undoubtedly shaped and influenced by his late father, Rev. Bernard Mead Wilson, who, in turn, was influenced by his father, Rev. A. S. Wilson, who was Mead's son-in-law and mentee, co-pastoring and working alongside Silas Mead in later life. Torrey's desire to be a minister grew in him as a young boy and stayed with him through his teenage years as he sat under his father's ministries in five states of Australia. He was ordained to the Christian ministry in South Australia in March 1984. He was a pastor in six SA churches before retirement, and his final ministry was to be an Associate Minister in the Flinders Street Baptist Church, Adelaide, where the South Australian story of Silas

Mead began. After retirement, Torrey became an Associate Minister of Trinity Baptist Church, formerly Colonel Light Gardens Baptist Church, Adelaide, where his father ministered from 1960 and where he and his sister Raewyn were both baptised. He is married to Elizabeth and has three adult children and five grandchildren to date.

Index

Taylor, Rev James 57, 71n16
temperance 77, 199
Temperance Alliance 121
Temperance League 96, 121
Thomas, Helen Rosetta 54
Thomas, Mary 54
Thomas, Mary Jane 54
Thomas, Mary Maria 54
Thomas, Robert (brother of WK Thomas) 51
Thomas, Robert (son of WK Thomas) 127
Thomas, Rosetta Jane *see* Birks, Rosetta Jane (née Thomas)
Thomas, William Kyffin 50, 54, 55, 63, 65, 86, 105, 121, 127
Tirhoot, West Bengal 148
Todd, Charles 50
Trick, Mrs 64–5
trustees 53
Truth and Progress 3, 71–3, 81, 107, 136, 259, 310
Tsong Gyiaou School, McLaren Vale, SA 255–6
Tuck, Bertha 93, 97, 134, 138, 144
    photograph of 143
Tuck, Rev HL 134–5
Tuck, Rev and Mrs HL 54, 90
Tucker, Frank 14, 22, 25, 29, 103–31, 340
Tudball, Dr Pauline 15, 17, 30–1, 211–29, 341
Tunbridge Wells, Kent 180, 203

Union Church, Angaston, SA 104
Union College of South Australia 110
University of Adelaide 120, 187, 196–7, 212, 238, 291–2
    Union College in 3, 43, 120, 311
University of London 39–40, 197
University of Western Australia 250–1
Uttermare, Bessie 204
Uttermare, Honor *see* Mead, Honor (née Uttermare)

Varley, Henry 91
Victorian Baptist Association/ Union 18, 149n92, 175
Victorian Baptist Missionary Society 136, 140, 145–6, 151
Victorian Baptist Theological College 43, 81
Victorian Baptists 139, 141, 175
Victorian Presbyterian College 110
Vincent, Henry 77
visitation 62–4, 88, 89
voluntaryism 24

Walker, Rev Dr John 14, 21–31, 95, 307, 310, 341
Wall, James 78
Webb, Rev Allan 55, 61, 125, 148
Wesleyans 70, 110
West Australian Health Society 246
West End Mission, Adelaide 97
Western Australia, history of 167–8
Western Australian Baptists 151–2, 172–80
Western Australian Council for the Australian Aborigines Mission 183
Western Australian Emigration Commissioner 180
Whately, Mary Louise 78
Whately, (Church of Ireland) Archbishop Richard 78
White, Walter F 152, 175
White's Assembly Hall, Adelaide 51
Whiting, Isabella 54
Whiting, James 54, 62
Whitley, Dr William T 81, 100, 143, 146, 149, 151, 168, 218, 315–16
    photograph of 143
Wilkin, Ruth 145, 147
    photograph of 147
Williams, George 125
Wilson, Albion Staple Colin ('Colin') 4, 242–3, 250, 262, 264
    as church musician 275
    eulogy for 277

fatally ill with Spanish flu 277
military service of 265, 276–7
photographs of 265, 266, 274, 275 (honour roll), 276, 280
as a 'PK' (pastor's kid) 274
schooling of 274
Sunday School and 277
YMCA and 275, 276
Wilson, Rev Alfred Samuel 96, 100, 151, 164, 169–70, 171, 172, 173, 178, 183, 188–9, 249, 251
death of 268
on death of son, Colin 278
early life of 260–1
ministry of 261, 263–4, 266–7, 298
open membership and 29, 261
photographs of 98, 172, 262, 266, 280, 281
wedding of 260
YMCA and 263–4, 265, 266–7
Wilson, Annie Blanche ('Blanche') (née Mead) 4, 31, 36, 59, 87, 89, 91, 100, 171, 173, 198, 204, 232
baptism of 234, 256
birth and early years of 254
burial of 268, 299
Cecil and 258–9
character of 253, 260, 267
Christian activities of 254, 256
death of 253, 268, 299
death of two sons and 265–6
health of 237, 255
at Keswick Convention 258
mission and 257, 259–60
in New Zealand 263–4, 266–7
obituary of 268
Perth household of 263
photographs of 67, 89, 98, 193, 236, 257, 259, 262, 265, 266, 267, 281, 298, 305
schooling of 255–6
as 'shining saint' 267
Silas memorial and 308
speeches of 256, 260
travel to Britain by 258, 262
travel to East Bengal by 259

Endorsements

Silas Mead was a man of profound lasting influence. He was a distinguished Australian Evangelical, who displayed adaptability, being drawn into the holiness movement of his day. He championed the role of women inside and outside the churches. He dedicated his life to global mission. Perhaps his most striking memorial was the persistent moulding power of his priorities over his descendants. Mead's ministry was almost as influential after his death as it had been in his lifetime.

Professor David Bebbington
University of Stirling

Silas Mead is one of the giants of our mission story. He models for us attentiveness to God's leading, bold faith, a spirit of innovation and a strong commitment to the place of women in ministry. As we learn from our past, this study of Mead's life and his descendants is a valuable contribution to our collective Australian Baptist mission story.

Scott Pilgrim
Executive Director, Baptist Mission Australia

A leading figure in the history of our movement and mission, the name Silas Mead is recognisable to many South Australian Baptists. But the scope of his story is far less known, and most would be unaware of how his faith shaped the next generation and bore fruit in the lives of his descendants. In particular, his advocacy and desire to make space for women in the life of the church is embodied in the remarkable lives of his daughters and granddaughters. This study of the Mead family should inspire all those who seek to faithfully follow Jesus in ways that unfold for generations to come.

Rev Dr Melinda Cousins,
Director of Ministries, Baptist Churches of SA